Habitus in Habitat III

Synaesthesia and Kinaesthetics

natur, wissenschaft und die künste
nature, science et les arts
nature, science and the arts

Volume 8

Edited by

Julia Burbulla
Bernd Nicolai
Ana-Stanca Tabarasi-Hoffmann
Philip Ursprung
Wolf Wucherpfennig



PETER LANG
Bern · Berlin · Bruxelles · Frankfurt am Main · New York · Oxford · Wien

Joerg Fingerhut, Sabine Flach & Jan Söffner (eds)

# Habitus in Habitat III

## Synaesthesia and Kinaesthetics

PETER LANG
Bern · Berlin · Bruxelles · Frankfurt am Main · New York · Oxford · Wien

**Bibliographic information published by Die Deutsche Nationalbibliothek**
Die Deutsche Nationalbibliothek lists this publication in the Deutsche Nationalbibliografie; detailed bibliographic data is available on the Internet at ‹http://dnb.d-nb.de›.

British Library and Library of Congress Cataloguing-in-Publication Data:
A catalogue record for this book is available from *The British Library*, Great Britain.

Library of Congress Cataloging-in-Publication Data

Habitus in Habitat III: Synaesthesia and Kinaesthetics / Jörg Fingerhut, Sabine Flach & Jan Söffner (eds). -- 1st ed.
p. cm. -- (Nature, science, and the arts, ISSN 1663-6007; v. 8)
ISBN 978-3-0343-0532-7
1. Synesthesia. 2. Human ecology. I. Fingerhut, Jörg. II. Flach, Sabine. III. Söffner, Jan. IV. Title: Habitus in Habitat three. V. Title: Habitus in Habitat 3. VI. Title: Synaesthesia and Kinaesthetics.
BF495.H33 2011
52.1'89--dc23

2011040564

The proceedings are result of a conference which was supported by the German Federal Ministry of Education and Research (promotional reference: 01UG07129).
The authors of this publication are responsible for its content.



Cover illustration: Suzanne Anker: *The Glass Veil (Lonely Planet)*, 2009, Digital print on watercolor paper, 24" x 36" / 61cm x 91.4cm .

Cover design: Thomas Jaberg, Peter Lang AG

ISBN 978-3-0343-0532-7


Hochfeldstrasse 32, CH-3012 Bern
info@peterlang.com, www.peterlang.com, www.peterlang.net

*Dedicated to John Michael Krois*

# Content

*Spatialities*



*Modernities*



*Arts of Synaesthesia*

# Introduction

JOERG FINGERHUT

Synaesthetic experience and kinaesthetics, the experience of the posture and the movement of the body, are key concepts in the understanding of the interplay between the habitus of the organism and its habitat. Both denote synthetic achievements of the sensing human organism. As Maurice Merleau-Ponty famously noted: "[s]ynaesthetic perception is the rule, and we are unaware of it only because scientific knowledge shifts the centre of gravity of experience, so that we have unlearned how to see, hear, and generally speaking feel […]."[1] The original unity in sense perception, in his view, was grounded in the living body constituting a 'système synergique' linked together in the action of being in the world and thus constituting the kinaesthetically experienced 'lived body' of the embodied subject.

## Habitus in habitat

The present third volume of the series *Habitus in Habitat* does not just address synaesthesia and kinaesthetics from the point of view of the organism or a psychologically and phenomenologically construed philosophy of perception and the knowledge that this perspective brings. It also aims at an understanding of the several interfaces of habitat and experience. A theoretical approach that intends to include the sensually and emotionally charged environment (i.e. what it affords, what it offers and the interaction it enables) brings into view artistic, cultural, and social renderings of synaesthetic and kinaesthetic phenomena. It is the very habitus of the human organism to engage, to share, to express itself, and by following this habitus it creates a social and cultural habitat. This habitat, the social structures and urban patterns of cities, the complex unfoldings of artworks, the sensual environment of everyday life, all mark elements of synthesis which can be enlightened by theories of organismic capabilities, but also mark phenomena in their own right. The knowledge embedded in these ways of differentiating and combining modalities and the ways of making their interplay explicit in multimodal artworks and kinaesthetic artistic practices, transforms our experiences in various ways and calls for specific scientific and intellectual means to bring this specific knowledge into view. The *Habitus in Habitat* project aims to take both

1 Merleau-Ponty: *Phenomonology of Perception*, p. 229.

the specific ways of constructing this habitat and its very properties as well as the theories concerned with the engaging organism and its habitus into focus without committing the error of unheedingly foregrounding only one of these two intrinsically intertwined aspects.[2]

This only recently has come to be appreciated within the growing field of the cognitive sciences and has found expression in their recognition of the need for a new science of the mind which takes the embodied, embedded, enactive, extended and affective subject seriously, as has been proposed in the philosophy of the embodied mind.[3] For example, in philosophy itself, this approach has been put to work in understanding social and political phenomena by bringing together social constructivism and biological foundations, the social and the somatic.[4] This alternative picture of the human mind distances itself from the methodological solipsism and the strict boundaries of the neuroscientific disciplines that investigate local phenomena and generalize about the human mind and nature based on these findings. No comprehensive theory of mind and human practice can evolve by turning away from the embeddedness of its results in the wider biological, social or cultural settings. The social sciences, political theory, art history, media theory, and film studies – among many others – also have to be taken into account. It is fair to say that the very disciplines just mentioned have already gained in influence (as the limitations of a too narrowly construed biological theory have become manifest) and nowadays are seen more and more as what they are and always have been: congruent theories of human nature. As such they restore insight into humans as bio-cultural beings and correct the shortcomings of some neurobiology and its view of the 'naked brain' as the single explanans. In taking the more comprehensive stance, the boundaries of the sciences are becoming more and more permeable, though not without keeping the methodological principles of the respective disciplines intact. Those principles sometimes even are more fully explicated when adjacent theoretical achievements of different disciplines are compared and differentiated. The present volume of *Habitus in Habitat* follows such a line of thought with its transdisciplinary endeavour to explore *synaesthesia and kinaesthetics.*

## Synaesthesia

Two general uses of the concept of synaesthesia can be separated. There is the rather liberal use of the word 'synaesthesia' that also figures in some of the con-

2 For a more detailed discussion of the phenomena, foundational texts and methodological considerations underlying the *Habitus in Habitat* series see the "Introduction" in: Flach/Margulis/Soeffner: *Habitus in Habitat I*, pp. 7–15.

3 See Rowlands: *The New Science of the Mind.*

4 For such an approach and an introduction to what has been labelled the '4EA' view of cognition see: Protevi: *Political Affect.*

tributions to the present volume, as the idea of a fusion of the senses in experience, art or metaphoric language. Also in the philosophy of perception there has been a focus on cross-modal influences and integrative or binding effects in normal perception. Following Merleau-Ponty's use of the term, synaesthesia can be seen as the standard form of perception, and the synaesthetic kind of cross-modal integration thus constitutes the most basic form of our meaningful, value-laden engagement with the world. These approaches deal with synaesthesia as a, so to speak, productive phenomenon that makes valuable contributions to our cognitive lives and every-day experiences, but is also brought to bear and directly addressed in the experience of art.

There is also a more narrow use of the term that describes a specific neuronal condition that has been named 'genuine perceptual synaesthesia'. Narrowly defined, synaesthesia is a condition in which stimulation in one sensory modality (or sensory aspect) systematically and automatically leads to experiences in a different modality (or sensory aspect). The graphem→color synaesthesia is by far the most common form, in which e.g. a specific letter or number reliably and involuntarily triggers a specific colour response.

In 1880, in an article published in the journal *Nature,* Sir Francis Galton systematically described this condition for the first time, hence making it available to a broader scientific community. Research done in Germany and especially in Hamburg in the 1920s and early 1930s can be regarded as the heyday of synaesthetic research, particularly because its achievements were made possible by the collective efforts of a transdisciplinary endeavour, sustaining a level of intellectual interaction and discourse that has yet to be reached since. At the time, experimental psychologists, neurologists, musicologists, artists, and philosophers engaged in an intense and extensive dialogue on synaesthesia and related phenomena, developing a comprehensive account of it as a biological and artistic phenomenon.[5] Over the past twenty years, synaesthesia has regained a lot of interest, which is to a large extent due to the monographs of Richard E. Cytowic and the research conducted in cognitive neurosciences on this condition – research which combined phenomenological, behavioral, and neuroimaging methods and has begun to identify parts of the cognitive and neural basis of synaesthesia.[6]

In contrast to other neuropsychological conditions, synaesthesia does not primarily represent a cognitive breakdown or a pathology and thus does not constitute an impaired subjective state. It is rather a positive symptom, sometimes opening up

5 See e.g. Rösch: "Albrecht Wellek", Lewanski: "Die neue Synthese des Geistes". For the interaction of experimental psychologist Heinz Werner, neurologist Kurt Goldstein and the philosopher Ernst Cassirer see Krois: "Synaesthesia and the Theory of Signs", pp. 155–159.

6 Cf. Cytowic: *Synesthesia,* the first edition of which was published in 1989. See also his most recent book: Cytowic/Eagleman: *Wednesday Is Indigo Blue.* Both give a comprehensive overview of phenomena and theories of genuine perceptual synaesthesia and related phenomena as well. For an overview with a focus on recent findings in the neurosciences see also: Ward/Mattingley: "Synaesthesia".

a rich phenomenal world for the subjects of this condition that does not seem to be available for non-synaesthetes. This makes synaesthesia a specifically interesting phenomenon for the scientific study of differences among subjects, though one that is hard to gain access to and that forces us to embrace the otherness of our conspecifics within the scientific paradigm. All types of the condition of genuine synaesthesia share common features that are used in tests of authenticity and make synaesthesia distinguishable from comparable phenomena, like cross-modal interactions in non-synaesthetes. Without going into detail here,[7] it is worth looking into three of these features that make synaesthesia such an interesting phenomenon and that also relate synaesthetic experience to elements that have been considered throughout the *Habitus in Habitat* series like emotions and imaginations.

One important feature in this respect is that genuine synaesthetic experience is in many cases loaded with affect and strongly related to emotional states. This would suggest that research into synaesthesia might also shed light on the highly interesting field of the 'emotional brain', which in recent years has taken evolutionary more basic brain structures and their contributions to emotional, sensory and even homeostatic experiences into their focus.[8] This same interest in emotion is also one key aspect of the philosophy and science of the embodied mind, in the sense that it is becoming more and more clear and empirically trackable in what profound ways emotional and bodily mediated processes underlie and inform our decision-making and even constitute our most abstract thoughts and ideas. Thus in tying together sensory experience and emotion, synaesthesia might open up new paths for research that were not yet envisioned.

The second interesting feature of synaesthetic experience is its phenomenal specificity. As already Galton has noted in 1883, colour synaesthetes "are never satisfied, for instance, with saying 'blue', but will take a great deal of trouble to express or match the particular blue they mean."[9] This taken together with the third feature, 'idiosyncrasy' (no two synaesthetes seem to have the same 'matching' between elements in the trigger domain and the elements in the response domain), makes this condition extremely interesting for related questions of how to approach experiences of other minds and the qualitative feels of their mental lifes. This line of thought and the awareness of the problem of how to gain access to the mental states of others that seem to differ in such an extensive way has been prevalent from the beginning of research into synaesthesia and has led to a specific sensitivity towards the idiosyncrasy of the experiences of synaesthetic subjects: "The psychologist should inquire into the minds of others as he should

7 But see Cytowic/Eagleman: *Wednesday Is Indigo Blue*, pp. 47–56 and the 'test of genuineness' proposed in Baron-Cohen et al.: "Hearing Words and Seeing Colours".

8 For such approaches to emotionality cf. Panksepp: *Affective Neuroscience;* Damasio: *Self Comes to Mind.* The 'emotional loop' involved in synaesthesia figures prominently in Hinderk Emrichs approach, see e.g. his: "Synästhesie als 'Hyper-binding'".

9 Galton: *Inquiries Into Human Faculty and Its Development,* p. 107.

into those of animals of different races, and be prepared to find instances of much to which his own experience can afford little, if any, clue."[10]

It might have been these three features in conjunction with the renewed scientific interest in phenomenal consciousness, the realm of private, subjective experience, which has led to an increase in research and attention given to the field of synaesthesia in recent years. But beyond these rather general points, synaesthesia has also become an explanatory feature in theories of aesthetic responses and the highly interesting, though also highly problematic, field of neuroaesthetics via the element of transfer in metaphor. This has been investigated by Vilayanur S. Ramachandran, who argued that to a certain extent, we are all synaesthetes since we are immediately able to understand notions like 'sharp cheese' or that of a 'dark tone'. He accordingly uses synaesthetic capabilities as a stirrup for what he calls the synaesthetic 'bootstrapping theory of language origins' and implements the transfers enabled by synaesthesia into his neurological theory of art.[11]

## Kinaesthetics

Kinaesthetics have also figured prominently, albeit for an arguably longer time period, in theories of aesthetic responses to artworks. In his *Prolegomena to a Psychology of Architecture* from 1886, Heinrich Wölfflin argued (already reviewing an existing literature on the topic and esp. citing Robert Vischer's notion of 'Einfühlung') that every physical form possesses a character only because we possess a body through which we engage with forms and structures in the environment. He used this insight to answer his main question: "[h]ow is it possible that architectural forms are able to express an emotion or a mood?"[12] In this way, he brings bodily sense, kinaesthesia and empathy together in the immediate emotional appreciation of art works and form elements even beyond architecture – theoretical elements that have been picked up in recent debates on the role of embodied, emotional underpinnings of aesthetic experience.[13] The link between kinaesthetics and emotions can be made palpable by looking at the fundamental role both play in the interaction with the world – but what might be the specific kind of sensing that is constituted by kinaesthesia?

As the ecological psychologist James Gibson noted, what had traditionally been called the 'five senses' and their respective modality-specific feels did not hold up in any of the psychology textbooks of his time (the early 1960s), in

10 Galton: "Visualised Numerals", p. 85.

11 Cf. Ramachandran/Hubbard: "Synaesthesia", and Ramachandran/Hirstein. "The Science of Art", for the passages on metaphor see pp. 30–32.

12 Cited from Mallgrave: *Modern Architectural Theory*, p. 199.

13 See e.g. the contemporary debate on that topic that started with the paper by Freedberg/Gallese: "Motion, Emotion and Empathy in Esthetic Experience", see, for a short review and an enactive reading of their theory, Gallagher: "Aesthetics and Kinaesthetics".

which from 6 to 12 senses were mentioned. He himself refrained from the futile task of separating senses based on modes of conscious qualities and focused instead on the modes of activity which different perceptual systems enable human beings to engage in. He found five such 'systems' of interaction, five external senses (he combined taste and smell and added the vestibular system as basic orientation mode). What he referred to as kinaesthetics is even more fundamental and important and therefore has not been entrusted to just one group of sensory perceptors but "cuts across the functional perceptual system."[14] With its focus on the outward-reaching abilities of the organism and in accordance with a theory of direct perception of environmental 'affordances' (i.e. offerings of the surroundings like e.g. a tree being perceived as 'climb-able' by a squirrel) Gibson's notion is particularly interesting for questions regarding the specific interplay between habitus and habitat. It should be included in the debate alongside related questions, for example those related to 'motor intentionality' that have been mostly derived from the phenomenological tradition, e.g. following Merleau-Ponty or Edmund Husserl.

Husserl's treatment of the relation between kinaesthesia and perception, e.g. in his 1907 lectures on *Thing and Space*, also deserves mention. He describes the interdependence between the kinaesthetic experience and perceptual consciousness in a way that foreshadows current sensorimotor approaches to experience.[15] It is only through the kinaesthetic system and the movement of the whole body that perceptual disclosure of the world is constituted, putting the focus on the active body which guarantees the unity of experience but often recedes from experience in favour of the world. Especially in the phenomenologically informed philosophy and science of the embodied mind, there are ongoing debates over the question whether the concept of kinaesthetics should include the conscious awareness of the body parts and their movement or just their subpersonal tracking.[16] This relates to questions of how kinaesthesia should be defined and specified with regards to proprioception or e.g. the somato-sensory cortex and other comparable systems. For the purpose of the present volume of the *Habitus in Habitat* series, a useful definition but one that is still too unspecific for the questions just introduced would conceive of kinaesthetics along the following lines: kinaesthesia is not the perception of the body as an object; instead it pragmatically defines the body in its activities and as the center of interaction. It is through this proprioceptive awareness that the human subject is able to navigate

14 Gibson: *The Senses Considered As Perceptual Systems*, p. 111.

15 In Husserl's terms perception is 'kinaesthetically motiviated'; see the chapters including this notion in *Thing and Space*. For a detailed outline of a more recent kinaesthetic approach to visual consciousness that is informed by cognitive science see O'Regan/Noë: "A Sensorimotor Account of Vision and Visual Consciousness".

16 Cf. Gallagher: *How the Body Shapes the Mind,* for an overview of debates related to the questions raised in this paragraph, with a specific focus on the role of 'body image' and 'body schema' in these debates.

its environment. In this sense kinaesthetic experience is also directly and prominently situated at the very interface of habitus and habitat.

The various ways in which the moving body constitutes and shapes our conscious experience of the world is thus only one part of the story to be told. How social or cultural scaffolding and artistic practice evolve and unfold, and how they might impress themselves on the human body, constitutes a fascinating question. It was again Wölfflin who anticipated this line of thought, although shying away from its execution: "Whether it is the physical history of the human body which determines the forms of architecture *or* whether this body is determined by them, is a question that goes beyond what we are willing to discuss here."[17] As far-fetched as such questions seem to be, they lie at the heart of understanding the various interrelations and constraints between habitus and habitat, of engaging and being embedded in a richly structured cultural world.

## The essays

Synaesthesia, bringing into focus the complex, rich phenomenal life of the subject, and kinaesthetics, mediating the environment with the personal coordination and emotive system, play a key role in understanding our peculiar relation to the natural as well as cultural environment. An extended discussion of these phenomena will help us to gain a deeper understanding of both our engaging habitus, and the structuring and structure of the habitat.

The first part of this volume investigates the *Phenomenologies of Synaesthesia* and kinaesthetics as an integrative ground for perception and embodied activity. Caroline Jones, in her opening essay, shows how those two phenomena merge into a sixth sense, a sense of the viscera – a unification and an enhancement of the senses at the same time – and argues that it could be claimed with some right that they give contemporary art its 'Urgrund' and object. The story to be told here is one of a shift from 'aesthetic experience' to the 'aesthetics of experience' exemplified by contemporary works of art which set themselves against the bureaucracies of the senses. That is: in opposition to the 20th century modernisms' emphasis on form, the work of the artist includes and transforms the art-goer who is engaged and embodied. Hinderk Emrich's insightful thoughts about the 'world of synaesthesia' start off with the question of how constructivity and perceptuality fit together. Emrich argues that the interaction of 'bottom-up' and 'top-down' processes with a 'ratiomorphous apparatus' plays a key role in synaesthesia – and he concludes that the oscillation between different types of synthesis and analysis are crucial for both synaesthetic experiencing and a

17 Cf. Wölfflin: *Prolegomena*, p. 28: "Ob aber nun die physische Geschichte des menschlichen Körpers die Formen der Architektur bedingt oder von ihr bedingt ist, das ist eine Frage, die weiter führt, als wir hier zu gehn beabsichtigen." Translation into English by the author.

broader phenomenology of human perception. In an approach, informed by contemporary theories of phenomenology and embodiment as well as by practical and artistic knowledge, Gabriele Brandstetter dedicates her essay to the phenomenon of 'listening' in contact improvisation. Listening, here, is not limited to the auditory sense, but it is rather a 'metaphor we live by', referring to a broader sense of kinaesthetic awareness, which – as the metaphor indicates – is synaesthetic in essence. On this basis Brandstetter develops a theory of how the phenomenologies of attention relate to those of kinaesthetics, how kinaesthetic sensuality is shared in space and – furthermore – brings forth its own spatiality, and how listening – in the broad sense of the word – reaches the synaesthetic-kinaesthetic quality of 'being moved' in both the emotional and the sensual meaning of the word.

The second part, *Feeling and Cognition*, approaches synaesthesia by focusing on theories of art and by looking at the elements of disruption and unification with respect to visuality in these theories. Sabine Flach's chapter is dedicated to the question of art experience as a profoundly synaesthetic and kinaesthetic phenomenon. With reference to the involvement of the whole body, its motion, its sensuality and its emotionality on the one hand and to subjective experience on the other, she develops a theory of both visuality and imagination based on a concept of 'images in agitation', closely related to the interaction of habitus and habitat. This approach to visual arts (but not only to those) is then exemplified with a study on Olafur Eliasson, which concludes her essay. In his close reading of Gilles Deleuze's *Francis Bacon. The Logic of Sensation* Sven Spieker investigates the different strategies of de-centering and de-stabilizing vision and the eye. Since Bacon tries to paint the sensation and not what is sensational, he – according to Deleuze – directly tackles invisible and deformative forces in order to liberate the eye and give it a pure presence and, in a sense, its own body.

The third part, *Framing Synaesthesia*, combines three approaches that specify synaesthesia by relating it to adjacent phenomena. The three papers follow the questions of how synaesthesia can be integrated into a general theory of perception, how it relates to other phenomena of binding, and how it is related to broader theories of mental imagery maintained in the $19^{th}$ century. In his discussion of the research on colour-experiences in cases of 'genuine perceptual synaesthesia', Joerg Fingerhut discusses two challenges such cases might constitute for a theory of enactive perception. First, colour experiences in synaesthetic responses seem to track, not something in the world, but rather another experience within the perceiving subject. And second, genuine synaesthesia persists as a perceptual phenomenon without having a world-involving role. Each of these claims challenges the enactivist assumption that the human mind and brain is in a strong sense determined by interactions with the world and is in this sense supposed to be extremly plastic. Enactivism, he argues, has to reflect on the timescales in the explanations it uses and has to emphasize a normative element in order to deal with limiting cases as synaesthesia. Paul Cumming's contribution follows the question of what kind of perturbation of sensory channels synaesthesia consists of. He treats synaesthesia as a special case of binding and reviews several neurobiological and psychological studies dealing with phenomena of integration within the human brain. In contrast to cases like Parkinson's disease or schizophrenia, in which binding fails in certain respects, he argues that synaesthesia constitutes a case of excessive binding related to insufficiently pruned connectivity between neuronal pathways. Karl Clausberg, in his essay, goes beyond the phenomenology of genuine perceptual synaesthesia and shows that in the 19th century, the binaries which are at work for example in cases like graphem→colour synaesthesia would have been treated only as second order or derived forms of a more general variety of mental imagery. He follows the lead of Ernst Kapp's concept of 'organ-projection' and Karl Bühler's 'deictic fields' and brings those ideas to bear in a fascinating interpretation of scrolled voices in medieval art works that constitute synaesthetic gestures of sound and writing. Clausberg relates his insights to the contemporary discussions of the 'extended mind', thereby giving this debate a historical underpinning.

Both synaesthesia and kinaesthetics are intrinsically connected to questions of *Spatialities*, to which the fourth part of this volume is dedicated. In a broad and insightful approach including phenomenology, semiology and research on synaesthesia, Heinz Paetzold argues for a synaesthetic approach to atmospheric phenomena. In dedicating his study to 'flânerie' and to the kinaesthetics of the 'rhythm' of cities, he takes up concepts of both habitus and habitat in order to integrate them into a broader concept of atmospherical synaesthesia as a kind of 'symbolic pregnance' (in Ernst Cassirer's meaning of the word). A cinematic approach to synaesthesia – based on a broad understanding of sensuality and what Cretien van Campen calls 'The Hidden Sense' – is then put forth by Robin Curtis' rich text on filmic ways of modeling spatial kinesis and visual abstraction. Curtis exposes a new approach to sensual engagement with images in motion by relating them to recent psychological concepts such as 'immersion' and 'presence', but most of all in offering a highly insightful discussion of the concept of 'Einfühlung' (in the tradition of Robert Vischer and Theodor Lipps). Isabelle Moffat, in her contribution, offers an analysis of the role 'hermeneutic effort' can play in Jackson Pollock and Cy Twombly. Neatly re-tracing and criticizing Clement Greenberg's approach to Pollock's diverging ways of confronting the 'madeness' of art works and the kinesis of the artist's stroke, she offers an alternative understanding, pointing to the question of self-expression, or, more precisely, of "how to continue as an artist after painterly gesture had become a sign, a trope in the Abstract Expressionist vocabulary." This question, she argues, becomes very prominent in Cy Twombly's divergent approach, whose artistic practice is explicitly set against the illusion of pure self-expression.

The three papers assembled under the title *Modernities* shed some light on paradigmatic figurations of modern aesthetics and literature as well as modern media formats and theory. In his essay Gerhard Scharbert follows the visions of a cosmic, synaesthetic body in the thoughts and writings of Charles Baudelaire and

Arthur Rimbaud. By laying out possible influences of the theories of his time concerning the psychological effects of drugs and physiological treatises of the nervous system, he draws a comparison to similar effects in music – an element which would influence Baudelaire through his exposure to the works of Richard Wagner. This essay provides a sense of the rich knowledge and artistic renderings concerning synaesthesia in the late 19th century. Jan Söffner dedicates his contribution to Rainer Maria Rilke's work. He argues that especially the *Sonnets to Orpheus* were shaped by a poetics of *synaesthesia* as opposed to, but at the same time intrinsically linked with, *referential* concepts of meaning. In discussing the *Sonnets to Orpheus*, he argues for a poetics of immediacy beyond the problem of referential meaning. Rilke's poems are, in his view, as much about the 'synaesthesias of reading' as they are about its 'allegories'. In a media-archeological approach, Wolfgang Ernst's rich paper looks at the divergent temporalities of synaesthesia. In exposing the asynchronies of sensory and technical channels, of neuronal and technical signal processing and the generative codes implied in these processes, Ernst offers an overview of the 'temporal gaps' in the integration of the modality of senses. By taking temporal sense to be at the core of these questions, his chapter succeeds in integrating the history of science with phenomenological, technical, and media-theoretical elements that are implied by the phenomenon of synaesthesia.

The volume closes with two interventions on the discourse about synaesthesia and kinaesthetics, focusing on the *Arts of Synaesthesia*. Two artists express their view of synaesthetic experiences and their importance for artistic phenomena. Ditte Lyngkær Pedersen's reflects on synaesthesia as a special form and method of artistic exploration of the senses. In explaining her own works and projects, she clarifies how a different, creative and open exploration of synaesthetic phenomena can lead to a deeper understanding of human senses. The volume ends with an interview of Kate Hollett (conducted by Sabine Flach and Jan Söffner) in which she explains her work 'Mind Chatter', which she also presented during the conference underlying this volume: a work profoundly concerned with the intermodal aspects of mental activity.

## Acknowledgments

The conference *Habitus in Habitat III – Synaesthesia and Kinaesthetics* was the third major event organized by the research project *Habitus in Habitat*. It took place in October 2010 at the *Zentrum für Literatur- und Kulturforschung* (ZfL) in Berlin and was organized in cooperation with the *Collegium for the Advanced Study of Picture Act and Embodiment* and the *Berlin School of Mind & Brain*. We wish to thank all the participants and all of our colleagues at these three institutions for the fruitful discussions about the topic and for participating in the conference as speakers or chairs. Our special thanks go to the director of the ZfL, Prof. Dr. Dr. h.c. Sigrid Weigel, for her confidence in our research and her commitment to the project and to Prof. Dr. John Michael Krois (†) – who discussed the concepts and ideas of *Synaesthesia and Kinaesthetics* intensly with us in the last years – and Prof. Dr. Horst Bredekamp for their support from the side of *Picture Act and Embodiment*. We are equally grateful for the collaboration with our colleagues from the *Berlin School of Mind & Brain* – and we thank the directors Prof. Dr. Arno Villringer and Prof. Dr. Michael Pauen for being long-term collaborative partners on the project and for discussing with us the insights of cognitive sciences, of philosophy and neurosciences. We also wish to express our gratitude to Patrizia Unger for final proofreading and to Franck Loric for editorial work done on this volume. Special thanks are due to Caroline Schopfer, who assisted our work at the Peter Lang Verlag in Berne.

Berlin, May 2011
Sabine Flach, Jan Soeffner and Joerg Fingerhut

## References

Baron-Cohen, Simon / Maria A. Wyke / Colin Binnie: "Hearing Words and Seeing Colours: An Experimental Investigation of a Case of Synaesthesia", in: *Perception,* 16 (1987) 6, pp. 761–767.

Cytowic, Richard E.: *Synesthesia: A Union of the Senses*, Cambridge, Mass. (MIT Press) 2002.

Cytowic, Richard E. / David Eagleman: *Wednesday Is Indigo Blue: Discovering the Brain of Synesthesia,* Cambridge, Mass. (MIT Press) 2009.

Damasio, Antonio R.: *Self Comes to Mind: Constructing the Conscious Brain,* New York (Knopf Doubleday Publishing Group) 2010.

Deleuze, Gilles: *Francis Bacon. The Logic of Sensation*, Minneapolis (University of Minnesota Press) 2004.

Emrich, Hinderk: "Synästhesie als 'Hyper-binding'", in: Adler, Hans / Ulrike Zeuch (eds.): *Synästhesie: Interferenz, Transfer, Synthese der Sinne,* Würzburg (Königshausen & Neumann) 2002, pp. 25–30.

Flach, Sabine / Daniel Margulies / Jan Söffner: *Habitus in Habitat I: Emotion and Motion,* Bern / New York (Peter Lang) 2010.

Freedberg, David / Vittorio Gallese: "Motion, Emotion and Empathy in Esthetic Experience", in: *Trends in Cognitive Sciences,* 11 (2007) 5, pp. 197–203.

Gallagher, Shaun: "Aesthetics and Kinaesthetics", in: Bredekamp, Horst / John M. Krois: *Sehen und Handeln,* Berlin (Akademie Verlag), forthcoming.

Gallagher, Shaun: *How the Body Shapes the Mind,* Oxford / New York (Clarendon Press) 2005.

Galton, Francis: "Visualised Numerals", in: *Nature,* 21 (1880), pp. 494–495.

Galton, Francis: "Visualised Numerals", in: *The Journal of the Anthropological Institute of Great Britain and Ireland,* 10 (1881), pp. 85–102.

Galton, Francis: *Inquiries Into Human Faculty and Its Development,* London (Macmillan) 1883.

Gibson, James J.: *The Senses Considered As Perceptual Systems,* Boston (Houghton Mifflin) 1966.

Husserl, Edmund: *Thing and Space: Lectures of 1907,* ed. by Richard Rojcewicz, Dordrecht/Boston (Kluwer Academic Publishers) 1997.

Krois, John M.: "Synesthesia and the Theory of Signs", in: Clausberg, Karl / Elize Bisanz / Cornelius Weiller (eds.): *Ausdruck, Ausstrahlung, Aura: Synästhesien der Beseelung im Medienzeitalter*, Bad Honnef (Hippocampus) 2007, pp. 151–160.

Lewanski, Jörg: "Die neue Synthese des Geistes. Zur Synästhesie-Euphorie der Jahre 1925 bis 1933", in: Adler, Hans / Ulrike Zeuch (eds.): *Synästhesie: Interferenz, Transfer, Synthese der Sinne,* Würzburg (Königshausen & Neumann) 2002, pp. 239–248.

Mallgrave, Harry F.: *Modern Architectural Theory: A Historical Survey, 1673–1968,* New York (Cambridge University Press) 2009.

Merleau-Ponty, Maurice: *Phenomonology of Perception*, translated from French by Colin Smith, London (Routledge) 1962.

O'Regan, Kevin J. / Alva Noë: "A Sensorimotor Account of Vision and Visual Consciousness", *The Behavioral and Brain Sciences,* 24 (2001) 5, pp. 939–73.

Panksepp, Jaak: *Affective Neuroscience: The Foundations of Human and Animal Emotions,* New York (Oxford University Press) 1998.

Protevi, John: *Political Affect: Connecting the Social and the Somatic,* Minneapolis (University of Minnesota Press) 2009.

Ramachandran, Vilayanur S. / William Hirstein: "The Science of Art: A Neurological Theory of Aesthetic Experience", in: *Journal of Consciousness Studies,* 6 (1999) 7, pp. 15–51.

Ramachandran, Vilayanur S. / Edward M. Hubbard: "Synaesthesia – A Window Into Perception, Thought and Language", in: *Journal of Consciousness Studies,* 8 (2001) 12, pp. 3–34.

Rösch, Gabriele: "Albert Wellek: Synästhesie als kulturbildendes Phänomen", in: Clausberg, Karl / Elize Bisanz / Cornelius Weiller (eds.): *Ausdruck, Ausstrahlung, Aura: Synästhesien der Beseelung im Medienzeitalter*, Bad Honnef (Hippocampus) 2007, pp. 13–28.

Rowlands, Mark: *The New Science of the Mind: From Extended Mind to Embodied Phenomenology,* Cambridge, Mass. (MIT Press) 2010.

van Campen, Cretien: *The Hidden Sense: Synesthesia in Art and Science*, Cambridge and London (MIT Press) 2008.

Ward, Jamie / Jason B. Mattingley: "Synaesthesia: An Overview of Contemporary Findings and Controversies", in: *Cortex,* 4 (2006) 2, pp. 129–36.

Wölfflin, Heinrich: *Prolegomena zu einer Psychologie der Architektur,* Berlin (Gebr. Mann) 1999.

*Phenomenologies of Synaesthesia*

# Embodied Experience

CAROLINE A. JONES

The turn to experience is a notable feature in contemporary art. There has been a sustained critique of $20^{\text{th}}$ century modernism's emphasis on forms (canonized in mid-century by "formalism" as a critical framework), and an intellectual and artistic targeting of visuality, opticality, and disembodied transcendence as problematic aspects of an older episteme. Contemporary biennial culture is one zone in which aesthetic experience has given way to an aesthetics *of* experience, and artistic strategies increasingly prize the embodiment and multi-sensory activation of the visitor. I will conclude by questioning to what extent this recent aesthetics of experience returns to a prior avant-garde's infatuation with synaesthesia; speculating, on the one hand, about instrumental modalizations of the senses in late capitalism, and on the other, about radical sensory transfers accomplished in new media art.

> [...] there can be no doubt that all our cognition begins with experience [*Erfahrung*]. For what else might rouse our cognitive power to its operation if objects stirring our senses did not do so?
>
> – Kant, 1790[1]

> The forming of the five senses is a labor of the entire history of the world down to the present.
>
> – Marx, 1844[2]

## Introduction

My topic is embodied experience – what that might be taken to mean, which senses might be involved, and why it becomes an issue today.[3] Already in his first critique, Kant was thinking hard about how sensory experience was the *a*

1 Kant: $2^{\text{nd}}$ edition of *Critique of Pure Reason*, p. 43.

2 Marx: *Economic and Philosophic Manuscripts of 1844*, pp. 108–109.

3 This essay works out a theory of the aesthetics of experience that will form the conclusion of my forthcoming book on contemporary art in the global circuit. A related version will also be published in Dumbadze/Hudson, eds.: *Contemporary Art*, (in preparation). I am grateful to the organizers of the "Habitus in Habitat III" conference on Synaesthesia (particularly Sabine Flach and Jan Söffner) for allowing me to develop the more speculative scientific aspects of this argument, and to benefit from the extraordinary work of participating philosophers and neuroscientists.

*priori* to reason; fifty years later Marx reasoned that this primary level of sensory experience had already been deeply marked by industrial capitalism. Far from being rendered obsolete by the collapse of both dreams – Enlightenment reason and state-sponsored socialism – Kant and Marx are still useful to think with. They are emblematic of an historical trajectory not unlike our own, marked by dramatic surges in the international exchange of knowledge and upheavals in the economic order of labor and production. But if theirs were industrial shifts, ours are surges in economies of information and its modes of circulation. Building on Marx's theory of free-floating and available 'General Intellect' – what we would call the general knowledge produced by humans (and what Kant called the *sensus communis)* – theorists of *capitalisme cognitif* (cognitive capitalism) are examining how the instruments of economic time management and intellectual property have come to penetrate our bodies and minds – through every mobile device that is pulsing in our pockets, tapped by our fingers, ringing in our ears.[4] Merging Kant and Marx (via Antonio Negri), these thinkers push us to ask whether the very work of reason – human pattern recognition applied to website security protocols, for example – has become a mode of distributing unpaid cognitive labor over many bodies, labor which can then be harvested as surplus value for Google Books. So if the working of the body's senses must be examined in light of the labor of human history from its origins to our present, then we must also acknowledge, *pace* Marx, that there has been a complete transformation of both labor and the subject during that span of time. From specific bodies working in place-bound industries tied to coal, steel, shipping lanes and railroad right-of-ways, for whom art became a site of transcendent individuation (Monet's *Nymphéas*, for example), we have been sucked by the flows of capital into a world-spanning yet mottled distribution system demanding new post-industrial orders of information and 'experience economies'.[5]

4 Moulier Boutang: *Le capitalisme cognitif.*

5 Pine/Gilmore: *The Experience Economy*, drawing on the work of German sociologist Gerhard Schulze, *Die Erlebnisgesellschaft: Kultursoziologie der Gegenwart.*

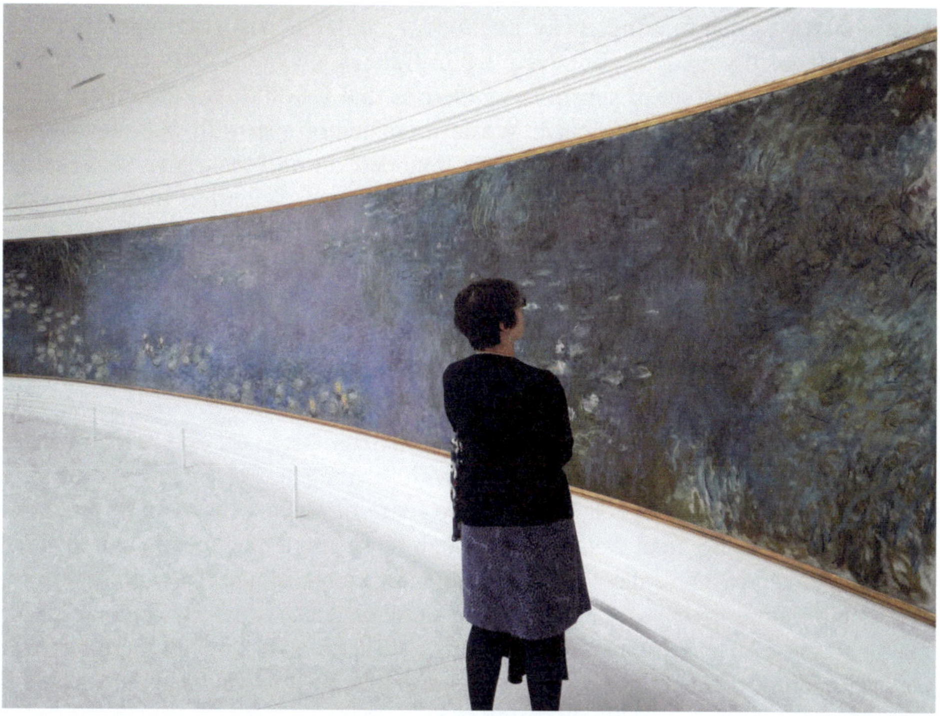

Fig. 1: Visitor with *Les deux saules*, part of Monet's *Les Nymphéas*.

The drift of artistic developments after the second world war (often carried on under the name of Duchamp) has participated in this trajectory, leading us away from objects of art to what I argue is an aesthetics of *experience itself.*

The aesthetics of experience does not entirely collapse into capitalized and instrumental culture. Art, in this argument, is not mere reflection or superstructure. Art *works* to produce new kinds of subjects in many different kinds of bodies; exhibitions aggregate this activity and become subject-making assemblages. As part of my longer project examining two centuries of desires for world pictures, I examine how the contemporary art world subject is increasingly positioned as *produced* by experience, particularly the experience on offer in contemporary biennial exhibitions.[6] How might we understand this now robust aesthetics of experience? First I will offer a summary of its emergence. Then I will explore its dual aspects of embodiment and virtuality – addressing the hermeneutics, the politics, and the paradox of embodied experience and mediation for the publics of contemporary art.

Explicit in my argument is a theory of the senses. Appropriately for this volume, I forward a critique of the disproportionate attention paid by philosophy, art, and science to the sense we call sight, and I celebrate other perceptual modes.

6 In preparation Jones: *Desires for the World Picture: the global work of art.*

Postmodernists' hammering away at modern ocularcentrism during the 1980s certainly feeds my analysis, but even that critique was vision-obsessed. So let me set out an intriguing set of sensory symmetries that I would like to keep in mind as I explore embodied experience. Western epistemologies still operate with an elaborated chart of perceptual pathways, mapped on an essentially Aristotelian schema but updated in light of contemporary physics. Scientists understand the senses to operate through three sets of forces: mechanical, chemical, and electromagnetic. The body meets each of these forces with perceptual apparatuses adjusted to detect either proximate or distant stimuli. That is, *touch* and *hearing* are the mechanical senses, with *hearing* registering sound waves coming from a distance, and *touch* operating through proximate contact to read sense data of pressure and thermal change. Chemistry governs *smell* and *taste* – molecules wafting from a distance are captured by smell, whereas taste can only capture these molecules if they make proximate contact with the tongue. Celebrated as crowning the sensory hierarchy is the electromagnetic sense of *sight,* which can register single photons traveling great distances, although those single photons do not count as 'seen' unless at least 5 of them strike the retina in a tenth of a second.[7]

But if nature loves symmetries, then where, or what, is the *proximate* electromagnetic sense? There are numerous theories "[…] by analogy with the other sensory pairs one expects that the sixth sense operates on low-frequency electromagnetic forces, namely relatively slow-varying electric and magnetic fields."[8] Scientists search for creaturely examples of such proximate electromagnetic detection. In addition to the magnetite in pigeon brains and butterfly wings, there is cryptochrome in bees; such materials (deposited through the metabolic activity of key bacteria) serve these species as visceral navigation aids – but for non-proximate signals from the earth's magnetic core and distant poles; perhaps more suggestive are the electroreceptors in the heads of sharks, which allow them to perceive the proximate and thus very weak electromagnetic signals given off by other living things – prey – that have approached close enough to be seized and eaten.

| **Stimulus at a distance** | | **Proximate Stimulus** | |
|---|---|---|---|
| mechanical: | *Hearing* | mechanical: | *Touch* |
| chemical: | *Smell* | chemical: | *Taste* |
| electromagnetic: | *Sight* | electromagnetic: | ***Kinaesthesia?*** |

Is there a human electromagnetic system that could be imagined to work at the proximate scale? Although I am far from being a physiologist, I venture to specu-

7 Gibbs: "Can a Human See a Single Photon?".

8 Davis: "A Sixth Sense?" cf. article #352, *Alaska Science Forum*, November 8, 1979, online at http://www.gi.alaska.edu/ScienceForum/ASF3/352.html.

late that it would be the somato-sensory systems of the viscera, suggested by the scientific and aesthetic term, *kinaesthesia*. In the 1990s, magnetite was discovered in human brain tissues as well as in tissue extracts of the meninges (membranes surrounding the brain and spinal cord); it has been known for even longer that there are some electrical capabilities in human bones, whose fractures repair more quickly when modest amounts of electrical current are applied.[9] What if we finally came to understand the human musculo-skeletal system as an intimate electromagnetic sensory apparatus, the proximate analogue to sight, the long-imagined 'sixth sense'? In this analysis, somato-sensory nerve systems would work through the viscera and bones to sense minute magnetic and electrical oscillations. Some of these oscillations are produced internally, through the contractions of muscles and the pulsing of nerves. Indeed, this internal electromagnetic stimulus may be the everyday source of the hypothesized sixth sense. Feeling 'electrified' or exhilarated by an art experience, knowing something 'in your bones' or having 'a gut instinct' would all be vernacular names for this proximate electromagnetic sense. On the basis of this somewhat playful set of speculations, I propose that what I am calling *embodied experience* can be posited as the knowledge produced by such as yet under-theorized proprioceptive, visceral, embodied cognitive operations.[10] And what role do the much-hyped mirror neurons play in this? "Human brain activity consistent with that of mirror neurons has been found in the premotor cortex, the supplementary motor area, the primary somatosensory cortex and the inferior parietal cortex."[11] Although the only confirmation of the existence of mirror neurons has come from experiments with small primates, such neurons have been speculated to fire in motor areas of the brain when humans *observe* action or emotion, when humans *hear* a familiar action being performed, and perhaps even when humans read about, listen to narratives about, or otherwise 'imagine' actions or feelings.

Much of this mimetic stimulation falls into the realm of art – a cultural activity specifically developed by humans to engage these powerful systems of empathetic cognition and body knowledge. We can agree to this premise with or without 'mirror neurons' per se, and can imagine embodied and visceral responses whether they might be triggered by a figurative, representational, and visual art (directed to the primary visual cortex), or whether they lodge in the contemporary aesthetics of experience (and involve the entire somato-sensory system). Visceral response would not be confined to representational art, in this argument; it is my thesis that the body's electro-magnetic sensory system can be

9 Kirschvink/Kobayashi-Kirschvink/Woodford: "Magnetite biomineralization in the human brain".

10 In support of such speculation, see the wild and woolly new-age articles of "The Academy for Future Science" particularly Coetzee: "Biomagnetism and Bio-Electromagnetism: The Foundation of Life".

11 This standard definition can be found in the "Mirror Neuron" entry of Wikipedia, http://en.wikipedia.org/wiki/Mirror_neuron, accessed September 2010.

triggered by abstract forms or vague immersive atmospheres just as easily as a landscape painting (and the enormous art historical, scientific, and philosophical literatures on empathy, abstraction, the *ganzfeld*, and Gestalt can be cited here). To be straightforward about it, my claim is that we needn't forbid science from joining our investigations of embodied aesthetic experience. But neither do I believe in a so-called 'neuroaesthetics' that would *explain* the contemporary turn to experience or 'decode' its subject-making procedures with a magnetic resonance image taken from a head in a vise. Let us assume instead that there is a scientifically trackable but experientially polymorphous human capacity for response, distributed across multiple sensory domains, located in moving ambulatory bodies enmeshed in particular social relations, given 'binding' force by compelling political contexts – and that we need to pursue fully cultural explanations to understand their histories.

In my account, there was a precise split between mid-century modernism and the present in these histories. As I have examined elsewhere, modernism (at least as it came to be hegemonic in the postwar U.S.) encouraged an understanding of art as vigilantly *outside* the economic and corporeal systems that rule our lives – high modern art was to be self-reflexive and avant-garde in pursuing the logic of its own medium.[12] The point of this self-reflexivity was to transcend the body through the higher cognition mediated by 'eyesight alone', a practice instantiated in critic Clement Greenberg's writings about Jackson Pollock. To be sure, large-motor masculine labor, a labor empathetically felt to be working class, was part of what mattered in the uptake of Pollock, and in turn became crucial to the installation of late modernism in the American case – but that visceral way of 'knowing' was invoked only to be immediately called away from the specific body of the artist, and sublimated into the civilizing of universal man. In Greenberg's words, we needed an 'Apollonian' culture of 'Athena', not the embodied *agon* of Dionysus. But Greenberg's very success at putting the viscera in its place stimulated a return of the repressed – artists of the 1960s began to critique the epistemic isolation of what Greenberg had called 'our modern sensibility'. They inserted physical bodies into the white cube, into art documentation, and into the space of art history, a conceptualized onslaught that bore fruit in the emergence of Fluxus, Happenings, performance and body art. By the 1990s this legacy had mutated to incorporate new imaging and distributing technologies (among them video and web), and to respond to the demands of postcolonial bodies and narratives – juxtaposing an emerging bodiless virtuality that disguised the source of its labor, with the stubborn reality of marked 'foreign bodies' that refused to disappear. Thus the experience of video and virtuality could be tied to a peculiarly local and situated kind of body, as in the laparoscopic cameras through which we view and explore the orifices of Mona Hatoum's sedated body in *Corps étranger*.

12 Jones: *Eyesight Alone*.

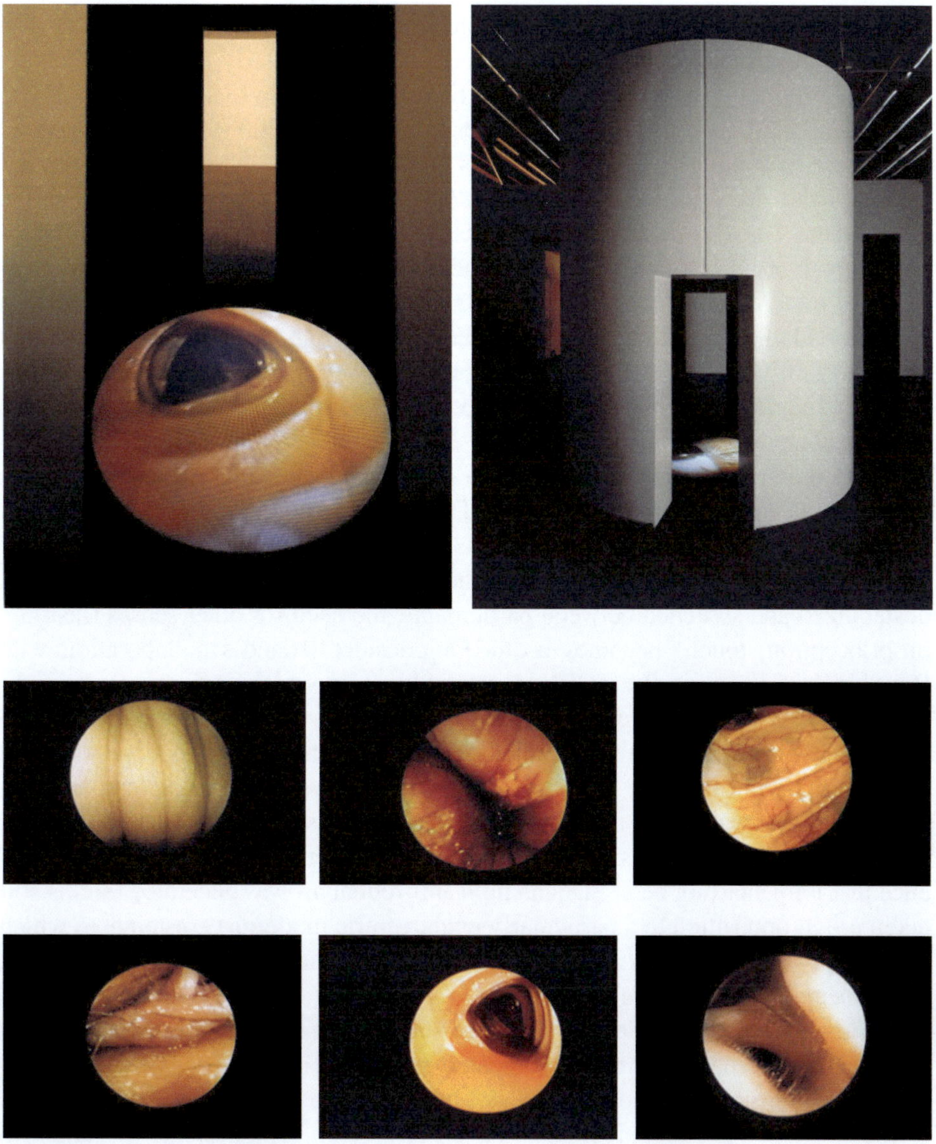

Fig. 2.1–2.8: Mona Hatoum, *Corps étranger*, 1994.

Although we viewers enter this body by virtual means, that journey is experienced as vertiginous and unstable. Viscerally twisting and turning through unnamable invaginations of this other's body, we are empathetically dis-oriented from mastery of our body-world coordinates. This is the present-day dialectic I am interested in charting: the tension between a virtual digital spectacle that seems to forget the body, and the body "remainder" that insistently re-emerges in the aesthetics of experience, an aesthetic of visceral, empathetic, kinaesthetic mirroring in the participant/observer.

How does the historical turn from form to experience announce itself? The art world obsession with embodied experience is particularly notable in biennial culture, offered by installations that are literally located in biennials, such as Cai Quo Gang's *Cultural Melting Bath* (Biennale de Lyon, 2000) but also measured by the rise in popularity of artists such as Olafur Eliasson, whose biennial reputation was the precondition for commissions at major art museums such as the Tate, where *The Weather Project* was staged. The emerging aesthetics of experience signals itself through what Raymond Williams would call the 'residual' ideology of material objects, elemental stuffs, and biomimetic technologies – but this unspoken ideology of thingness, embodiedness, and enhanced presence is sutured together with virtuality and mediation, forming a newly theorized encounter with the body in all of its sensory modes. Expanding the site of knowledge production beyond what modernism fetishized as 'eyesight alone', the contemporary aesthetic of experience also wants a brave new world of amplified and prosthetic supplements for the human apparatus. This is evident in Matthieu Briand's *Sys* installations, which offer schizo-headsets, worn by visitors who then find their vision intermittently reassigned to another's point of view. As vision becomes destabilized and switched between participants, the need for other senses (hearing, proprioception, touch) becomes acute. Or consider Briand's collaboration with Prue Lang in *Fleur de Peau* ('Blossom of Skin'), in which performers and audience alike are submerged in a hazy sea of pulverized talc, across whose airborne particles lasers cut to illuminate bodies and activate what the artists hope will be a Duchampian 'inframince', per Lang: "Something overriding logic and moving between the senses."[13] The invocation of Duchamp by such artists, and the call to a multi- or infra-sensuality, is a significant part of the trend toward embodied experience that I am charting here.[14] Duchamp's anti-retinal art was generated (and is still taken up) in opposition to a particularly ocularcentric modernist episteme, to which it confronts a set of radical cultural alternatives in bodies that are gendered, queer, experimental, or prosthetically enhanced.

This is part of my polemic: when we speak of an aesthetics of experience or embodied participation, it must be located in specific cultural, political bodies – subjects of discourses and visibilities, subjects who cannot be constructed as elemental, essential, or universal. 'We' in any given sentence may be taken to refer to the general art world visitor, but is always in the final analysis only the body of the speaking art historian, a subject spoken in turn by the art and installation she has in-corporated as her 'experience'. But if it must always be understood as localized in this way, how can 'experience' be generalized to an aesthetic? How can we insist on its embodiedness, when digital convergence and accelerated knowledge production are present realities in a networked world of

13 Epigram citing Duchamp on the website of Prue Lang, with reference to the collaborative project with Matthieu Briand, *La Fleur de Peau*, 2005–06.

14 I include myself in this poly-sensorial turn of the zeitgeist, with the 2006–07 exhibition and book project *Sensorium: Embodied Experience, Technology, and Contemporary Art* at MIT.

distributed 'artificial' intelligence? Precisely because it is in such flux, I suggest, embodied experience is a compelling trope, a deeply desired physicality in a mediated, digital contemporaneity so unprecedented that our theories can barely catch up. Amidst all of this, we turn again and ambivalently, to corporeal experience, with the rarefied virtuality of the 'extra-' (supra, infra) human prompting a rethinking of what '80s cybertheorists once denigrated as 'meat machines' – those biopolitical, evolutionary processing units we call the body.

Art is the place we do some of our best thinking and feeling, and curatorially, there has been an efflorescence of interest in kinaesthetics, and in histories and objects of synaesthesia, from the 2005 show *Visual music: synaesthesia in art and music since 1900* (Los Angeles and Washington D.C.) to New York Eyebeam's *What Sound Does a Color Make?* that same year.[15] The Biennale de Lyon provided a self-consciously hippie gloss on kinaesthesia and embodied experience in 2005, with a room of green fog from Ann Veronica Janssens, a meditation lounge from La Monte Young, nerve-stimulators from Carsten Holler, a crystalline visual pod from Eliasson, and a claustrophobic (and hairily static) installation of pink balloons from Martin Creed. The Sensory obsession continued through Rob Storr's curation of the 2007 Venice Biennale, which he called "Think with the Senses, Feel with the Mind."

Many of these exhibitions with their experiential tropes have been staged within biennials. In place of what previous centuries had positioned as 'aesthetic experience', I argue, biennial culture has produced 'an aesthetics *of* experience'. This aggressively departs from Western philosophy's hard-won theory of the aesthetic as a progressively refined system of discrete experiences, beginning with the Greeks' hierarchies of rhetoric, the medieval separation of human activity into the seven liberal arts, and the first explicit theory of aesthetics by Alexander Baumgarten in 1750. This development reached a high point in the German Enlightenment, with Gotthold Lessing's genre enforcements on the sculpted body of Laocoön and his sons, whom Lessing made the eponymous subjects of his essay on the border between the arts in 1766.[16] The Laocoön, in fact, became an icon for sensory regulation, in which aesthetics code for an entire moral universe – beginning with Lessing chastising Winckelmann for his excessive libidinal attachment to the forms of these writhing male bodies in pain, Romantic poet William Blake translating the sculpture's pagan eroticism into a Christian struggle, and Harvard literature scholar Irving Babbitt carrying on the whole sublimatory project into his 1910 book *The New Laokoön: an essay on the confusion in the arts.* Warning his Anglo-Saxon readers against the French Romantics' "breaking down of all barriers and boundaries" Babbitt railed against a dangerous 'mingling of the flesh and spirit', culminat-

15 The academic community has also risen to embrace senses other than sight, evinced by the new journal, *Senses and Society*, and the recently founded doctoral field of "Sensory Studies" (in Canada and England).

16 Gotthold Ephraim Lessing: *Laokoon*.

ing in what he astonishingly termed a "priapism of the soul."[17] It was this screed against an embodied, visceral aesthetics of experience that in turn prompted Clement Greenberg's definitive enforcement of genre purity in his 1940 essay *Towards a Newer Laocoön.*[18] Greenberg brought the late modernist regulation of the senses to their apogee in formalism's dictum that painting was intended for, and should be experienced by, "eyesight alone". This was how reduced aesthetic experience had become in the modernist 20th century, when the transcendent Kantian subject emerged only by isolating aesthetic perception from embodied experience – coming to a peak with Michael Fried's 1967 *Art and Objecthood*[19] essay, which attacked theatricality and everyday literalism, concluding with the famous dictum, 'Presentness is grace'. Presentness in this context meant floating free of the body and its visceral demands.

The aesthetics of experience emerged as a fleshy and theatrical rejection of all this throughout the '60s – from Carolee Schneemann's *Meat Joy* in New York and Paris to Robert Smithson's rovings in New Jersey and the Ruhr Valley. But if such embodied practices staged themselves implicitly against the late modernist bureaucracies of the senses in a variety of international contexts, the result of this emerging aesthetics of experience and embodiment, so much of it located in biennials, documentas, or festivals, was to stimulate a reappraisal of pre-existing histories – the longer experiential histories that have wrapped around art or been referenced by it, but have rarely been understood to be its *medium*, until now. With this in mind, we can see how even the isolated art of painting, so fiercely protected by modernist theory, was pressured to record the onslaught of new experiences in the industrializing city and its numerous grand expositions, a new pictorial regime captured by Edouard Manet and apostrophized by Baudelaire (ably historicized by T.J. Clark) as "the painting of modern life."[20] The point I would add to this well-established critical and art historical literature is that the culture of expositions was not merely a reflection of modern life, but an intensified form of it, one that codified the embodied conjunction of aesthetics and experience that has recently come to be so characteristic of contemporary art. Moreover, it was not simply that artists had to depict this emerging expositionary culture, the very notion of art was altered by it. Technology had a visceral impact *on the body* in these fairs – massive new architectures of steel and glass, streamlined propellers, throbbing industrial engines, automobiles, electric light. It was American historian Henry Adams who experienced all this as an epiphany in the machine hall of the 1900 *Exposition Universelle de Paris*, later narrated in his autobiography as a confrontation he felt in his bones between "The Virgin and the Dynamo."[21] As Adams was writing these memoirs, it would be Duchamp who

17 Babbitt: *The New Laokoön*, pp. 105–106.
18 Greenberg: *Towards a New Laocoön.*
19 Fried: *Art and Objecthood.*
20 Clark: *The Painting of Modern Life.*
21 Adams: *The Education of Henry Adams.*

turned to his fellow artists Leger and Brancusi, standing in front of an enormous propeller at the 1912 aviation fair in Paris to announce: "This is the end of painting. Who could do better than this propeller? Tell me, can you [...]?"[22] Answering his own question, Duchamp first attempted to hybridize the Virgin and the Dynamo in his mechanomorphic bride, later turning from painting altogether to capture the inframince of a non-retinal art in his 'Rotoreliefs'. These strange devices rejected eyesight alone to pulse into the uncanny realms of the human perceptual apparatus, achieving what Babbit would certainly have experienced as a *priapism of the soul.*

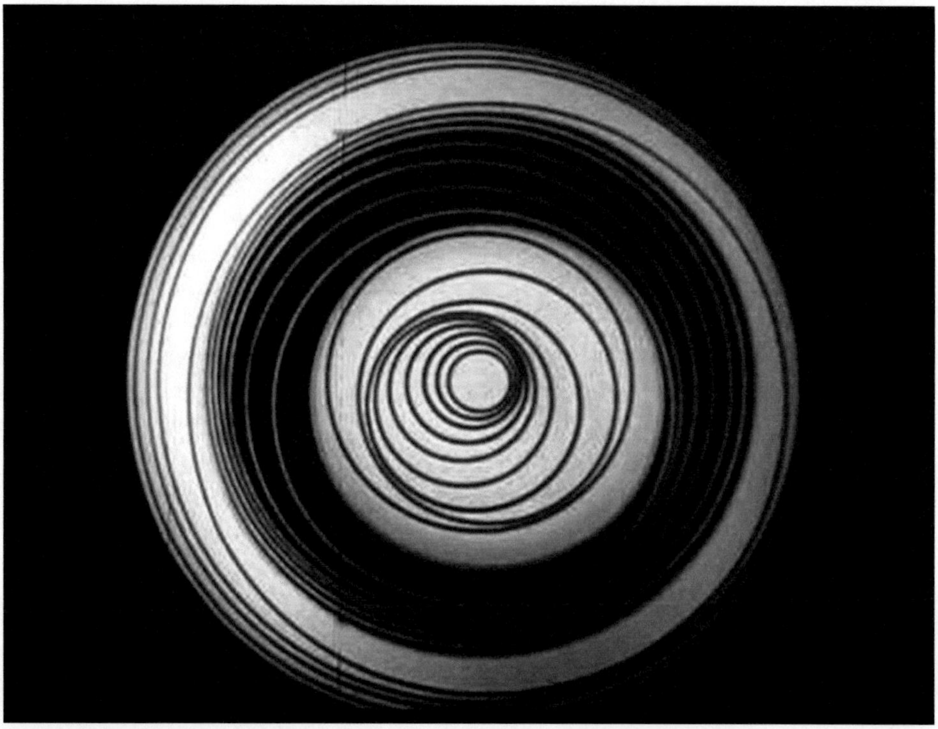

Fig. 3: Still from Marcel Duchamp's film *Anemic Cinema* (1926), showing one of his Roto reliefs in motion. © Succession Marcel Duchamp / VG Bild-Kunst, Bonn, 2011.

In this account, it is no surprise that Duchamp attempted to present the Rotoreliefs at an international fair of inventors in the late 1930s – the biennial art world had not yet caught up with him in observing that the shift from portable art objects to generators of experience was well underway.[23]

22 It was the 1912 *Salon de la Locomotion Aérienne* in Paris, with Duchamp's encounter reported in various sources, among them the foundational Cabanne: *Entretiens avec Marcel Duchamp*. This exposition also had a huge impact on Pablo Picasso and Georges Braque, who began to refer to themselves as "Orville and Wilbur", incorporating fair souvenirs into their Cubist collages.

23 For an excellent introduction, see Betancourt, "Precision Optics/Optical Illusions".

In the kinaesthetics of the rotorelief's pulsating and mesmerizing patterns, Duchamp demonstrated that the electromagnetic sense of sight, so convinced of its mastery of the universe, would be undone by a profound "carnalization of vision" – the viscera claiming its own response.[24] The retina could no longer be master of its house, as Duchamp intended the body to experience these illusory pulsations as three-dimensional phallic probes, their seemingly austere geometries firing the mirror neurons in cascades of empathetic muscular movement, as if color in motion could code directly for the erotics of being. Duchamp was a Dadaist, and the early twentieth-century's tropism for kinaesthesia and synaesthesia can be understood in this light – as a constant if not always noticed alternative to the patriarchal austerities of established aesthetics, a confounding of formalism, a vernacular counter-philosophy to positivist protocols of knowledge. Significantly, it was often film or performance art that solicited this embodied experience, as if tunneling out from static vision to reach that deeper, mirroring electromagnetic sense deep within. Pursuing my original notion, we can imagine this sixth sense of embodied experience asserting itself as the *urgrund* of all art, the place where sight, touch, and hearing anchor themselves in the inchoate electromagnetism generated by the humming of the viscera, Being in the world. On this account, synaesthesia, when it is not a medical but a cultural condition (as it seems to have been for Kandinsky), reveals itself as the space of yearning for this aesthetic *urgrund*, this site of unification and confusion where the senses productively mix, and where creative being can aspire to rebuilding a subject from the ground up. Kinaesthesia is the more organized form in which such sensory stimuli bind to visceral 'experience'.

This returns us to the aesthetics of experience in contemporary art, and the necessarily political questions of *whose* experience we are talking about, where and in what bodies politic. Embodied experience can be profoundly populist, or can be as elite as any part of the art world, as class-bound as the experience economy itself. As I conclude this short essay, we must also address the philosophical questions prompted by routine contemporary curators' invocations of experience. How widely can such experience be shared? If I describe entering and participating in Mariko Mori's *Wave UFO* at a Venice Biennale called 'the Experience of Art', do you believe we have shared one? As a term in English, experience can assert the presence of either immediate or cumulative impacts, 'lived' or 'acquired' knowledge, freshness or seasoned professionalism. In Western philosophy, 'experience' has been buffeted by centuries of competing claims, made all the more complicated by its splitting in German between an earlier *Erfahrung* (from a root for movement) and a later *Erlebnis* (from the word for living). It is further confounded by its double meaning in the French, where *expéri-*

24 For Duchamp's "carnalization of vision" see Krauss: *The Optical Unconscious*. I have also been informed by Scott Richmond's recent work on Duchamp's *Anemic Cinema*, especially his talk "Philosophical Problems of Modernist Aesthetics", presented at MIT in the Spring of 2010.

*ence* is both experience and experiment.[25] Polemically, 'experience' is usually interjected to interrupt the flow of thought and theory, and to stage itself against 'bookish' philosophy and received tradition. The art world wants embodied experience to be populist, accessible, entertaining. Claims to experience act as space holders, allowing something (we will call it 'an experience') to form in the bodies of visitors to this hypothetically neutral, safe space. What the aesthetics *of* experience leads me to claim is that the activities occurring in this space of fluid negotiation can be called the *work* of art, where work is a verb rather than a noun.

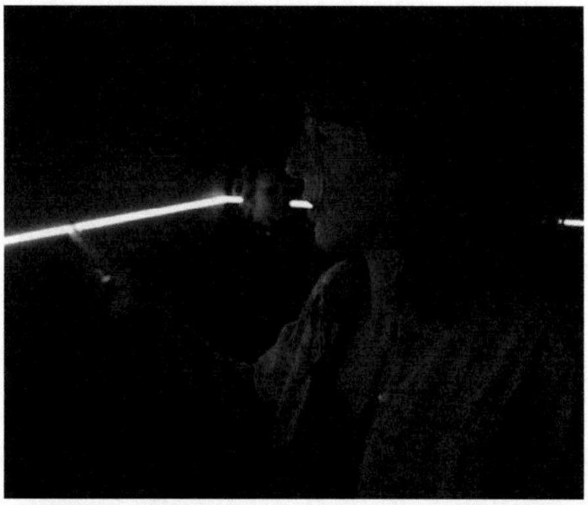

Fig. 4: Visitor with Olafur Eliasson, *Your black horizon*, 2005.

This ongoing-ness, this working in the body of the engaged biennial-goer, is what Olafur Eliasson means to evoke in the repetitions of his titles: *Your foresight endured, Your sun machine, Your inverted veto, Your black horizon.*[26] Without the viewer, as Saint Duchamp pointed out, the creative act is unconsummated. But if Duchamp would emphasize the cerebral and intellectual work of reception, Eliasson wants to foreground the work that begins in the experiencing body of a visitor. Not that the working ends here; this is merely one node in the multiplied processes involving the staging of the work, the slow dawning of situated knowledge from experiencing, and the revisiting of those experiences through mediated discourse. It is not enough to have installed the strip of led-lights at standard viewing height in a blackened interior at the 2005 Venice Biennale for *Your black horizon*. Biennial culture ensures that wall labels, webchat, exhibition catalogue, press coverage, and word of mouth are part of the production, in addition to the expectations about Eliasson (and black cubes in biennials) that the viewer brings along. Further, we needed to learn that the lights which waxed and waned in this installation did so as a function of photon levels emitted by the city of Venice from dawn to dusk, the data compressed and transmitted in a repeating twelve-minute cycle. Suddenly the embodied experience of wandering in the near dark is amplified by thinking and feeling. We wonder about the algorithm.

25 For a magisterial summary, see Jay: *Songs of Experience: Modern American and European Variations on a Universal Theme*.

26 See also Eliasson: *Your Engagement has Consequences, on the Relativity of Your Reality*.

(A temporal compression? Or a stochastic sampling?) *Your black horizon* may even begin worming its way into a darker space of anxiety about a global future without oil, an 'event horizon' of black nights and scary strangers. Experience thus blossoms out from the individual body, potentially to inform a body politic.

This oscillation between micro and macro scales – the subject and the system, the individual and the group – characterizes the claims to experience in biennial culture. But remember that "Experience" is both a utopian aspiration *and* a marketing tool in the 'Experience economy'.[27] It is an authentic yearning and a discursive feint; it is a claim to innocence and an assertion of professional authority – it can be both sacral, and a scam. But if it is always at risk of commodification, it is also in some sense *all we have* to build our communities of action and contemplation. At its simplest, 'experience' is the first stage of a history – the not yet fully examined data set for all readings of art. Here we are advised to recall the critical historiography of Joan Scott from the 1990s: "Experience is a subject's history. Language is the site of history's enactment. Historical explanation cannot, therefore, separate the two."[28]

My brief essay can hardly do justice to the range of philosophers embedded in the history of embodied experience – the seemingly unlikely connections linking John Dewey, a US educator, philosopher, and pragmatist, with the Husserlian and Merleau-Pontyan phenomenology that saturates an Olafur Eliasson installation, both rooted in the branching tree of phenomenology seeded by Wilhelm Wundt in Leipzig, with whom both Dewey's mentor William James and Edmund Husserl himself once studied.[29] And it is no accident that it was students of Dewey who became key theorists and practitioners of Happenings, particularly in the person of artist Allan Kaprow during the 1960s, championing action and agency over disembodied contemplation in the aesthetic field.

Dramatically complicating the white cube, refusing the phenomenological certainty it implies, and putting into question the whole Kantian concept of 'sensus communis', performance and body artists of the '60s actively rejected the bureaucratic separation of the body's sensory portals. Even the rarified domains of Minimal or Systems art began to contend with the social and phenomenological in newly complex ways – if they conceptualized art as never before, they were also grappling with the underexamined 'sixth' sense of visceral embodiment along the way. Today's artists (such as Eliasson) are indebted to the stirrings of participation and body engagement that came out of this crucible of the '60s; particularly the early systems art set-ups of an artist such as Hans Haacke

27 Pine/Gilmore, op.cit.

28 Scott: "The Evidence of Experience", p. 779–793.

29 See Shook: "Wilhelm Wundt's Contribution to John Dewey's Functional Psychology", p. 347-369.

have been revisited and retooled by the '90s generation of experiential artists, inserting the viewer/participant actively into the formula.[30]

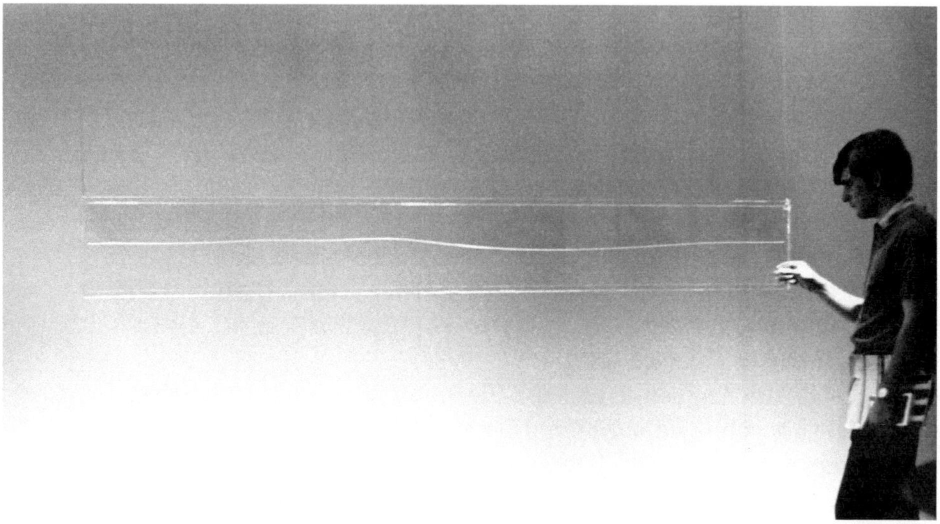

Fig. 5: Participant manipulating one of Hans Haacke's systems art works, *Wave* (1965), in 1967. © VG Bild-Kunst, Bonn, 2011.

The long arc of embodied experience has taken us from the modernist sensorium as it was bureaucratized in the mid-20th century, through the '60s critique of ocularity and aesthetic regulation, to the current hyper-mediated art world of embodied experience – a shift from 'eyesight alone' to visceral knowing. The art of our contemporaneity invites viewers to trust in a momentary suspension of some repressive systems, to entertain a willingness to be surprised and 'reprogrammed'. The question, as always, is what happens afterwards, when the re-oriented visitor reenters the world outside the gallery. Artists today are actively seeking to produce new kinds of subjects; Mariko Mori hopes that the brain waves her subjects generate with their eyes closed will merge into a 'hive mind' of higher consciousness; Eliasson wants us to 'see ourselves seeing'. Such artists welcome the paradigm of the avant-garde, but only so they may fragment the subject of art and reconfigure it to view/smell/hear/feel/taste the world differently. Splitting proliferates as an aesthetic in its own right. Whose glance am I seeing in Briand's headset? Whose mind am I melding with in Mori's? How am I sensing the flux of Eliasson's light? Leaving us open, unbounded, or 'split' is not meant to produce us as psychotic, but to leave us available for re-organ-ization in terms we might be able to negotiate for ourselves, through a new awareness of visceral knowing and the embodied experience of art.

30 This will be explored in depth in the forthcoming exhibition catalogue, *Hans Haacke 1967*, due from the MIT List Visual Art Center in October 2011.

## References


Adams, Henry: *The Education of Henry Adams: An Autobiography*, Boston and New York (Houghton Mifflin) 1918.

Babbitt, Irving: *The New Laokoon: An Essay on the Confusion of the Arts*, Boston and New York (Houghton Mifflin) 1910.

Betancourt, Michael: "Precision Optics / Optical Illusions: Inconsistency, Anemic Cinema, and the Rotoreliefs", in: *toufait* 2 (2003), http://www.toutfait.com/issues/volume2/issue_5/articles/betancourt/betancourt.html.

Cabanne, Pierre: *Entretiens avec Marcel Duchamp*, Paris (Belfond) 1967.

Clark, Timothy. J.: *The Painting of Modern Life: Paris in the Art of Manet and His Followers*, New York (Knopf) 1985.

Coetzee, H.: "Biomagnetism and Bio-Electromagnetism: The Foundation of Life", originally published in *Future History*, Vol. 8, now online at the *Academy for Future Science* website, http://www.affs.org/html/biomagnetism.html.

Davis, T. Neil: "A Sixth Sense?" in article n°352, *Alaska Science Forum*, (1979), http://www.gi.alaska.edu/ScienceForum/ASF3/352.html.

Eliasson, Olafur: *Your Engagement has Consequences, on the Relativity of Your Reality,* Baden, (Lars Müller Publishers) 2006.

Fried, Michael: "Art and Objecthood" (1967), in Michael Fried: *Art and Objecthood. Essays and Reviews*, Chicago (The University of Chicago Press) 1998, pp. 148-172.

Gibbs, Philip: "Can a Human See a Single Photon?" (1996), http://obscure.org/physics-faq/Quantum/see_a_photon.html.

Greenberg, Clement: Towards a Newer Laokoon, in: *Clement Greenberg. The Collected Essays And Criticism*, vol I, ed. by John O'Brian, Chicago (The Univiserity of Chicago Press) 1986, pp. 23-37.

Jay, Martin: *Songs of Experience: Modern American and European Variations on a Universal Theme*, Berkeley (University of California Press) 2005.

Jones, Caroline A.: *Eyesight Alone: Clement Greenberg's Modernism and the Bureaucratization of the Senses*, Chicago (The University of Chicago Press) 2005.

Kirschvink, J. L., Atsuko Kobayashi-Kirschvink, Barbara. J. Woodford: "Magnetite biomineralization in the human brain" in *Proceedings of the National Academy of Science U S A,* 89 (1992) 16, pp. 7683–7687, http://www.ncbi.nlm.nih.gov/pmc/articles/PMC49775/.

Krauss, Rosalind: *The Optical Unconscious*, Cambridge (MIT Press) 1993.

Lessing, Gotthold Ephraim: *Laokoon: oder, Über die grenzen der mahlerey und poesie*, Berlin (C.F. Voss) 1766.

Marx, Karl: *Economic and Philosophic Manuscripts of 1844*, translated by Martin Milligan, Mineola, N.Y. (Dover Publications) 2007.

Moulier Boutang, Yann: *Le capitalisme cognitif: la nouvelle grande transformation*, Paris (Éditions Amsterdam) 2007.

Pine, Joseph B., James H. Gilmore: *The Experience Economy*, Boston (Harvard Business School Press) 1999.

Richmond, Scott: "Philosophical Problems of Modernist Aesthetics: The Unfinished Business of Modernism in Film Theory" talk presented at MIT in the Spring of 2010. http://lit.mit.edu/audio/scottrichmondlecture-01-15-10-edited.mp3.

Schulze, Gerhard: *Die Erlebnisgesellschaft: Kultursoziologie der Gegenwart*, Frankfurt am Main and New York (Campus) 1992.

Scott, Joan: "The Evidence of Experience" in *Critical Inquiry,* 17 (1991) 4, pp. 779–793.

Shook, John Robert: "Wilhelm Wundt's Contribution to John Dewey's Functional Psychology", in: *Journal of the History of the Behavioral Sciences,* 31 (1995) 4, pp. 347–369.

## List of Illustrations

Fig. 1: Visitor with *Les Deux saules* panel of Claude Monet's suite of paintings *Les Nymphéas*, donated to the French people in 1922 and installed at the Musée de l'Orangerie, Paris.

Fig. 2.1–2.8: Installation set-up and details from Mona Hatoum, *Corps étranger*, 1994, Video Installation with cylindrical wooden structure, video projector and player, amplifier, four speakers, 350 x 300 x 3000 cm. © Mona Hatoum. Coll. Centre Pompidou, diffusion RMN, photo Philippe Migeat. Images: présentation dans les Collections Permanentes, MNAM/CCI, Centre Pompidou, 1994–1995.

Fig. 3: Still from Marcel Duchamp's film *Anemic Cinema* (1926). © Succession Marcel Duchamp / VG Bild-Kunst, Bonn, 2011.

Fig. 4: Olafur Eliasson, *Your black horizon*, 2005, Thyssen-Bornemisza Limited Edition Art Pavilion on Isola San Lazzaro, Venice, Italy.

Fig. 5: Hans Haacke, *Wave*, 1965, Howard Wise Gallery, New York. © VG Bild-Kunst, Bonn, 2011.

# The World of Synaesthesia
# Subjectivity and the Brain – Synthesis

HINDERK EMRICH

## 1. Introduction

The topic of my chapter intends to contribute to the understanding of what I call the 'world of synaesthesia'. Do synaesthetes really live in another world, compared to the subjective selves of other individuals? Are individuals experiencing synaesthesia really generating other types of habituations in some perceptual cognitional and emotional respects? And how can these habituations be characterized in the understanding of the nomenclature of this volume?

The phenomenology of synaesthesia is greatly related to the problems of unifying processes in perception, and my 18 years of research in subjectivities and objective brain correspondences of synaesthetes led me to come to this conclusion: there is not one world of synaesthesia but there is a great diversity of so to speak synaesthetic sensory habituations. It means there are many different worlds of synaesthetes, which imply different types of synaesthetic couplings and unifications in sensory processes as well as differences in the emotional awareness of synaesthetic experiences, and lastly the challenging phenomena of emotional synaesthesia. How can we cope with this great number of highly differentiated types of synaesthetic subjective worlds? How can we – from a neurobiological point of view – explain in neuropsychological terms the so to say 'synaesthesia-spectrum'? In order to better understand this subject, one has to raise the questions of interaction, superimposition, and perceptual processes as well as of the constructivity of the brain.

## 2. Aisthesis: constructivity and perceptuality: how do they fit together?

In the recent past, evolutionary biology of vertebrates has shown that the process of so to speak 'encephalisation' (in the sense of Taillard de Chardin) has evolved simultaneously from perceptual and volitional processes within the so called *rhinencephalon*, which is the part of the brain in which perception, by way of smelling and tasting environmental elements, gives rise to processes of seeking or avoidance. In higher mammalian brains this structure has evolved to the 'prefrontal cortex', a region which is related to, so to speak, 'curiosity', interest, novelty-seeking, the generation of conceptualizations of possible realities, the ability of reality-constructions and the formation of 'intentionality' in both senses of the neuropsychological term.

Recent understanding of aisthesis points to the view that the superimposition of two major basic functionalities represents the matrix of aisthesis, on the one hand the so called 'top-down' (i.e. conceptualizing) component and on the other hand the purely sensory faculty within the brain which has been characterized as being 'bottom-up'.

If we try to conceptualize the bottom-up component, one should be aware of very elementary perceptual functions, e.g. in the vegetative system the monitoring of sugar concentration or $CO_2$ tension within the blood circulation of the brain. This would be an example of 'pure sensitivity', whereas on the other hand an example of 'pure constructivity' might be represented e.g. by the 'a colour within a dream'. Interestingly, when we hear about experiences of synaesthetes, who claim that sometimes they experience synaesthetic colours (e.g. Martian colours) which cannot be represented by any obvious colour, it becomes clear that this – philosophically – so to speak 'idealistic' top-down component, apparently exerts its own autonomous neuropsychological rights in opposition to the so to speak purely 'sensualistic' components of 'bottom-up' processes within the functionality of the human brain.

The famous book of Thomas Nagel, *The View From Nowhere*[1], construed a world in which an "objective self" might exist and could be elaborated from a perspectiveless perspective. Common sense neurobiology, however, is 'naïve' in the description of the philosophical problems regarding the question on how the subjectivity of persons and the objectivity of brain processes may belong together. Due to these unresolved problems, neurobiology of aisthesis, the so to speak 'neurosciences of sensate cognition' is still a nascent field of research. It rather tries – within an iterative asymptotic approximation – to establish some innovative ideas about how – due to a complex interaction of subcomponents within the investigable brain – the subjective experiences are generated in sensory cognition. The present paper aims at outlining my personal view in this regard, elaborated in the context of basic clinical research.

In his well-known book on aisthesis in Aristotle, Wolfgang Welsch[2] points out that aisthesis belongs to the domains of understanding, of intelligence, of recognition. However, as he shows, it is a "lower form of understanding" in the conceptualisation of Aristotle. Why is such a lower form of cognition – aisthesis – of

1 Nagel: *The View from Nowhere.*
2 Welsch: *Aisthesis: Grundzüge und Perspektiven der aristotelischen Sinneslehre.*

such great interest in basic psychiatric research? For the elucidation of the causal factors of mental disorders, perceptual processes (of aisthesis) are very important, since they may represent the only possible window – an interface – to enter the disturbed subjective cognitive sphere of mentally ill individuals, which can be used in an operational and quantifiable manner.

Ernst Pöppel, in an article about the neurobiology of aisthesis[3] has pointed out the relevance of so called 'bottom-up' processes in data processing of perceptual patterns in the CNS and that additionally 'top-down'-components have to be considered. He claims that "the brain is not a passive filter" but it has conceptualizing and shaping creative power. That aisthesis is not only passively processing data but is an active process which can be demonstrated in many ways, e.g. in optical illusions or in ambiguous figures. This statement can be considered as an outline of the research-concept, relevant to basic clinical research on aisthesis.

The interaction of these two components of aisthesis (poiesis and data-processing) under normal and pathological circumstances is the main subject of my research in psychiatric cognitive neurosciences. The 'bottom-up' components have been very elegantly discovered in the visual system by the pioneering work of Hubel and Wiesel.[4] Their papers demonstrate that primary sensory data are analysed step by step by highly specialized neuronal assemblies which detect e.g. the direction of a movement, a contour, the colour or another quality of a retinal excitation/inhibition-pattern. If one considers naïvely the physiology of perception; one may anticipate that this is the whole story regarding perception and aisthesis. This is demonstrated in the cartoon in figure 1a as a paradigm of 'naïve realism', or so to speak 'radical sensualism'. In this view, aisthesis is nothing else but the computational evaluation of an outer reality (in this instance of a tree) by a computer using sensory inputs (a camera, a microphone). The brain would – in this metaphor – be a pure 'sink', not a 'source' of information (and meaning). However (c.f. fig. 1b), as Immanuel Kant already pointed out, an interpretation of reality is only possible if a leading conceptualisation (a "world model") is applied to the raw material of sensational inputs. (Fig. 1a/1b)

3 Pöppel: "Zum formalen Rahmen des ästhetischen Erlebens".
4 Hubel/Wiesel: "Brain mechanisms of vision".

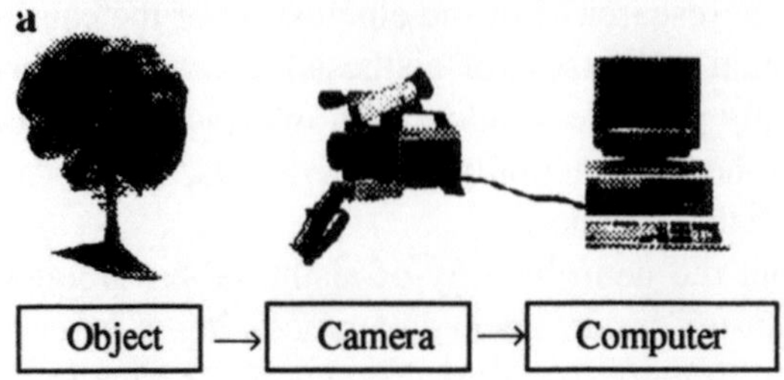


Fig 1a: Representation of "naïve realism".

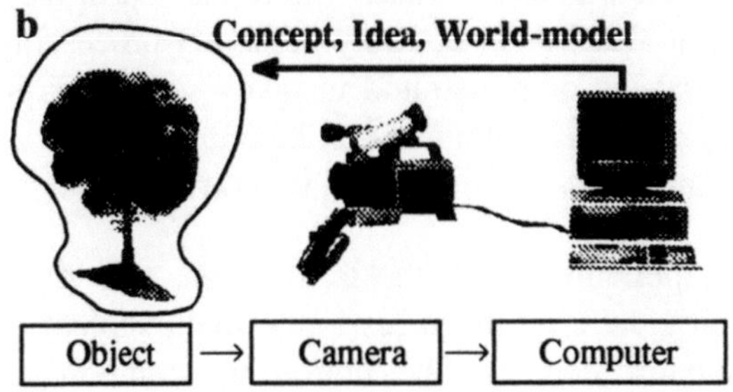


Fig 1b: Representation of the primary role of conceptualization in aisthesis.

Referring to Immanuel Kant, the philosopher Wolfgang Welsch[5] wrote in an article on aisthesis, that "we recognize" only these "aspects of things apriori in which we project ourselves" (Kant: *Kritik der reinen Vernunft*) and these are primarily aisthetic preconditions of, namely the recognition-categories of space and time.

As a consequence, we can construe an interactional circuit in which the interpretation of sensory data is only possible by the conceptualization of hypotheses on possible realities; so to speak nuclei of pre-categories which are – for experimental purpose – used to test the applicability of hypothetical world-models. The 'top-down-components' might also be interpreted as the manifestation of a constructivistic part within the neuronal basis of aisthesis. Recently, a cartoon was published in the famous textbook of neurobiology edited by Gazzaniga, Desimone[6] (Fig. 2), in which the superimposition of bottom-up- and top-down-components is conceptualised as a manifestation of two streams of excitation, antagonizing each other.

5 Welsch: *Die Aktualität des Ästhetischen*.
6 Desimone et al: "Multiple Memory Systems in the Visual Cortex".

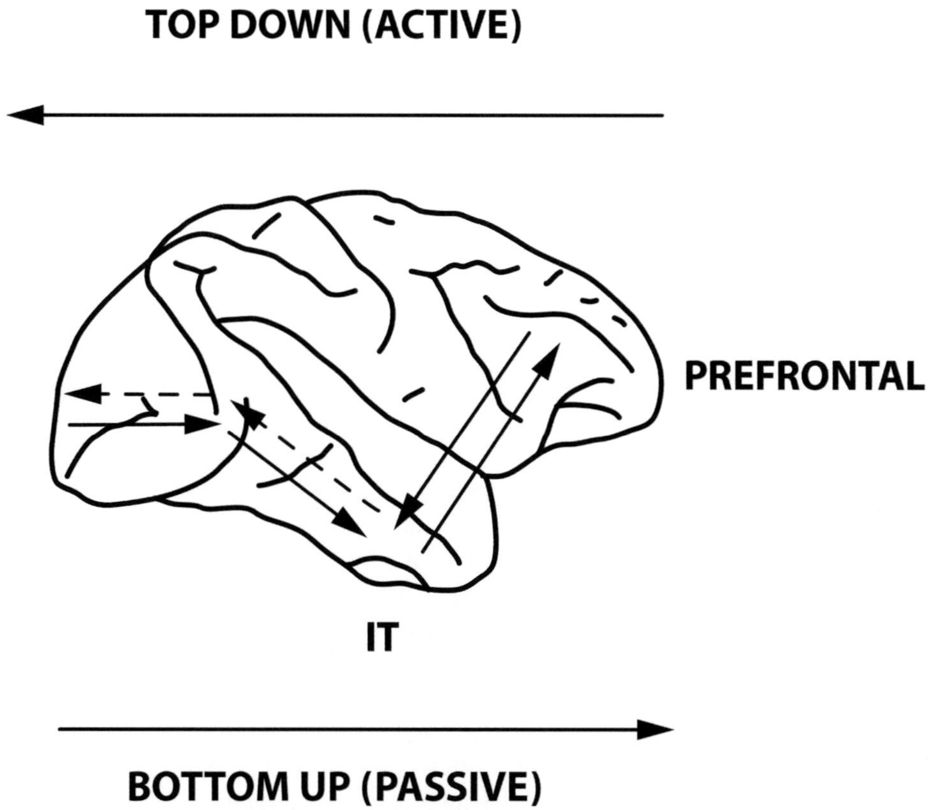


Fig. 2: Cartoon illustrating the processing-strategies of 'top-down' vs. 'bottom-up'.

From a 'neuro-philosophical' point of view, the interesting fact in this cartoon, is that the human brain is apparently able to represent a whole spectrum of representations, starting from pure sensitivity (occipital cortex, 'bottom-up') over a great number of mixed states to pure constructivity (frontal cortex, 'top-down'). It also appears that oscillations between the different types of representation are possible.

I would like to especially focus on the area in the middle, the temporal brain, where these two streams converge, since a particular concept regarding the functional meaning of these temporal brain-structures in aisthesis can be proposed. This function is related to a third component, relevant in processes of conceptualisation of 'reality', namely internal 'censorship'. This component is also attributed to plausibility control, to stabilization of internal data processing, if ambiguity and instability of percepts in emergency-situations occur. It is attributed to a component, which may operate on incongruences in percepts and thus may induce a predominance of fictional and internal reality over the intricate un-assimilated raw material of information on the outer reality.

Consequently, one may propose the 3-component-hypothesis-model about aisthesis:

1.: Sensitivity ('bottom-up')
2.: Constructivity ('top-down')
3.: Censorship ('ratiomorphous apparatus')

The main work of my neurophysiological research group about psychiatric cognitive neuroscience deals with a quantification of these types of interactions under normal and pathological conditions.

In his article about neurobiology of aisthesis, Ernst Pöppel claims that knowledge about functional meaning of special assemblies within the human brain has mainly been deduced from pathological conditions, local brain injuries and disturbances due to stroke, thus leading to maps of functional localizations, which grosso modo have been replicated by functional imaging of the brain. In the particular environment of psychiatry, functional defects are not easily localizable disorders but represent a series of functional psychotic decompensations, especially in schizophrenia. This concept makes possible the investigation of the results of cognitive and perceptual changes induced by the intoxication of probands with hallucinogens like cannabinoids and e.g. ketamine (Emrich 2006).[7]

An elaborated research about this subject has to combine two different approaches: one is a refined, operationalized and quantifiable investigation on subjective events in particular modes of aisthesis; the other is an objectivation of the brain-events correlated to these internal subjective experiences.

My research group has implemented this double-strategy and will continue in that direction in the near future.

## 3. Aisthesis and synaisthesis: the problem of intermodal integration

The phenomenology of synaesthesia deals with the topic of intermodal or transmodal integrations, which can be so intensely experienced by the subject that the impression of a 'unifying process in the sensing' occurs. Therefore it appears not to be a composition or an association, but a new complex entity with all the characteristics of a *Gestalt*, of a new qualitative item, a holism. The sentence "why is the A red?" can be understood as pointing to a coupling in which a decomposition, a deconstruction seems impossible. Examples are the impressions during musical events (Fig. 3), in which complex visual structures are experienced for the duration of the performance.

7 Emrich: "Systems-Theory of Psychosis – the Relevance of 'Internal Censorship'".

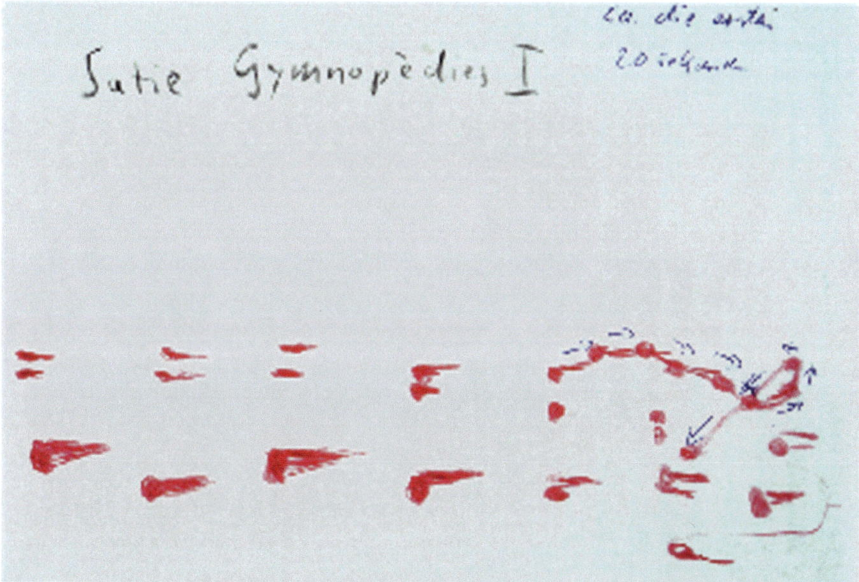


Fig. 3: Visualization of visual synaesthetic impressions, hearing music (M. Waldeck).

Or in another example we find the description of an emotional synaesthesia induced by an organ concert in a church (Fig 4).

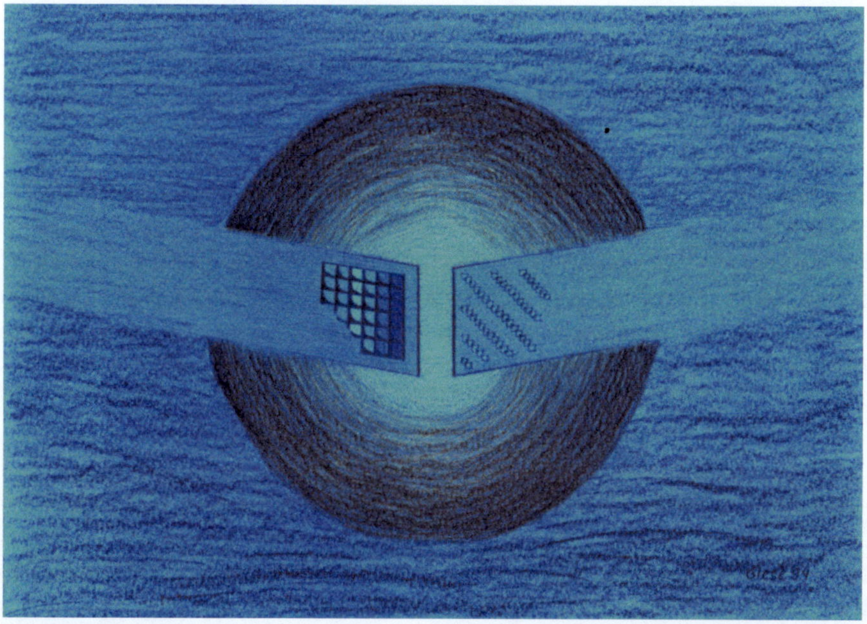

Fig. 4: Graphical representation of a synaesthetic perception while hearing a church organ (G. Giese).

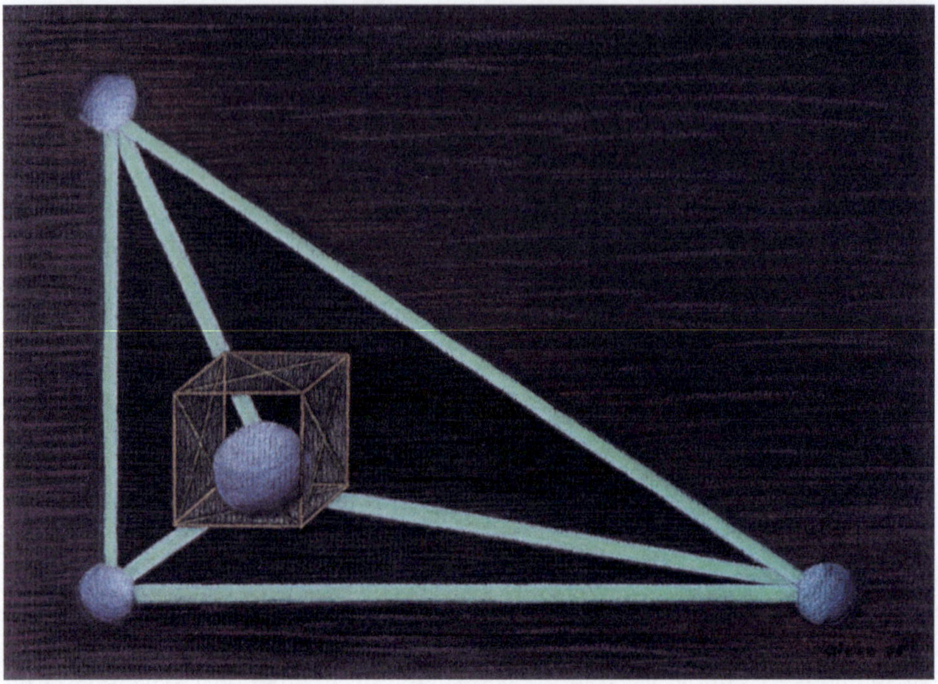

Fig. 5: Depicts the impression of an impression of taste, represented by a geometrical visual percept.

Some years ago, I proposed the idea that synaesthesia represents an unusual occasion and position in a process which normally generates transmodal integration in the brain, i.e. the ability of construing a multimodal object due to the neurobiology of the so called 'binding'-process within the brain. In this sense, synaesthesia would represent a 'hyperbinding' in the particular circumstance of perceptual processing.

From the point of view of Immanuel Kant's *Critic of pure reason* this has to do with the concept of 'synthesis'. According to Immanuel Kant the "I think" must always be able to accompany my propositions. This sentence does not mean that my propositions are always really accompanied by my "I think". But the postulate is, that – at least under normal conditions – any proposition can be accompanied by my cognition "I think this". One could question in which way and under which conditions our perceptions are representations of such types of synthesis? The problem of transmodal integration of senses, the generation of contexts – and thus the genesis of a unification of the multiple aspects of an intentional object into one single entity – represents one of the most challenging topics of contemporary neurobiology: how is the mechanism of transmodal integration constituted? For this fundamental neuroscientific question, the paradigm of synaesthesia may represent a crucial, so to speak, 'nature-experiment'. And therefore it may be extremely fruitful to perform this type of research using a sophisticated neurobiological method.

Under the condition of these working hypotheses about synaesthetic synthesis, the question may arise as to how complete is this synthesis? Many probands claim that their internal constructs of synaesthetic icons, their, so to speak, 'hyperobjects', have the quality of irreducibility: they cannot be decomposed into their constituents. On the other hand, they claim that they can think this construct without the colour or the colour without the cognitive symbolic meaning. Therefore I would think that there is a specific type of ambiguity within the understanding of the holism of synaesthetes' percepts; and my guess is that, like with the top-down and bottom-up processing, there is a 'spectrum of degrees of completeness of synthesis'.

## 4. Subjectivity and objectivity: loneliness within qualia

One of the major advances in contemporary neurobiology is the fact, that it is possible to simultaneously record objective functional events in the brain and the statements of the probands regarding their subjective experiences. For each synaesthete and under each environmental and subjective conditions the quantitative and qualitative events in synaesthetic experiences are highly divergent, hence my need for the voice of an artist.

In his fundamental book of 1910 *Concerning the Spiritual in Art*, Kandinsky describes the relation between music and art in a highly philosophical way. His understanding of the relation of music with painting and colour is due to very early impressions in Moskau. He described the city in a letter in which he refers to Claude Monet and the hearing of Lohengrin by Wagner. Kandinsky wrote:

> This impression does not last long. After a few minutes the sunlight becomes redder, redder and stronger, at first cold and then warmer and warmer. The sun is melting and the whole Moskau is condensed to one point, which like an expressive tuba induces a vibration of the inner world, of the totality of psyche. No, this red uniqueness is not the nicest hour, this is only the final tone of a symphony in which any colour is exaggerated to the highest type of life in a fashion which makes the whole Moskau sound like a giant orchestra and induces different colours like yellow, white and blue houses to have their own chant, their own voice ... the snow is singing with a thousand voices ...[8]

8 Kandinsky: *Concerning the Spiritual in Art*, p. xx.

## 5. Summary

The hypothesis is that conscious perceptual events in synaesthesia are driven by oscillations on the one hand between top-down and bottom-up processes and on the other hand by oscillations between different types of synthesis and – on the contrary – of analysis of the holistic *Gestalt* within synaesthesia.

## References

Desimone Rober / E. K. Miller / L. Chelazzi / A. Lueschow: “Multiple Memory Systems in the Visual Cortex”, in: Michael Gazzaniga (ed): *The cognitive Neurosciences*, Cambridge, Massachusetts (MIT Press) 1995, pp. 475–486.

Emrich, Hinderk M. / F. Markus Leweke / Udo Schneider: “Systems-Theory of Psychosis – the Relevance of ‘Internal Censorship’”, in: *Pharmacopsychiatry* 39 (2006) Suppl. 1, pp. 52–53.

Hubel, David / H. Torsten / N. Wiesel: “Brain mechanisms of vision”, in: *Scientific American* 241 (1979) 3, pp. 150–163.

Kandinsky, Wassily: *Concerning the Spiritual in Art.*

Nagel, Thomas: *The View from Nowhere*, Oxford (Oxford University Press) 1986.

Pöppel, Ernst: “Zum formalen Rahmen des ästhetischen Erlebens. Ein Beitrag aus der Hirnforschung?”, in: Wolfgang Welsch (ed.): *Die Aktualität des Ästhetischen*, Munich (Fink) 1993, pp. 227–246.

Welsch, Wolfgang: *Aisthesis: Grundzüge und Perspektiven der aristotelischen Sinneslehre*, Stuttgart (Klett-Cotta) 1987.

## List of Illustrations

# "Listening…"
# Kinaesthetic Awareness in Contemporary Dance

GABRIELE BRANDSTETTER

"Listen!"

This appeal is generally intended to attract the attention of another person. *LISTEN* was the title given to a series of 'lecture demonstrations' by the American musician and performer Max Neuhaus in the 1960s.

"What interested me at first," he wrote,[1] "was the imperative expressed by the word 'listen'." He goes on to tell a private anecdote about how he hit upon this theme: "My girlfriend at that time – who was of French-Bulgarian origin – used to shout this word when she got into a rage before proceeding to throw objects at me." His first work as a free-lance artist was to take people who wanted to attend a 'concert' of his on a 'walk' through Manhattan's 'Lower East Side'. He took a rubber stamp and stamped the word "listen" on the hands of those who had come to the concert and walked with them through certain streets and districts. Concentrating entirely on hearing, he "just set off"[2] and remained silent during this guided tour of the everyday environment. "At first people found it somewhat embarrassing," Neuhaus continues, "but my concentration was usually infectious." After this attentive walk through these everyday sonic landscapes, "many of them had found a new kind of hearing for themselves."[3]

So much for Max Neuhaus. But who could attend this 'Listen' lecture demonstration without being reminded of John Cage's performance of *4'33"*, that silent piece in which the solo instrument, the piano, was *not* heard? What happened instead was that a space of attention was opened for the numerous noises and sounds heard inside and outside the concert hall.

*Listen*: the reduction of sensory attention to an "act of hearing" was used in yet another way by Xavier le Roy in his solo performance *Self Unfinished* (1998). Le Roy begins the piece by entering a vacant white space and going towards a tape deck and pressing a button, as though starting the music for a (dance) piece. However, not a sound is heard, neither music nor noise. Le Roy makes the *gesture* of opening a sonic dimension and thus brings about an *act* of 'listening'. The drawing of the audience's attention to a *possible* hearing event changes the hearing *and* the attention. This focusing of an act of 'listening' facili-

1 Neuhaus: "LISTEN".
2 Ibid. p. 126.
3 Ibid.

tates – synaesthetically speaking – a *different* perception of space and movement. *Listen!*: listening to the movement, hearing the body-space movement, means that the seeing receives a different, an additional sensory (kinaesthetic) quality. As Paul Valéry, for whom the ear was the preferred sense for conveying attention, said, the ear "keeps watch, so to speak, at the frontier beyond which the eye does not see."[4]

'Listening' is a term belonging to the basic vocabulary of contact improvisation. The following remarks are intended to investigate the use of the concept and see how it ties in with the discussions and practices of 'kinaesthetic awareness'. Cheryl Pallant remarks in her introduction to "contact improvisation" as a "dance form"[5] that "listening," "listening to motion," is a term…

> […] regularly used in contact improvisation. Listening, according to contact improvisation's metaphorical use of the word, refers to paying attention to all sensory occurrences arising from touch, from the play of weight as partners move through space, and from the event of one body encountering the presence of another. Listening refers to noticing stimuli not only within oneself but also from another.[6]

The range of meanings covered by the word 'listening' refers to one of those – open – scenarios of the metaphorical, which Lakoff called "metaphors we live by."[7] Thus the image of a summons to an act of 'listening' refers to a field of perception of the sensory, which is not just limited to acoustics. It is a synaesthetic network of experiences of the body, of its internal and external states at rest and in movement. It involves awareness, which in contact improvisation is exercised and refined in a multitude of ways in and through synaesthetic-kinaesthetic addressings of perception. A selection of sentences that act as a guide to such (synaesthetic) perception could illustrate the range covered by 'listening' (quoted from Cheryl Pallant):

> – *Listen to the click of cartilage, the slap of skin, of the whisper of your will typically silenced by a shout.*
> – *Notice a part of your body for which you have no name, no history, no awareness* […]
> – *Feel weight push into your stubbornness, your expectations, against your habit of always yielding to aggression or constantly fighting it.* […]
> – *Sniff the circumstances, the leg extending into view, the hand urging direction* […]
> – *Watch time dissolve* […]
> – *Follow the sound into the garden past the bench in the corner on* […]
> – *Tend your body as if it were the body of a lover* […]
> – *Drink the elixir of expansion, the release within repose*

4 Valéry: *Cahiers*, Vol. II, p. 934; cf. Waldenfels: *Phänomenologie der Aufmerksamkeit*, p. 198.
5 Cheryl Pallant: *Contact Improvisation.*
6 Ibid., p. 31 f.
7 Lakoff and Johnson: *Philosophy in the Flesh*; Johnson: *The Body in the Mind.*

> *– Find the edge between comfort and discomfort, the familiar and the unknown. Balance there, however precariously.*
> *– Devolve into protozoa.* [...]
> *– Let your body call you back into yourself* [...][8]

From this list of addressings of a sensory awareness that is important for the preparation and setting *in* contact improvisation it can be seen that 'listening' refers not so much to *hearing* as a sensory form of registering acoustic events (although this is part of it), but to a very broad and open state of sensuous/sensory perception. It also includes the sensing, the tactility of touching. Thus 'listen' does not refer primarily to a hearing event. It refers rather to an intersection of action and event (Ereignis) – which in German breaks down into the terms *zuhören, hören auf, horchen* and *lauschen* – thus implying the reference to the self as well as the reference to the other and to space.[9] In contact improvisation 'listening', 'listen' to motion, refers to synaesthetic and kinaesthetic forms of *awareness*, which embrace both conscious and unconscious 'subliminal' perceptions.

## I. Contact improvisation and kinaesthesis

Contact improvisation is a dance practice in which two (or more) moving partners, always in contact, explore their possibilities of movement. Curt Siddall, an "early exponent of contact improvisation" defines this dance form as "a combination of kinaesthetic forces: contact improvisation is a movement form, improvisational in nature, involving two bodies in contact. Impulses, weight, and momentum are communicated through a point of physical contact that continually rolls across and around the bodies of the dancers."[10] Historically this movement *praxis* goes back to Steve Paxton's movement and improvisation explorations at Oberlin College in 1972. Since then this dance form has established itself internationally and assumed different forms, whether as performance improvisation or social dance in the shape of regular jams, or as a means of exercising in combination with various release techniques, which in turn determine the aesthetics of contemporary dance. "The physical training of contact improvisation emphasizes the release of the body's weight into the floor or onto a partner's body [...]," writes Ann Cooper Albright. "The experience of internal sensations and the flow of the movement of two bodies is more important than specific shapes or formal posi-

8 Ibid. p. 7 f.
9 Cf. Nancy: *À l'écoute*, p. 15 f and p. 38 f. Nancy argues that "listening" relates to the whole register of the senses, being touched, and within a difference of the interior and the exterior.
10 Quoted after Albright/Gere (eds.): *Taken by Surprise*, p. 206.

tions."[11] In an early article in *The Drama Review* (1975) Steve Paxton identifies the six main elements of contact improvisation: "attitude, sensing time, orientation to space, orientation to partner, expanding peripheral vision, and muscular development, which includes centring, stretching, taking weight, and increasing joint action."[12]

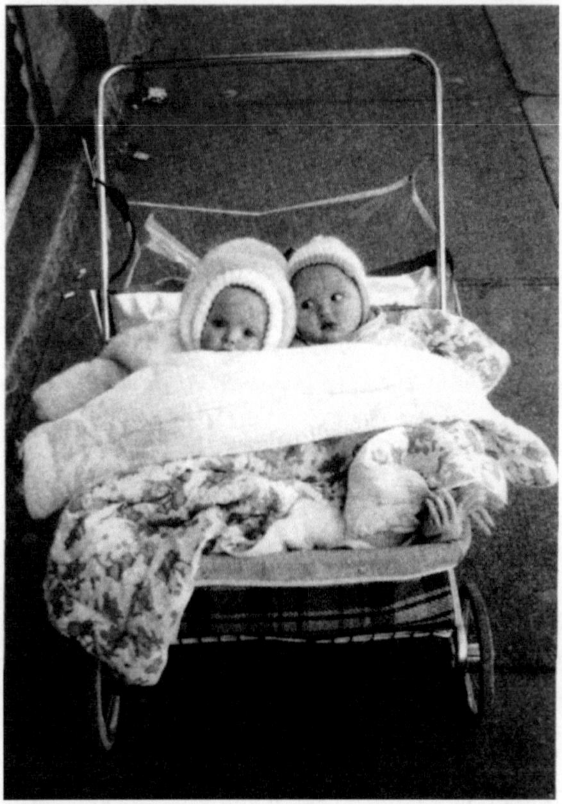

Fig. 1: Bill Arnold.

11 Ibid., p. 206. – This is not the place for a more detailed examination of the historical development and aesthetic structures of contact improvisation. Albright has pointed out that it is a "tricky business" to give a coherent description of contact improvisation: "the form has grown exponentially over time and has travelled through many countries and dance communities. Although it was developed in the seventies, contact improvisation has recognisable roots in the social and aesthetic revolutions of the sixties" (ibid., p. 205). On the history of contact improvisation see: Novack: *Sharing the Dance*.

12 Steve Paxton, quoted after Pallant: *Contact Improvisation*, p. 12 f.

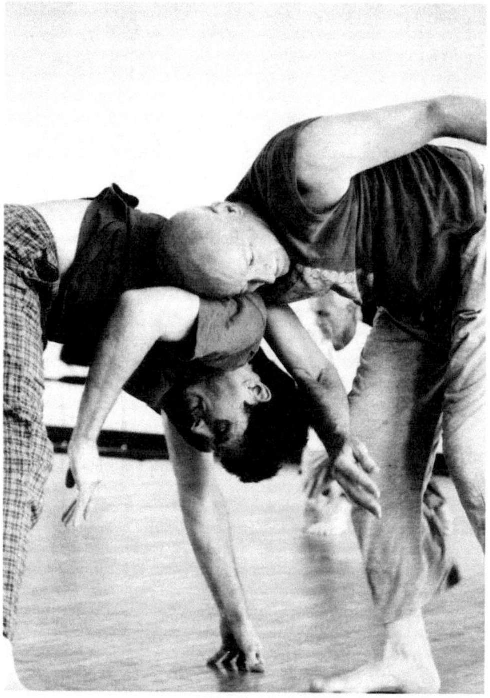

Fig. 2: Who leads? Andy Wichorek and Kelly Lane. *Contact Improvisation: An Introduction to a Vitalizing Dance Form*, p. 81. © 2006 Cheryl Pallant by permission of McFarland & Company, Inc., Box 611, Jefferson NC 28640.

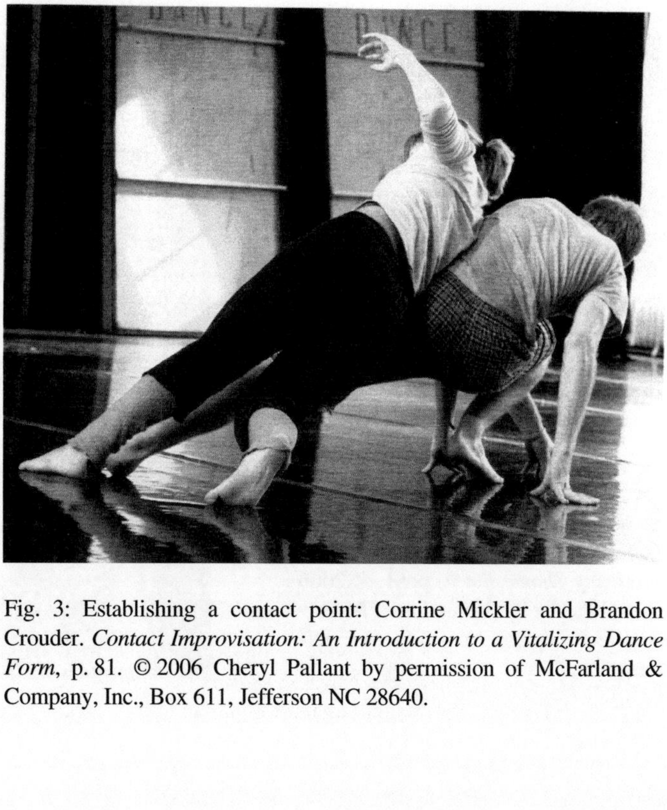

Fig. 3: Establishing a contact point: Corrine Mickler and Brandon Crouder. *Contact Improvisation: An Introduction to a Vitalizing Dance Form*, p. 81. © 2006 Cheryl Pallant by permission of McFarland & Company, Inc., Box 611, Jefferson NC 28640.

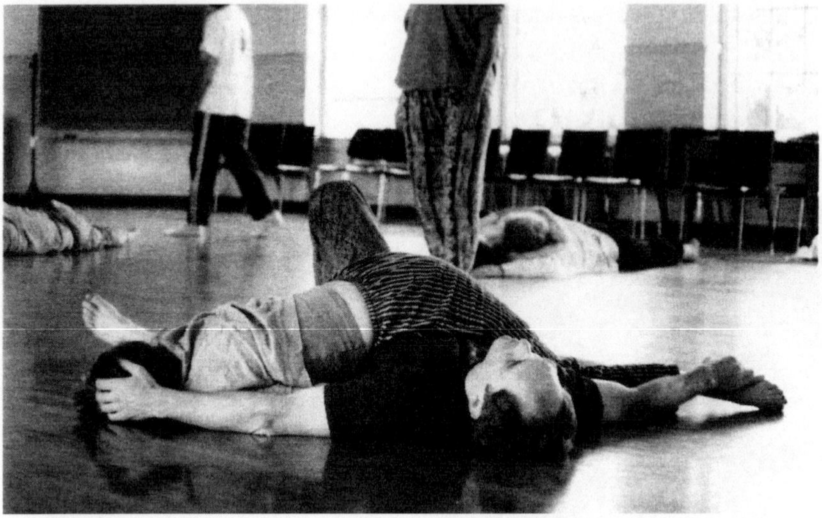

Fig. 4: Ease in stillness: Susan Singer and Keith Winston. *Contact Improvisation: An Introduction to a Vitalizing Dance Form*, p. 81. © 2006 Cheryl Pallant by permission of McFarland & Company, Inc., Box 611, Jefferson NC 28640.

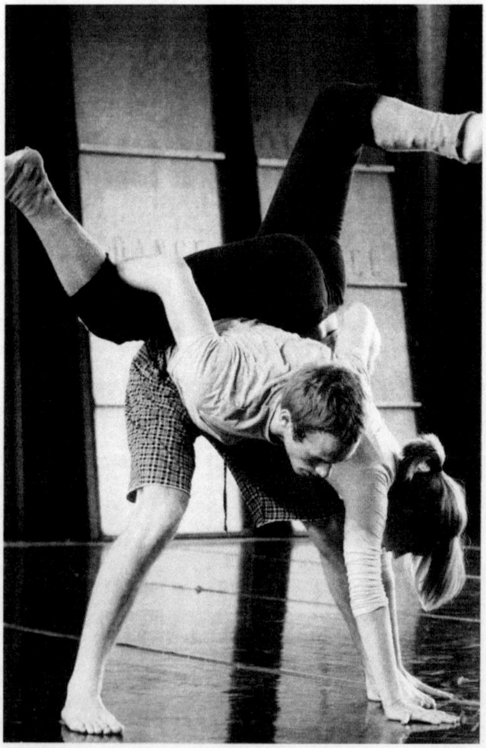

Fig. 5: Following impulses: Brandon Crouder and Corrine Mickler. *Contact Improvisation: An Introduction to a Vitalizing Dance Form*, p. 81. © 2006 Cheryl Pallant by permission of McFarland & Company, Inc., Box 611, Jefferson NC 28640.

The emphasizing of the motor aspects of movement – such as working with 'momentum', 'gravity', 'mass/weight', 'chaos', 'inertia', the attention to highly differentiated states of muscle tone between release/inertia and contraction, and finally the shifting of spatial perception between the focus on the interior of the body and the exterior of space make clear that an accent of the overall concept of contact improvisation lies on the conscious work with the 'sixth sense', kinaesthesia.

This is where two fields of the kinaesthetic mesh together: kinaesthetic proprioception and working with kinaesthetic communication – contact and shifts of weight and spatial position, which are shifts of the dynamically interacting dancer-bodies.

"Both the gross motor awareness of kinaesthesia and the less conscious sensory feedback mechanism of proprioception form the basis of the physical dialogue which is so pivotal to creating dance," writes Cheryl Pallant.[13] That is why experienced 'contacters' like Nancy Stark Smith constantly stress the spatial orientation created not only by vision but by the entire physical perception, a condition which Nancy Stark Smith calls "telescoping awareness,"[14] a "shifting between narrow and wide views, from up-close sensation to perceptions of the wider world,"[15] accompanied by the "sensation of dropping through space, [...] the forces of gravity, momentum, and mass."[16]

There has been a delay between the highly differentiated *praxis* with kinaesthesia in dance and theoretical references to the results of physiological, phenomenological and neuroscientific research into kinaesthesia. This research has only recently attracted more attention in the field of dance studies.[17] The initial impetus for this discussion was provided in the 1980s by an article by Mary M. Smyth: *Kinesthetic Communication in Dance.*[18] The researches and discoveries connected with 'kinaesthesia' as the ability to feel movement of the limbs and body, from Sherrington (1906)[19] to Gibson (1966),[20] are examined by Smyth to see if they yield an answer to the question as to how "watching someone dance could link to the movement system of the observer."[21] For Smyth this question ultimately remains unanswerable.[22] Her work reviews several hypotheses, all of

13 Ibid., p. 32.

14 Cf. in Albright/Gere: *Taken by Surprise*, p. 153.

15 Ibid., p. 154

16 Ibid., p. 157.

17 Cf. Montero: "Proprioception as an Aesthetic Sense" and cf. Coleman/Montero: "Affective Proprioception".

18 Smyth: *Kinesthetic Communication in Dance.*

19 Sherrington: *The Integrative Action of the Nervous System.*

20 Gibson: *The Senses Considered as Perceptual Systems.*

21 Smyth: *Kinesthetic Communication in Dance*, p. 19.

22 Mary M. Smyth notes that "Somehow" remains as a gap in the process. Even if dancers were happy that such a process could in any way relate to the experiences which they called 'kinaesthetic communication', we still do not know how it is effected [...] We do not yet know how seen movement can do this." p. 22.

which arose before more recent research findings on the function of "mirror neurons" were discussed in dance and dance studies.[23] The subject of 'kinaesthesia', on the other hand, is a topical one in dance research, since interest has become focused on the meaning of 'energy', 'rhythm', 'synchronization' of movements in Modern and Contemporary Dance. Thus Dee Reynolds has devoted her study of "Rhythmic Subjects"[24] to the "uses of energy" and the question of kinaesthesia, not only in relation to bodily position, muscle tension and movement, but also with regard to kinaesthetically 'embodied' cultural 'imaginations' of and attitudes to the kinaesthetic. Rudolf von Laban's concept of "effort" and Edmund Husserl's and Maurice Merleau-Ponty's phenomenological theories inform her approach. By using the concept of "kinaesthetic imagination" – which refers not only to the subjective aspects of proprioception, but also to questions of cultural imprint and transfer of energy – she manages to detach the phenomenon of kinaesthesia from the issue of self-perception in dancer *praxis* and open it up to questions of (syn-)aesthetic perception by the observer.[25]

In the practice of various body techniques, which are of relevance to contemporary dance (though not only to it), the subject of kinaesthesia is of increasing importance, even if the term itself is not part of the vocabulary of the discourse. Thus in a newly held series of interviews not a few representatives of body techniques – such as Feldenkrais and proponents of the Alexander technique and Body-Mind Centering – admitted to having worked with the basic principles of kinaesthesia long before they became aware of the term and the research associated with it. The dancer Julyen Hamilton, for example, stated that his work was very spatially oriented. "This spatial sense is highly informed through the kinaesthetic sensing of the inner body."[26] Furthermore, the "choices," which are always movement decisions, are influenced by the fact that they are not made from outside – "via an outside eye," but are "choices made from the proprioceptive abilities within the body as it senses itself and its environment." The result is a "radically spatial event permitted by the public and performers sharing of space." Susan Klein, the founder of the "Klein Technique™," stresses the extraordinary importance of "kinaesthetic," both as a "tool that allows us to understand the body" and as an aid to artistic work.

23 Rizzolatti et al.: *Mirrors in the Brain*.

24 Reynolds: *Rhythmic Subjects*.

25 On kinaesthesia and empathy see also: Foster: *Movements Contagion*; cf. Foster: *Choreographing Empathy*.

26 Cf. *Corpus* (28.9.2010): *Kinesthetics: Four questions* – http://www.corpusweb.net/kinesthetics-four-questions.html, p. 2.

> For me the beauty and excitement in kinaesthetics is bringing a body-felt understanding of movement to consciousness. It is fine-tuning our ability to feel, on subtle levels. [...] Kinaesthetics is our tool to bring the body into a deep state of balance, to its optimal state of movement potential.[27]

The associated 'process of discovery', which is able to trigger a periphrasis of fixed blockades, of postures of muscles, bones and tissue, leads to a kinaesthetically informed "internal knowing."[28] The aim is – as in most concepts of body techniques, which operate with Body-Mind Centering, "ideokinesis" or "functional integration" (such as the Feldenkrais method) – "body alignment, ease of movement and overall body harmony in dance," as Linda Rabin puts it.[29] Here, as in all works of kinaesthetically oriented practices, it is not a 'beautiful' bodily form resulting from a course of training dictated by an aesthetic style or movement code that is the guiding principle of the idea of dance and choreography, but the question posed by Linda Rabin: "What would dance performance be like if dancers drew from this essential source?"[30]

## II. Attention: kinaesthetic awareness

A key concept, which plays a pivotal role in nearly all texts and discourses of the above-mentioned body techniques and contact improvisation is that of attention – in the double sense of attention and awareness, of directed attention (perception) and 'noticing', a distinction made by the philosopher Bernhard Waldenfels on the basis of the phenomenological theory of Husserl and Merleau-Ponty.[31]

"It all starts with paying attention," says Linda Rabin.[32] "Kinaesthetics, the sense that tells us where and how we exist in our internal environment and how we connect and relate to our external environment,"[33] can lead to a conscious perception. Of particular interest in this connection is the *division* of attention. According to Susan Klein:

27 Ibid., p. 3.

28 Ibid.

29 *Corpus*, p. 4. Linda Rabin worked with Lulu Sweigard on "ideokinesis", learned the Alexander technique (through Rika Cohen), practised "Body-Mind Centering®" (founded by Bonnie Bainbridge Cohen), and finally became a teacher of the "Continuum Movement" (founded by Emile Conrad).

30 Cf. Ibid.

31 Cf. Waldenfels: *Phänomenologie der Aufmerksamkeit.*

32 *Corpus*, p. 5.

33 S. Klein in: *Corpus*, p. 3.

> It requires a split level of consciousness: one level is doing while the other level is observing what is done. Kinaesthetic awareness allows us to keep track of what we are doing with our bodies as well as how we are doing it.[34]

Attention – as attention and awareness – embraces the entire sensory and action scenario which is addressed, for example, in the movement explorations of contact improvisation. Attention implies attentiveness – both to the processes of one's own physicality and to the experience of contact with the Other. Attention thus opens up the entire range of the concept as it might be described in an anthropological-phenomenological specification. Waldenfels points out with recourse to Immanuel Kant that the boundaries between the deliberate direction of attention (*attentio, abstractio, distentio*), noticing (*animadvertere*), and observing (*observare*), are fluid.[35] To this must be added the mode of self-affection, i.e. "the affection of the inner sense by ourselves with an 'Actus of attention'."[36] It is this doubling of only partially controllable awareness and self-affection by images in the (inner) perception that marks the potential of kinaesthesia and "kinaesthetic imagination" (Dee Reynolds). This is where the key formula "*listening*" opens the synaesthetic-kinaesthetic spectrum of possible modes of attention: perception and awareness. A small episode may serve to illustrate the shifts and transfers between movement and (observer) perception.

This summer I drove with two colleagues through the Brandenburg landscape to a village where there was a kind of 'Dance Land' farm called *Ponderosa*, where a workshop on contact improvisation was being held by Nancy Stark Smith, one of the best-known personalities in this field. We had announced our arrival and had permission to observe the workshop as a small research team. The workshop was taking place in a large, somewhat dilapidated barn set amidst an overgrown, elderberry-scented 'Paradise' – like a relic of the hippy 1970s: in a large, light-filled room supported by wooden beams, whose atmosphere had put all the 'participants' into the right mood, thanks to its spaciousness, openness, conduciveness to concentration, calm *and* dynamic character, and the rhythmical division of the space by windows and beams. The nineteen participants of the workshop – and we as observers – distributed ourselves about this space. What was striking was how much this space and its divisions actually helped to promote the whole process of the workshop, with its various action centres of movement and 'contact'. Here *participation* was not just about 'sharing' the place, but also and equally a constituting of 'space' in (inter-)action, in motion, and in watching-listening.

The question of the relationship between movers (workshop participants) and observers was in the air throughout the entire process – and it changed! Relationships transform perception.

34 Ibid.
35 Waldenfels: *Phänomenologie der Aufmerksamkeit*, p. 230 f.
36 Ibid., p. 231.

The workshop was intended

> [...] to pay special attention to the delicate transition from intimate, private authenticity to making art intended to be viewed by the public. [...] Are the subtle experiences of perception and action inside improvised dance visible to the watcher?[37]

These *experiences* and these *questions* were shared. At the end we were asked: "What did you see?" – with regard to a process of movement involving constant changes between "dancing, watching, listening, and being watched." It is remarkable that all themes and processes that occurred in the workshop were linked with the question of 'attention': attention as a sensory-kinaesthetic mode of participation.

In reply to the question that all participants put to us in the closing interview: "What did you see?" One participant of our research group said that entering into (and sharing of) this workshop on *space* and *framework* had been a striking experience. Why? Because of the difference between a stress situation (one's normal job, university life, an arduous journey) and this space offering opportunities of meeting people, lots of peace and quiet, freedom to organize one's own affairs, and release from perfection constraints. This feedback was very well received by the workshop participants. It was clear that the experience of release from tensions in everyday life, scope for selective contacts, and the remoteness of output-oriented tasks, unconsciously responded to the concept of the workshops and contact improvisation. In addition, however, it was the experience of difference itself in this case, which caused the outside observer to be accepted as a participant – in the sense of 'sharing' – in the group of 'movers'.

Our questions lead us to consider whether and in what way these parameters, which constitute the *kinaesthetic sharing*, could be reconsidered. In this case this would also mean, for example, that the mutual 'responsiveness' between workshop-movers and workshop-observers was not the 'answer' to the question of participation. But it does raise a question concerning context-dependent changes. The question is: What does this tell us about forms of kinaesthetic and synaesthetic empathy, if the relaxing of tension or a change in breathing is seen as an emergent effect of such a transference? And in what way are different dimensions of experience and knowledge addressed in such processes? Was this, in the case of our example, addressing a "tacit knowledge" (Michael Polanyi) of a liminal attention? It is hard to describe a state in which one is receptive to signals on which one is not – intentionally – focused and which are received in a distracted, casual manner.[38]

37 Nancy Stark Smith in the Programme note.

38 Our questions, on the other hand, focus on *modes of participation* with such formulas and criteria that are inadequate to describe: for example, in what way do I belong or am "included" in a process of actions, exercises, movements – as in that contact improvisation workshop in "Dance Land" Ponderosa – even if I as "audience," observer, spectator am "there" and yet remain outside, a situation that is not accurately reflected in the words "exclusion," or "not belonging."

## III. "Listening": "Small Dance"

The questions, which were to be illuminated by this episode of a 'contact' between dancers and observers at a contact improvisation workshop, are complex. Neither in a neuroscientific nor in an aesthetic-theoretical sense is the multiplicity of aspects easy to solve. There is, for example, the question of *how* the intricate and microscopic kinaesthetic processes, which take place during an hour of Susan Klein technique or in a sequence of contact improvisation, are perceptible to an observer.

In the context of contact improvisation discourse it is 'listening' – as a quality of attention *and* awareness – in which 'voluntary' and 'involuntary' movement processes are open both to *mover* and *observer*: "Remaining present and listening go hand in hand."[39]

As the phenomenological studies by Husserl, Merleau-Ponty and Waldenfels show, kinaesthesia is a physical embodied space-time experience. As such it assumes a particular shape within a hear-sound space.[40] This implies an 'acoustic epoché', i.e. a breach (in) the resonance. 'Listening' thus means (to follow Waldenfels)[41] that a 'different kind of hearing' (ein *Andershören*) is needed to break through the hearing order and reach the synaesthetic-kinaesthetic quality of that *movere* (in the sense of a sensory and emotional 'being moved') which is involved in the "contact," the touch play of contact improvisation. Thus the concept of *Kinästhese*, as Edmund Husserl introduces the term, is not "to be understood as a sensation of movement that is only distinguished from other sensations by a special sensibility, but 'Kinästhese', which the ego ascribes to itself, means a moving sensation before a sensing movement, the chiastic formulation indicating that kinesis and aisthesis are not fully congruent either in a phenomenal or a neuronal sense."[42]

This hesitation, this delay – that kinaesthetic epoché that keeps open a gap in the relationship between movement and (self-)perception[43] – is constantly registered in the descriptions of kinaesthetics and contact improvisation. Linda Rabin poses the question: "What is movement within the movement?"[44] Nancy

Does this not show how potentially interesting it might be to rethink *participation* on the basis of experience and performance theory? Should we not recognize that the attributions of active and passive and the semantic range of the concepts of action and performance cannot ultimately be determined, and that the shifting nature of relationships (e.g. between performers and spectators) and changes in the background against which they play out, give rise to all sorts of temporary possibilities of participation? – cf. Rancière: *The Emancipated Spectator*.

39 Pallant: *Contact Improvisation*, p. 34.

40 Cf. Waldenfels: *Phänomenologie der Aufmerksamkeit*, p. 199; cf. Taylor: "The Body in Husserl and Merleau-Ponty".

41 Ibid., p. 194.

42 Cf. Waldenfels: *Sinnesschwellen*, p. 68 ff.

43 Waldenfels: *Phänomenologie der Aufmerksamkeit*, p. 221.

44 In *Corpus*, p. 5.

Stark Smith constantly emphasizes the elementary significance of the kinaesthetic experience of 'disorientation' for contact improvisation and of a 'gap' which interrupts the control of movement orientation. At this point the – long since obsolete – question may be raised again as to where the boundary work with kinaesthetic perception between the *praxis* of 'social dance' and artistic performance runs, shifts, becomes diffuse. The orientation to "flow," to "coordinating falling, following momentum, blending with 'partner's movement'" turns – according to Nancy Stark Smith – into a game "against":

> [...] making myself heavy instead of light when a lift starts, [...] insisting instead of yielding, adding no to yes. [...] I've been in the harmony business a long time now. [...] As much as I love running around, I think I'm going to try running *into* things more often, or at least against them.[45]

This refraction – on the part of a counter force, a kinaesthetic resistance – reflects the pendulum, the balancing between motion and stillness, in which the potentiality/reflexivity of the kinaesthetic is articulated. The extreme reduction of movement as a "deep inner dance" – and the question of what happens "by reducing the outer movement to a minimum, and by slowing down the speed to a degree, I continued to explore the *inner* world of the dance," as Linda Rabin relates.[46] She was eager to learn 'what' the audience would perceive when all extraneous movement was removed, if the simplicity of a dancer's walk, sitting or raising an arm, could communicate the intriguing world of sensations and feelings coursing through the performer.“[47] Even if this inner journey, this 'inner dance' cannot be comprehensible in every detail, there are links in kinaesthetic perception – a 'sharing' between 'mover' and 'observer' – which is a vital aspect of a syn- and kinaesthetic (empathic) movement synchronization in contact improvisation and other body practices mentioned here.

This reduction, the attention to the microscopic 'inner dance', opens a specific field of (kin-)aesthetic movement experience bordering on 'standstill'; a standing still that is not a standstill, but a scenario full of risky inner movement: "Even standing, we execute a continuous fall."[48] Where would we find beginning and end, rest and movement in a dance which consists of nothing but a standing still? Nancy Stark Smith describes that 'dance' that Steve Paxton invented in the 1970s and which he called *small dance*.[49]

45 N. Stark Smith in an article in *Contact Quarterly*, 1984, quoted in Albright/Gere: *Taken by Surprise*, p. 162.

46 In *Corpus*, p. 5.

47 Ibid.

48 Ann Woodhall formulated this central paradox, quoted in Albright/Gere: *Taken by Surprise*, p. 157.

49 On Steve Paxton's instructions on "small dance" see the "reconstruction" by Nora Heilmann (2006): in *Rupture in Space* (http://www.ruptures.wordpress.com); cf. Erin Manning, who comments on "A Mover's Guide to Standing Still," referring to Steve Paxton's "Small Dance", in: *Relationscapes*, p. 43–49.

A dance that consists of nothing but 'standing'? She comments on her experience as follows:

> Relaxing erect, the intelligence of the body is revealed as it fires the appropriate muscles just enough to keep the body mass hovering within the range of its vertical supports. The micromovements that occur to keep me balanced are so tiny and yet so magnified, and arise from such a deep feeling of stillness and space, that I get giddy, tickled by the impossible magnitude of such subtle sensations. The disorientation in the stand comes from the feeling that inside the apparent solidity and stillness of standing, there is nothing but movement and space![50]

Disorientation, the intensity of movement – a tumult in the heart of standing still – these moments of the kinaesthetic experience of an act of 'listening' are what open and transmit the potential for inventing movement in contemporary dance.

## References

Albright, Ann Cooper / David Gere (eds.): *Taken by Surprise: A Dance Improvisation Reader*, Middletown (Wesleyan University Press) 2003.

Coleman, Jonathan / Barbara Montero: "Affective Proprioception", in: *Janus Head* 9 (2007) 2, pp. 299–317.

*Corpus* (28.9.2010): *Kinesthetics: Four questions* – http://www.corpusweb.net/kinesthetics-four-questions.html.

Foster, Susan Leigh: *Movement's Contagion: The Kinesthetic Impact of Performance*, online publication of: University of California, International Performance and Culture Multicampus Research Group, June 2008 – http://uc-ipc.com/wp-content/uploads/2008/06/movementcontagion-11.pdf.

Foster, Susan: *Choreographing Empathy. Kinesthesia in Performance*, Routledge (London) 2010.

Gibson, James J.: *The Senses Considered as Perceptual Systems*, Boston (Houghton Mifflin) 1966.

Manning, Erin: *Relationscapes. Movement, Art, Philosophy*, Cambridge (Massachusetts), London (MIT-Press) 2009.

Johnson, Mark: *The Body in the Mind: The Bodily Basis of Meaning, Imagination and Reason*, Chicago (University of Chicago Press) 1987.

Lakoff, George / Mark Johnson: *Philosophy in the Flesh*, New York (Basic Books) 1999.

Montero, Barbara: "Proprioception as an Aesthetic Sense", in: *The Journal of Aesthetics and Art Criticism* 64 (2006) 2, pp. 231–242.

50 Quoted in Albright and Gere: *Taken by Surprise*, p. 162 f.

Nancy, Jean-Luc: *À l'écoute*, German: *Zum Gehör*, translated from French by Esther von der Osten, Berlin-Zürich (Diaphanes) 2010.

Neuhaus, Max: "LISTEN", in: *Welt auf tönernen Füßen. Die Töne und das Hören*, ed. by Kunst- und Ausstellungshalle der BRD (Bonn), Göttingen (Steidl-Verlag), 1994, pp. 125–127.

Novack, Cynthia: *Sharing the Dance. Contact Improvisation and American Culture*, Madison (University of Wisconsin Press) 1990.

Pallant, Cheryl: *Contact Improvisation: An Introduction to a Vitalizing Dance Form*, North Carolina, London (McFarland) 2006.

Rancière, Jacques: *The Emancipated Spectator*, London (Verso) 2009.

Reynolds, Dee: *Rhythmic Subjects. Uses of Energy in the Dances of Mary Wigman, Martha Graham and Merce Cunningham*, Hampshire (Dance Books) 2007.

Rizzolatti, Giacomo et al.: *Mirrors in the Brain: How our Minds Share Actions, Emotions, and Experience*, Oxford (Oxford University Press) 2008.

Sherrington, Charles: *The Integrative Action of the Nervous System*, New Haven (Yale University Press) 1906.

Smyth, Mary M.: "Kinesthetic Communication in Dance", in: *Dance Research Journal* 16 (1984) 2, pp. 19–22.

Taylor, Carman: "The Body in Husserl and Merleau-Ponty", in: *Philosophical Topics* 27 (1999), pp. 205–286.

Valéry, Paul: *Cahiers*, Vol. II, Paris (Gallimard) 1974.

Waldenfels, Bernhard: *Phänomenologie der Aufmerksamkeit*, Frankfurt am Main (Suhrkamp) 2004.

Waldenfels, Bernhard: *Sinnesschwellen*, Frankfurt am Main (Suhrkamp) 1999.

## List of Illustrations

Fig. 1: Ann Cooper Albright and David Gere: *Taken by Surprise. A Dance Improvisation Reader*, p. 251, Photo by Bill Arnold.

Fig. 2: Who leads? Andy Wichorek and Kelly Lane. *Contact Improvisation: An Introduction to a Vitalizing Dance Form*, p. 81. © 2006 Cheryl Pallant by permission of McFarland & Company, Inc., Box 611, Jefferson NC 28640.

Fig. 3: Establishing a contact point: Corrine Mickler and Brandon Crouder. *Contact Improvisation: An Introduction to a Vitalizing Dance Form*, p. 103. © 2006 Cheryl Pallant by permission of McFarland & Company, Inc., Box 611, Jefferson NC 28640.

Fig. 4: Ease in stillness: Susan Singer and Keith Winston. *Contact Improvisation: An Introduction to a Vitalizing Dance Form*, p. 23. © 2006 Cheryl

Pallant by permission of McFarland & Company, Inc., Box 611, Jefferson NC 28640.

Fig. 5: Following impulses: Brandon Crouder and Corrine Mickler. *Contact Improvisation: An Introduction to a Vitalizing Dance Form*, p. 133. © 2006 Cheryl Pallant by permission of McFarland & Company, Inc., Box 611, Jefferson NC 28640.

# Feeling and Cognition

# Feel the Feeling
# Media-Installations as Laboratories of Senses

SABINE FLACH

In 2004, in an interview titled "The image as anthropological phenomenon," the art historian Hans Belting was asked the question: "Do you mean that experiencing an image is *always* a synesthetic experience?" To which he playfully gave the convincing and short answer: "Yes."[1]

This simple *yes* is the basis and argument of the following reflections. I assume that the experience of an artistic work is *fundamentally synesthetic* and consequently, the basic assumption of my remarks is that in terms of image act theory as a Habitus in Habitat, this "Yes" clearly reveals one thing: the artwork is not experienced by the eye alone. It is always the *entire body* which perceives and is perceived.

The self-awareness of the person who uses his body as a medium, allows him to react to the materiality or the immaterial materiality of images in a specific way, based on its physicality. It means that the question to ask: "What is an image?" cannot be answered from what is thought of the image *alone*, but first of all *demonstrate* the compelling interdependency between the body that perceives an image, remembers an image, shows or produces it and the material image itself.

This combination is more remarkable in installation spaces of contemporary art, which are more and more distant from the classical concept of image – as the traditional iconicity – and present us with sensations, light effects; visibilities which *can* be pictorial, but cannot be experienced with the sense of sight *alone*.

The question facing us now would concern the nature of the relationship between a body and what *constitute* these installations visibilities? How can these presumed interdependencies be more precisely determined?

How does this reciprocal relationship appear? How is it experienced and where does it take place?

It is clear that this interaction cannot be conceived outside of a *spatial dimension* and becomes more obvious in installations, on which I will now focus.

When viewers enter such a space, the very first thing that the so-called *black box* does is provide a *concrete site* for the interaction between habitus and habi-

1 Belting: "Das Bild als anthropologisches Phänomen", p. 122.

tat. *Then, however*, this concrete installation space between the viewer and the image of the installation generates an *intermediate space*. Temporary, transitory, and unfolding in the interplay between perception, imagination, remembrance and feeling,[2] this space defies any attempt to determine its location. On the contrary – it *marks out the space* in which these specific experiences can first *occur*.

My argument would be that in these installation spaces, the senses assume a double nature: they are present and are presented, i.e. they *show* themselves and *are shown*. In other words, the focus is always on giving senses a *presence*. It appears, and this would be another argument for my statement, that it is a more specific *mediality* – which should be further examined – a mediality which binds the body and the artwork consistently together in their *phenomenological* constitution, and thus – and this is crucial for my next argument – according to their sinnliche Erscheinung – their *perceptible (sensual) appearance (phenomenon)*,[3] which – as Maurice Merleau-Ponty developed it in his "Phénoménologie de la Perception" on the connection between the body and the aesthetic experience of art – brings the unity of senses at the core of the synthesis rather than the conceptual discursive thought: "Les sens se traduisent l'un l'autre sans avoir à passer par l'idée."

An aesthetics, setting the aisthetic experience of art closer to the core, focuses on the *perceptible phenomenon* and the *perceptible perception of aesthetics,* which in turn detaches the artwork from pure materiality and rather leads to the concept of *dispositif.* I would like to interpret such a dispositif in the same way Foucault did in his book "The Confessions of the Flesh"[4] as a more specific way to see, i.e.

2 The strong relations between these concepts and also their distinctions cannot be discussed here.

3 And because of that, an image is not a sign if a sign is understood in the sense of a *sprachliches* sign. See also for that argument Belting, ibid. p. 120.

4 "What I'm trying to pick out with this term is, firstly, a thoroughly heterogeneous ensemble consisting of discourses, institutions, architectural forms, regulatory decisions, laws, administrative measures, scientific statements, philosophical, moral and philanthropic propositions – in short, the said as much as the unsaid. Such are the elements of the apparatus. The apparatus itself is the system of relations that can be established between these elements" (Michel Foucault "The Confession of the Flesh"). Siegfried Jäger defines the term as "the interaction of discursive behavior (i. e. speech and thoughts based upon a shared knowledge pool), non-discursive behavior (i. e. acts based upon knowledge), and manifestations of knowledge by means of acts or behaviors [...]. Dispositifs can thus be imagined as a kind of Gesamtkunstwerke complexly interwoven and integrated dispositifs add up in their entirety to a dispositif of all society." Giorgio Agamben wrote: "Further expanding the already large class of Foucauldian apparatuses, I shall call an apparatus literally anything that has in some way the capacity to capture, orient, determine, intercept, model, control, or secure the gestures, behaviors, opinions, or discourses of living beings. Not only, therefore, prisons, madhouses, the panopticon, schools, confession, factories, disciplines, judicial measures, and so forth (whose connection with power is in a certain sense evident), but also the pen, writing, literature, philosophy, agriculture, cigarettes, navigation, computers, cellular telephones and – why not – language itself, which is perhaps the most ancient of apparatuses – one in which thousands and thousands of years ago a primate inadvertently let himself be captured, probably without realizing the consequences that he was about to face." (Agamben: "What is an Apparatus?", p. 14).

a *device*. It means that a *materiality* can be the agent of images – or visibility – for the respective media, which makes possible to combine a theory of visibility with a theory of perception.[5]

Such analysis is not as crucial anymore for the factuality of the visual itself, as it is for the relationship between a specific image or visual production and the way it is perceived. It is possible to avoid – this was my idea – a purely historical perspective in images or visual history. This means – it does not involve only artifacts in terms of physical images, but also as *mental images and images of memories* – that addressing the *interaction between the imaginary and the respective image production*, i.e. the *individual, subjective, mental production and perception of images* and what can be conceived of the social space as an image product. These arguments can be methodically conceived and analyzed as Habitus in Habitat.[6]

For such an expanded and expanding concept of image, one thing is obvious: a discourse on the signification of sensory experiences and the ensuing numbering, classification and attempt to de-cipher the *number 5*, is not only a semiotization of the body and its perception. Sensory experiences could *not* arise from a purely symbolic reading, which is also far too restrictive as it would be a restriction of the categorical connection of the sensory experiences to the organs of the body. A simplification always fails to establish the references – the numerous references, like spatiality or the responsibility (function) of an organ and the fact that a single sense is not a single sense if considered as a stable entity, but that a perception can have several basic qualities – to the necessary interdependency between the body and the experience. This relation is less biologically determined than culturally. Louise Vinge wrote in her book *The Five Senses*[7]: "The number and order of the senses are fixed by custom and tradition, not by nature" which lift all doubts raised by the constant anthropological dominance on the very limited diversity of sensory experiences and thus showed the true *nature* of sensory experiences.

In 1689, John Locke, in his "Essay Concerning Human Understanding," already conjectured about the fact that God could have created more than five senses in the infinite universe:

> [...] we cannot believe it impossible to God to make a Creature with other Organs, and more ways to convey into the Understanding the notice of Corporeal things than those five, as they are usually counted, which he has given to Man: Yet I think, it is not possible for any one to imagine any other qualities in bodies, howsoever constituted, whereby they can be taken notice of, besides Sounds, Tastes, Smells, visible and tangible Qualities [...][8]

5 Meant in a phenomenological theoretical approach, which has to be differentiated from an anthropological one. See for that argument: Wiesing: "Das Bild aus phänomenologischer Sicht".

6 See: Flach: "On Twilight".

7 Vinge: *The Five Senses*, p. 7.

8 Locke: *Essay Concerning Human Understanding*, p. 120.

Locke's description of a God created "extra terrestrial being,"[9] was not so far from the sensory perception of earthlings – and among them human beings. Common sense already suggested that many bodily perceptions make the five senses system fragile, because it cannot explain all the bodily noticeable perceptions – all actions and interactions – just with these five senses. Modern research on senses in psychology, physiology and neurology also came to the conclusion that the limitation of the number of senses was an "oversimplification."[10]

> The perception of the complex self referentialities of the different parts of our body, its high level of exchange with external stimuli as well as the concentration of internal relationships between neurons, which prove to be a broken dialogue with the exterior, all these elements are forced to dissolve in the organo-logically fixed number of five senses.[11]

It seems less useful to speak about one sense, such as *the* sense of sight or the visible *than about senses*, such as *senses* of sight and visibilities. It appears that the five based system of the senses is a construction, which is culturally orientated by optically discriminated criterion (eye, ear, hand etc.) was induced by visibility.

This artificiality gave the impulse to increase the number of senses taken into account for the study of a particular perception, from an aesthetic point of view.[12] The goal was always to search for new – so called *sensitive qualities* – perceptive systems in the body. Replacing the criteria of visibility by a functional one[13] would allow to explore the observable apparatus and the seemingly indirect senses, even if they function invisibly and are not linked to any particular organ. A non-organologic use of the senses leads – in the sense of Plessner's Aesthesiology – to ask the question "What are the specific opportunities for a man (as a person) to attain his own senses?" and then focus on the *tension between* sensibility, experience and behavior.[14]

One should also take notice of the intricate relationship between aesthetics and aisthesis – the Greek etymology of synaesthesia, syn-aisthesis, refers to a complex system, a *sensation-with*, and this means it is not only reduced to a dichotomy such as color-hearing. This relationship between aesthetics and aisthesis did *not* ignore what is known as the inner sensorium, Einbildungskraft, imaginatio sive phantasia, sensus communis, mind, inner emotions and so on.

In the Polylog *Simon ou les facultés de l'âme*, Socrates recapitulates a conversation he had with Diotima, who told him the story of Prometheus accepting

9 Nauman-Beyer: *Anatomie der Sinne*, p. 8. See for my following argument this excellent key-study on senses. Regarding my arguments I mostly follow Nauman-Beyers' explanation of the five-senses-schema.

10 Rivlin/Gravelle: *Deciphering the Senses*. p. 9–28.

11 Nauman-Beyer: ibid. p. 3.

12 See for example Olswald Külpe: *Vorlesungen über Psychologie* and Marinetti: *Tattilismo*.

13 See Nauman Beyer: ibid., p. 13.

14 Plessner: *Die Einheit der Sinne*, p. 198. Generally I do not follow his theoretical approach because it is too much of an anthropological position, but here, his argument is correct.

the task Zeus gave him to create the soul through Zeus as a *essence pure*, to prepare the first man for his existence on earth. To fulfill this task, Prometheus gave the first man Einbildungskraft. Einbildungskraft was a container for receiving and storing all kinds of perceptions, sensations, ideas and actions which would then be imprinted: "[...] un receptacle de toutes les actions, de toutes les sensations, perceptions ou idées qui devoient y entrer de dehors, et s'y imprimer."[15]

Therefore, perception cannot be separated from imagining. I call Einbildungskraft the productive activities of the sense of sight, in which appear the works of cognitive and mental faculties.[16] Their activities do *not* consist – contrarily to sensualist perception theories – in mediating between various current and remembered image perceptions, which would connect together various additive or associative sensory fields, in other words to assume a quasi passive unity of senses as a condition of synaesthetic perceptions. Einbildungskraft – as a modal plurality of senses – makes possible the emergence of images of perception in which it shapes the constitutive activities of the subject for the emergence of the mental images interacting with the material images and vice versa. Thus, senses and body are always a synergic system in which these Images are to be understood as "Ereignisbilder"[17] – 'images of an event' or even better: as "Erregungsbilder" – images of an *agitation*, in which Aisthesis and Kinesis cannot be thought of separately. What is relevant to an iconic episteme's concept is also equally addressed: the internal proximity between imagination and imago, between imaginativeness and image. In this sense, it is the imagination itself that uses the internal image sense to create external images. The mental image and *l'image objet* are two aspects of one and the same phenomenon; the difference, if there is one at all, is that one picture is ephemeral and the other can be of an undetermined duration. Or, as Jacques Derrida and Bernhard Stiegler described it in the *Échographies*:

> L'image en général n'existe pas. Ce que l'on appelle l'image mentale et ce que j'appellerai ici l'image-objet, [...] sont deux faces d'un seul et même phénomène qui ne peuvent pas plus être séparées [...]. La différence qui s'impose le plus immédiatement est que l'objective dure, tandis que la mentale est éphémère.[18]

From this perspective, as Merleau-Ponty thought, the synaesthetic perception would not be the exception but the rule. Even the everyday perception seems by no means different from the atomic sensory qualities, but if "je me tourne vers ce regard lui-même," then my gaze becomes a part of the visual field, and thus irrevocably intertwined with the other fields – or spatial structure – of the senses of touchs, smells, sound perceptions. The problem lies in the fact that too few are

15 Hemsterhuis: *Simon ou des facultés de l'âme*, p. 124.
16 See: Hüppauf/Wulf (ed.): *Bild und Einbildungskraft*, p. 24.
17 Waldenfels: "Von der Wirkmacht und Wirkkraft der Bilder", p. 57.
18 Derrida/Stiegler: *Échographies*, p. 165.

aware of the interaction and the elasticity of the focusing or of the 'wandering' of the gaze to consciously follow the "vibration de mon regard."[19]

## Hyperseeing

In this second part of my paper I will present you artworks by Olafur Eliasson. The aim is to present, how and in which way an artist shows through and with his artwork, that every perception of art is always related to the whole body and therefore synaesthetic per se and in this way deeply related to Einbildungskraft. I want to illustrate the situation developed in the first part and prove that inner senses are constitutive of synaesthesia.

This part of my paper has 4 sub-chapters. Every chapter is 'guided' by a quotation from Olafur Eliasson.

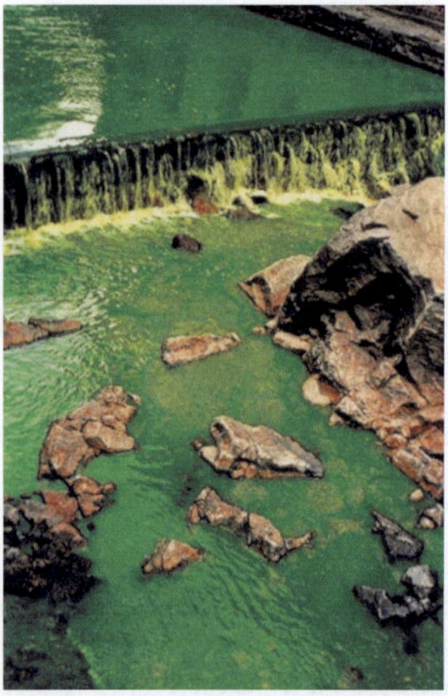

Fig.1: *Green river*, 1998, Moss, Norway, 1998.

19 Merleau-Ponty: *Phénoménologie de la perception,* p. 263.

## *Jemanden Rück-Augen geben – to give backward eyes*

Olafur described this as the enabling: "to observe our own gaze or to be aware that we see, and to see that we are aware. In this way, our knowledge is efficiently filtering our sense of sight." For Eliasson, this process was like providing "someone a rear eye."[20]

Fig. 2: *Your black horizon*, 2005, Thyssen-Bornemisza Limited Edition Pavilion, 51st Venice Biennale, 2005.

Therefore a dimension has to be opened, in which *gaze* itself has an optical value and the certainty to *know,* that art does not *necessarily renders the visible*, but what has not been seen *before*. Given that an artistic practice does not only refer to something, but first of all, shows itself, one has to ask how.[21]

Thus, the essence of art is *differentiation*. It can neither be regarded as a piece of reality, nor can the gaze lose its capacity of being represented. Art in itself, has always been an internal reflection and a relevant approach for addressing the questions of the modalities of perception. If the characteristic essence of art comes out of the discharge of tension between the medium of representation and the

20 Eliasson: *The Mediated Motion*, p. 32.

21 See also: Boehm: "Vom Medium zum Bild".

represented, this relation can be discussed only after the specific conditions of visibility – the requirements for the visibility of the specific structure – are produced.[22]

## Contextualization or: "My work is very much about positioning the subject"

In 1922, Walter Benjamin wrote in his text about the "psycho-physical question":

> For all living reactivity is bound to differentiation, whose preeminent instrument is the body. This is an essential function of the body. Only the body can be viewed as an instrument with which to differentiate between the vital reactions and at the same time can be comprehended in terms of its psychic animation. [...] One of the body's most important organs of differentiation is perception."[23]

The fact that looking at your own gaze makes the non-visible visible, determines essentially that gaze is linked to the concept of perception, because it does not only depend – as Walter Benjamin wrote – "on what is seen but also on what is felt of the structures."[24] The gaze does absolutely not hinges on the classical authority of visuality and scopophilia, but is related to the density and materiality of the body.

In the art work of Eliasson, this structural insight leads the perception to oscillate between the fields of aesthetics and aisthesis, between outer and inner sensory data. His work is no longer about the perception itself, but about the *sensation* of perception. Perception is no longer subordinated to a pure equivalent of visuality, but Eliasson links it to a model of perception and subjectivity, so the vision of his reduction of a pure retinal reproduction of an external visual impression *creates* and *connects* it to the concept of embodiment. This reconnection of the senses of sight to the body, where gaze is no longer just a layer in the body and in the subject, but is not entirely and *univocally* determined by the construct of the senses of sight, rather by a choir of *all* senses which shape the senses of sight. Therefore, the subject becomes aware of the inextricably mingled modalities and contingencies of the exercise of perception.[25] To explain these sensations aroused by the structures, which are the basic condition of his works, Eliasson wrote: "you are not only seeing or experiencing a piece but you are also experiencing yourself experiencing the piece."[26] Such a concept of the sense of sight, as perceptual activity, incorporates the idea of a subject observing his own per-

22 Cf. also Flach: *'Körper-Szenarien'*. By answering this question, one also finds an approach to complex perception systems.

23 Cf. Benjamin: *Schemata zum psycho-physischen Problem* (ca. 1922), here quoted after Weigel: "Passagen und Spuren des Leib- und Bildraums in Benjamins Schriften", p. 61.

24 Benjamin: "Strenge Kunstwissenschaft", p. 368.

25 Eliasson: *The Mediated Motion.*

26 Ibid.

ception, but, this subject is also aware that the sense of sight and the perception are historical processes, where cultural codes determine all the contemporary perception processes; or, as Eliasson wrote "History is not external and objectified in a situation but is inside the spectator. I expect the spectator to bring history or memory and culture with them. I take it for granted that the memory of the spectator is a part of the project."[27]

In Eliasson's view, perception is also a process, a dynamic constellation of events, in which, for each constitutive element of the processes of perception and memory, time and space are non-linear and are organized around floating rhythms and dazzling pulsations.[28] The body cannot be reduced to an optical system providing a penetrating view of the world. It is rather a *zone of tension* where external surfaces absorb and generate sensory experiences at the same time. Eliasson's artistic practice is characterized by this nuanced procedure with the physiological and subjective conditions of perception on the one hand and the material objects of perception on the other hand.[29] This brilliant handling demonstrates that consciousness arises in the same way as objects: through and with relations.[30]

Then, one can understand Eliasson's practice as an effort to bring back in the senses of sight and perception, something from the latin word *perceptio,* which not only referred to the senses of sight, but rather to the *mastering* of the subject, in the sense of *seizing* or *capturing*.[31]

## "Today I feel Prismatic"

*A warning:*
"Be very cautious during these observations!
Do not overstrain your eyes!
Do not carry out more than two tests in succession!

And: Take a close look at the setting sun and then close your eyes!"

Reminders of Titchener's experimental psychology and of the possibility for experimental subjects of physiological experiments to produce after-images, in Goethe's theory of colors.

And Herman von Helmholtz wrote in his Physiological Optics:

> When one stares into the distance and scans the horizon, while standing on the beach at nightfall, there comes a moment, when the difference between the light sky and the dark sea is no

27 Ibid, p. 16.
28 Crary: "Olafur Eliasson: Visionäre Ereignisse".
29 Ibid.
30 Stafford: "Die kombinatorische Ästhetik der Neurobiologie", p. 44.
31 For the etymology of *perceptio*, see: Crary: *Aufmerksamkeit*, p. 15.

> longer really visible. This is clearly due to the fact that the longer a light excites the eye, the weaker its stimulating effect becomes the retina grows fatigued. That this is indeed true is shown the moment we transfer our gaze a little higher; the negative afterimage of the sea takes the form of a light streak against the sky. If we let our gaze descend a little, we can see the dark afterimage of the sky against the sea.[32]

Experiments with phantom images, which in rare cases relaxed the eyes, often caused pain, disabilities and even permanent blindness. They belong to the history of optical and psycho-physical experiments which fathomed the relation between outer and inner vision.

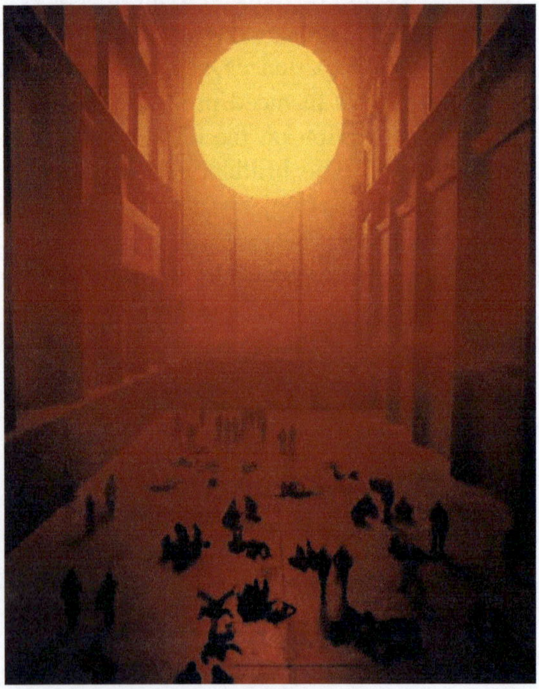

Fig. 3: *The weather project*, 2003, Turbine Hall, Tate Modern London (The Unilever Series), 2003.

Olafur Eliasson titled his installations "Experimental setups."[33]

It proposes similar psycho-physical situations in which visitors experience the experimental observation of themselves.

An experiment within an experiment, a double perspective on observation in which one is equally an observer of oneself and an experimental subject. The audience itself becomes the producer, the generator of its own luminous phenomenon of seeing, which – provoked by an external impulse – is transformed in a subjective sensory phenomenon. The visual space of the eye will be transformed

32 von Helmholtz: *Physiologische Optik.* Vol II. p. 202.

33 Eliasson: *The Mediated Motion.*

in an emphatic place displaying itself, similar to a theatre stage on which is showed the exciting spectacle springing from a solitary bodily sensation.[34]

The eye undergoes unprecedented experiences, prismatic and hallucinatory effects emphasizing the experience rather than the object, an experience which hypnotic movements can display a previously unknown ecstatic vision.

Eliasson's objects refer to other objects as well as to themselves, they show the receptivity of the senses of sight and the strain of the eye. The art of Eliasson is the result of a productive effect of perceptual activity, causing definite sensations. An intense, blinding bright light does not produce colored experiences of the inner perceptive world. Quick flashes of light, which undermine (exceed) the physiological limits of the eye, produce a staccato of visions, seemingly *still* images and *broken up* movements – consequently an *immobilized vision*. What emerges is a permanent distinct oscillation: a swing, the result leaves an *echo chamber*, created by an oscillating movement between a perceiving subject and the exploration of his inner feelings.

Eliasson calls such effects provoked by seeing: "hyperseeing," on which he declares: "The fact is, that we see more than we think we are seeing, and so this refers to the line of representation."[35]

Objectifying such a visual effect allows the experience to reach a condition he calls "hyperrepresentational" which he describes as follow:

> But since we are in the picture and in fact experiencing it, and since we don't exactely know it and recognize it, it becomes real again. By making it hyperrepresentational, we have a real experience – so that you see something that you don't normally see.[36]

The afterimages produced by the works of Olafur Eliasson demonstrate that stimuli, sensation and perception are not purely mechanical and univocal understanding processes, but allow comprehending the *Eigensinn* – or strong innate character – to the *Augensinn* – namely, the senses of sight.

34 It is possible to draw a comparison with experiments executed by Jan Evangelista Purkinje. For a description of the experiments and their effects, see: Müller-Tamm: "Die 'Empirie des Subjektiven' bei Jan Evangelista Purkinje", p. 155.

35 Eliasson: *The Mediated Motion*, p. 20.

36 Ibid.

## "To see yourself seeing and to sense yourself sensing"

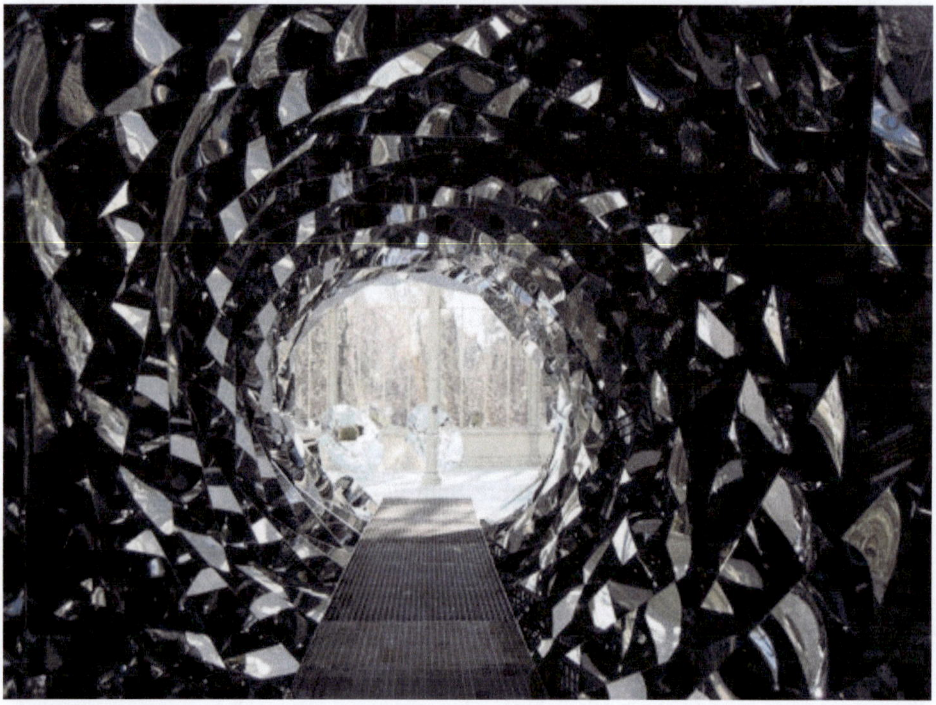

Fig. 4: *Your spiral view*, 2002, Palacio de Cristal, Museo Nacional centro de Arte Reina Sofia, 2003.

> [My interest lies] in how we see and how we sense [...] which goes beyond how we organize ourselves in our surroundings and how we have tried to organize our surroundings in order to orient ourselves properly[37] [...] I think one of the most important (levels of representation) is our sensual involvement. I would say that the engagement of our senses is proportional to our level of representation.[38]

Imagination, as the general capacity to picture to oneself the subjects of senses and sensations, appears in the brilliant combination of gaze, perception and thinking with the effects of emotion and invention. A form of perception is produced in which vision is no longer bound to a a priori of the visible, but visibility is postponed to make way for what is *conceivable* and *tangible*.

Relations between traces in the memory and direct vision: the easiest is to correlate them with the effect on the visual image, without taking the risk to investigate what really *produces* the effect. The question Frederico Zuccari asked in 1607 remains without an answer: what is the *disegno interno* and how is it different from, and relates to the *disegno esterno* on the canvas? As remains un-

37 Ibid, p. 21.
38 Ibid.

answered the question Rafaello asked, in the famous letter wrote to the count Baldassare Castiglione, in which he struggled to define the *certa idea*, which has its source in inner visions, before they find their expression on the canvas.[39]

The answer is the 'produktive Einbildungskraft' – the *productive* imagination, which makes possible to picture the internal organization of mental images, themselves connected to the outer images, because they depend on the goodwill of the perceiving subject to produce his *own* reality and his *own* sensory phenomena. If reality is not limited to the visible, then imagination is the condition of the possibility of a *pictorial* vision,[40] a visual *thinking*, which allows to think *consciousness* as inherently visual.

This creative role of the inner and outer images in the description of a thought, which is inherent to the emotion, seems to be Olafur Eliasson's ambition. What is generated, is not primarily objects, but event fields, zones and passages in which nothing objective is produced, but in which arise conditions of visibility, possibilities and options allowing floating zones of virtual experiences on the verge of achievement.[41] In these visionary experiences, an important role is played by fiction, which does not mean the contrary of facts but includes the whole range of meanings of *fingere*, i.e. forms, images, designs, suppositions, produces and representations. This touches a concept of image in which images are not effigies but configurations, in which, in the first place, representations of the thought meet with things from the outer world.

Olafur Eliasson reached this point of convergence through the radical disclosure that transparency would create the artificial means to give a psychological process a visual expression. But this disclosure of the means will be deliberately introduced to create the connection to an illusion, which becomes obvious if one thinks about the fact that the disclosure is showing the observer a moment of the creation of reality.

The visibility of the production of the image lets the image fall back on the plane of reality. This intrusion, or infiltration into the real world does not create at any moment the impression of an illusion, because it never leaves the plane of reality of the viewer. The reason of the large size of this *intrusion* in the real world is because such images belong to the proper reality of the viewer.

It creates a persistent shift between object and subject, and indistinguishable zones of experience, which Eliasson describes as follow:

> [...] I always begin to work from the point of view of the spectator. And then I try to list the conditions of the relationship between the piece and the spectator and all the layers between them.[42] [...] Sensing one-self sensing is our [...] ability to see oneself in a situation. [...] Works of mine might even suggest that the reading makes more sense the other way around. Such that the spectator puts herself in the position of the object, which then becomes the sub-

39 Arnheim: *Anschauliches Denken*, p. 99.

40 Cf. Müller-Tamm: "Vision und Visualität", p. 180.

41 Crary: "Olafur Eliasson: Visionäre Ereignisse".

42 Eliasson: *The Mediated Motion*, p. 17.

ject, such that the spectator is being looked back at by the object – a reversal of the subject and the object. And that is, I think, a generous gesture.[43]

## Epilogue

Fig. 5: *Your strange certainty still kept*, 1996, Tanya Bonakdar Gallery, New York, 1996.

The conditions of perceptions and the emotional realization of perception are also territories that Olafur Eliasson's pieces explore. He describes his pieces as "devices for the experience of reality,"[44] in which seeing and reflecting on yourself, memories, perceptions, stimuli, emotions, actions and activities are mapping a complex territory where the subject must find its place. Eliasson's artworks are researches, they are research labs on the status and knowledge of a subject, for whom artworks are systems of experience and of self observation.

43 Ibid. p. 23.
44 Eliasson, in: Grynszstejn/Birnbaum/Speaks: *Olafur Eliasson*, p. 39.

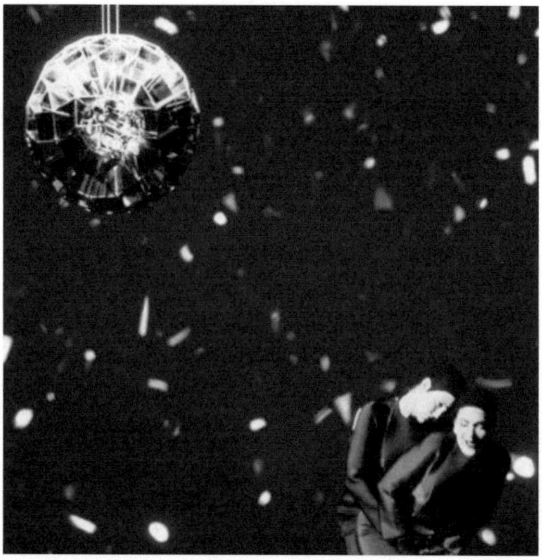

Fig. 6: *Phaedra*, 2007, Staatsoper Unter den Linden, Berlin, 2007.

In these models of perception, Eliasson alludes again and again to the infiltration of specific conditions between a person and the surrounding situation[45] – or, as he puts it: "I think there's a subliminal border where suddenly your representational and your real position merge, and you see where you 'really' are, your own position."[46]

45 Eliasson, in: Burchhart: "Wie in der Pop Art klaue ich direkt Naturphänomene und wissenschaftliche Darstellungen", p. 195.

46 Olafur Eliasson, in: Grynszstejn/Birnbaum/Speaks (ed.): *Olafur Eliasson*, p. 11.

## References


Agamben, Giorgio: "What is an Apparatus?", in: *What is an Apparatus? And Other Essays*, Stanford (Stanford University Press) 2009.

Arnheim, Rudolf: *Anschauliches Denken. Zur Einheit von Bild und Begriff*, Köln (DuMont) 2001.

Belting, Hans: "Das Bild als anthropologisches Phänomen", in: Klaus Sachs-Hombach: *Wege zur Bildwissenschaft*. Interviews. Köln (Herbert von Halem), 2004.

Benjamin, Walter: "Schemata zum psycho-physischen Problem" (ca. 1922), in: Sigrid Weigel: "Passagen und Spuren des Leib- und Bildraumes in Benjamins Schriften", in: Sigried Weigel (ed.): *Leib- und Bildraum. Lektüren nach Benjamin*. Köln/Weimar (Böhlau), 1992.

Benjamin, Walter: "Strenge Kunstwissenschaft. Zum ersten Bande der 'Kunstwissenschaftlichen Forschungen'", in: *Gesammelte Schriften*, vol. III, ed. by R. Tiedemann und W. Schweppenhäuser, Frankfurt am Main (Suhrkamp) 1972.

Boehm, Gottfried: "Vom Medium zum Bild", in: Yvonne Spielmann / Gundolf Winter (eds.): *Bild – Medium – Kunst*, München (Fink) 1999, pp. 165–179.

Burchhart, Dieter: "Wie in der Pop Art klaue ich direkt Naturphänomene und wissenschaftliche Darstellungen: Olafur Eliasson – ein Gespräch", in: *Theorien des Abfalls* Kunstforum 168 (2003), pp. 190–207.

Crary, Jonathan: "Olafur Eliasson: Visionäre Ereignisse", in: *Olafur Eliasson. Kunsthalle Basel*, Basel (Schwabe) 1997, pp. 5–13.

Crary, Jonathan: *Aufmerksamkeit. Wahrnehmung und moderne Kultur*, translated by Heinz Jatho, Frankfurt a. M. (Suhrkamp) 2002.

Derrida, Jacques / Bernhard Stiegler: *Échographies de la télévision. Entretiens filmés*, Paris (Éditions Galilée) 1996.

Foucault, Michel: "The Confession of the Flesh" (1977), Interview, in Colin Gordon (ed.): *Power/Knowledge. Selected Interviews and Other Writings*, translated by Colin Gordon, New York (Pantheon) 1980, pp. 194–228.

Flach, Sabine: *'Körper-Szenarien' Zum Verhältnis von Bild und Körper in Videoinstallationen*, München (Fink) 2003.

Flach, Sabine: "On Twilight", in: Sabine Flach, Jan Söffner (ed.): *Habitus in Habitat II Other Sides of Cognition*. Bern. u.a. (Peter Lang) 2010.

Grynszstejn, Madelaine / Daniel Birnbaum / Michael Speaks (eds.): *Olafur Eliasson*, London (Phaidon), 2002.

Helmholtz, Hermann von: *Physiologische Optik. Vol II*, 1867.

Hemsterhuis, François: "Simon ou des facultés de l'âme", in: *Hemsterhuis, François oeuvres philosophiques*, Vol. 2, ed. by Louis Susan Meyboom, Leuwarden 1846–1850.

Hüppauf, Bernd / Christopher Wulf (ed.): *Bild und Einbildungskraft*, München (Fink) 2006.

Katalog: *Olafur Eliasson. The Mediated Motion,* Boston/Köln (Institute of Contemporary Art) 2001.

Külpe, Oswald: *Vorlesungen über Psychologie,* ed. by Karl Bühler, Leipzig (Hirzel) 1920.

Locke, John: *Essay Concerning Human Understanding* (1690), ed. by Peter H. Nidditch, Oxford (Clarendon) 1975.

Marinetti, Filippo Tommaso: "Tattilismo" (1924), in: Marinetti, Filippo Tommaso: *Teoria e invenzione futurista*, ed. by Luciano de Maria Milano (Mondadori) 1983.

Merleau-Ponty, Maurice: *Phénoménologie de la perception,* Paris (nrf, Gallimard) 1945.

Müller-Tamm, Jutta: "Die 'Empirie des Subjektiven' bei Jan Evangelista Purkinje: Zum Verhältnis von Sinnesphysiologie und Ästhetik im frühen 20. Jahrhundert", in: Gabriele Dürbeck et al.: *Wahrnehmung der Natur – Natur der Wahrnehmung*, Dresden (Verlag der Kunst) 2001, pp. 153–165.

Müller-Tamm, Jutta: "Vision und Visualität. Zum Verhältnis von Wahrnehmungswissenschaft und Poetik bei Hermann Bahr und Robert Müller", in: Bernhard J. Dotzler / Sigrid Weigel (eds.): *fülle der combination. Literaturforschung und Wissenschaftsgeschichte*, München (Fink) 2005, pp. 173–189.

Nauman-Beyer, Waltraud: *Anatomie der Sinne im Spiegel von Philosophie, Ästhetik, Literatur*, Köln/Weimar/Wien (Böhlau) 2003.

Plessner, Helmuth: *Die Einheit der Sinne. Grundlegung einer Ästhesiologie des Geistes*, vol. 8, Bonn (Friedrich Cohen) 1923, reprint 1965.

Rivlin, Robert / Karen Gravelle: *Deciphering the Senses. The Expanding World of Human Perception*, New York (Simon and Schuster) 1984.

Sachs-Hombach Klaus / Bernhard Waldenfels: "Von der Wirkmacht und Wirkkraft der Bilder", in: Boehm, Gottfried, Birgit Mersmann, Christian Spies (eds.): *Movens Bild, Zwischen Evidenz und Affekt*, München (Fink) 2008, pp. 47–65.

Spielmann, Yvonne: "Schichtung und Verdichtung im elektronischen Bild", in: Id. / Gundolf Winter (eds.): *Bild – Medium – Kunst*, München (Fink) 1999, pp. 59–75.

Stafford, Barbara: "Die kombinatorische Ästhetik der Neurobiologie", in: Jörg Huber (ed.): *Interventionen. Darstellung: Korrespondenz*, Zürich/Wien, New York (Springer) 2000, pp. 3–59.

Vinge, Louise: *The Five Senses, Studies in a Literary Tradition*, Lund (CWK Gleerup) 1975.

Waldenfels, Bernhard: "Von der Wirkmacht und Wirkkraft der Bilder", in: Gottfried Boehm / Birgit Mersmann / Christian Spies: *Movens Bild: Zwischen Evidenz und Affekt*, München (Fink) 2008, pp. 47–63.

Weigel, Sigrid: "Passagen und Spuren des Leib- und Bildraumes in Benjamins Schriften", in: *Leib- und Bildraum. Lektüren nach Benjamin* vol. I, Köln/ Weimar (Böhlau) 2001, pp. 49–64.

Wiesing, Lambert: "Das Bild aus phänomenologischer Sicht", interview in: Klaus Sachs-Hombach (ed.) *Wege zur Bildwissenschaft*, Köln (Herbert von Halem) 2003, pp. 152–69.

## List of Illustrations

Fig. 1: *Green river*, 1998, Moss, Norway, 1998. Courtesy the artist; neugerriemschneider, Berlin; Tanya Bonakdar Gallery, New York. © 1998 Olafur Eliasson

Fig. 2: *Your black horizon*, 2005, Thyssen-Bornemisza Limited Edition Pavilion, 51st Venice Biennale, 2005. Photographer: Cameraphoto Arte, Venezia / T-B A21, Vienna. Thyssen-Bornemisza Art Contemporary (T-B A21), Vienna. © 2005 Olafur Eliasson.

Fig. 3: *The weather project*, 2003, Turbine Hall, Tate Modern London (The Unilever Series), 2003. Photographer: Andrew Dunkley & Marcus Leith. Courtesy the artist; neugerriemschneider, Berlin; Tanya Bonakdar Gallery, New York. © 2003 Olafur Eliasson.

Fig. 4: *Your spiral view*, 2002, Palacio de Cristal, Museo Nacional centro de Arte Reina Sofia, 2003. Boros Collection, Berlin. © 2002 Olafur Eliasson.

Fig. 5: *Your strange certainty still kept*, 1996, Tanya Bonakdar Gallery, New York, 1996. The Dakis Joannou Collection, Athens. © 1996 Olafur Eliasson.

Fig. 6: *Phaedra*, 2007, Staatsoper Unter den Linden, Berlin, 2007. Photographer: © Ruth Walz Photography. Staatsoper Unter den Linden, Berlin. © 2007 Olafur Eliasson

I wish to thank Studio Olafur Eliasson for giving me the permission to use the images.

# Radical Inactivism: Gilles Deleuze on Inert Motion in Francis Bacon's Painting (*Logique de la Sensation*)

Sven Spieker

With its emphasis on painting and on sensation as what animates it, Gilles Deleuze's *Francis Bacon. The Logic of Sensation* (1981) is not a good match for customary accounts of modernism with their reductive emphasis on the medium and its specificity. As a philosopher Deleuze is not interested in the conditions under which painting progressively elaborates its own medium but in the conditions under which it de-centers seeing by treating the eye as an organ without a fixed position in the organism, thus creating the condition for its own becoming. Unlike accounts of modernism that view the abandonment of representation in terms of a concomitant move away from the body, Deleuze establishes an intense connection between painting and the organism. Deleuze's argument is that painting, and Francis Bacon's painting in particular, focuses on the production of *sensation* as a form of experience that acts "directly on the nervous system," circumventing the brain. This is what distinguishes Bacon's questioning of representation from figurative painting and from abstract painting alike: "The same criticism can be made against both figurative painting and abstract painting: they pass through the brain, they do not act directly upon the nervous system, they do not attain the sensation, they do not liberate the Figure."[1]As a result, in Deleuze mind, they question representation less effectively than Bacon who does not abandon the body: "Everywhere there is a presence acting directly on the nervous system, which makes representation, whether in place or at a distance, impossible."[2]

Pioneers of abstraction such as Mondrian or Malevich avoided figuration by severing the link between sensation and the nervous system. In this spirit Malevich for one tied Suprematism to what he referred to as *oshchuchshenie,* a word that signifies sensation or what in German goes by the term *Empfindung*. However, the sensation Malevich associates with *oshchushchenie* is not beholden to any specific body or object, it is a disembodied affect the artist associated with the 4$^{th}$ (cosmic) dimension. From Deleuze's perspective, this compromised its ability to move beyond figuration, since such abandonment should never simply be a form of negation, which remains as such linked to the very thing it hopes to overcome. This also separates Deleuze sharply from Adorno for whom the *Ver-*

1 Deleuze: *Francis Bacon*, p. 32.
2 Ibid., p. 44.

*mitteltsein* of the artwork – its mediated nature – results in the progressive abandonment of expression and sensuousness, both of which can only appear in art in the most sublimated form.[3]

According to Deleuze, Bacon practiced an intermediate path in between the extremes of abstract painting and figural painting. As Bacon himself said of one of his works, "this image is a kind of tightrope walk between what is called figurative painting and abstraction."[4] Bacon's paintings, which are generally read as expressive gestures focused on the figuration of an existential experience of violence and despair, use color to produce affect and an experience of utter immediacy (sensation) that is as incompatible with traditional figuration as it is at odds with avant-garde abstraction: "Bacon has always tried to eliminate the 'sensational', that is, the primary figuration of that which provokes a violent sensation."[5]

The term *figure* as it is used by Deleuze can be explained with reference to what Bacon himself referred to as *pulverization*: "I think of myself as a kind of pulverizing machine into which everything I look at and feel is fed."[6] Commenting on his practice of using found photographs, Bacon continues:

> I believe that I am different from the mixed-media jackdaws who use photographs etc. more or less literally or cut them up and rearrange them. [...] In my case the photographs become a sort of compost out of which images emerge from time to time. Those images may be partly conditioned by the mood of the material which has gone into the pulverizer.[7]

It is the 'pulverization' of figuration – which I want to understand as an instance of a successful, lasting binding of a mimetic form to a meaning – in the name of a more immediate access to sensation that is at stake here: "I don't want to avoid telling a story, but I want very, very much to do the thing that Valéry said – to give the sensation without the boredom of its conveyance. And the moment the story enters, the boredom comes upon you."[8] In other words, what Bacon wants to achieve is not the sublimation of the sensuous that Adorno thought of as essential in (modern) art, yet he also does not want to return to traditional figuration and representation.

According to Deleuze, Bacon achieves his goal of 'pulverizing' and disrupting figuration in a variety of ways, from the isolation of his figures (by placing them into a closed box or space, or on a kind of stage) to the frequency with which he places his paintings in series of three (triptychs) and then introduces

3 "Whereas to a certain extent these functions may be attributed to sensual immediacy [...] artworks nevertheless achieve a critical point where this immediacy ends; where they must be 'thought'.", Adorno: *Aesthetic Theory*, p. 89.
4 Sylvester (ed.): *Interviews with Francis Bacon. 1962–1979*, p. 12.
5 Deleuze: *Francis Bacon. The Logic of Sensation*, p. 34.
6 Quoted after Russell: *Francis Bacon*, 1979, p. 71.
7 Ibid.
8 Sylvester (ed.): *Interviews with Francis Bacon. 1962–1979*, p. 12. See also p. 22.

breaks between the canvases which isolate the different figures from each other. As Bacon himself has said in one of the conversations with David Sylvester that Deleuze used extensively for his study, "they [the vertical breaks between the canvases of a triptych, S.S.] isolate one from the other. And they cut off the story between one and the other. It helps to avoid story-telling if the figures are painted on three different canvases."[9] It will be crucial then not to interpret this proceeding thematically, i.e. as a way of telling a story of isolation, emotional distance, or existential solitude. As Michel Leiris has written, the point is not the intense expression of the figure's isolation rather than "to isolate this figure in order to express it [the figure, S.S.] intensely."[10] This intensity is directly linked to Deleuze's – and Bacon's own – idea that the painter's figures are not, or not fully, representational. Bacon himself has often invoked chance as one of the means by which he seeks to replace figuration with intensity. Overall, what is perhaps most important in this context is the deformation of his figures. Such deformation might occur when Bacon wiped over parts of his paintings with brushes or pieces of cloth; through the literal throwing of paint at the canvas; or through the application of insignificant lines meant to cancel figuration and enhance intensity.[11] In all these cases, the point was to avoid the impression that Bacon was attempting to simply *represent* intense states of being.

Art as sensation, or what he calls "blocs of sensations" is key to Deleuze's thinking about art. In *What is Philosophy* (1991) Deleuze and Guattari write that "The artist creates blocs of percepts and affects, but the only law of creation is that the compound must stand up on its own. The artist's greatest difficulty is to make it *stand up on its own.*"[12] Artists are "presenters of affects, the inventors and creators of affects."[13] This does not mean, however, that artists or for that matter anyone else can own an affect or a sensation. Instead, according to the authors, affects and sensations exceed the individual that experiences them: "Percepts are no longer perceptions; they are independent of a state of those who experience them. Affects are no longer feelings or affections; they go beyond the strength of those who undergo them. Sensations, percepts, and affects are *beings* whose validity lies in themselves and exceeds any lived. They could be said to exist in the absence of man because man, as he is caught in stone, on the canvas, or by words, is himself a compound of percepts and affects. The work of art is a being of sensation and nothing else: it exists in itself."[14]

Given that we have come to take it as a given that post-avant-garde art rejects art's autonomy and social insulation, Deleuze's remarks here may strike us as strange. He does, however, raise a tantalizing question, namely the question as

9 Ibid., p. 23.
10 Quoted from Ruf: *Fluchtlinien der Kunst*, p. 69.
11 Ibid., p. 69.
12 Deleuze/Guattari: *What Is Philosophy?*, p. 175.
13 Ibid.
14 Ibid., p. 164.

to whether affect can exist outside, and independently from, a subject that experiences it. This indeed is the very question Deleuze asks in his book on Bacon and the "logic of sensation." Deleuze begins the central chapter ("Painting and Sensation") with an analysis of Cézanne's critique of Impressionism. In the history of modernism, Impressionism is generally associated with a regime of pure opticality, a disembodied way of seeing that concentrates on the recording of conditions under which objects appear at a specific point in time. However, what Cézanne championed under the term "sensation" was not limited to the representation of the object or to the impressions to which it gives rise. Instead Cézanne's idea was not to copy the object but paint ('actualize') its *own* sensation. Deleuze comments on this statement when he writes: "This was Cézanne's lesson against the Impressionists: sensation is not in the 'free' or disembodied play of light and color (impressions); on the contrary, it is in the body, even the body of an apple."[15] To Cézanne, color mediates between sensation and objects. Deleuze takes up this equation when he argues that "color is in the body, sensation is in the body, and not in the air. Sensation is what is painted. What is painted on the canvas is the body, not insofar as it is represented as an object, but insofar as it is experienced as sustaining *this* sensation…"[16] What is being proposed here is that sensation in Cézanne is a synthetic event ("something happens") which produces its perceiving subject as it unfolds. In his conversations with David Sylvester Bacon expressed somewhat similar ideas, arguing that a form related to a sensation is the opposite of a form related to the object that it is meant to represent. Bacon also speaks of different "orders" of sensations in painting, orders that result in the deformations that are so characteristic of his work (as opposed to abstraction where, according to Bacon, sensations remain on one and the same level). Deleuze takes up this point when he argues that in Bacon's painting sensations never stay on the same level, adding that each sensation may within itself contain different orders or levels: "It is each painting, each Figure, that is itself a shifting sequence or series (and not simply a term in a series). […] Hence the irreducibly synthetic character of sensation."[17]

Deleuze rejects the idea that these different levels of sensation can be associated with the different stages or intervals in an ongoing motion or movement. This hypothesis is based on the fact that Bacon was demonstrably fond of Muybridge's chrono-photographs and that he used them in his paintings. Many of Bacon's paintings do indeed contain movements or motions, often in such a way that it appears as if the figures were put in motion by the round area that isolates them so that they seem to be "making their daily round." However, as Deleuze points out, in these cases, movement does not explain sensation since Bacon's figures never make it beyond the boundaries of the contour that holds them in. Their feet, often swollen, are not made for walking: "According to Becket's or

15 Deleuze: *Francis Bacon. The Logic of Sensation,* p. 31.
16 Ibid., p. 32.
17 Ibid., p. 33.

Kafka's law, there is immobility beyond movement: beyond standing up, there is sitting down, and beyond sitting down, lying down, beyond which one finally dissipates. The true acrobat is one who is consigned to immobility inside the circle."[18]

For Deleuze, sensation is neither fully on the side of the subject (it transcends the subject) nor is it fully on the side of the object (it goes beyond the impressions created or evoked by an object). Instead sensation "has one face turned toward the subject (the nervous system, vital movement, 'instinct', 'temperament') […] and one face turned toward the object (the 'fact', the place, the event)."[19] The consequence of this is that the state of pure opticality which was a characteristic of impressionism has to be given up since the separation between the object and its spectator can no longer be maintained: "I *become* in the sensation and something *happens* through the sensation. […] [I]t is the same body that, being both subject and object, gives and receives the sensation."[20]

These thoughts link Deleuze to the late 19th century physicist, mathematician and philosopher of science Ernst Mach.[21] Mach's radically anti-metaphysical attitude; his insistence on the primacy of change over immutability; his focus on sensations over the brain and on the impossibility of transcending the body make him a crucial precursor to Deleuze's critique of figuration. With Mach, Deleuze shares a suspicion not only of representation and narrative, but also of an understanding of sensation that views it as a primarily reactive, mono-lateral physical affect. Mach believed that it was our habitual, language-based inclination to prefer stable concepts over constantly changing sensations that prevented us from seeing the world for what it is: a forever changing conglomerate of clusters of sensations. In *The Analysis of Sensations* (1885) Mach writes:

> My friend can put on a different coat. His face can become serious or serene. The color of his face can change through changing light or affects. His figure can change through motion or permanently. The sum total of what is permanent here remains big enough when compared to

18 Ibid., p. 36. Deleuze's idea of inert motion in Bacon can be related to Einstein's theory of general relativity and his contention that in a gravitational field being in accelerated motion and being at rest are physically identical states. Einstein concluded that if this were true then the free fall of an object had to be considered an inertial motion.

19 Ibid., p. 71.

20 Ibid., p. 31.

21 On possible links between Mach and Deleuze, see Schmidgen: "Begriffszeichnungen. Über die philosophische Konzeptkunst von Gilles Deleuze", in: Gente/Weibel (eds.): *Deleuze und die Künste*, pp. 26–53. Cf. also Schmidgen's definition of Deleuze's understanding of concepts (*Begriffe*): "What then is a concept according to Deleuze and Guattari? […] On the one hand a concept is not independent of the perceptions and sensations from which it is extracted. It should be borne in mind, however, that perceptions and sensations are not apprehended, registered, and summarized from an elevated observer's position but that they are deduced from the themes that are as it were implicit in the perceptions and sensations […]. However, a concept does not only produce a summary. It also has a regressive effect back on the perceptions and sensations, changes them or produces them." (p. 47).

> these daily changes that these fade into the background. It is the same friend with whom I go on my daily walk.[22]

As Mach writes, "there are only sensations," a statement that is designed to throw us back beyond the stage at which sensations become figurative by entering into 'sensible' relations with each other.

Deleuze's ideas regarding the role played by sensation in Bacon are close to Mach's, in that Deleuze insists that the binding or integration of sensations into meaningful clusters is temporary and cannot durably sustain seemingly stable notions such as that of the organism or the subject. And yet, in his insistence that sensation in itself is not, as Mach seems to imply, a homogenous concept but is instead characterized by a multitude of levels, thresholds, and intensities, Deleuze goes beyond Mach. In fact, he does everything to persuade us that nothing is as difficult to achieve as the binding of the different levels internal to every sensation. Sensation may be a form of synthesis, but this does not mean that the differences between its levels and intensities can be erased.

The unity of sensation cannot, according to Deleuze, be located in the represented object, since Bacon is interested in painting sensation but not what is 'sensational'. Or, in Bacon's own words, he wants to "paint the scream but not the horror" because painting the horror would mean to remain tied to the order of narrative and representation: "[E]ither I paint the horror and I do not paint the scream, because I make a figuration of the horrible; or else I paint the scream, and I do not paint the visible horror, I will paint the visible horror less and less, since the scream captures or detects an invisible force."[23] Invisible forces are forces that are not in themselves subject to being experienced, even though they represent the particular conditions necessary for a sensation and incite our sense faculties to become active.[24]

As an example of the deformative effect of such invisible forces Deleuze cites Bacon's series of heads and his self-portraits:

> [T]he extraordinary agitation of these heads is not derived from a movement that the series would supposedly reconstitute, but rather from the forces of pressure, dilation, contraction, flattening, and elongation that are exerted on the immobile head. They are like the forces of the cosmos confronting an intergalactic traveler in his capsule. It is as if invisible forces were

22 Mach: *Die Analyse der Empfindungen und das Verhältnis des Physischen zum Psychischen* (Jena, 1885), p. 2. Translation mine, S.S.

23 Deleuze: *Francis Bacon. The Logic of Sensation*, p. 51. Cf. also: "I wanted to paint the scream more than the horror. I think, if I had really thought about what causes somebody to scream, it would have made the scream that I tried to paint more successful. Because I should in a sense have been more conscious of the horror that produced the scream. In fact they were too abstract." In: Sylvester (ed.): *Interviews with Francis Bacon. 1962–1979*, p. 48.

24 Ruf: *Fluchtlinien der Kunst. Ästhetik, Macht Leben bei Gilles Deleuze.* Ruf defines *force* in Deleuze as "that which cannot be sensed from an empirical point of view and what from a transcendental point of view (i.e. as the particular and concrete condition for every sensation) can only be sensed." (p. 82)

> striking the head from many different angles. [...] This is why the problems Bacon faces are indeed those of deformation and not transformation.[25]

Deleuze views painting as an effort to make invisible forces visible: "Bacon's Figures seem to be one of the most marvellous responses in the history of painting to the question, How can one make invisible forces visible?"[26] If that proposition seems outlandish, it loses some of its strangeness when we consider that Deleuze did not consider the deformations to which Bacon's figures are subject to be the result of identifiable (visible) causes whose consequence would then be a visible distortion. However, at the same time, the invisible forces he invokes are not simply metaphysical either, they are not, say, the forces of death or evil.

We might place Deleuze's understanding of these forces in the context of the late 19th century critique of Newtonian mechanics, of which Ernst Mach was a prominent representative. That critique proceeded on the grounds that traditional mechanics was incapable of accounting for invisible forces, including the electric waves whose existence had been deduced by Clerk Maxwell and then experimentally proven by Heinrich Hertz. Hertz was also able to show that a flow of current in one electrical circuit could result in a corresponding flow in a similarly tuned circuit not directly connected with the first. In a famous example from the preface to his textbook on mechanics, Hertz advances a striking example of hidden forces, the stars in the sky whose movements can be observed even

25 Deleuze: *Francis Bacon,* p. 50. Deleuze regards Bacon as a painter of heads rather than faces. The face, in his reading, is part of the body's spatial organization and integration. As such it is part of the order of representation, not the order of intensity for which he has Bacon strive. The face conceals the head and can exist independently from the body, while the head depends on the body. Through his rubbing and wiping Bacon literally de-faces the figure and strips it of its form, with an intensity that is that of an animal spirit, a becoming-animal: "The marks or traits of animality are not animal forms but rather the spirits that haunt the wiped-off parts, that pull at the head, individualizing and qualifying the head without a face." (p. 19) This remark should not be misunderstood to mean that a human being becomes an animal; rather that "in place of formal correspondences, what Bacon's painting constitutes is a *zone of indiscernability or undecidability* between man and animal. Man becomes animal but not without the animal becoming spirit at the same time..." (p. 20) Deleuze's argument here is reminiscent of a passage in Rainer Maria Rilke's novel *The Notebooks of Malte Laurids Brigge* (1910) in which the protagonist muses upon the fact that people do not have one face but many ("I am learning to see. Yes I am starting. [...] Why for example did I never become conscious of how many faces there are. There are a lot of people, but many more faces because everybody has several." Rainer Maria Rilke: *Die Aufzeichnungen des Malte Laurids Brigge*, p. 111. Rilke believes that once we approach reality from a rigorously sensation-based viewpoint the idea that there could be such a thing as a stable subject that disposes of a static face becomes untenable. However, Deleuze goes beyond what Rilke argues. With him it is not simply a matter of pluralizing the face, or of accepting the instability of the subject, but of abolishing it as an agent of sensation altogether. Again, the question Deleuze asks is if there can be sensations or affects that are independent of the normative integrity of a sensing subject, of the idea that we own ourselves, our body, and the sensations that are channeled by its organs.

26 Ibid., p. 49.

though the force behind these movements never becomes visible.[27] Yet, while the original force remains invisible, its effects are subject to observation and sensation. Clearly, once physics turns in a serious way to the forces behind such movements it will be a science concerned not only with registration or archivization of past motions but also with the anticipation of future ones, with a form of becoming. Ballistic experiments might be said to be dealing, similarly, with such a mechanics of the future. And this makes them similar to Deleuze's invisible forces which at one point he indeed labels "the forces of the future."[28] This orientation in Deleuze's understanding of sensation towards the future is crucial. There is always an element in sensation that exceeds the positivist insistence on immediacy. Or rather, the feeling of presence and immediacy that we associate with sensation is not mono-temporal; it consists both of present perceptions and of anticipated forces that are not subject to perception in the present. It is these forces or rather the sensations to which they give rise that painting seeks to register – archives of future traces.

Simon Ruf has noted that the deformations caused by Deleuze's invisible forces do not mark a transition from one aggregate state to another (say, from a state of physical integrity to harm; or from happiness to despair). Any such transition would after all remain firmly tied to the order of narrative and story. The point is not to express emotions or states of being that are caused by invisible forces and that change over time but *these forces themselves*, or rather the sensations to which they give rise. Again, Bacon is interested in painting the scream but not the horror. But what exactly does this mean?

Deleuze explains (in what he himself calls a "phenomenological" key) that even though the different levels of sensation may depend on different sense organs every single sensation or level of sensation refers us to the other levels. This happens independently from the represented object that these sensations may have in common. This "non representational moment" in sensation (*le moment non-représentatif*) might imply that whenever flesh is represented in Bacon's paintings "on la touche, on la sent, on la mange, on la pèse."[29] In one sense, this is synaesthesia, the common exercise of all the senses, an original unity. However, such a unity is dependent on the invisible forces, a kind of *vis activa* that traverses these individual sensations. Deleuze calls this power "rhythm" and argues that it is "more powerful than vision, hearing, etc." "[C]ette opération n'est possible que si la sensation de tel ou tel domaine (ici la sensation visuelle) est directement en prise sur une puissance vitale qui déborde tous les domaines et les traverse."[30] The ideal division of the senses into five, neglects the possibility

27 Heinrich Hertz: *The Principles of Mechanics*.

28 Gilles Deleuze: *Francis Bacon*, p. 51.

29 Ibid., p. 31: "We touch it, smell it, eat it, weigh it." Translation by the author, S.S.

30 Ibid. "This operation is only possible if the sensation of this domain or another [here visual sensation] is in close contact with a vital force that overflows all the domains and moves

of interferences that can cloud such arithmetic precision. At their most general level, such interferences would be nothing but the pulse of life itself: life here understood not as a metaphor but in its pure state, a pure presence. In this sense what we are dealing with is synaesthesia understood not as metaphor, not as the ideal unity of the five senses or as a Kantian synthesis on a higher level but instead as an instance of unbinding. The senses sense, there is synthesis, but they are not ideally in sync with each other.

Rhythm, Deleuze explains, appears as music on the auditory level, and as painting on the visual level. Only at the point where sensation establishes a relationship with this *vis activa* can, and must, sensation become a pulse: "C'est diastole-systole: le monde qui me prend moi-même en se fermant sur moi, le moi qui s'ouvre au monde, et l'ouvre lui-même."[31]

At this point the deformations and contortions endured by Bacon's figures are to be understood as the effects of contractions or expansions of the flat field that surrounds them – of rhythm – rather than as expressions of anguish or despair. Bacon said of himself that he was intellectually a pessimist but at the same time a nervous optimist who only believes in life. Deleuze takes the painter at his word: from the point of view of sensation, the nervous system, being touched by rhythm is to experience its deformations not in the order of representation – as anguish – but as the pulse of life itself. Where rhythm touches on sensation, it introduces if not sound – there can be such a thing as a silent rhythm – then at least an element of time. And perhaps this element of rhythmic time is crucial when it comes to the disruption of figuration. Perhaps what Deleuze wishes to argue is that representation – the idea that there can be a binding unity of form and meaning – is disrupted precisely by the introduction of rhythmic intervals into an otherwise purely static visual regime. Bacon's paintings break with representation, achieving a sensation that "acts directly on the nerves," precisely at the point where rhythm intervenes in their visual forms in ways that recall avant-garde film of the 1920s. This is also why Bacon's paintings would not qualify as synaesthetic, let alone sympathetic: they do not integrate different sensations such as sound and the visual; instead they use the one to "space out" the other.

At this point Bacon's figures are no longer to be understood as organisms but as what Deleuze and Guattari called a body without organs, quite literally a non-organic body. The body without organs is, crucially, not without a body. Nor is it a subject that has lost his or her body, or that can no longer exercise control over its individual parts. On the contrary, the body without organs is the body outside of any claim to ownership or normative possession. It is a body not dominated by sequence, by structure, or by the hierarchy of organs (beginning with the brain). The body without organs, much like the invisible forces in Ba-

across them." Translation mine, S.S. I thank Elisabeth Weber for her assistance with this translation.

31 "It's diastole/systole: the world that takes me on by closing in on me, the I that opens to the world and opens it itself." Translation mine, S.S. Ibid.

con, is not in need of interpretation or analysis. It is not defined by lack, or by a relationship between cause and effect. Nor is it really a body subjected to radical dissociation or to the kind of sceptical analysis to which Ernst Mach subjected the world. From the perspective of the body without organs, the zones of indeterminacy that Bacon introduces into his painting through brushing and wiping and the deformations his figures undergo are not marks of cruelty. They rather mark the figures' liberation from the rigid representational regime of the organism towards a life that is at the same time non-life because it is non-organic in the literal sense of that word.

In the hierarchical order of the organism, the eye has always occupied a privileged position. By contrast, the eye associated with the non-organic body without organs – the eye that Deleuze associates with Bacon's painting – is neither the privileged organ of a disembodied registration of exterior phenomena, as is the case in impressionism, nor is it the privileged organ of an organized, organizing body that has, ever since the Renaissance, been at the center of figuration in art (ever since Brunnelleschi's peephole). Instead, the eye, in Deleuze's understanding, leaves its assigned place in the organism so that painting can become a blind art:

> [Painting] *does not treat the eye as a fixed organ.* It liberates lines and colors from their representative function, but at the same time it also liberates the eye from its adherence to the organism, from its character as a fixed and qualified organ. [...] Painting gives us eyes all over: in the ear, in the stomach, in the lungs (the painting breathes....). This is the double definition of painting: subjectively, it invests the eye, which ceases to be organic in order to become a polyvalent and transitory organ; objectively, it brings before us the reality of a body, of lines and colors freed from organic representation. And each is produced by the other: the pure presence of the body becomes visible at the same time that the eye becomes the destined organ of this presence.[32]

Painting is retinal in a perverted sense: it makes us see with *all* our senses. The abandonment of figuration then is not the abandonment of seeing, on the contrary. It is as if we were to take leave of ourselves *through our own eyes* so that we can see ourselves freed from the prison of binocular eyesight. The sensation that corresponds with this is a vibration, the extension of a sound in space, what Bacon calls an "intensive reality," in relation to which forms are "contingent or accessory."[33] What happens, in other words, is that we *hear the painting by seeing it.*

One might here feel reminded of Dziga Vertov's camera eye, which was made prominent in his famous film *The Man With a Movie Camera* (1929). In that film, the camera comes to inhabit even the most hidden spaces in the city as it moves (and sees) where the human body cannot go. The reason the camera can do this is that it is detached from the body; it cannot die. Only at the point where the camera attaches itself to the human body like a prosthesis (a technical sup-

32 Ibid., p. 45.
33 Ibid., p. 39.

plement) are the limitations of human eyesight overcome.[34] Deleuze's understanding of the relationship between painting and the eye, however, goes beyond the progressive avant-garde. Where with Vertov the detached camera eye takes its rightful place in a newly formed techno-physical organism in which it occupies the central position, this kind of stratification and organization—with the technical camera eye in a position n of superiority—is given up by Deleuze. Instead, the eye in painting, once it has been liberated from the organism, returns us to the body (without organs) as a pure presence.

The body without organs has only a head but no face since the very idea of a face would immediately place it in the order of binding, of metonomy, metaphor, and synaesthesia understood as an ideal unity that precedes the body or that affects it from outside. Also the sensations correspond to the body without organs are not categorized by the different organs from which they originate (nose, eye, mouth, etc.): "The insistence [...] of a body that survives the organism, the insistence of transitory organs that survive the qualified organs. [...] Everywhere there is a presence acting directly on the nervous system, which makes representation [...] impossible."[35] The body without organs is the body in the grasp of invisible forces. However, it does not resist these forces, nor does it really suffer from them; it is simply *shaped* (deformed) by them.

## References

Adorno, Theodor W.: *Aesthetic Theory*, Minneapolis (University of Minnesota Press) 1970.

Deleuze, Gilles: *Francis Bacon. The Logic of Sensation*, Minneapolis (University of Minnesota Press) 2004.

Deleuze, Gilles / Guattari, Félix: *What Is Philosophy?* New York (Columbia University Press) 1994.

Hertz, Heinrich: *The Principles of Mechanics, Presented in a New Form*, New York (Dover) 1956.

Mach, Ernst: *Die Analyse der Empfindungen und das Verhältnis des Physischen zum Psychischen*, Jena, 1885.

Ruf, Simon: *Fluchtlinien der Kunst. Ästhetik, Macht Leben bei Gilles Deleuze*, Würzburg (Königshausen & Neumann) 2003.

Russell, John: *Francis Bacon*, London (Thames and Hudson) 1979.

34 See Spieker: "Orthopädie und Avantgarde. Dziga Vertovs *Filmauge* aus prothetischer Sicht *(Der Mann mit der Kamera)*", pp. 147–169.

35 Deleuze, *Francis Bacon. The Logic of Sensation*, p. 44.

Schmidgen, Henning: "Begriffszeichnungen. Über die philosophische Konzeptkunst von Gilles Deleuze", in: Peter Gente / Peter Weibel (eds.), *Deleuze und die Künste*, Frankfurt/M (Suhrkamp) 2007, pp. 26–53.

Spieker, Sven: "Orthopädie und Avantgarde. Dziga Vertovs *Filmauge* aus prothetischer Sicht *(Der Mann mit der Kamera)*", in: N. Drubek-Meyer / J. Murasov (eds.), *Apparatur und Rhapsodie. Zu den Filmen des Dziga Vertov*, Munich (Fink) 1999.

Sylvester, David (ed.): *Interviews with Francis Bacon. 1962–1979*, London (Thames and Hudson) 1975.

# *Framing Synaesthesia*

# Sensorimotor Signature, Skill, and Synaesthesia. Two Challenges for Enactive Theories of Perception

JOERG FINGERHUT

## Introduction

The condition of 'genuine perceptual synaesthesia' has been a focus of attention in research in psychology and neuroscience over the last decades.[1] For subjects in this condition stimulation in one modality automatically and consistently over the subject's lifespan triggers a percept in another modality. In hearing→colour synaesthesia, for example, a specific sound experience evokes a perception of a specific colour. In this paper, I discuss questions and challenges that the phenomenon of synaesthetic experience raises for theories of perceptual experience in general, and for theories that see the content and modality of conscious experience as being constituted and determined by the active and skilful exploration of the environment in particular. The focus of my paper will be on the latter, 'enactive' view of perception and its theory of what determines the modality-specific 'feel' of a perceptual experience.[2]

In genuine synaesthesia a local element – e.g. another percept – reliably and sufficiently triggers a specific response experience: no involvement of the body that is related to the response percept (like eye saccades for visual experience) seems to be needed. This constitutes the first challenge to enactivism: in cases of hearing→colour synaesthesia colour experiences are elicited that are not related to the normal sensorimotor signature of vision. The strong correlation between skill and experience that is predicted by enactivism does not hold in these cases.

1 It has been argued that this is due to the use of non-invasive neuroimaging techniques that enable scientists to verify synaesthesia beyond phenomenological reports as well as the new general scientific interest in consciousness. Cf. Cytowic/Eagleman: *Wednesday is Indigo Blue,* pp. 235–237; see also the introduction to this volume, pp. 10–13.

2 In its general form this view dates back to the embodied conception of the mind put forth by John Dewey in the 19th century and has found a contemporary expression in the sensorimotor contingency theory of visual awareness. A precise and extensive formulation of this theory is Alva Noë's and Kevin O'Regan's "A Sensorimotor Account of Vision and Visual Consciousness". See also Myin/O'Regan: "Perceptual Consciousness, Access to Modality and Skill Theories" for an enactive account with a specific focus on the modalities of experience that is close to the topic of my paper.

A second but related challenge is constituted by the fact that the established correlations between trigger and response percept seem to be stable over the life-span of the synaesthete without the response modality ever being related to its 'normal' sensorimotor signature. Yet, experiments with visually distorting goggles and sensory substitution systems have been cited by sensorimotor enactivists to show that the human perceptual system is in a strong sense adaptive. The question with regard to synaesthesia is: why doesn't the extra synaesthetic experience *adapt away* like it would do in normal perceptual cases? Why can a visual experience that is unrelated to vision not be unlearned?

In the first part of the paper I introduce the phenomenon of 'genuine perceptual synaesthesia'. I then, in the second part, sketch a theory of active perception that I want to endorse: enactivism. This is done by focussing on two basic assumptions underlying enactivism, and by defining two claims that a rather narrow 'sensorimotor enactivism' derives from these assumptions. These claims are: (a) the modality of a perceptual experience is constituted by the sensorimotor signature (i.e. the specific dependencies relating movements to stimulations) and the larger body-involving cycle underlying this modality; and: (b) distorting elements get integrated and become transparent for the perceptual systems over a learning time span. As indicated above, these claims are challenged by cases of genuine synaesthesia. In part three, I discuss possible replies of the more narrowly defined sensorimotor enactivism to the first challenge and show that those replies either fail or betray important enactive insights. I will argue in particular that a promising way to meet the challenge (i.e. to claim that synaesthetic colours lack the properties of 'bodiliness' and 'grabbiness' of normal perceptual experience) fails. In part four, I suggest that enactivism, because it is unable to explain the perception-like experiences in cases of genuine perceptual synaesthesia, has to focus, instead, on typical realizers of perceptual experiences and on a more general enactivism in order to meet the two challenges. I show that this goes hand in hand with the inclusion of other adaptive time spans (in the course of which the perceptual system of an organism is shaped) in the explanations of phenomena like synaesthesia. In my view enactivism has not made this recourse to longer time spans as opposed to the 'here-and-now' explicit enough, though it is inherent to enactivism, even in the narrower, sensorimotor version of the theory. In order to explain and integrate certain atypical expressions of a perceptual mechanism – as I will argue in the last part of the paper – it is necessary to also take into view the embodiment of cognitive solutions shaped over evolutionary time spans and to adopt a heuristics and engineering perspective on such phenomena. This, I conclude, allows us to meet the challenges and hold on to central tenets of an enactive theory of perception.[3]

3 For a take on enactivism and synaesthesia that also embraces a version of enactivism see Dan Hutto's talk: "Understanding Synaesthesia, Radically Enactively", presented at the conference "Habitus in Habitat III: Synaesthesia and Kinaesthetics", 22nd October 2010.

## 1. What is 'genuine synaesthesia' and why should it be accounted for in theories of perception?

The prevalence of synaesthesia is nowadays assumed to be 1 in 23 of the normal population. The variety of types of synaesthesia is fascinating – 61 variants reported to date – and the growing public awareness of synaesthesia has led subjects to come forth and report more and more different forms, adding to the already known varieties. The graphem→colour synaesthesia is by far the most common type, a condition most likely shared by over 60% of all synaesthetes, and there is a high chance that a subject with one type of synaesthesia will also present another. In general, colour is the most common response, with different triggers ranging from sounds to even perceived personality. The response characteristics differ widely from synaesthete to synaesthete. There are reported cases of complex three-dimensional forms projected into space, or smells and felt temperatures as synaesthetic responses.[4] In what follows, I will focus on two specific features of the synaesthetic condition: *automaticity* and *consistency over time*, which cover two central aspects of genuine synaesthesia.

In genuine synaesthesia there is an experienced element that automatically triggers another sensory experience. The triggered sense modality (or aspect) is different from the triggering modality (or aspect). In other words: given a certain perceived or imagined triggering element, the response percept occurs involuntarily and cannot be suppressed. Consider again the case of graphem→colour synaesthesia. Once a synaesthetic subject is aware of a certain number or letter, she can't help but see at the same time (and in all cases) a specific colour or hue. It is important to notice that the automatic trigger is perceived and has to some extend to be consciously present itself. The trigger is not just another element in the causal chain that might, under normal conditions, lead to a specific experience, like retinal input or neuronal excitations in the pathways involved, leading to the activation of specific brain areas. It is a percept itself that elicits the cooccuring synaesthetic experience.[5]

Besides the automatic and involuntary response to a specific experienced trigger, consistency over time has become *the* defining element of genuine sy-

4 For the numbers concerning the general prevalence see Simner et al.: „Non-random associations of graphemes to colors in synaesthetic and normal populations". For a good introduction to the phenomenon and an overview on the variety of synaesthesia and the prevalence of the different types see chap. 2 of Cytowic/Eagleman: *Wednesday is Indigo Blue*, pp. 23–62. Cf. also Dixon et al.: "Not All Synaesthetes Are Created Equal".

5 Cf. Mattingley: "Attention, Automaticity, and Awareness in Synesthesia" for a good discussion of this topic. The latter point – that an experienced percept or concept has to be present in order to elicit the response – has been long disputed and is not part of the definition of genuine perceptual synaesthesia in classical papers like e.g. Ramachandran/Hubbard: "Synaesthesia", and "The Phenomenology of Synaesthesia".

naesthesia. It has been used to separate genuine synaesthesia from other forms like acquired or drug-induced synaesthetic experiences, and as such it has become part and parcel of the standardized behavioural test to verify synaesthesia. This test has shown that pairings of triggers and responses, for example the pairings of specific numbers with specific colours in synaesthetes, are persistent over time to a much higher degree compared to control groups exposed to those pairings during extensive associative learning phases. Consistency in synaesthetes has been proven in large test-retest scenarios by using refined computerized colour matching paradigms, and has now become the 'gold standard' for determining genuine synaesthesia.[6]

Both aforementioned criteria are behaviourally determined and partly also make use of subjective descriptions as hetero-phenomenological data. Given the variety of cases, no single neuronal mechanism or condition has yet been identified which sufficiently characterizes synaesthesia, but some attempts have been made to replace the behavioural criterion with a neurobiologically based one.[7] Independently of such attempts, neural correlates have been identified for the respective modality or aspect of trigger and response percept (e.g. the ventral temporal lobe, including colour-selective area V4/V8, for colour as a response).[8] It is contested whether synaesthesia constitutes a case of hyperconnectivity established by extra-connections between different brain areas, or a lack of inhibition of crosstalk between the regions with the same amount of connections. I won't go into this debate here, but it is of great interest for the study of consciousness, since synaesthesia constitutes a case where two hetero-phenomenologically determined conscious percepts can be looked into at the same time, while (a) searching for their neural correlates and (b) looking at cross-influences of the necessary treshold levels of activation underlying these conscious experiences. One can also expect to learn a lot about cross-modal interactions and attention – to just name a few of the issues – by using insights from research on synaesthesia.

By contrast, I want to treat synaesthesia as a kind of limiting case for theories of perception, comparable to cases of imagination and hallucination. These cases nevertheless deeply shape our understanding of what perception is. A theory of perception has to explain how the world appears to us in the way it does – and the commonalities of perceptual experiences of the world and those in cases of hallucination or synaesthesia have to be accounted for. In subjects experiencing synaesthesia, something works fascinatingly different. The way I treat synaesthesia with respect to theories of perception is in this sense more akin to how cognitive

6 The standardized 'test of genuineness' (TOG) was developed in 1987, see Baron-Cohen et al.: "Hearing Words and Seeing Colours". For a more recent version and contemporary refinements see Asher et al.: "Diagnosing and Phenotyping Visual Synaesthesia".

7 See e.g. Simner: "Defining Synaesthesia".

8 For an overview on recent evidence from brain imaging studies see Mattingley: "Attention, Automaticity, and Awareness in Synesthesia", pp. 158–161.

science might look into the phenomenon: synaesthesia as a small but interesting 'breakdown' of a cognitive or perceptual mechanism.

I will briefly introduce why I think this is worthwhile for philosophy. I consider it to be a philosophical endeavour to treat perception in terms of biological solutions. These solutions can be addressed in terms of the demands a specific 'Umwelt' poses to the organism, as well as in terms of the biologically realized ways the organism meets these demands. In this sense, perception does not have to be treated as enabling an ideal mirroring of the environment, but rather as based on a system that works pretty well overall but sometimes produces errors, and these errors tell us something about the system. Perceptions in this sense are heuristics for action. Errors produced by using a heuristic are not random, but systematically biased and allow us to learn something about the workings of perception by understanding the design of the system underlying it.[9] The design in question includes the morphological structure of the whole organism, the specific sense organs and means of locomotion, as well as the neural mechanisms – something I will discuss in the final sections of this paper.

These elements constitute an important part of a full-fledged theory of perception that in the end also has to explain what structures and interactions underlie our conscious percepts and the ways the world shows up for us. But what about the phenomenology of experience itself? Is it not the commonality between the perceptual and synaesthetic colour experience that is the starting point for the topics discussed in this paper? For the context of what I am doing here I will consider the phenomenology as more or less unproblematically given. This sounds like more of a concession than it actually is. It does not mean that one has to avoid the question of what determines the content and quality of a conscious percept. All it means is that reports by subjects are a sufficient reason (if some refining conditions are met) to assume the presence of a phenomenal state of a specific kind or modality.[10] I thereby dispense with the 'hard problem of consciousness' and confine myself to discussions on intermodal, comparative gaps of the following form: why does (neuronal, bodily, worldly) activity give rise to visual experiences rather than auditory ones?[11] Here, as I will show, synaesthesia has something to add to our development of a biological theory of perception.

9 Cf. for the relation of heuristics and design: Wimsatt: *Re-Engineering Philosophy for Limited Beings*.

10 For this account of heterophenomenology cf. Dennett: *Consciousness Explained*, pp. 66–98. In my paper I focus on the modalities and qualities and not, as Dennett does, on the contents of perception.

11 See Hurley/Noë: "Neural Plasticity and Consciousness" for these and related comparative gaps. In my paper I sometimes also discuss what should be called intramodal gaps, since the most common und thus best studied type of synaesthesia is graphem→colour synaesthesia (called weak synaesthesia) in which the transfer is within one modality: vision. These findings are, for the relevant aspects of this paper, transferable to intermodal gaps e.g. of the hearing→colour type (also called strong synaesthesia). See Chalmers' *The Conscious Mind* for question related to the 'hard problem' and for a thorough treatment of the question of how the

## 2. Enactivism and synaesthesia: the first challenge

I take two assumptions to underlie enactive theories, each of which has specific enactivist claims as consequences that will be scrutinized and challenged in light of the insights gained in synaesthesia research. The first of these assumptions captures the general idea that any theory of perception has to start with the whole human organism and its involvement with the world. As a consequence – and this is an important follow-up to the former, rather uncontested claim – other parts besides the brain (i.e. the body and to some extent the world itself) will participate in a nontrivial way in explanations of what determines our perception. More will have to be said regarding the nontrivial ways in which these extra-cranial elements are involved, but it is important to see that it goes further than the content of experience being determined by what is 'out there'. The very machinery that realizes a specific conscious experience extends beyond elements that can be located in the brain.[12] In this sense John Dewey had already argued against what he saw as ill-conceived dualisms between periphery and centre, between action and cognition, between the physical act of moving and the psychical idea: "The sensory quale gives the value of the act, just as the movement furnishes its mechanism and control, but both sensation and movement lie inside, not outside the act."[13]

The second assumption is that every life form is situated and embedded in a structured as well as destabilizing environment. Consequently every organism has to cope with an ongoing change between stable and precarious conditions. In the case of human beings these interactions not only have shaped the body, sensory system, and brain in the course of phylogenetic adaptation, such that their structures were selectively developed. Moreover, these changes are ongoing throughout the course of an ontogenetic lifespan. The human brain is extremely plastic and can alter its structure in a way that was only recently fully acknowledged in the cognitive neurosciences.[14] Studies in neuroplasticity have been used to show that subjects with a loss or absence of the 'normal machinery' of perception in one modality (e.g. sight in congenitally blind people) can nevertheless experience this modality to some degree. They can do so just in case they are

qualitative feel of mental life can or cannot be integrated into our theory of nature and what 'absolute gap' the acknowledgment of conscious experience might force upon such a theory.

12 See e.g. Dewey: "The Reflex Arch Concept in Psychology", pp. 358 f.: "Upon analysis, we find that we begin not with a sensory stimulus, but with a sensori-motor coordination, the optical-ocular, and that in a certain sense it is the movement which is primary, and the sensation which is secondary, *the movement of body, head and eye muscles determining the quality of what is experienced*. In other words, the real beginning is with the act of seeing; it is looking, and not a sensation of light." (My italics).

13 Ibid., p. 359.

14 For an accessible but nevertheless comprehensive overview of research done in the field of plasticity cf. Doidge: *The Brain that Changes Itself*.

enabled to engage in the respective modality-specific interaction with the world – when they perform the relevant sensorimotor signature, e.g. learn to interact with distal objects in their environment. Cases of sensory substitution are used to prove this point: congenitally blind people equipped with a head-mounted camera connected to a vibration array on their skin learn to see through these devices. After a short period of interaction with the environment (e.g. after learning to grasp or to avoid an approaching object), they report experiencing not a sense of touch on the skin but something like sight or, to be more neutral, a distal sense.[15]

Specific local machinery and specific sensory pathways are not necessary for the occurrence of a modality-specific experience like vision, but the mastery of a specific kind of interaction with the world is. Based on the second assumption, I claim that the reliance on cases of brain plasticity makes it indispensable for enactive theories to extend the time-frames under consideration beyond the here-and-now over the time period of learning or adaptation. As I would argue, elements that exert their influence over a learning time span should be granted explanatory priority over the here-and-now. From my point of view, this has not been made explicit enough in the enactive literature. Maybe because this methodological claim does not directly attack or contradict statements of other theories, it has not been regarded as constitutive and definitive for the enactive approach, unlike claims based on the first assumption. This extension to longer time spans beyond the unfolding in the here-and-now is nevertheless central and used in arguments to vindicate the sensorimotor theory of perception and consciousness.[16]

In the remainder of this paper, I will tackle the two challenges that synaesthesia represents for an enactive theory of perception. Let's start with the first and postpone the second (lack of perceptual adaptivity) for now. In genuine synaesthesia, local triggers (percepts) elicit a visual experience without any world-engaging visual activity at its basis. For example, in cases of hearing→colour synaesthesia, the experience of a heard sound, or of the syllables of a spoken word, triggers a visual colour experience. In this case the subject does not engage in any sensorimotor contingencies related to vision. In order to understand why this might be considered a challenge, it is important to call to mind again one of sensorimotor enactivism's central tenets: intrinsic character of neural events does not provide the appropriate means to explain experiential quality; local properties of neuronal assemblies are not sufficient to explain the character of our experiences. They do play an important role, though, but one they can only play because they are recruited into world-engaging loops of the organism. Seeing is an activity, a process of active, exploratory engagement mediated by the possession and exercise of a certain body of knowledge concerning sensorimotor dependencies, dependencies that link potential actions (eye saccades, head movements)

15 Cf. the studies on visual sensory substitution with TVSS-devices conducted by Bach-y-Rita. See also, for the specific use of these studies that is relevant to the present paper, the treatment in O'Regan/Noë: "A Sensorimotor Account of Vision", pp. 957 f.

16 See especially Hurley/Noë: "Neural Plasticity and Consciousness".

and their sensory consequences. In short: seeing is a skill and the mastery of this skill is necessary and sufficient for one or the other modality of conscious experience to occur. It is the exercised sensorimotor skill that determines the character and modality of what is experienced.

We can now make the challenge explicit by showing that the following two claims cannot hold at the same time:

(1) For any strong sensorimotor difference in a domain of interaction with the environment associated with a conscious experience, there must be a discriminable difference in the experience (intra/intermodal)
(2) In genuine hearing→colour synaesthesia, subjects with no skilful interaction with the environment related to the visual response modality have a visual colour experience.[17]

Genuine synaesthesia is a condition in which, despite a strong sensorimotor difference and very different sensorimotor expectancies, a conscious visual experience is generated that is similar to a normal, veridical visual experience. The second claim contradicts the first because the same modality seems to be associated with two different functions: "Given [the sensorimotor] conceptual framework, there should be no case in which one quale is associated with two disparate functions. Yet this is exactly what happens in coloured-hearing synaesthesia. Colour qualia, affirmed by the synaesthete herself to be closely alike, occur in response to both heard words and seen coloured surfaces."[18]

Let us look at the second claim first and raise the question: is the visual experience of colour really the same in perceptual and synaesthetic experiences, or at least similar enough to call it a 'visual colour experience'? If not, the challenge would not hold. There are reliable hetero-phenomenological reports of colour identification and comparison to 'normal' colours in synaesthetes, i.e. they consistently identify colours of the synaesthetic and veridical variety. So the 'identification criterion' gives prima facie plausibility to the sameness claim. But do synaesthetic experiences have the same 'feel' as veridical ones? This question has been tackled and answered in two recent replies to a comparable challenge with verdicts against sufficient similarity, since, it has been argued, synaesthetic subjects would never confuse synaesthetic and veridical colour.[19] On the other hand, synaesthetes do report that synaesthetic colours 'look' like those in normal perception. One might also suspect that synaesthetes can distinguish veridical from synaesthetic colours, due to the fact that they have learnt some additional

17 This is a version of an argument put forth by Gray et al.: "Evidence Against Functionalism From Neuroimaging of the Alien Colour Effect in Synaesthesia", Gray et al.: "Implications of Synaesthesia for Functionalism" and see esp. Gray: "How Are Qualia Coupled to Functions?" for a discussion of sensorimotor accounts.

18 Gray: "How Are Qualia Coupled to Functions?", p. 194.

19 See Hurley/Noë: "Can Hunter-Gatherers Hear Color?" pp. 70 f. See also the criteria and negative verdict in Macpherson: "Synaesthesia, Functionalism and Phenomenology", pp. 73–77.

facts about their condition. It has been reported that younger synaesthetes often are astonished to learn that not everybody is sharing their experiences because their perception of, say, every number '2' as red feels completely natural to them. And even after learning to separate more clearly what might be called the synaesthetic and the perceptual colour synaesthetes still experience disconcerting effects when, for example, they see a letter written in a colour conflicting with what is synaesthetically associated with this specific letter.[20] The latter, in my view, suggests something like perceptual conflict in these cases and favours the claim of sufficient similarity between perceptual and synaesthetic colour experience.[21] If this is so the first challenge to sensorimotor enactivism still holds: synaesthesia constitutes a case where sufficiently similar experiences occur despite strong diffences in sensorimotor signatures related to these experiences.

## 3. Can bodiliness and grabbiness of perception help to meet the first challenge?

Two elements have not yet been emphasized in the debate, but might help to separate the experience of extra-colour in synaesthesia from normal experiences of colour in perception. These elements have the advantage of defining a rather general perceptual feature and hence not putting too much weight on otherwise marginal elements. As O'Regan and Noë make clear, there are additional phenomenological components included in their sensorimotor theory relating to the specific presence of perceptual experiences: 'bodiliness' and 'grabbiness'.[22] 'Bodiliness' emphasises the tight link to body motions: movement produces immediate changes in input, which are accounted for in perceptual experience. This can be seen as a kind of control condition; it reassures the organism that something is a 'normal' object. When we move the object's perceivable properties change and, for example, elements of the objects surface become vivid and present. The other element is 'grabbiness', which is based in an alerting capacity that allows transient elements in the environment to grab the subject's attention. Our visual system is contrived in such a way that sudden changes or movements in the environment are easily detected and the organism can become aware of them.

20 See Cytowic/Eagleman: *Wednesday is Indigo Blue*, p. 63.

21 This goes beyond Stroop-like inferences which can also occur when there is a conflict between the meaning of a written word and its colouring, e.g. a 'red' written in green ink. Here the conflict does not become conscious. See MacLeod/Dunbar: "Training and Stroop-Like Interference".

22 In response to the commentaries to their 2001 paper, they mark these two elements as their "most important clarification"; see Noë/O'Regan: "A Sensorimotor Account of Vision and Visual Consciousness", author's response, p. 1011.

Before I get to the comparison of those 'normal' features of perceptual experience with synaesthetic experiences, I should note a possible problem. Introducing those additional elements as part of the phenomenology of colour seems to be a circular move by the enactivist. It presupposes what it seeks to show. In our case, the enactivist seems to include bodily movements and behavioural criteria in the description of the phenomenology in order to prove that the non-body-involving synaesthetic colour experience misses out in terms of this description. The circularity can be avoided if it can be shown that it is in fact a characteristic of *all* perceptual colour experiences of non-synaesthetes to be accompanied by such experiences of bodiliness and grabbiness, for example by collecting sufficient hetero-phenomenological data to support this claim.

As it turns out, however, one can grant this move (to include bodiliness in the phenomenology of perception) to the enactivist, because it does not threaten the similarity claim after all: synaesthetic colours seem to be sufficiently similar to normally perceived colours, even with regard to bodiliness. In a review article, David Eagleman and Melvyn Goodale have collected data showing that other object-like features (including surface properties like texture) are also experienced in synaesthetic colour.[23] These extra features have been used to account for the reported vividness of the synaesthetic colour experience. By attending thoroughly to subjective descriptions of colour-response synaesthetes, they have found references to texture even when this was not specifically asked for in the experimental paradigm. In conjunction with that, they report that larger regions of the medial ventral stream (that have been associated with the processing of texture properties)[24] are activated in colour-synaesthesia. One can expect to get more results supporting this in the near future, for the simple reason that these areas have not yet been the main areas of interest for neuroimaging studies of colour-synaesthesia. One preliminary result is that even if one allows the enactivist to include bodiliness as part of the phenomenology of normal perception, she cannot rule out synaesthetic experiences on this basis. This is why synaesthesia is such a problematic case: one seems to get the feeling of bodiliness without interactions, or without any bodily activity involved. You get it for free, and this goes against the heart of the enactivist account.

It seems doubtful that similar things can be shown for grabbiness. In this case it would be necessary for the defender of the challenge against enactivism to fall back on the first strategy of showing a circularity in the enactivist response to the challenge, namely that of stipulating a behavioural feature as part of the phenomenology. One would then also have to show that grabbiness does not accompany all visual experiences, and I do think that this is a possible way to go. Yet, again, one might not need to do so since some features of synaesthetic experience have also been associated with grabbiness.These features are pop-out phenom-

23 Eagleman/Goodale: "Why Color Synesthesia Involves More Than Color".

24 That is besides the traditional colour area V4, which recently has to be known to process texture information as well. Cf. Arcizet et al.: "Natural Textures Classification in Area V4".

ena reported to occur in synaesthetes.[25] Pop-out is an effect that enables subjects to easily pick out a target from an array of distractors when the target is constituted by different elements than the distractors. Synaesthetes are better than non-synaesthetes at identifying a target (a triangle of 2s) among distractors (randomly arranged 5s) of the same colour [fig. 1a] when the target induced a different synaesthetic colour than the distractors [fig. 1a synaesthetically experienced as fig. 1b].

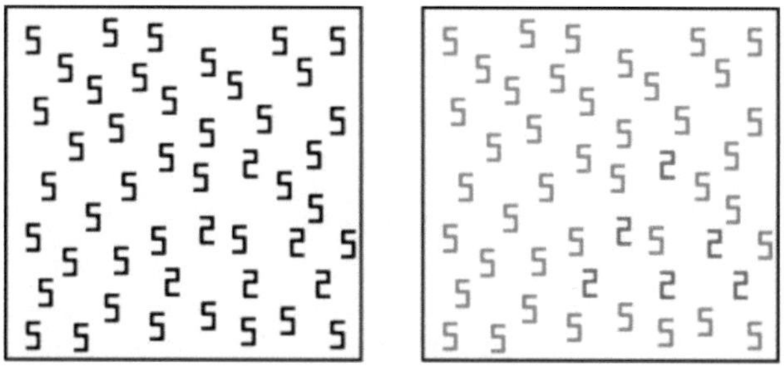

Fig. 1a, 1b: The figure on the left shows how non-synaesthetes would experience the field, the figure on the right how a number→colour synaesthete might experience the same field.

Here a salient feature of the environment seems to attract or 'grab' the attention of the synaesthete. But these results are more than disputed: "As it turns out, despite initial excitement, synesthetes are generally not able to spot the hidden shape any better than nonsynesthetes. This result is important, because it demonstrates the stage at which synesthetic colours are perceived: the number must be attended to for it to be synesthetically coloured – it does not evoke colour before the viewer is conscious of the number's identity."[26] It has been convincingly shown that number→colour synaesthetes only sometimes perform better in tasks of identifying targets [such as the triangle hidden in fig. 1a], because they 'anchor' their search-pattern in the first oddball '2' they find (which appears red to them among the green 5s) as they go on searching for the other oddballs. In these cases the synaesthetic colour does not seem to be attention-grabbing in the first place.

But even if some elements of the perceptual feature of grabbiness are missing, the case of bodiliness shows that compared to cases of mental imagery or cases of remembering synaesthetic experience has an enhanced vividness and forcible presence that is comparable to real perception. So even if the results are still tentative, the vividness that the enactivist account links to skill and active sensorimotor encounters with the environment is to some extent present in both perceived and synaesthetic colours. Yet, in synaesthesia no visual-like interaction with an object, no sensorimotor testing of conditions of the environment seems to be necessary to experience an enhanced visual vividness. In short: the narrow version of enactivism that I just sketched is unable to explain why the vividness is present in *both* cases.

25 Cf. Ramachandran/Hubbard: "Synaesthesia".

26 Cf. Cytowic/Eagleman: *Wednesday is Indigo Blue*, p. 49; they cite Edquist et al.: "Do Synaesthetic Colours Act As Unique Features in Visual Search?".

## 4. Normative enactivism and the second challenge from synaesthesia

So, if one grants sufficient similarity in the experience, the phenomenon of hearing→colour synaesthesia contradicts the claim that characterizes enactivism and the problem persists: there is a strong sensorimotor difference but nevertheless the same look. But should enactivism hold such strong claims in the first place? Couldn't it give up the strong reading of claim (1) and allow for two signatures triggering one kind of experience? In this case there might not be one common but rather *two* different world-exploring roles realizing visual colour experience. This would be tantamount to giving synaesthetes their own 'extra' enactive signature (or a disjunctive signature underlying veridical *and* synaesthetic colour experiences).

The first immediate problem one would have to face is that colour-experiences in hearing→colour synaesthetes do not seem to have environment-exploring functional descriptions at all: there seems to be no sensorimotor feedback-loop at work. Instead the experience is triggered automatically by a local percept or concept. So this move to weaken claim (1) is excluded for enactivists if they want to keep the actionist vein of the theory.[27] This also holds for the suggestion to combine the visual experience of the hearing→colour synaesthetes with the auditory sensorimotor pattern and to say, that the disjunctive base for all visual colour experience is, besides the visual skill, an auditory skill as well. The option seems valid but is not very satisfying as it undermines the claim that modalities are determined in terms of mastery of a specific skilful interaction, that is to say by the specific *sensorimotor signature* underlying the modality. Consequently, this suggestion reinforces the local (neuronal) supervenience base theory against enactivism because this theory offers a much simpler explanation of why in both cases a visual experience arises: the local neuronal activation in V4.

The more promising strategy for enactivism is to strengthen a normative element. This is to say that there is a *typical* realizer of a perceptual state, which is the larger sensorimotor cycle. Once done so, one can allow for exceptions when the normal conditions that are at work in typical occurrences are disturbed in one or another way. Like in hallucinations and misperceptions, something can go wrong. In cases of synaesthesia, this means that something as vivid and perceptual as in the veridical situation can be experienced. This is also a substantial weakening of claim (1) because now a strong difference in interaction (even the lack of such interactions) is allowed to generate a similar look in some cases. To make this weakening of the claim bearable, enactivism must now come up with

27 The same holds for focusing on the one core functional role played in both cases. In this case the underlying activation loop would for example include only V4 and adjacent brain area activity as a common core; see Macpherson: "Synaesthesia, Functionalism and Phenomenology", p. 73. But this works against the wide enactivism including action and body and would leave us with the local constitutionism enactivism wants to avoid.

an explanation of what makes these cases less interesting or less binding for explanations of perceptual experience, and it has to give alternative reasons that speak in favour of the typical roles played in the cases of perception. Ultimately, or so I will argue, those reasons lie in the enactivist endorsement of a biological theory of the human organism as expressed in the two assumptions I introduced in part two. I'll come to those in a moment, but for the first challenge there is an argument for a typical role that does not have to refer to these rather general considerations.

One possible way to go is to point out the necessity of engaging in the relevant sensorimotor interactions – of learning them – at least once during an ontogenetic lifespan. Explanations of how someone comes to experience a specific modality in the first place, as e.g. shown in the cases of sensory substitution systems, always involve the element of engaging in the relevant sensorimotor skill. This gets the specific experience running in these subjects, and without it the experience would not occur. This is also true for colour-synaesthetes: in early childhood they have at least to learn to engage visually. One explanation of what happens in cases of synaesthesia is that during childhood development, the intensive crosstalk of early infancy between different brain regions (for example between those that process sound and those that process visual information) stays vivid and intense, though it is meant to decrease during the development with the pruning of the connections between the regions.[28] As a result colour experiences are elicited e.g. by activation of brain regions whose activity is related to sound or touch. Hence a normative element in enactivism can be maintained: in normal cases an experience occurs when a skill, a sensorimotor signature is learned. Skill explains even in these cases the onset of a modality of experience, something the biological organism is prepared for – it has the local elements ready to run and awaiting the skilful exposure – but which, lacking the relevant skilful engagement, might as well just not occur.

In standard cases, this also explains why a certain experience persists or not. Enactivism would predict that the synaesthetic colour should become transparent or fade away – to use an admittedly odd metaphor – like the way glasses become transparent after a short time of wearing them, because we do not interact visually with *them* and their properties do not show up in the contents and characteristics of our experience. If sounds (like in hearing→colour synaesthesia) are sometimes bound to visual experiences, this is no problem at first since the theory just would predict that the visual experience would disappear as we do not interact visually with these sounds. But what defines synaesthesia is that these correlations do persist over the ontogenetic lifespan. This is the *second challenge from synaesthesia*: its persistence over time.

This point has been raised in a paper against Hurley & Noë's view of enactive perception and their prediction that in the course of development and within

28 Cf. Maurer/Mondloch: "Neonatal Synesthesia".

a learning time scale, such activity should become integrated into normal activity and the perceptual colour effect should vanish. This should especially hold since the 'extra colours' in synaesthesia sometimes have confusing and cognitively interfering effects.[29] In classical examples of perceptual adaptation and visually distorting prisms in non-synaesthetes, such elements *do* adapt away.[30] So the question is, how can the theory explain both the 'adapting away' in these cases and the life-long persistence in cases of genuine synaesthesia? Hurley and Noë, in a response, strike sail and declare that one would have to "go beyond" the pure interactionist account and suggest not to expect that the character of experience will be explained "either just in terms of what happens in the brain, or just in terms of the active subject's relations to the world;" and conclude: "[t]he sensorimotor dynamics that govern experience are in principle distributed across brain, body, behaviour, and environment (though they can be so distributed to different degrees)."[31]

Here, again, it seems to me that it is necessary to point out a normative element, but one of a second-order: adaptivity. Many more cases and studies would have to (and can) be cited in favour of the profound adaptivity of the human perceptual systems to vindicate this point. But for the time being the examples of cognitive integration and the already mentioned sensory substitution cases have to suffice as support of the claim that adaptivity is the standard, and persistence without a world-engaging role the derivation. So adaptivity on this level is in itself a cognitive 'mechanism' that has a normal outcome but can be disturbed as well.

Two short, but interesting notes on the side: some adaptivity, albeit to a much smaller degree, seems to be at work in synaesthetes as well: despite the strong consistency of the pairings in synaesthesia they do nevertheless change, although much more slowly.[32] Furthermore it has been shown that under specific experimental conditions, something like synaesthetic consistency over time can also be induced in non-synaesthete subjects: in posthypnotic situations, subjects consciously experience black ink letters in a colour after having learned to pair

29 See Gray: "How Are Qualia Coupled to Functions?" He quotes studies of behavioural disadvantages of graphem-colour-synaesthetes because of Stroop-like inferences due to an 'alien colour effect'(ACE), in which synaesthetes e.g. see the written word 'green' as synaesthetically red and their response-speed for certain tasks is reduced.

30 Most famously cited are experiments by researchers like Stratton, Taylor, and Kohler with distorting goggles, where the subjects after short adaptation time learn to see 'normal' again. See the discussion in Hurley: *Consciousness in Action*, pp. 346–351.

31 Hurley/Noë: "Can Hunter-Gatherers Hear Color?" p. 80. One promising way to go beyond their account of sensorimotor enactivism, which I will not discuss in this paper, is to extend it towards a theory of the organism and the dynamics of the autopoietic systems it constitutes in order to explain the occurrence of certain kinds of experienes. This variant of enactivism follows Varela/Thompson/Rosch's *The Embodied Mind.*

32 See the case of Erica F. described in Cytowic/Eagleman: *Wednesday is Indigo Blue*, p. 237.

them with the respective colour during hypnosis.[33] These experiences are reported to persist and, if at all, only seem to slowly vanish. This might suggest that the pressure to adapt away is just not strong enough in colour-response synaesthesia (otherwise it would go away in the non-genuine hypnosis cases) and that the adaptation system might be just slowed down by a lot in these genuine cases. But even this in itself would not suffice to meet the challenge: the consistency and persistence in the genuine synaesthesia cases would be still so strong that we could not say enactivism accounts for it – especially, and this is decisive, since only the pattern of the one-to-one pairings (specific sound to specific colour) might change to some extent but the general intermodal pairing, e.g. of sound percepts with vision percepts, stays fully intact.

## 5. A heuristics and engineering perspective on perception

What I have shown so far is that synaesthesia indeed poses a twofold challenge that cannot be easily discarded. Strengthening the normative claims in enactivism in response and allowing synaesthesia to be a derivation offers a way to meet the challenges – all the more so if one can show how enactivism could sustain the assumptions introduced earlier (the first being that perception is an activity of the whole organism, the second highlighting the adaptivity of organisms over different time spans) and nevertheless integrate synaesthesia into such a view. In concluding this paper I will sketch a way in which this could be done.

Enactivists would never deny that neuronal elements are to a large degree involved in the processes that determine the character of an experience. But they claim that this is completely different from assuming that those internal features in principle are better suited to provide an explanation of why certain phenomenal features arise and persist, and thus why an experience is of this modality or another. In this respect references to body- and world-involving dynamics provide more satisfying and richer explanations. Yet, questions concerning the metaphysics of consciousness have traditionally focused on local supervenience bases of mental states (as opposed to wider realizations that include the body and the environment of the organism) and they have focused on the here-and-now time scale – almost exclusively dealing with what realizes a mental state at those levels. Sensorimotor enactivism already takes a step in the right direction by taking into consideration the time scales of ontogenetic integration, and by claiming that the ability to interact with an environment is a necessary element in explaining why certain conscious experiences arise. It should thereby focus on a

33 Cf. the preliminary results in Cohen et al.: "Induced Cross-Modal Synaesthetic Experience Without Abnormal Neuronal Connections".

theory of constitution that includes as integral theoretical elements the interaction-based changes that are realized over such time spans. But Hurley and Noë have already suggested that in order to deal with the obstacles raised by phenomena such as synaesthesia, one might have to go beyond this kind of sensorimotor enactivism "to bring brain activity and the extended dynamics in which it is embedded within a unified explanatory framework."[34] Although they did not specify how to do so, they did say that the aim would be to hold on to the insights of their dynamicism and at the same time to seriously consider the constraints of the brain and nervous system.

The envisioned explanatory framework should be extended, I would argue, especially in terms of the time scales of the dynamics that shape these interactions and the underlying biological structures. As we have seen, sensorimotor enactivism highlights learning and ontogenetic adaptivity. But the way I introduced the general assumptions of enactivism, it also takes into account the organism-environment couplings that shape the organism (and the environmental niche) over larger time scales. These elements and the powers they exert on cognitive systems have been specifically acknowledged by theories of embodied cognition that include our 'contingent embodiment', and the 'tinkering' of nature at the level of evolutionary design, something that enactivism does not specifically account for. One then can highlight the different levels of adaptivity of organisms and the specific 'design' underlying the cognitive and perceptual solutions. Such accounts also go hand in hand with what I would call the view of perception as heuristics, because they acknowledge that heuristics are especially telling with regard to engineered solutions in physical and biological systems. Extended time scales for organismic perceptual designs in this perspective might include at least four different levels with specific properties and ways of exerting influence on cognitive solutions embodied in organisms:[35] the evolutionary time scale (t3), the developmental time scale (t2), the learning time scale (t1), and the time scale of the here-and-now (t0). Adaptivity and design solutions of organisms on the first three time scales explain the behaviour and experience of subjects in the here-and-now.

Back to perceptual systems in the human case: We saw that what allows the perceptual unfolding in the present is mediated by structures acquired on (t2) and (t1) especially, which are in the narrower focus of sensorimotor enactivism. What makes genuine synaesthesia an exceptional and challenging case relates in particular to the childhood development time scale, and the learning time scale. This is to say that in a 'critical period' in childhood, pruning and inhibition do not get underway, and since then perceptual adaptivity is impaired and normal perceptual learning mechanism are disturbed. Under normal circumstances, enactive

34 Hurley/Noë: "Can Hunter-Gatherers Hear Color?", p. 80.

35 Time scales for design and their specific properties have entered theories of embodied cognition esp. via the research and engineering done in robotics, cf. Pfeifer/Bongard: *How the Body Shapes the Way We Think.*

explanations of underlying sensorimotor skills for perceptual experience should focus on these ontogenetic time scales. But in this special case and if we want to posit further normative elements as well as to include the specific implementations or embodiments of cognitive solutions, it might be necessary to defer to elements that are shaped in course of (t3).

These theoretical elements taken together might offer a way to deal with both 'breakdowns' constituted by genuine perceptual synaesthesia: (a) the disturbance of the 'normal' relation of sensorimotor signature and modality of experience, and (b) the lack of 'normal' adaptivity. If we do understand perception in general as a heuristic for actions, and take up the engineering or 'contingent embodiment' perspective, it is possible to explain both of these as instances of breakdowns at two different levels of analysis and also explain what happens in synaesthesia without giving up the central claims of enactivism. Here it is important to see that this embodiment thesis includes body, environment, and, last but not least, the neuronal structures and mechanisms, all of which put constraints on the unfolding of a cognitive solution. Heuristics of cognitive solutions can go wrong, and heuristics are also realized in systems that can break down. Focusing on the way implementations work, but also on how they can go wrong, can bring brain activity (that leads to untypical experiential effects) into a larger framework.

In order to give a hint at how the engineering and heuristics perspective might help to deal with a phenomenon like synaesthesia, I want to conclude with a genuine insight stemming from this perspective: One has to be careful not to confuse the part that causes the breakdown with the elements and dynamics that constitute the cognitive or perceptual solution. Neither (a) non-world-involving local activation nor (b) non-adaptive persistence over time figure prominently in the explanation of what constitutes a perceptual experience. Nor do they explain what determines the modality of such an experience. Both highlight elements that are causally responsible for the specific 'breakdown' of a perceptual solution. But the part responsible for this atypical expression, despite having a big effect, might not show up among the key features that explain the mental phenomenon in the first place.

## Conclusion

In the light of the heuristics and engineering perspective, the insights of enactivism can be sustained even in the face of the challenges constituted by synaesthesia. Visual perceptual awareness or consciousness, although dependent on the brain, is not just a property of an event in the brain, and atypical functioning on this level does not contradict the underlying assumptions of enactivism and its basic claims concerning perceptual experience. But to be able to integrate these atypical effects one has to take the level of implementation seriously and thereby also the role of neuronal expressions of perceptual solutions that are embedded in a larger supervenience base. Otherwise one might end up exaggerating the theoretical role of those phenomena. These elements do not by themselves provide the resources for a comprehensive theory of perceptual experience, though they should be given a place within the theory.

*References*


Arcizet, Fabrice / Christophe Jouffrais / Pascal Girard: "Natural Textures Classification in Area V4 of the Macaque Monkey", in: *Experimental Brain Research,* 189 (2008), pp. 109–120.

Asher, Julian E. / Michael R.F. Aitken / Nasr Farooqi et al.: "Diagnosing and Phenotyping Visual Synaesthesia: A Preliminary Evaluation of the Revised Test of Genuineness (TOG-R)", in: *Cortex,* 42 (2006) 2, pp. 137–46.

Baron-Cohen, Simon / Maria A. Wyke / Colin Binnie: "Hearing Words and Seeing Colours: An Experimental Investigation of a Case of Synaesthesia", in: *Perception,* 16 (1987) 6, pp. 761–767.

Chalmers, David J.: *The Conscious Mind. In Search of a Fundamental Theory,* New York (OUP) 1996.

Cohen Kadosh, Roi / Avishai Henik et al.: "Induced Cross-Modal Synaesthetic Experience Without Abnormal Neuronal Connections", in: *Psychological Science,* 20 (2009) 2, pp. 258–265.

Cytowic, Richard E. / David Eagleman: *Wednesday Is Indigo Blue: Discovering the Brain of Synesthesia,* Cambridge, Mass. (MIT Press) 2009.

Dennett, Daniel C.: *Consciousness Explained,* Boston (Little, Brown & Co) 1991.

Dewey, John: "The Reflex Arc Concept in Psychology", in: *Psychological Review,* 3 (1896) 4, pp. 357–370.

Dixon, Mike J. / Daniel Smilek / Philip M. Merikle: "Not All Synaesthetes Are Created Equal. Projector Versus Associator Synaesthetes", in: *Cognitive, Affective, & Behavioral Neuroscience,* 4 (2004) 5, pp. 335–343.

Doidge, Norman: *The Brain That Changes Itself. Stories of Personal Triumph From the Frontiers of Brain Science,* New York (Viking) 2007.

Eagleman, David M. / Melvyn A. Goodale: "Why Color Synesthesia Involves More Than Color", in: *Trends in Cognitive Sciences,* 13 (2009) 7, pp. 288–292.

Edquist, Jessica / Anina N. Rich / Cobie Brinkman et al.: "Do Synaesthetic Colours Act As Unique Features in Visual Search?", in: *Cortex,* 42 (2006) 2, pp. 222–231.

Gray, Jeffrey A. / David M. Parslow / Michael J. Brammer et al.: "Evidence Against Functionalism From Neuroimaging of the Alien Colour Effect in Synaesthesia", in: *Cortex,* 42 (2006) 2, pp. 309–318.

Gray, Jeffrey A. / Susan Chopping / Julia Nunn et al.: "Implications of Synaesthesia for Functionalism: Theory and Experiments", in: *Journal of Consciousness Studies,* 9 (2002) 12, pp. 5–31.

Gray, Jeffrey A.: "How Are Qualia Coupled to Functions?", in: *Trends in Cognitive Sciences,* 7 (2003) 5, pp. 192–194.

Hurley, Susan / Alva Noë: "Can Hunter-Gatherers Hear Color?", in: Brennan, Geoffrey / Robert Goodin / Frank Jackson et al. (eds.): *Common Minds: Themes From the Philosophy of Philip Pettit,* New York (OUP) 2007, pp. 55–83.

Hurley, Susan / Alva Noë: "Neural Plasticity and Consciousness", in: *Biology and Philosophy,* 18 (2003) 1, pp. 131–168.

Hurley, Susan: *Consciousness in Action,* Cambridge (HUP) 1998.

Hutto, Daniel D.: "Understanding Synaesthesia, Radically Enactively". Talk at the conference "Habitus in Habitat III: Synaesthesia and Kinaesthetics", Berlin, 22nd October 2010 (http://itunes.apple.com/gb/podcast/philosophical-psychology-2/id386952605?i=87011854).

MacLeod, Colin M. / Kevin Dunbar: "Training and Stroop-Like Interference: Evidence for a Continuum of Automaticity", in: *Journal of Experimental Psychology: Learning, Memory, and Cognition,* 14 (1988) 1, pp. 126–135.

Macpherson, Fiona: "Synaesthesia, Functionalism and Phenomenology", in: Marraffa, Massimo / Mario De Caro / Francesco Ferrett (eds.): *Cartographies of the Mind. Philosophy and Psychology in Intersection,* Dordrecht (Springer) 2007, pp. 65–80.

Mattingley, Jason B.: "Attention, Automaticity, and Awareness in Synesthesia", in: *Annals of the New York Academy of Sciences,* 1156 (2009), pp. 141–167.

Maurer, Daphne / Catherine Mondloch: "Neonatal Synesthesia: A Re-Evaluation", in: Lynn C. Robertson / Noam Sagiv (eds.): *Synesthesia: Perspectives From Cognitive Neuroscience,* Oxford / New York (OUP) 2005, pp. 193–213.

Myin, Eric / J. Kevin O'Regan: "Perceptual Consciousness, Access to Modality and Skill Theories. A Way to Naturalize Phenomenology?", in: *Journal of Consciousness Studies,* 9 (2002) 1, pp. 27–46.

Noë, Alva: *Action in Perception,* Cambridge, Mass. (MIT Press) 2004.

Noë, Alva / Susan Hurley: "The Deferential Brain in Action: Response to Jeffrey Gray", in: *Trends in Cognitive Sciences,* 7 (2003) 5, pp. 195–196.

O'Regan, J. Kevin / Alva Noë: "A Sensorimotor Account of Vision and Visual Consciousness", in: *The Behavioral and Brain Sciences,* 24 (2001) 5, pp. 939–73; discussion pp. 973–1031.

Pfeifer, Rolf / Josh C. Bongard: *How the Body Shapes the Way We Think. A New View of Intelligence,* Cambridge, Mass. (MIT Press) 2007.

Ramachandran, Vilayanur S. / Edward M. Hubbard: "Synaesthesia – A Window Into Perception, Thought and Language", in: *Journal of Consciousness Studies,* 8 (2001) 12, pp. 3–34.

Ramachandran, Vilayanur S. / Edward M. Hubbard: "The Phenomenology of Synaesthesia", in: *Journal of Consc. Studies,* 10 (2003) 8, pp. 49–57.

Simner, Julia: "Defining Synaesthesia", in: *British Journal of Psychology,* (2011, forthcoming).

Simner, Julia / Jamie Ward / Monika Lanz et al.: "Non-random associations of graphemes to colors in synaesthetic and normal populations", in: *Cognitive Neuropsychology,* 22 (2005) 8, pp. 1069–1085.

Varela, Francisco J. / Evan Thompson / Eleanor Rosch: *The Embodied Mind: Cognitive Science and Human Experience,* Cambridge, Mass. (MIT Press) 1991.

Wimsatt, William C.: *Re-Engineering Philosophy for Limited Beings. Piecewise Approximations to Reality,* Cambridge, Mass. (HUP) 2007.

# Synaesthesia As a Natural Aberration of Sensory Pathways. Evidence from Anatomic and Functional Imaging Studies

PAUL CUMMING

Contemporary techniques for structural and functional imaging are being applied to the study of the phenomenon of sensory synaesthesia. It seems intuitively obvious that synaesthesias arise from a perturbation of normal sensory processing, resulting in a mixing of channels that are normally distinct. However, the integration of multiple sensory systems is the main task of the human brain, resulting in a coherent experience of the external world. It follows that synaesthesias may be rare manifestations of this normal function of the nervous system; while being inaccessible to most people, they might be recognizable as being similar in kind to more commonplace experiences. Functional connectivity models of the nervous systems predict that the conflation of sensory channels may occur such that the conscious experience of synaesthesia emerge only when a certain threshold for cross-talk is exceeded, and that this threshold may be defined by the trajectory of development of the nervous system. As such, synaesthesia has some relation to the phenomenon of neuronal plasticity, whereby learning engraves a pathway in the nervous system, resulting in binding of sensory channels into a unitary experience. In this paper, I attempt to place synaesthesia in this context, citing and discussing instances where a normal sensory pathway is perturbed, due either to experimental manipulation of the developing brain, or accidents such as in congenital blindness, in which the visual cortex is appropriated for the use of alternate cognitive and sensory processes. I will argue that, in effect, the blind see with their visual cortex, in the sense that they execute a class of sensory integration particularly related to spatial orientation, but obtained through other means, in the absence of visual input. A certain capacity for reorganization of sensory processing and integration is retained by the adult brain, but certain pathologies may arise from failures of the normal binding of sensory and affective experiences into a singular experience. In particular, Parkinson's disease, schizophrenia and Capgras syndrome present aspects of failed binding.

While failure of binding may be an aspect of a number of disabling brain disorders, anecdote suggests that synaesthesia enriches the lives of those who experience it, while otherwise bringing no particular benefit, except in the performance of some specific cognitive and perceptual tasks. Synaesthesia likewise brings no great impediment, except under special circumstances of sensory interference. In a single case study of an individual with color/grapheme synaesthesia, superior recall in a word naming task was apparently encoded through color memory, but performance of an object memorizing task was only average.[1] From an evolutionary perspective, this scenario would not predict selection for or against the transmission of the synaesthesia trait. The considerable over-representation of synaesthesia among women initially suggested a linkage to the X-chromosome, imparting excess mortality to males. However, study of synaesthesia families failed to reveal excess male mortality, implying that males are less likely to recognize or report their synaesthesia experience.[2] Color/grapheme synaesthesia is the most common variety, attaining an incidence of 7% among Swiss art students, versus only 2% in a control sample.[3] We cannot conclude from this observation that synaesthesia furthers the career or enhances the talent of artists. Instead, the overrepresentation of color synaesthetes among artists may rather indicate a self-selection process, whereby those who experience a broader incorporation of the color sense into their world experience may be guided by that experience towards involvement in the visual arts (excluding black and white photography, one would presume). As arbitrary as color/grapheme synaesthesias, let alone some of the more rare synaesthesias, may seem to non-synaesthetes, they represent natural variants of the essential attribute of normal brain function, which is the integration of multiple sensory and cognitive processes into a unitary experience of the self and the external world.

Insofar as synaesthesia brings no great benefit or handicap to those who experience it, synaesthesia seems to be an epiphenomenon, presumably arising as an uncommon variant of some essential developmental process or cognitive attribute. As such, synaesthesia might be compared to absolute pitch, which is over-represented among musicians, but is not universally considered to be useful, except for tuning an instrument by ear. Indeed, absolute pitch can cause discomfort to musicians who must switch between the conventions of American and European concert pitch. The comparison may extend further, since it is known that absolute pitch, like synaesthesia, is in part hereditary. Nonetheless, environmental and cultural factors certainly play a role in the accessibility of absolute pitch; fluency in a tonal language is associated with significantly increased incidence of absolute pitch among music students.[4] Here the metaphor fails, since cultural determinants of synaesthesia have not been firmly established, and there is no evidence that the synaesthesia trait can be acquired through practice, in the manner of relative pitch. Nonetheless, it remains true that synaesthesia resembles a special case contiguous with the normal range of human sensory function and integration.

At this point it would be appropriate to consider the classical anatomy of this visual pathway, so as to provide a model for how cross-talk between sensory

1 Mills et al.: "Effect of a synesthete's photisms on name recall".
2 Ward/Simner: "Is synaesthesia an X-linked dominant trait with lethality in males?".
3 Rothen/Meier: "Higher prevalence of synaesthesia in art students".
4 Deutsch et al.: "Absolute pitch among students in an American music conservatory".

channels may arise from the proper function of sensory integration. The brain is an input-output device, receiving inputs from several sensory channels, and sending commands to the skeletal muscles and a number of other output devices. Whatever happens in-between lies in the realm of pure reflex, but also that of cognition, and conscious experience. Sensory input channels are by definition narrow, resembling a cable input from a detector. This is particularly well established in the visual system at the level of the retina, where the cellular architecture is relatively simple. Small groups of primary sensory neurons, the rods and cones of the inner retinal layer, communicate via horizontal cells to an equally small number of retinal ganglion cells of the outer retinal layer, which themselves give rise to projections in the optic nerve, and thence to the central nervous system. This architecture ensures that the coding of visual signals in individual axons of the optic nerve closely matches the activity of a small number of sensory neurons, which are responsive to a domain of visual space mapping to a small part of the retinal surface. However, upon entering the brain, the visual pathway immediately segregates into channels destined for the optic tectum, which mediates a kind of blind sight outside the realm of conscious experience, and the pathway ascending to the visual cortex. The primary visual cortex receives the visual inputs, and initially conducts simple processing characterized by conservative retinotopic mapping. This means that sensory neurons in a very circumscribed locus of the retina are able to inform a specific domain of the primary visual cortex. Using voltage sensitive vital dyes, the state of activity of the visual cortex can be mapped, resulting in an actual representation, albeit distorted, of a geometric shape projected upon the retina of an experimental animal. The further processing of this input entails the concerted activation of higher order visual cortices, which conduct ever more complex processing of the raw signal, resulting in the identification of edges and other features, and the perception of movement of objects in space. A very advanced form of visual processing manifests in the phenomenon of face constancy; a familiar face is recognized irrespective of its orientation, and also its distance and corresponding retinotopic size; the brain representation of a familiar face exists outside of real world coordinates. Put another way, a rose is a near rose, is a far rose.

Infant humans soon acquire the ability to recognize faces, and we may tend to assume that face recognition is a particularly human attribute. However, sheep are also skilled in the recognition of faces, at least those of other sheep. This task engages the high order visual cortex embedded in the temporal lobe. High order processing is delayed in proportion to the number of synapses between the primary sensory cortex and the site of high order processing. Consequently the response latency of neurons activated by presentation of familiar faces was much slower in the left temporal cortex than in the right, suggesting that a more complex emotional and contextual judgement of recognized faces is made in the left hemisphere in sheep,[5] just as in monkeys and humans.[6] A familiar face does not exist in isolation, but is perceived within a historical context, in conjunction with the recollection of congruent sensory experiences, such as a voice, or the scent of a particular kind of soap.

Consideration of the visual pathway for face recognition suggests how conscious experience entails the integration of multiple sensory channels and memories into a unitary experience. A simpler example of this phenomenon is presented by the motion-sensitive region of the middle temporal cortex, which is also responsive to sounds moving in space.[7] In fact, this is a synaesthesia cortex, the proper function of which is to integrate auditory and visual channels, so as to produce a coherent experience. Imagine a bird flying past your head, entering into your visual world while simultaneously evoking an auditory experience of beating wings, following a matching trajectory. This experience might be termed everyday synaesthesia, as distinct from Synaesthesia with a capital S, to designate exotic forms of sensory integration.

The convergence of sensory channels into an integrative sensory experience is sometimes expressed as binding, an elusive property of our brain, which has yet to be emulated by computers. Conjecturally, Parkinson's disease and a number of neuropsychiatric disorders may be interpreted as failures of the normal binding process. The main symptoms of Parkinson's disease are rigidity of the skeletal muscles, slowness to initiate movement, and, at least at some stage of the disorder, a particular tremor of the hands. The symptoms arise from the core neuropathology of Parkinson's disease, which consists of degeneration of the dopamine neurons of the midbrain, and consequent loss of dopamine innervation in parts of the basal ganglia. Key motor symptoms are alleviated with dopamine replacement therapy, but current treatments do not interfere with the ongoing degeneration. The basal ganglia are a network of brain structures constituting the extrapyramidal motor pathway, as distinct from the pyramidal system arising in the motor cortex. The pyramidal motor pathway mediates voluntary movement via myelinated fibres arising in the cerebral cortex and descending to a confluence known as the pyramids, and thence to the spinal cord, where they convey a command to the primary motor neurons. The pyramidal pathway is an innovation of the mammalian brain, but it is inseparable from the phylogenetically more primitive extrapyramidal pathway. In the mammalian brain, the basal ganglia serve to inform and modulate the output of the pyramidal pathway, based on an integration of sensory and motor inputs.

Parkinson's disease manifests as impairment of voluntary movements, in association with increased muscle tone. This may seem upon first consideration to be a disorder of an output pathway, a disengagement of a command system from

5 Peirce/Kendrick: "Functional asymmetry in sheep temporal cortex".
6 Perrett et al.: "Specialized face processing and hemispheric asymmetry in man and monkey".
7 Bedny et al.: "Sensitive period for a multimodal response in human visual motion area MT/MST".

its servomechanisms in the skeletal muscles. This cybernetic notion is certainly an oversimplification, or even a misconception. The basal ganglia may more properly be considered to be a key site for the comparison of the command to move with its consequences, as conveyed by the proprioceptive sense, i.e. the sense of position of the body in space. Robots of science fiction move jerkily, since they operate through servomotors, without benefit of sensory and proprioceptive feedback. The paralysis of Parkinson's disease, in which the pyramidal pathway is intact, may be an expression of failed integration of proprioceptive feedback into the planning and execution of commands to move. This impairment can in some cases be circumvented, without recourse to pharmacology. For example, Parkinson's disease patients can learn to improve their gait though training with visual targets placed on the floor as targets.[8] Here, the visual pathway can partially replace the function of a defective sensorimotor system, although at the expense of great effort, and the risk of interference in other tasks. Training in mental singing can also improve the gait of Parkinson's disease patients.[9]

When rehabilitation and pharmacological treatments fail, surgical interventions can be used for alleviating Parkinson's disease symptoms. In the past ten years, the favoured strategy has employed electrical stimulation of the subthalamic nucleus, a component of the basal ganglia, which is normally inhibited by dopamine release elsewhere in the circuit. This treatment can be highly effective in reducing muscle rigidity, translating into a substantial improvement in quality of life of the patient. The precise mechanism of action of this approach is still rather mysterious, and the subject of much study and controversy. We have investigated the effects of this treatment, known as deep brain stimulation, on cerebral energy metabolism, using an imaging technique based on the cerebral uptake of radioactive oxygen, as measured by positron emission tomography (PET). The procedure entails the inhalation of a neutron-deficient isotope of oxygen gas ([$^{15}$O]-oxygen), which is absorbed in the lungs, binds to haemoglobin, and is deposited in brain. Even at rest, the brain has an appetite for oxygen as voracious as that of the leg muscles of a sprinting athlete. This radiotracer oxygen enters the respiratory pathway of living cells, but decays in a matter of minutes, giving rise to the emission of energetic photons. These gamma photons are detected by the PET scanner, and are then reconstructed into a source image showing the pattern of energy metabolism.

Our hypothesis was that activation of the electrodes would result in a net inhibition of neurons in the overactive subthalamic nucleus, manifesting in a local decline in the uptake of radioactive oxygen. Our observations were contrary to this expectation; turning on the stimulator, which is controlled by a power supply

8 Sidaway et al.: "Effects of long-term gait training using visual cues in an individual with Parkinson disease".

9 Satoh/Kuzuhara: "Training in mental singing while walking improves gait disturbance in Parkinson's disease patients".

implanted under the skin, immediately improved muscle rigidity and tremor in the patients, but had no discernible effect on oxygen uptake at the site of stimulation.[10] Instead, a number of unexpected foci of increased oxygen metabolism were detected, but not in the basal ganglia. These foci were in high order visual cortical regions. One of the sites of activation was the lingual gyrus, which had earlier been implicated in the perception of biological motion. This term refers to the sense of movement of a human body that is conveyed by watching the movements of an actor in a dark room, to whose joints are affixed illuminated patches: the motion of a stick man. Another site of activated oxygen consumption was located in the so-called V5 motion cortex, the same region activated by the convergence of visual and auditory stimuli arising from a moving object, as mentioned above. We interpreted these results to indicate that the beneficial effects of deep brain stimulation were obtained through a re-integration (or re-binding) of high order visual and proprioceptive sensory integration imparting the sense of the position of one's body in space. This may be precisely what is lacking in Parkinson's disease, here considered to be a failure of normal synaesthetic sensory processing. If you don't know where your body is, you cannot move it.

Schizophrenia, a condition which is partially alleviated by blockers of dopamine, would seem to be a polar opposite of Parkinson's disease, which is best treated by dopamine replacement. Nonetheless, schizophrenia may present another instance of failed binding. It has long been appreciated that a command to move the skeletal muscles, arising in the motor cortex, gives rise to collateral discharge of the adjacent sensory cortex. This message prepares the sensory cortex to interpret the sensory experience yet to be evoked by the voluntary movement. Thus, when the sensory feedback arrives, it comes as no surprise, and the brain can make a rapid comparison between the intended consequence, and the actual outcome. This process also allows the agent to retain its sense of agency, since the sensory feedback is recognized as belonging to the agent, and not arising from some external source. However ones' own inner voice can seem alien to patients with schizophrenia, as if thoughts and sensations arise without warning.

Collateral discharge in the sensorimotor cortex of humans can be measured using high-resolution electroencephalography during performance of a simple paced motor task consisting of button pressing. In one such study, the initiation of voluntary movement was preceded by 20 and 40 Hertz discharges occurring in the sensory cortex about one tenth of a second before the beginning of the movement.[11] However, the same task failed to evoke these anticipatory discharges in people with schizophrenia, as if their sense of the present encompasses a narrower temporal domain than that of the healthy. Perhaps a general failure of

10 Vafaee et al.: "Focal changes of oxygen consumption in cerebral cortex of patients with Parkinson's disease during subthalamic stimulation".

11 Ford et al.: "Out-of-synch and out-of-sorts: dysfunction of motor-sensory communication in schizophrenia".

binding obliges people with schizophrenia to misattribute their own thoughts as arising from capricious and hence menacing, others.

Capgras syndrome, the delusion that a relative or friend has been replaced by a sinister Doppelgänger, may be yet another manifestation of a particular failure of binding. The delusion can arise as a result of traumatic brain injury, and has 12% prevalence among patients with Alzheimer's disease, likely reflecting a collapse of intracortical communication in that disease. In Capgras syndrome, the recognition of familiarity in appearance and behavior of the other is retained, but is now infused with a sense of the alien. The experience resists rational argument and has been attributed to a particular class of brain lesions involving anatomic pathways for visual recognition of emotional response. In a case report employing fMRI, presentation of familiar faces evoked reduced activation in the fusiform face-detection cortex, and an abnormally large (fearful) response in the amygdala of a Capgras patient.[12] Grandmother brings a tray of cookies, but her warm smile is a simulation, devoid of real emotional content, as experienced by the viewer; who would not react fearfully to a Zombie-grandmother? The phantom limb phenomenon may present a variant of Capgras syndrome, wherein a particular type of brain injury obliges the subject to experience their own body, in part or in whole, as belonging to another. This concept has been explored in the fiction of Stanislaw Lem, who imagined a sanatorium for disturbed robots, one of whom was convinced that its lustrous, imperishable metal body had been replaced by a disgusting vessel of soft flesh, such as is inhabited by human beings. In Andrei Tarkowski's film of the eponymous Stanislaw Lem novel Solaris, the alien projections from a sentient ocean suffer from an inverse Capgras syndrome, wherein they imagine themselves to be real. The film ends on an optimistic note, in which true recognition and reconciliation occur, due to the re-establishment of binding through the agency of love.

I have argued that failure of normal binding of sensory, motor, and cognitive functions may manifest in symptoms of a number of devastating diseases of the nervous system. In contrast, synaesthesia, the conflation of one cognitive or sensory modality with another, may be an expression of excessive binding. Here, excessive means surpassing some normal or perhaps normative limits to the extent of binding which is necessary or useful for living in the world. Synaesthetes, never having known the bland experience of ordinary people, are often taken by surprise to learn that their experience is considered unusual. Everyday synaesthesia, arising from the normal integrative function of the nervous system, might consist of associations, which are actually part of ordinary experience. It seems in no way exotic to say that the lemon flower is sweet, even though we mean that it smells as if it should taste sweet (I ate a lemon blossom yesterday as a kind of experiment; it tasted bitter). Here, synaesthesia might be considered to be a

12 Cf. the abstract in: Naasan et al.: "The social cognition of attachment: Preliminary results from functional imaging of Capgras delusion".

metaphor, but one that strikes others as something very strange. Imagine invariably experiencing the numeral five (5) as being blue, either blue in its essential nature, or suffused by a cloud of blueness, as in so-called projection synaesthesia.

Whereas failures of binding may be an aspect of disabling brain disease, synaesthesia is not commonly reported to bring with it any notable handicaps. For example, the relatively common color/grapheme synaesthesia benefits only in the context of particular neurocognitive tasks, to be revealed by careful testing. Thus, this trait facilitates the detection of geometric patterns represented in a field of black and white numerals, when the idiosyncratic color experience of these synaesthetes makes the hidden pattern stand out in sharp contrast from the surround.[13] I use the word idiosyncratic without any prejudice, only to indicate that there seem to be no general rules for the mapping between color and grapheme, as if each synaesthete has a unique code or look-up table for their personal paint-by-numbers world. In this respect, color/grapheme synaesthesia differs from the commonplace musical/emotional synaesthesia of attributing differing emotional valences to major and minor keys, at least in western countries. While color/grapheme synaesthesia may impart very few benefits, its disadvantages may be equally subtle, if the detection of some object just happens to suffer from interference from a synaesthesia experience. For example, were ripe red apples on a tree perceived as if surrounded by an unpleasant smelling blue cloud, this might dampen the comfort to be derived from apples.

Ramachandran and Hubbard speculated that color/grapheme synaesthesia may be related to the proximity of the V4 colour cortex and the adjacent grapheme cortex,[14] presumably reflecting the close collateral connectivity between neurons on adjacent cerebral gyri. This proposal has recently been substantiated on the basis of fMRI findings.[15] However, grapheme cortex, must have assumed its current function only with the advent of graphic representations, some 20,000 years ago. The appropriation of that particular lump of cerebral cortex by graphemes must surely be a socially-determined, learned phenomenon. This conundrum might be solved if functional correlates of that structure could be assigned in preliterate humans who make no use of symbols, if such people still exist somewhere, or if indeed they ever existed. One very well trained and clever border collie is able to distinguish several hundred object by name, and invariably fetches the correct one upon command.[16] We cannot get into the head of that dog, but it seems clear that it has succeeded in binding the auditory experience of a word with the visual appearance of physical objects. Being a dog, it may for all we know also be guided by olfactory cues in addition to visual form. The humble chameleon, clinging to branches in the vanishing forest of Madagascar, and de-

13 Ramachandran/Hubbard: "Psychophysical investigations into the neural basis of synaesthesia".

14 Ramachandran/Hubbard: "Synaesthesia".

15 van Leeuwen et al.: "Synaesthetic colour in the brain: beyond colour areas. A functional magnetic resonance imaging study of synaesthetes and matched controls".

16 Kaminski et al.: "Word learning in a domestic dog: evidence for fast mapping".

spite its lack of cerebral cortex, is likewise an everyday synaesthete, able to associate visual/spatial cues with the expectation of eating a prey item, and consequently project its tongue with uncanny precision to the intended target.

The integrative function of the cerebral cortex is obtained through connectivity between different functional domains. The cerebral cortex, at least the neocortex of the mammalian brain, is a sheet of neurons containing a rather uniform microstructure. This sheet is folded upon itself, so as to maximize the surface area that can be contained within the bony skull. The human cerebral cortex is as convoluted as the neck of a sharpei dog. Irrespective of its position in the sheet, most areas of cerebral cortex consist of six cellular layers; one layer receives the majority of sensory and collateral inputs, while another layer gives rise to most of the outputs, including collateral projections to adjacent cortical regions. The computation performed in a small cortical module occurs via interconnections with the other layers. I confess a certain ignorance of the nature of the computation performed within a cortical module, but expect that, whatever it may be, the computation is nearly the same everywhere in the cortical sheet, which is pluripotent in its function. Thus, the function of a given cerebral cortical region is more determined by the coding of its inputs and outputs, rather than particular aspects of the local cortical architecture. Of course, cytoarchitectonic (to use the technical term) differences exist between cortical regions, notably in the primary visual cortex. However, the particular input/output connectivity of a given cortical region is something that arises during brain development, when ascending sensory pathways find their way to the destined cortical region, the functional maturation of which is informed by that same connectivity, once established. News agents crop up around subway stations, not the other way around, pax Times Square and Piccadilly Circus.

The trajectory of ascending sensory pathways towards their appropriate cortical targets, and the establishment of intra-cortical connectivity are driven by complex factors. Molecular biology techniques are providing new insights into the regulation of brain development. For example, the genesis of our inner worm is revealed through studies of the Hox gene, which determines body segmentation in Annelids and Hominids alike. In the course of brain development, the ultimate state of connectivity is determined by the influence of poorly understood trophic factors, and various kinds of overshoot can occur early in development. An initial phase of superabundant connectivity is followed by a process very much like pruning a rose bush, such that particular information channels reach their preferred target, and come to avoid alternate targets. It might be expected that individual differences in the extent of pruning may underlie certain kinds of synaesthesia. This seems to be indeed the case: using fMRI for mapping the anisotropic diffusion of water within bundles of narrow axonal fibres, it has been shown that the connectivity between the relevant cortical regions is indeed increased among color/grapheme synaesthetes.[17] However this is certainly an oversimplification of the matter. A recent functional activation study showed that the pattern of cerebral activation associated with color/grapheme synaesthesia was not completely suppressed by exposure to real colors, implying that the anatomical substrates of color experience in synaesthesia are not identical to those which subserve ordinary color perception.[18] Furthermore, a very recent MR-based correlational analysis of the thickness of several thousand cortical regions in color-grapheme synaesthetes has shown that the greater connectivity between cortical regions may be a global phenomenon,[19] not just restricted to the culprit regions postulated by Ramachandran. It then becomes a question why a globally increased binding should manifest specifically in cross-talk between grapheme and color perception.

In normal mammals, the auditory and visual sensory pathways are highly segregated in the thalamus, which serves as a routing station for projections ascending to the cerebral cortex. The integration of auditory and visual information, an instance of everyday synaesthesia, is a proper function of the multimodal cortices, where information from the primary sensory cortices converges. However, experimentally induced brain lesions can force an aberrant trajectory, which reveals the pluripontiality of cerebral cortex. For example, neonate hamsters can survive a surgical destruction of their nascent visual cortex, but they do not necessarily grow up blind. Alternate pathways can take over some of the visual processing. If the inferior colliculi of the brainstem are also destroyed, the auditory cortex is deprived of its normal input. The visual pathway, likewise bereft of its normal target, then densely innervates the auditory cortex.[20] These animals eventually open their eyes and grow up as normal-behaving, sighted, although presumably deaf, hamsters. Behavioural testing shows that they can make certain kinds of visual discriminations using the hijacked auditory cortex, seeing with their hear-brain.

The specific brain injury inflicted on the neonate hamsters is unlikely to arise spontaneously, but serves as an example for the potential of brain to develop along alternate lines, and to establish functional connectivity that serves as a metaphor for the phenomenon of synaesthesia. Congenital blindness presents the opportunity to study alternate lines of brain development and sensory processing in humans. The visual cortex of the congenially blind seems nearly normal in structural images, even though it has developed without any retinal input. The metabolic activity of cerebral cortex has recently been investigated in such individuals using PET with the synthetic glucose analogue [$^{18}$F]-fluorodeoxyglucose

17 Rouw/Scholte: “Increased structural connectivity in grapheme-color synesthesia”.

18 van Leeuwen et al.: “Synaesthetic colour in the brain: beyond colour areas. A functional magnetic resonance imaging study of synaesthetes and matched controls”.

19 Hänggi et al.: “Globally altered structural brain network topology in grapheme-color synesthesia”.

20 Frost et al.: “Surgically created neural pathways mediate visual pattern discrimination”.

(FDG). Rather like [$^{15}$O]-oxygen, as discussed above, the uptake of FDG reveals the local rate of energy metabolism, since the oxidation of glucose is normally the main energy source for brain work. Remarkably, the visual cortex in the congenitally blind is metabolically hyperactive (Professor Ron Kupers, University of Copenhagen, personal communication). It is clearly doing something, and is perhaps paying a penalty in metabolic efficiency, due to having been hijacked along an alternate developmental line; scissors make a poor hammer, but will serve to drive in a small nail, albeit inefficiently.

One might expect that the visual cortex in the congenitally blind has been recruited into the service of spatial perceptions, but through other means. This too has been investigated in functional imaging studies. The sighted and the congenitally blind can both learn to perceive a certain kind of spatial navigation, through stimulation of the tongue using a matrix of electrodes. This stimulation would normally evoke activation of the part of sensory and motor cortex representing the surface of the tongue, but with training, the message can be rerouted. After training, the performance of this task results in activation of the hippocampus, which normally encodes spatial learning, and also activates parts of the visual cortex, but only in the congenitally blind.[21] This suggests that their visual cortex continues to participate in perception of the external world, but under the influence of alternate sensory pathways. The plasticity of the healthy brain is such that the tongue can assume a role normally undertaken by the retina, while making use of visual cortex. It seems unlikely that the primary sensory fibres from the tongue can be re-routed by training. Either a small, pre-existing tongue input to the visual cortex can assume a larger than normal role in spatial awareness, or alternately, the somatosensory cortex representing the tongue can strengthen pre-existing intracortical pathways for informing the visual cortex. Either model could be interpreted as an acquired form of synaesthesia.

The taxonomy of possible synaesthesias is incomplete, but it seems that any permutation of mixing is possible; more than 60 varieties have been described. There is a recent report of colour synaesthesia evoked by swimming stroke; the butterfly is sky blue.[22] The theme of this chapter is that synaesthesias should properly be considered as unusual manifestations of normal sensory integrative functions of brain. Indeed, the normal sensation of the integrity of the self and the coherence of the external world is itself a familiar type of synaesthesia, without which we could scarcely survive. Associative learning may also be a kind of synaesthesia; if the smell of freshly baked cookies never fails to evoke the recollection of one's grandmother, this type of experience may also qualify as synaesthesia in the everyday sense. Synaesthesia with a capital S then refers to uncommon varieties of the mixing of the normal sensory and cognitive channels, which seem strange to the majority of people. These traits seem to be inborn, or at least

21 Kupers et al.: "Neural correlates of virtual route recognition in congenital blindness".
22 Nikolić et al.: "Swimming-style synesthesia".

manifest themselves early in life, and remain stable experiences throughout life. However, there are anecdotal reports that certain drugs can transiently evoke synaesthesias; the visual/auditory mixing sometimes reported by users of LSD implicates brain serotonin as a mediator of the suppression or expression of latent synaesthesia. The normal integration of sensory experience may represent a kind of optimization, aiming to minimize interference from competing sensory channels, while maximizing the construction of a coherent world view. In an anatomic and developmental sense, competition may be precisely the word, since the wiring of the developing brain results from neuronal Darwinism, whereby neurons compete for connectivity with target neurons: lesion studies, and brain function among the congenitally blind indicate that alternate plan B pathways can arise, and present functional alternatives to plan A. We don't presently know many of the players in the establishment of neuronal circuitry, but it can be safely assumed the growing neurites follow a concentration gradient in some humoural factors, much as a bacillus can follow a glucose gradient to its source, or perhaps more aptly, much as a salmon finds its way home from the broad ocean to the gravel riverbed where it was spawned.

After having made these reflections, I conclude with an account of a rather rare vision/touch synaesthesia, which nonetheless exemplifies the notion that synaesthesia can properly be regarded as an outlier in the range of ordinary sensory experience. A perfectly healthy informant had always experienced the sensation of touch whenever observing the touching of another.[23] So, if a conversant scratched his nose, she experienced the scratching of her own nose. Functional activation studies in which this synaesthete observed videos while reclining in the MR scanner showed that her visually evoked tactile sensations were associated with activation of the appropriate segment of the somatosensory cortex. More surprisingly, perhaps, a group of ordinary (as distinct from normal) volunteers also revealed functional activation of the same sensory cortical regions upon viewing the same video, but these activations were of lesser magnitude, and were (of course) not associated with explicit experience of the corresponding sensation. This implies a threshold phenomenon, whereby a certain degree of mirroring of neuronal activity between observer and observed may be essential for the interpretation of that class of sensory experience. But not too much; 'I feel your pain' is in moderation an expression of compassion, but in excess, would be insupportable unless one's compassion were a bottomless ocean.

23 Blakemore et al.: "Somatosensory activations during the observation of touch and a case of vision-touch synaesthesia".

## Acknowledgements

The author thanks Dr. Søren Dinesen Østergaard for a critical reading of the manuscript and Professor Ron Kupers for sharing unpublished results.

## References

Bedny, M. / T. Konkle / K. Pelphrey: "Sensitive period for a multimodal response in human visual motion area MT/MST", in: *Curr Biol.*, 20 (2010), pp. 1900–1906.

Blakemore, S. J. / D. Bristow / G. Bird: "Somatosensory activations during the observation of touch and a case of vision-touch synaesthesia", in: *Brain*, 128 (2005), pp. 1571–1583.

Deutsch, D. / K. Dooley / T. Henthorn: "Absolute pitch among students in an American music conservatory: association with tone language fluency", in: *J Acoust Soc Am*, 125 (2009), pp. 2398–2403.

Ford, J. M. / B. J. Roach / W. O. Faustman: "Out-of-synch and out-of-sorts: dysfunction of motor-sensory communication in schizophrenia", in: *Biol Psychiatry*, 63 (2008), pp. 736–743.

Frost, D. O. / D. Boire / G. Gingras: "Surgically created neural pathways mediate visual pattern discrimination", in: *Proc Natl Acad Sci U.S.A.*, 97 (2000), pp. 11068–11073.

Hänggi, J. / D. Wotruba / L. Jancke: "Globally altered structural brain network topology in grapheme-color synesthesia", in: *J. Neuroscience*, 31 (2011), pp. 5816–5828.

Kaminski, J. / J. Call / J. Fischer: "Word learning in a domestic dog: evidence for fast mapping", in: *Science*, 304 (2004), pp. 1682–1683.

Kupers, R. / D. R. Chebat / K. H. Madsen: "Neural correlates of virtual route recognition in congenital blindness", in: *Proc Natl Acad Sci U.S.A.*, 107 (2010), pp. 12716–12721.

van Leeuwen, T. M. / K. M. Petersson / P. Hagoort: "Synaesthetic colour in the brain: beyond colour areas. A functional magnetic resonance imaging study of synaesthetes and matched controls", in: *PLoS One*, 5 (2010) 8, p. e12074.

Mills, C. B. / J. Innis / T. Westendorf: "Effect of a synesthete's photisms on name recall", in: *Cortex*, 42 (2006) 2, pp. 155–163.

Naasan, G. / R. Hudson / R. Cesaro: "The social cognition of attachment: Preliminary results from functional imaging of Capgras delusion", abstract in: *American Society for Neurology, April 9–16,* Hawaii 2010.

Nikolić, D. / U. M. Jürgens / N. Rothen: "Swimming-style synesthesia", in: *Cortex*, (2011) [Epub ahead of print].

Peirce, J. W. / K. M. Kendrick: "Functional asymmetry in sheep temporal cortex", in: *Neuroreport*, 13 (2002), pp. 2395–2359.

Perrett, D. I. / A. J. Mistlin / A. J. Chitty: "Specialized face processing and hemispheric asymmetry in man and monkey: evidence from single unit and reaction time studies", in: *Behav Brain Res*, 29 (1988) 3, pp. 245–258.

Ramachandran, V. S. / E. M. Hubbard: "Psychophysical investigations into the neural basis of synaesthesia", in: *Proc Biol Sci*, 268 (2010), pp. 979–983.

Ramachandran, V. S. / E. M. Hubbard: "Synaesthesia: A window into perception, thought and language", in: *Journal of Consciousness Studies*, 8 (2001) 12, pp. 3–34.

Rothen, N. / B. Meier: "Higher prevalence of synaesthesia in art students", in: *Perception*, 39 (2010), pp. 718–720.

Rouw, R. / H. S. Scholte: "Increased structural connectivity in grapheme-color synesthesia", in: *Nat Neurosci*, 10 (2010), pp. 792–797.

Satoh, M. / S. Kuzuhara: "Training in mental singing while walking improves gait disturbance in Parkinson's disease patients" in: *Eur Neurol*, 60 (2008), pp. 237–243.

Sidaway, B. / J. Anderson / G. Danielson: "Effects of long-term gait training using visual cues in an individual with Parkinson disease", in: *Phys Ther*, 86 (2006), pp. 186–194.

Vafaee, M. S. / K. Østergaard / N. Sunde: "Focal changes of oxygen consumption in cerebral cortex of patients with Parkinson's disease during subthalamic stimulation", in: *Neuroimage*, 22 (2004), pp. 966–974.

Ward, J. / J. Simner: "Is synaesthesia an X-linked dominant trait with lethality in males?", in: *Perception*, 34 (2005), pp. 611–623.

# Scrolled Voices
# Synaesthetic Encounters of a Different Kind

KARL CLAUSBERG

Research focussing on synaesthesia has come up with a carefully groomed nomenclature of basic phenomena. They have been called *photisms, phonisms* etc originally and then were replaced by even more meticulous terms like *chromatic-lexical, chromatic-phonemic* and so forth, where the first item designates the additional synaesthetic experience. In the 19$^{th}$ century, however, such elementary binaries of sensation seemed to be only second-order qualities of visions, phantasms, number-forms and *mental imagery* in general. Diving even further down into the vast archives of art history one is bound to encounter truly strange varieties of apparent synaesthetic cross-breeding: scrolled voices. They were presented not only like oversized tongues, but were used as well manually as snares, maces etc. Speech-bubbles are the remote and reduced descendants of this high-medieval zoo of artificial limbs and tools engaged in imaginary behaviour.

Medieval scrolls originally depicted the standard book-type of antiquity: the *rotulus*, a lengthy roll of papyrus-sheets glued together. The material was brittle and ripped easily, readers had to be very observant in handling the precious handcrafted editions of literature. To use book rolls like flags or sails would have been considered utterly inappropriate.[1] Nevertheless this ostentatious manner of brandishing scrolls became increasingly popular in pictorial representation. Late Roman consuls let the expensive writing-material fall down carelessly to the ground to show their elevated official status, and Christian authors adopted this negligence, although the esteemed rank of Holy Scripture should have prevented them from doing so. Throwing-around the revered book rolls *in effigie* eventually turned into a general mode of signalling and pointing and this in turn brought synaesthetic allusions into play.

1 Birt: *Die Buchrolle in der Kunst*.

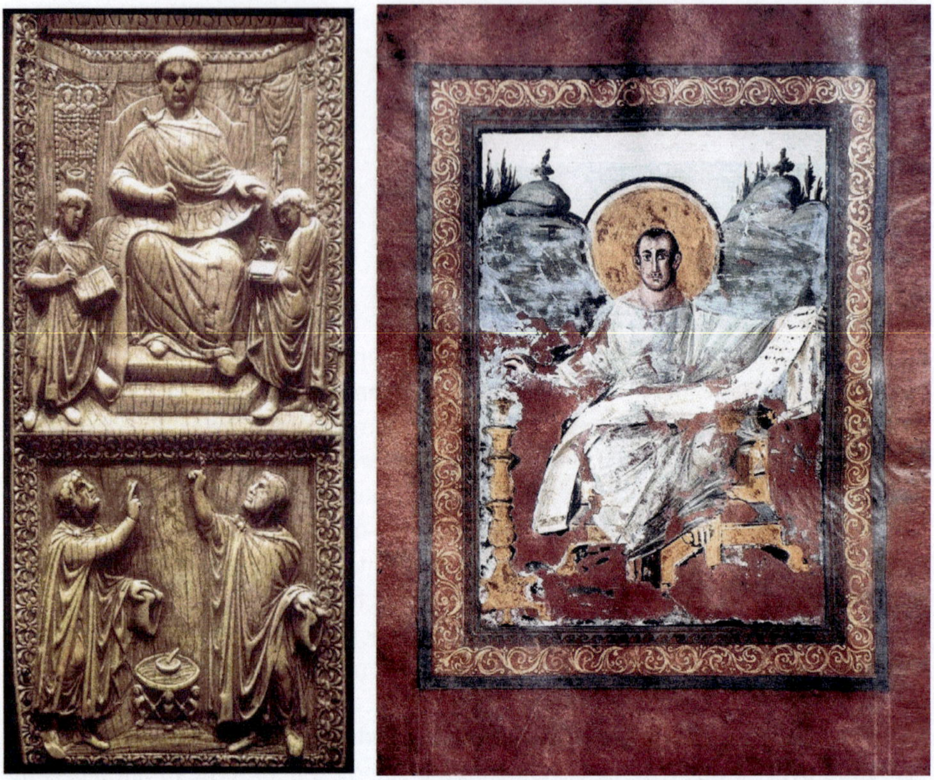

Fig. 1: *Probianus-Diptych*, ~380, Berlin. – *Schatzkammer-Gospels*, 9th century, Wien.

Texts written on scrolls acquired acoustic connotations and tended to be left away. Thus we find medieval authors rubbing their nimbi and heads with blank tape-towels or putting on scrolls like earphones. Scriptural letters apparently were replaced in tacit understanding by cross-modal equivalents of sonic impact. Scrolls could even be used as guided missiles aimed at the ears of adversaries. – This virtual transformation of scripture into terms of hearing eventually evoked the obvious corollary: strips of language issuing from the mouths of speakers. One of the finest examples is preserved in the famous 13th century Veldeke-Eneït, where the face of the gruesome ferryman-of-souls *Karo* (Charon) was doctored to release his fiery breath into the scroll blowing overhead. This astounding metamorphosis anticipated and forecast the course of development leading up to the speech-bubbles of modern times. A further ingredient was added to the repertoire of visualisation when tobacco entered the stage in 16th century. Early addicts were apparently able to embed their utterances in exhaled smoke. Henceforth we see 'dry drunkards' spouting clouds of aerosols and old-fashioned scrolls side by side. The onsetting age of 'bubble-prints' finally brimmed over with *fumetti and ectoplasmes*; the latter, a French term, insinuating almost spiritual powers of materialization.

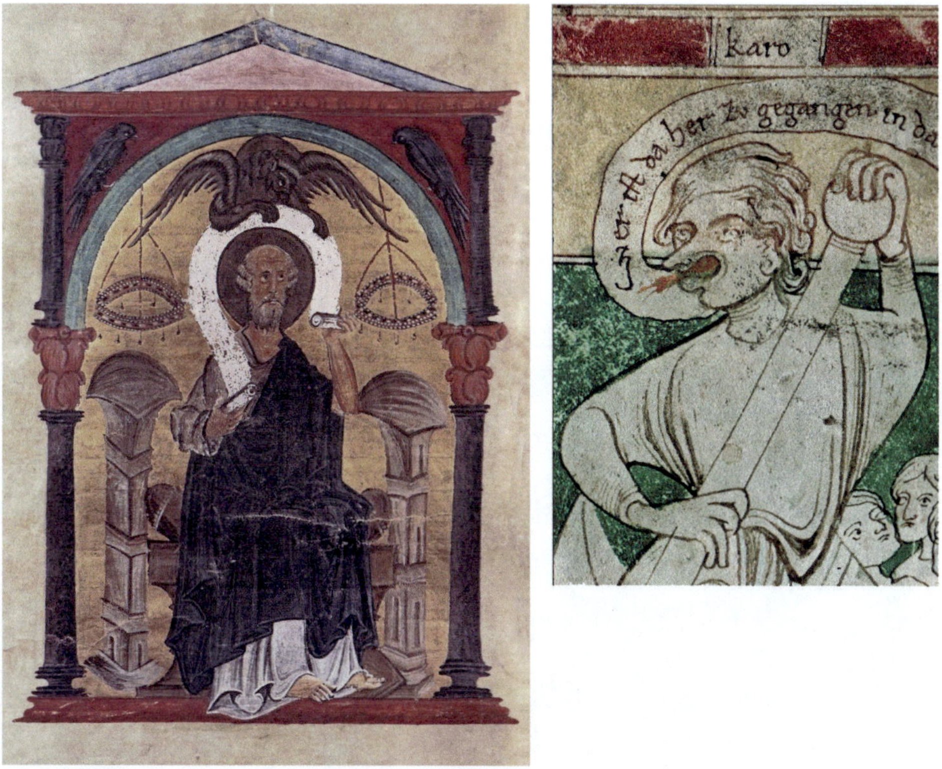


Fig. 2: *Marc*, *Gospels of Henry III*, ~990, Aachen. – *Karo* (Charon), *Veldeke-Eneït*, ~1230, fol. XXIIIr, Berlin.

Obvious conclusion of this very brief overview must be that material book rolls were transformed by imaginary evolution first into virtual multi-purpose tools, bodily extensions and aura-like envelopes and then into gaseous exhalations containing written characters. Although situated in pictorial space these mutations cannot be treated satisfactorily within the frameworks of single academic disciplines like history of art or literature alone. Altering the transportation vessels of written letters included a switch-back to insinuated auditory channels as well. The celebrated story of writing, which started from pictographic representations and culminated in truly phonetic alphabet-code, had a smaller offspring taking the opposite direction: it re-introduced the sound of language – or, put more precisely, visible indicators were engaged: blank scrolls acting as acoustic connectors and second-order signalling-devices.

Does it suffice to assume that cross-modal understanding or even synaesthetic perceptions were addressed? I think a new type of concept what to expect from bodily representations is needed. We have to proceed from corporeal likeness 'in the flesh' to pictorial similes of psychic attitudes and extensions. The well-known term *organ-projection* coined by Ernst Kapp in 1877 seems uniquely appropriate, and we may add Lazarus Geiger's slightly earlier (1868) notion of *secondary tools* to find a precise model for the transformations of book rolls. On the other hand the recent *philosophy of extended mind* – Clark and Chalmers, 1998 etc – offers a striking analogy: "Where the fish flaps its tail to set up the eddies and vortices it subsequently exploits, we intervene in multiple linguistic media […]." – Isn't it obvious that human figures did the same in the pictorial seas of art history using scrolls and balloons as 'tails' and tools? But does this suggestive comparison amount to anything more than a beautiful metaphor?

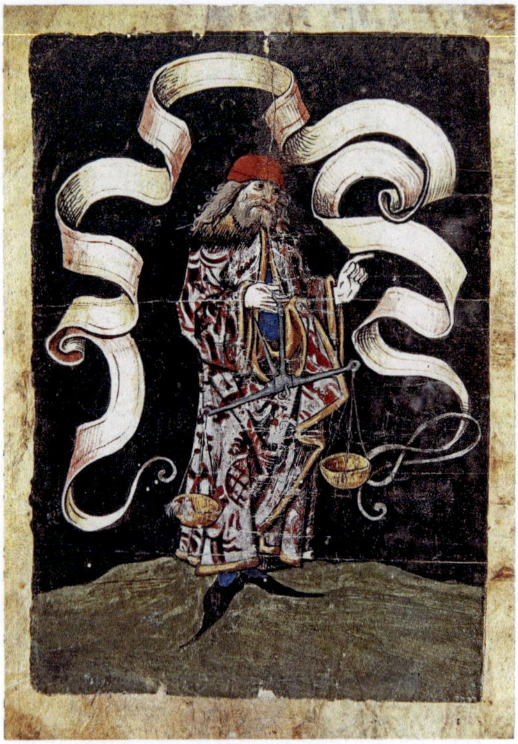

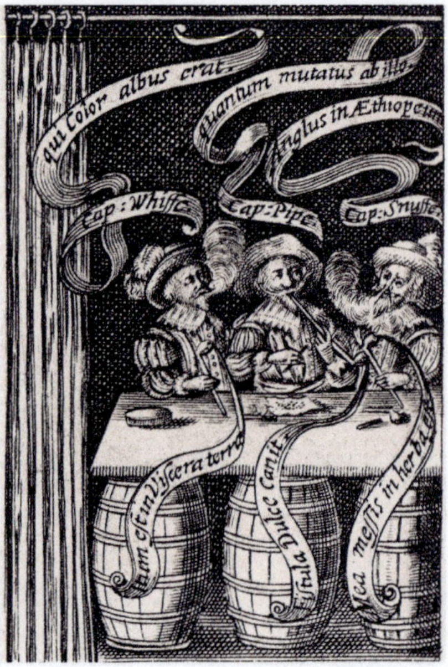


Fig. 3: *Avenzoar*, ~1480, München. – William Marshall, *A Tobacco Shop*; in: Richard Brathwait, *The Smoaking Age*, London 1617, Detail.

*

Andy Clark and David Chalmers had launched their short essay in 1998 by posing a blunt question: "Where does the mind stop and the rest of the world begin?" According to the authors this question invited two standard replies. Some would accept the demarcations of skin and skull, and say that what is outside the body is outside the mind. Others would appear to be impressed by arguments suggesting that the meaning of our words "just ain't in the head," and would hold that this externalism about meaning carries over into an externalism about mind. – Clark and Chalmers proposed to pursue a third position. They advocated a very different sort of externalism: an *active externalism*, based on the active role of the environment in driving cognitive processes.[2]

To emphazise their argument Clark and Chalmers resorted to a highly provocative comparison: What would be the difference between a normal person relying on his memory and an Alzheimer-patient using a notebook?[3] According to the authors there would only be *shallow* differences setting the two cases apart. Active externalism would see them on almost equal footing as minds using slightly different means to negotiate their affairs. Both cases would resemble externally enhanced or engaged cognitive units embedded in shared and activated surroundings. And in this line of argument Clark and Chalmers introduced the analogy of fish moving in a supportive environment.

> Now consider a reliable feature of the human environment, such as the sea of words. This linguistic surround envelopes us from birth. Under such conditions, the plastic human brain will surely come to treat such structures as a reliable resource to be factored into the shaping of on-board cognitive routines. Where the fish flaps its tail to set up the eddies and vortices it subsequently exploits, we intervene in multiple linguistic media, creating local structures and disturbances whose reliable presence drives our ongoing internal processes. Words and external symbols are thus paramount among the cognitive vortices which help constitute human thought.[4]

This beautiful philosophical layout of active externalism nevertheless evokes doubts and questions when projected onto the regime of visibility and visualization. How should normal people grasp and apply the idea of a 'sea of words'? Is it to be understood as a kind of Babbage's atmospheric ocean containing all utterances ever released or just as a cross-section of present statements? Or should we better restrict our approach to written material and its use? – And even if we resort to the epidemic appearance of scrolls and speech-balloons; are we not confronted with a very particular case due to special circumstances? – Last but not least even the distinction of 'inside' and 'outside' remains a thorny proposition.

Interestingly enough Ernst Kapp's *Principles of a philosophy of technology* of 1877[5] offer a wealth of insights and notions concerning the problems outlined above; but – as far as I can see[6] – these ideas were never introduced into the debates on 'active externalism'. In the following I shall try to bridge this obvious gap and, on the same route, introduce Kapp's concept of *organ-projections* into the survey of 'scrolled voices' and related phenomena.

2 Clark/Chalmers: "The Extended Mind", quoted in Clark: *Supersizing the Mind*, appendix pp. 220–232.

3 Clark: *Supersizing the Mind*, appendix pp. 226ff.

4 Ibid., p. 226.

5 Kapp: *Grundlinien einer Philosophie der Technik. Zur Entstehungsgeschichte der Cultur aus neuen Gesichtspunkten*. Facsimile with an introduction by Hans-Martin Sass.

6 My thanks to Jörg Fingerhut for confirming my suspicion.

*

After a mixed career as German school-teacher, geographer and Texan settler Ernst Kapp (1808–1896)[7] had combined his expertise in very different fields into a new approach towards theories and techniques of culture. Deeply entrenched in Hegelian ways of thinking he had set out to characterize the dynamic relation of the outside-world with its inner representations. Taking up a pivotal role consciousness would result from truly dialectic processes: knowledge of external things would propagate into awareness of their internal persistence, and this in turn would trigger a ceaselessly renewed to and from of outward attitudes and actions.[8] Depending on circumstances the Self would determine what should be regarded as belonging to the inside or to the outside. Limbs of the body might be considered to be part of the inner world; on other occasions our consciousness would decree that hands and feet should be seen as objects of the outer world.[9]

Right at the beginning Kapp expressed his conviction that current understanding of the 'Self' had outgrown earlier constructions of purely 'spiritual' existence. This peculiar illusion had dwindled with the insight that only the body can be the immediate and proper instantiation of the Self. What would remain of the appraised human Self if the entire corporeal assembly were removed? Just a ghastly spectre! Only through affirmation by our bodily existence the Self would be able to establish itself in consciousness.[10] On the same way the sphere of external activities would turn out to be a transmission of inner concepts and operative schemes. The entirety of cultural tools and works would be shaped in the image of corporeal models, and this unconscious mimicry would rebound to stipulate growing awareness of the rules governing the execution of *organ-projections*.[11]

With this powerful new term at hand Kapp set out to embrace the entire domain of cultural production: Not only material tools of craftsmen and scientist's instruments could be classified as organ-projections, even the molecules of air exited by human speech would fall into this category.[12] Language would therefore be, according to Kapp, the most universal tool comprising, among other phenomena, primeval gestures of sound (*Klanggebärden*), which would have their natural origin in elementary functions of the organism. 'Gestures of sound' would arise as and resemble lofty extensions of the body.[13] All ingredients of organ-projection seemed present in the creation and proliferation of soundwaves. Muscular modelling and mechanical transmission by vibrations of air,

7 Hantzsch: in: *Deutsche Rundschau für Geographie und Statistik*.
8 Kapp: *Grundlinien*, p. 23.
9 Ibid., p. 24.
10 Ibid., p. 2.
11 Ibid., p. 26.
12 Ibid., p. 27.
13 Ibid., p. 281.

originally an intuitive faculty of mankind, would become intelligible in comparison to brass- and string-instruments. Production of meaningful language would result from and coalesce into sensible units of means and ends: words could resemble thoughts, and vice versa.[14]

Kapp conceded that linguistics and literature had to deal with two forms of language, however. Language actually spoken had to be evaluated side by side with written texts. But even their fundamental difference should be somehow reconcilable in the light of a common origin. Kapp was convinced that emergent 'gestures of writing' were fostered by gestures of sound establishing a primeval code of primitive signs.[15] Scripture on the other hand preserved a kind of backwards-compatibility, because it resorted to manufactural tool-forming (*manufaktische Werkzeugbildung*). Thus language in toto, according to Kapp, was able to serve as a connective link between the material and spiritual spheres of human endeavour. – That the universal tool of language was capable to display its cross-modal properties as well and even far better in the virtual worlds of imagery and picturing didn't enter into Kapp's deliberations, however. Consequently his fruitful concept of organ-projections failed to reach the core of history-aided self-understanding: i.e. insight into the variability of enhanced human body-images, which is so overwhelmingly obvious in the virtual domain of scrolls and speech-bubbles.

*

Kapp's idea that organ-projections establish a cross-modal field of acoustic speech and scriptural language had evaded another obstacle of evolutionary dimensions as well: the apparent affliction with 'case-histories'. Particular tools evidently didn't arise just at a moment's notice as demanded by function. They had forerunners devoted very often to quite different tasks. Another savant of language-research had already discussed this aspect of tool-development: Lazarus Geiger (1829–1870).[16] In 1868 he had presented a lecture at the International Congress for Archaeology and History at Bonn titled *The Earliest History of the Human Race in the Light of Language, with Special Reference to the Origin of Tools*.[17] Geiger's main proposition was that man had language before he had tools, and before he practiced industrial arts. "On considering a word denoting an activity carried on with a tool, we shall invariably find it not to have been its original meaning, but that it previously implied a similar activity requiring only

14 Ibid., p. 298.
15 Ibid., p. 293.
16 Rosenthal: *Lazarus Geiger*, and Peschier: *Lazarus Geiger*, p. 507–508.
17 Geiger: *Die Urgeschichte der Menschheit im Lichte der Sprache*.

the natural organs of man."[18] This observation led Geiger to a crucial distinction between primary and secondary tools:

> The tool, observed in its evolution, marvellously resembles a natural organ; exactly like this it has its transformations and its differentiations. We should wholly misconceive the tool if we always wanted to find the cause of its origin in its immediate purpose, just as we should misconceive the webbed foot of the duck were we to think of it as unconnected with the formation of the feet of birds that cannot swim.[19]

Geiger was convinced that the history of language contained an immense treasure of utmost importance to the knowledge of our earliest history.

> Do not such developments of the productions of man's ideas and volition present a parallel to what happens in nature when, under altered conditions and necessities, the arm is, in the case of birds, converted into a wing?[20]

An interim conclusion based on this brief account of Kapp's and Geiger's concepts should not contend itself with the dismissal that they perhaps naively projected biologistic views onto the realm of human culture. The issues they raised are still open – and have a broader significance than they imagined. The history of book rolls turning into scrolls and speech-bubbles is one of the more obvious dossiers of evidence.

*

Gauged by the widespread attention paid to Geiger's and Kapp's publications it is rather astonishing that art historians took no notice at all of the bold schemes which reconnected language with corporeal operations. With the benefit of hindsight it becomes easier to identify the obstacles. "Homer treats two different classes of beings and actions," Gotthold Ephraim Lessing had ordained in his treatise on *Laocoon* in 1766, "[...] the visible and the invisible. This distinction cannot be made in canvas, where every thing is visible, and visible in precisely the same way."[21] To some extent this difficulty in representing the invisible could be overcome, but Lessing deemed the results highly questionable:

> The expedient to which painters have recourse to indicate that a certain character is supposed to be invisible, is a thin cloud veiling the side of the figure that is turned towards the other actors on the scene. [...] It always seems strange to me, therefore, to find this poetical expression embodied in a picture, and an actual cloud introduced, behind which, as behind a screen, the hero stands hidden from his enemy. This was not the poet's meaning. The artist in this exceeds the limits of painting. His cloud is a hieroglyphic, a purely symbolic sign, which

18 Geiger: *Contributions,* 1880, p. 34.
19 Ibid., p. 41.
20 Ibid., p. 43.
21 Lessing: *Laocoon*, p. 77.

> does not make the rescued hero invisible, but simply says to the observers, –"You are to suppose this man to be invisible." It is no better than the rolls of paper with sentences upon them, which issue from the mouth of personages in the old Gothic pictures.[22]

Obviously the idea that invisibility could be represented by custom-tailored clouds allowed Lessing to refer to another kind of, in his eyes, ill-advised visualisation: clouds of speech emerging from the mouths of speakers replaced by *rolls of paper* in paintings.

A similar prejudice was documented by Denis Diderot in 1765 when he voiced his utter disdain for allegorical paintings and came up with exactly the same comparison:

> Le mélange des êtres allégoriques et réels donne à l'histoire l'air d'un conte; et, pour trancher le mot, ce défaut défigure pour moi la plupart des compositions de Rubens. Je ne les entends pas. Qu'est-ce que cette figure qui tient un nid d'oiseaux, un Mercure, l'arc-en-ciel, le zodiaque, le sagittaire, dans la chambre et autour du lit d'une accouchée? Il faudrait faire sortir de la bouche de chacun de ces personnages, comme on le voit à nos vieilles tapisseries de château, une légende qui dit ce qu'ils veulent.[23]

Scrolls spouting from the lips of persons on old tapestries had the same repelling effect on the French Encyclopedian as on the German Aesthete. Finer taste and erudition were set internationally against such 'retarded' extravagances, and this judgement lingered on for more than a century.

Let us just call upon one of the most illustrious witnesses, Sigmund Freud. When he elaborated the means of representation of dreams in 1900 and set forth his famous diagnosis of their muteness he resorted to exactly the same comparison, i.e. old paintings:

> If dreams lack the ability to express [logical] relations [between the dream-thoughts], the psychic material of which they are wrought must be responsible for this defect. As a matter of fact, the representative arts – painting and sculpture – are similarly restricted, as compared with poetry, which is able to employ speech; and here again the reason for this limitation lies in the material by the elaboration of which the two plastic arts endeavour to express something. Before the art of painting arrived at an understanding of the laws of expression by which it is bound, it attempted to make up for this deficiency. In old paintings little labels hung out of the mouths of the persons represented, giving in writing the speech which the artist despaired of expressing in the picture.[24]

Six years earlier Freud's secret instigator, Carl du Prel (1839–1899), had already given the same verdict deploring the depiction of scrolls as a 'want of taste'.[25]

It must surprise therefore, at a first glance, that Aby Warburg felt tempted about the same time to invoke the despised explanatory powers of visualized

22 Lessing: *Laocoon*, pp. 80–81.
23 Diderot: *Essai sur la Peinture*, p. 471.
24 Freud: *The Interpretation of Dreams*, p. 203.
25 du Prel: *Die Entdeckung der Seele durch die Geheimwissenschaften*, p. 2.

speech: "I have to restore the scroll which issues from the mouth of mediaeval figures to the joyful personages of the Renaissance, brimming with life."[26] But that was only a sigh of momentary despair. Warburg had tried to identify persons in Ghirlandaio's frescoes in the Tornabuoni-chapel of Santa Maria Novella in Florence and failed. So his call for help was ambiguous and subtly condescending, since he believed that mediaeval art was seriously impaired by its incapacity of true expression. – Thus we have to acknowledge the singular fact that Warburg came, figuratively speaking, within a hair's breadth to incorporate scrolls into his repertoire of *accessories in motion* (bewegtes Beiwerk), but nevertheless remained a tacit adherent of a strange neglect uniting art historians and aesthetes around 1900. Although they cherished richly clad figures and even felt souls seeping through petrified garments they were utterly unable to 'see' scrolls as corporeal *organ-projections*. It has taken decades to slowly debase this predicament.[27]

*

Of the many authors worth mentioning in the context given I shall concentrate here on one person, who has paced research in many directions: Karl Bühler (1879–1963). His *Theory of Language* of 1934, at last translated into English in 1990,[28] still offers several fresh points of departure into the fields of cross-modal understanding. To outline briefly my following remarks two labels will suffice: *speech-acts* and the *deictic-field*.

Bühler felt a deep dissatisfaction with the canonical bipolar distinction of *language* and *speech*. Wilhelm von Humboldt had spoken of *energeia* and *ergon*, the linguist Saussure had picked up the opposition used in French between *la parole* and *la langue* (in English *speech* and *language*) in order to make it the topic of a *linguistique de la parole* running parallel to the traditional *linguistique de la langue*. Since Humboldt there had been practically no expert of any stature who did not sense that something quite remarkable had been touched with the terms *energeia* and *ergon*, and there had been none since Saussure who had not reflected on *la parole* and *la langue*.[29] – Bühler proposed instead a 'quadrifolium' of terms to account for the complexities of human communications: *Act, Work, Action* and *Structure* (*Sprechhandlung* und *Sprachwerk*, *Sprechakt* und *Sprachgebilde*). His crucial observation was that two of these terms designated *subject-related* phenomena, the latter meant phenomena *independent of a subject*, phe-

26 Gombrich: *Aby Warburg*, p. 120.

27 For a more comprehensive account see Clausberg: *Sichtbar gerollte Stimmen*.

28 Bühler: *Sprachtheorie*, translated by Donald Fraser Goodwin: *Theory of Language: The Representational Function of Language*.

29 Bühler: *Theory*, p. 57.

nomena that have an intersubjective fixation.[30] This farsighted distinction set the tap-root of speech-act-theory in its own course, which was introduced by John Langshaw Austin into the Anglophone world in the 1950s.[31] Needless to say that Austin's title *How to do things with words* easily lends itself to transpositions into the realm of visualization. One has just to replace *words* with *scrolls* to grasp the range of pictorial possibilities, when *locutionary*, *illocutionary* and *perlocutionary* modes of acting are considered in terms of observability. It would, however, require unduly extended space for closer scrutiny to substantiate particular findings. Instead I shall take up the other, more general topic raised by Bühler in his *Theory of Language*: the *deictic-field* that would act as a kind of carrier-system for possible visualizations.

To explain his views on language and speech Bühler engaged a telling comparison: The use of verbalized symbols and their mental handling would require a kind of distributive field just as painters would need a canvas, geographer's work would require a grid of latitudes and longitudes or musicians would write down their inventions on especially prepared sheets for musicography.[32] Even the very theatre-stage Bühler counted among the varieties of artificial symbolic fields. Main functions of the *symbolic field of language* would be to display syntactic and lexical elements resp. relations; not just in a mirror-wise representation of the real world, however, but indirectly by substituting the particular 'field equipment' (*Feldgerät*) of language.[33] Human language, understood in the sense of an assembly of virtual tools, had, according to Bühler, already detached itself from immediate imitation of reality. Pointing and 'painting' similes of external situations was not anymore a dedicated task of truthful verbalization. Having been released from specific situations the 'deictic field of language' (*Zeigfeld der Sprache*) still was able, however, to reconnect to circumstances given. The 'I am here now' coordinates of personal orientation (*hier-jetzt-ich-System subjektiver Orientierung*) would provide points of re-entry. This mixture of addressing real and imagined entities and situations Bühler tagged with the terms *demonstratio ad oculos* and 'Deixis by phantasm' (*Deixis am Phantasma*). The latter meant speaking *anaphorically*, i.e. pointing to things not present, but situated elsewhere, in the past or in the future. Thus the evolving contexts of situational speech would themselves become *deictic fields* reflecting their current positions of narration.[34]

These observations led Bühler to a conclusion that involved other forms of artistic creativity as well. Taken psychologically the use of deictic verbiage would presuppose that speakers and listeners alike were capable to envision the complete flow of narration (*Redeabfluß*). They should be able to observe whole

30 Ibid., p. 58.
31 Austin: *How To Do Things With Words.*
32 Bühler: *Sprachtheorie,* p. 254.
33 Ibid., p. 150–51.
34 Ibid., p. 121 ff., esp. p. 124.

events like objects visually present. Of course one is bound to instantly invoke the parallel of painting, but Bühler, strangely enough, didn't approve of this idea at all: "Neither in the realm of painting nor in music compositions exist properly specialized signs destined to function as signposts that might be compared to anaphorical signalling with words."[35] – Bühler could have known better. The Viennese school of art history had attained its particular rank by investigations into pictorial narrative. Franz Wickhoff's researches on the *Vienna Genesis* had been continued and enlarged by Otto Pächt, Hans Sedlmayr and Dagobert Frey in the 1920s, right at the time when Bühler was called to take the chair of psychology at the university of Vienna. Thus it remains a historical riddle that he never took notice of art historians working next door on narrative intertwining of diachronic signals. This is all the more mysterious since Bühler had already a finished manuscript in his travelling bags when he moved to Vienna. It dealt with the *Appearance of Colours* and had a special chapter on the *Optics of Painting,*[36] a theme that was to become a major topic of Viennese art history. For Bühler it served later to support his view of the symbolic field of language by quoting the *Paragone* (Italian: comparison), a Renaissance-debate devoted to the question which form of art was superior to all others. Leonardo da Vinci had emphasized in his *Treatise on Painting* that painterly work deserved the highest praise because, in contrast to sculpture and architecture, its inner lighting-conditions could be completely controlled by application of lustre and shadows. According to Bühler, painting had freed itself from external conditions in a similar manner as language had detached itself from particular circumstances.[37] Both cases would instead be governed by internal field-parameters, they would both come under the influence of a 'synsemantic surrounding field' (*synsemantisches Umfeld*).[38]

Bühler's views were obviously inspired by painterly illusionism and naturalism, and thus he never searched for other approaches to pictorial autonomy. In this respect he was still entrenched in aesthetic rules affirmed if not established in 19th century. He was convinced that Renaissance-art offered no place for *anaphorical Deixis* of any kind. The irony remains, however, that Viennese art historians had already explored quite different fields of narrative dilatation or contraction. Bühler could have found wonderful examples of pictorial self-extrication from the rules of external likeness: The far-reaching textures of mediaeval scroll-handling would have fitted his descriptions of resolved situational constraints and supplemented linguistic 'field-equipment' perfectly. – Matter of fact Bühler's *deictic fields* can be regarded as future theoretical 'green-houses' of cross-modal synaesthetics as well.

*

35 Ibid., p. 122.
36 Bühler: *Handbuch der Psychologie*, p. 183–209.
37 Ibid., p. 200 ff.
38 Ibid., p. 372.

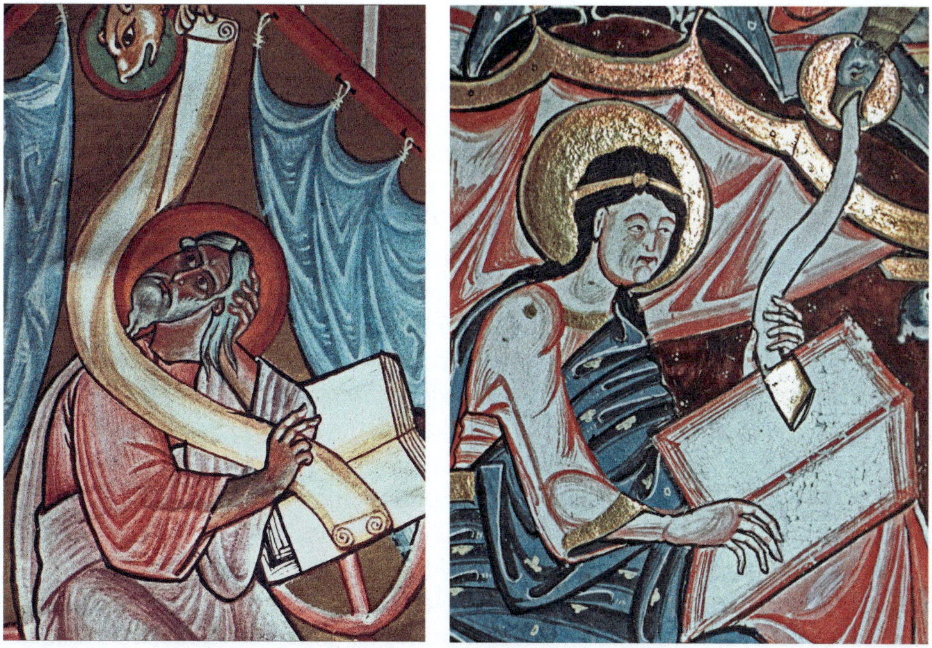

Fig. 4: *Marc*, 12th cent., Fulda. – *John, Gospels from Flandern,* Stuttgart, Middle 11th cent.

I shall restrict available evidence here to just two further examples of presumably synaesthetically enhanced presentations out of the vast archive of mediaeval book-illumination. In both cases these portraits of evangelists were obvious end-products of fairly long chains of copies and slight modifications: Marc receives his inspiration on a blank roll from his symbol, a lion; and on the other side John has to handle the empty outflow from his eagle's beak. In each of the two portraits the delivery of the holy message was conducted and supplemented in a peculiar way. Marc's roll curves around his nimb with the clear intent to visualize acoustic transmission – as already observed in other examples. The roll however, in this case, carries on and turns into a writing tool, coinciding with the pen's contours in the author's right hand. Or should we rather see it as a kind of hose that drains itself into the open book? That notion seems to have been the straightforward aim of the illuminators of John's portrait. They chose to install a short-cut by emptying the tongue-tube emerging from the eagle's beak right away into the codex, without bothering anymore to 'contact' and inform the scribe what he was transmitting. He had to content himself with steering the flow of wisdom.

First and foremost conclusion to be drawn, especially from the last two examples, is the notion that scrolls were indeed used as a kind of Bühlerian 'field-equipment' to move symbolic contents in highly artificial surroundings. Holy inspiration normally applied in the form of text was apparently 'liquefied' for easier transmission; written characters dissolved into cross-modal flow-charts that were outlined and guided by the contours of scrolls. Allusions of sound and touch seemingly supplemented or even replaced the standard-routines of message-reading. Mediaeval miniaturists may have subjectively aspired to give fairly naturalistic portraits of significant persons and events. What they actually created might be better characterized as *deictic fields* where *secondary tools* of transformed book rolls could be brought into play as imaginary *organ-projections*. And this in turn should lead us to address *The Image and Appearance of the Human Body* – to quote Paul Schilder's important book of 1935 – in a general way.

The human body as a physical object has been closely studied and subjected to subtle or exaggerating portraiture since Greco-Roman times. Physiognomics and Pathognomics addressed the outward appearance of fleshy surfaces supported by bony, skeletal frameworks. Understanding was derived from permanent traits, enduring habits or fleeting changes in the corporeal make-up and movements. One of the highlights in the history of this science was Karl Bühler's *Theory of Expression*[39] published in 1933 almost side by side with his *Theory of Language*. In a wide sweep Bühler discussed approaches to the phenomena of natural or enhanced expression starting with Johann Jacob Engel (1741–1802), an expert on improvements of theatrical play-acting, and finishing with Ludwig Klages (1872–1956) who had proceeded from graphological studies to debatable wholesale criticism of cultural profiles. – All these approaches relied more or less on quantifiable semiotics akin to medicinal diagnostics.

On the other hand psychiatry and psychoanalysis had endeavoured to bring the inner aspects of self-perception into sharper focus. One of the less well known Viennese experts worth mentioning was Paul Schilder (1886–1940). In 1914 he published *Consciousness of self and personality: a psychological study*[40] that dealt with a range of subjective distortions of personalities and, closely related to the latter, body images. Main term of Schilder's expositions was 'Depersonalization' (*Depersonalisierung*) supplemented by a chapter on 'Ecstasy, Duplication of the Self and Possessed States' (*Ekstase, "Ichverdoppelung" und Besessenheit*). In 1923 he proceeded to give a clear-cut view of the 'Body-Scheme' (*Körperschema*) especially turning to the symptoms of *Alloaestetics* and *Allochiria* that name the strange sensorial dislocations of body-parts.[41] – All in all Paul Schilder's writings, eventually crowned by his English bestseller of 1935,[42] stand for a heightened awareness that outward appearance and internal perception of one's own body can widely deviate from each other. This legacy from the Viennese 'sciences of the soul' provides a very good reason to transpose such distinctions fully onto the archives of art history. If done so in a sensible way a surprising range of subjective phenomena start to arrange themselves into powerful imagery. We are then at last enabled to observe the cross-modal workings of organ-projections in

39 Bühler: *Ausdruckstheorie*.
40 Schilder: *Selbstbewusstein und Persönlichkeitsbewusstein*.
41 Schilder: *Das Körperschema*.
42 Schilder: *The Image and Appearance of the Human Body*.

deictic fields in their own right – last but not least the scrolled voices of a lesser artistic milieu, which can reveal so much of our true bodily nature.

# References

Austin, John Langshaw: *How To Do Things With Words*. The William James Lectures delivered at Harvard University in 1955. J. O. Urmson (ed.), Oxford (Clarendon) 1962.

Birt, Theodor: *Die Buchrolle in der Kunst*, Leipzig (Teubner) 1907.

Bühler, Karl: *Sprachtheorie*, Jena 1934; translated by Donald Fraser Goodwin: *Theory of Language: The Representational Function of Language*, Amsterdam 1990.

Bühler, Karl: *Handbuch der Psychologie; Erster Teil, Die Struktur der Wahrnehmungen; 1. Heft, Die Erscheinungsweisen der Farben*, Jena (Verlag Gustav Fischer) 1922.

Bühler, Karl: *Ausdruckstheorie. Das System an der Geschichte aufgezeigt*, Jena (Verlag Gustav Fischer) 1933.

Clark, Andy / David J. Chalmers: "The Extended Mind", in: *Analysis* 58, pp. 10–23, 1998. Reprinted in (P. Grim, ed.): *The Philosopher's Annual*, 21 (1998).

Clark, Andy: *Supersizing the Mind. Embodiment, Action and Cognitive Extension*, Oxford (Oxford University Press) 2008.

Clausberg, Karl: "Metamorphosen am laufenden Band. Eine kurzgefaßte Entwicklungsgeschichte der Sprechblase", in: Michael Hein (ed.): *Ästhetik des Comic, Tagungsbericht zur ersten internationalen Fachtagung der Arbeitsstelle für graphische Literatur an der Univ. Hamburg*, Berlin (Erich Schmidt Verlag) 2002, pp. 17–36.

Clausberg, Karl: "Sichtbar gerollte Stimmen – Organprojektionen als Sekundärwerkzeuge für bildliche Sprechakte", in: Otto Brunken (ed.): *Erzählen im Comic*, Bochum (Ch.A. Bachmann-Verlag) 2011 (forthcoming).

Clausberg, Karl: "Spruchbandreden als Körpersprache im Berliner Äneïden-Manuskript", in: Thomas W. Gaehtgens (ed.): *Künstlerischer Austausch – Artistic Exchange*, Akten des 28. Int. Kongresses für Kunstgeschichte Berlin 15.–20 July 1992, vol. 1, Berlin (Akademie Verlag) 1994, pp. 345–355.

Clausberg, Karl: "Spruchbandaussagen zum Stilcharakter. Malende und gemalte Gebärden, direkte und indirekte Rede in den Bildern der Veldeke-Äneïde sowie Wernhers Marienliedern", in: *Städel-Jahrbuch*, NF 13 (1991), pp. 81–110.

Clausberg, Karl: "Stimmbänder der Bildphantasie. Synästhetische Rückwege der Schrift zur Sprache", in: Brigitte Felderer (ed.): *Phonorama. Eine Kulturge-*

*schichte der STIMME als Medium*, ZKM-Katalog, Berlin (Museum für Neue Kunst) 2004, pp. 71–84.

Clausberg, Karl: "Tabakrauch im Atemhauch", in: Annette Stahmer (ed.): *Parole # 1: The Body ofthe Voice l Stimmkörper,* Köln (Salon Verlag) 2009, pp. 24–31.

Diderot, Denis: *Essai sur la Peinture, Chapitre V. Paragraphe sur la Composition, où j'espère que j'en parlerai*, in: *Œuvres de Denis Diderot. Salons, Tome I*, Paris 1821.

Diderot, Denis: "Notes on Painting", in:. John Goodman (ed.): *Diderot on Art*, Vol. I. New Haven, Connecticut (Yale University Press) 1995.

Freud, Sigmund: *The Interpretation of Dreams*, translated by A.A. Brill 1911, 3rd Edition 1953.

Geiger, Lazarus: "Die Urgeschichte der Menschheit im Lichte der Sprache. Mit besonderer Beziehung auf die Entstehung des Werkzeugs", in: *Zur Entwickelungsgeschichte der Menschheit. Vorträge von L. Geiger*, Stuttgart 1871; Translated by David Asher, Ph.D.: *The Earliest History of the Human Race in the Light of Language, with Special Reference to the Origin of Tools*; in: Geiger. *Contributions to the History of the Development of the Human Race. Lectures and Dissertations*, Boston 1880.

Gombrich, Ernst Hans: *Aby Warburg. An Intellectual Biography*, London (Warburg Institute) 1970.

Hantzsch, Viktor: "Kapp, Ernst", in: *Deutsche Rundschau für Geographie und Statistik,* 20 (1898), in: *ADB*, 51 (1906), pp. 31-33.

Kapp, Ernst: *Grundlinien einer Philosophie der Technik. Zur Entstehungsgeschichte der Cultur aus neuen Gesichtspunkten*, Braunschweig 1877. Facsimile with an introduction by Hans-Martin Sass, Düsseldorf (Stern-Verlag Janssen) 1978.

Lessing, Gotthold Ephraim: *Laocoon. An Essay upon the Limits of Painting and Poetry* [1766], translated by Ellen Frothingham, Boston 1887.

Peschier C.: *Lazarus Geiger. Sein Leben und Denken. Augsburger Allgemeine Ztg. Beilage* 30. Dec. and 31. Dec. 1871. – With the same title, Frankfurt 1871. *ADB*, 8 (1878).

Prel, Carl du: *Die Entdeckung der Seele durch die Geheimwissenschaften*, Leipzig 1894.

Rosenthal, Ludwig A.: *Lazarus Geiger. Seine Lehre vom Ursprunge der Sprache und Vernunft und sein Leben*, Stuttgart 1884.

Schilder, Paul: *Das Körperschema. Ein Beitrag zur Lehre vom Bewußtsein des eigenen Körpers*, Berlin (Springer) 1923.

Schilder, Paul: *Selbstbewusstein und Persönlichkeitsbewusstein. Eine psychopathologische Studie*, Berlin (Springer) 1914.

Schilder, Paul: *The Image and Appearance of the Human Body*, London (Kegan Paul) 1935.

# List of Illustrations

# *Spatialities*

# Learning to Live with Abstraction
# Filmic Reception and Sensory Intermodality

ROBIN CURTIS

Popular interest in the cooperative functioning of the senses has made itself increasingly tangible of late, from the demand for 3D effects that has swept Hollywood since the premiere of James Cameron's blockbuster *Avatar* in late 2009, to the strategic reference to the immersive abandon made available when a given product – anything from a scoop of ice cream to the luxury of a hotel room – appeals to the human being in his or her sensory complexity. Even if only implicitly, rather than by name, synaesthetic phenomena have gradually regained a popular currency that they had not enjoyed since the beginning of the twentieth century.

A shift has also taken place in recent years within contemporary synaesthesia scholarship. The swell of writings that appeared in the late twentieth century (from those of Lawrence Marks and Simon Baron-Cohen, to Richard Cytowic's own) employed experimental methods to confirm the existence of synaesthesia. However, newer publications, such as *The Hidden Sense: Synaesthesia in Art and Science,* written by the Dutch social scientist, Cretien van Campen, or Richard Cytowic and David Eagleman's *Wednesday is Indigo Blue: Discovering the Brain of Synaesthesia,* have increasingly sought to move towards a better understanding of multisensory perception in general. Increasingly at issue is less the manner in which discrete senses are mingled, but rather a better understanding of the fundamental complexity of perception.

In *The Hidden Sense,* van Campen offers an extremely broad definition of synaesthesia that regards the distinction between the perceptual capacities of synaesthetes and those available to the general population as gradual rather than absolute. While careful to distinguish synaesthesia from the experience of blended senses offered by, for instance, classical program music or the LSD-inspired light shows offered at happenings such as Andy Warhol's Exploding Plastic Inevitable in 1966 and '67[1] which were then popularized in rock shows in the late sixties and seventies, van Campen nonetheless offers a more expansive perspective on the use value of synaesthetic phenomena than is generally found in contemporary literature. He suggests the correct approach within research

1 For an extremely detailed account of Warhol's contribution to intermedial practice and intermodal experience, situating the Exploding Plastic Inevitable within both the art practice of its time and the media theory of the twentieth century, see Branden Joseph's *My Mind Split Open: Andy Warhol's Exploding Plastic Inevitable.*

would be to enquire about the subject's *degree* of synaesthesia, rather than seeking to distinguish between synaesthetes and non-synaesthetes. He makes a case for synaesthesias in the plural form, citing Sean Day's research, which has found at least sixty-two types of synaesthesia in 871 case reports ranging from the familiar graphemes/colors to the unfamiliar tastes/sounds or vision/temperature combinations.[2] An overly restrictive notion of what constitutes synaesthesia, suggests van Campen, has hampered research into the multimodality of the senses.

The neuroscientists, Richard Cytowic and David Eagleman, come to much the same conclusion in their recent book entitled *Wednesday is Indigo Blue*. Like van Campen they are keen to highlight that, as they put it, "the normal brain is heavily cross-wired. The difference between the synesthetic and non-synesthetic brain is therefore not *whether* there is cross talk, but rather *how much* there is." (p. 205) On the basis of a cross-section of recent research employing various neuroimaging techniques, Cytowic and Eagleman emphasize the degree to which there are a huge variety of types of synaesthesic 'events' that each take place in different ways and, accordingly, leave different traces on neuroimagery. They thus challenge the notion of synaesthesia as a simple cross-modal perceptual experience that implies a standardization of discrete 'modes' of perception.

Both the prevalence of synaesthesia within the general population and the variety of forms that it takes have proven to be far greater than previously thought. Cytowic and Eagleman point in the former case to Julia Simner's ground-breaking research, which, by departing from self-reporting as a means of locating people with synaesthetic capacities, found that one in twenty-three individuals in the general population have synaesthetic capacities, and in the latter to the 152 varieties of synaesthesia catalogued in 2004 by the American Synaesthesia Association.

Ultimately, the prevalence and complexity of the phenomenon suggest the need for what Cytowic and Eagleman consider a paradigm shift in the study of perception away from a modular understanding of brain function. This is a shift that has repercussions for everything from an individual's ability to accurately self-report regarding her own perception on down to the manner in which the 'function' of a neuron is defined.

This nearly revolutionary perspective is shared by van Campen. In arguing that any attempt to define synaesthesia should be driven by the question what the benefits of such an overlap of the senses might be, he forces us all to re-evaluate the manner in which we speak about what and how we perceive. Van Campen's *The Hidden Sense* explicitly considers the implications of aesthetic experience in general and of twentieth-century audio-visual media in particular for the manner

2 Day compiles a list, which is continually updated, of types of synaesthesia encountered. His research has contributed to a better understanding of the vast range of inter- or cross-modal experiences that are possible, thereby suggesting the need for a re-orientation of expectations within synaesthesia research. See Day: http://home.comcast.net/~sean.day/html/types.htm (20.10.2010).

in which we define and distinguish the senses: van Campen goes so far to suggest explicitly that the rhythms perceptible in film viewing or in music, for instance, offer a means by which we may each become aware of this 'hidden sense'. He challenges us to re-educate ourselves to better perceive, for lack of a better word, 'intermodal' sensations, where they have lurked, at the periphery of our ability to name them, by means of aesthetic experience. The experience offered by film viewing could act as a form of 'rehearsal' in which aspects of everyday perception, otherwise hidden from our consciousness, may become more tangible.

But what kind of insight do such filmic 'rhythms' offer us? And where are they to be found?

## Film and Sensory Intermodality

Despite its obviously consisting of nothing more than oscillating areas of light, that are each dark, bright, or in-between, the spatial experience offered by the filmic medium has a striking palpability. For instance, in 1937 Erwin Panofsky remarked on the peculiar capacity of film to, quite literally, *move* the viewer, writing that in a movie theatre:

> [...] the spectator occupies a fixed seat, but only physically, not as the subject of an aesthetic experience. Aesthetically, he is in permanent motion, as his eye identifies itself with the lens of the camera, which permanently shifts in distance and direction. And as movable as the spectator is, as movable is, for the same reason, the space presented to him. Not only bodies move in space, but space itself does, approaching, receding, turning, dissolving and recrystallizing [...].[3]

The spatial fluidity of the spectatorial situation has profound implications for an understanding of the kinaesthetic complexity of the moving image. Filmic space should not be understood merely as a reproduction of architectural space, a documentation of space as a container of objects, in which various activities occur, but instead as a kind of kaleidoscopic space, in which the things of the world are tumbled, lose their shape and reform.

The advent of the cinema in 1895, at roughly the same time as the *fin-de-siècle* fascination with synaesthesia, is significant precisely because even the earliest film viewers understood that it introduced a very different spatial experience from that offered by any other medium. In his various texts exploring the form of engagement with early cinema termed the "cinema of attractions"[4] and the astonishment enjoyed by those viewers, Tom Gunning has noted the degree

3 Kracauer: *From Caligari to Hitler,* p. 6. This passage originally appeared in a somewhat different formulation in Erwin Panofsky. "Style and Medium in the Moving Pictures", p. 124 f.

4 Gunning: *The Cinema of Attractions: Early Film, Its Spectator and the Avant-Garde.*

to which that fascination was predicated on just such an abstract form of involvement. Blending the semantic identification of an undulating object (such as 'waves', 'smoke' or 'the leaves of a tree') with a pure kinetic pleasure that caused that object to dissolve into rhythmic intensity, the 'cinema of attractions' offered both an alternative form of visual pleasure and pointed to film's capacity to offer an aesthetic experience quite separate from the impulse towards semantic cohesion implicit in narrative film.

Film theorist Siegfried Kracauer's description of his own first experience with film is a testament to exactly this kind of fascination. He recalled,

> I was still a young boy when I saw my first film. [rc: he was born in 1889] The impression it made upon me must have been intoxicating, for I there and then determined to commit my experience to writing [...] I immediately put on a shred of paper, *Film as the Discoverer of the Marvels of Everyday Life*, the title read. And I remember, as if it were today, the marvels themselves. What thrilled me so deeply was an ordinary suburban street, filled with lights and shadows, which transfigured it. Several trees stood about, and there was in the foreground a puddle reflecting invisible house façades and a piece of the sky. Then a breeze moved the shadows, and the façades with sky below began to waver. The trembling upper world in the dirty puddle – this image has never left me.[5]

Kracauer's account of his experience has often been viewed as a description of the way in which film offers a very powerful kind of realist representation, an engagement with the world in a naturalistic sense; however, it might be more productively viewed as a description of the type of perceptual *experience* film offers to its viewers. 'The trembling upper world in the dirty puddle' offers a replication, but one that is muddied, obscured, kinetically altered – in a word, dispersed.

Rather than focusing attention on the circumstances of the human figures depicted in film, or the movement of human figures or objects through space, this paper seeks to address the potential for complex spatial engagement that is offered by the moving image – always and everywhere, even when there is no human figure in sight, or indeed even in the case of filmic abstraction. Despite the fact that this space cannot be entered physically, cinematic space is indeed strangely absorbing, calls forth a host of complex responses, and seems to be at the root of visceral effects that can be overwhelming, even while their perceptual source may remain somewhat inscrutable. Such features of filmic experience as these dwell at the heart of contemporary research into the experiences of 'immersion' or 'presence'.[6]

5 Siegfried Kracauer: *Theory of Film*, Preface p. li.

6 There is no consensus at the moment with regards to the meaning of immersion and presence. Within much of the humanities immersion tends to simply be understood as the capacity of electronic media to induce the experience of illusion that is usually based on naturalistic or realistic representations strategies (see for Grau's *Virtual Art* and Griffiths' *Shivers Down your Spine*). However perspectives within natural and social-scientific research on immersion and presence, especially within disciplines such as Communications and Media Studies, stand

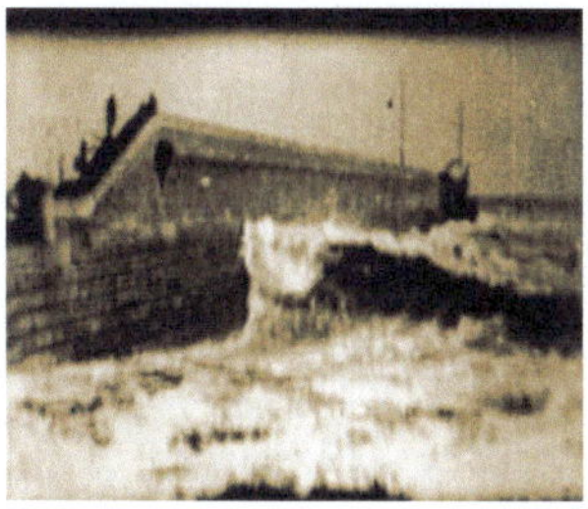

Fig. 1: *Rough Sea at Dover*, Birt Acres, Great Britain, 1895.

Immersion in particular seems to have become something of a contemporary placeholder for a very wide range of experiences of intense sensory engagement with other objects. An investigation of immersion is the topic of my own ongoing research. If, as is generally done, one understands immersion to be virtually synonymous with the simulation of the surroundings in which a viewer might find herself, and that this simulation is minimally or maximally achieved depending on the characteristics and capacities of a given medium, any investigation of the nature of immersion threatens to seem both self-evident and tautological at the same time: immersion is that which effaces the medium itself and is therefore, in essence, not available to analysis. However, by questioning the understanding of immersion as, simply, a contemporary form of illusion brought about by means of realist representational strategies employed by digital media, I seek to better understand the conditions of intense and palpable involvement brought about specifically by the moving image. In the case of the filmic medium it is as obfuscating (as it is tempting) to focus solely on its capacity for realistic reproduction as the basis for immersive experience; abstraction in the moving image – indeed the quality of movement itself – can present an opportunity for immersion, that is not simply based in a realist reproduction of space. Immersion likely has more to do with the reproduction of the conditions of human perception than with the reproduction of exterior space. I am therefore concerned here with the manner in

in contrast. There, in a more differentiated perspective, immersion tends to refer to technologies that induce the experience of presence, while presence in turn is the experiential counterpoint of immersive technology. Within this approach, media are understood to have greater or weaker immersive capacities (ranging from that evoked by virtual reality to the novel, for instance), but all media are capable of invoking the experience of presence. While Lombard and Ditton's popular text, "At the Heart of it All", offers a systemized perspective on presence, as the perceptual illusion of nonmediation in a variety of fields of research (generally remaining within the social and natural sciences) such a systemization can obscure the complexity of the wide range of experiences at issue here. For a more in depth overview of the distinctions between immersion and presence as they are used by a variety of authors within Communications and Media Studies see Giuseppe Riva, Fabrizio Davide, Wijnand A. IJsselsteijn' *Being There.* A similar approach that takes up the manner in which spatial involvement in particular is instilled by various media while helping to escape the media determinism of many discussions of presence and immersion, one that is more relevant for my own position, can be found in Wirth et al, "A Process Model of the Formation of Spatial Presence Experiences".

which synaesthesia, *Einfühlung,* (which I will describe more fully below) and immersion intersect, and how the clear distinctions between subject and object are challenged by such experiences, but also how these kinds of blendings have taken quite different forms at various moments since the advent of the filmic medium.

I focus here on extremely minimal forms of film, all of which are silent and with barely any editing, in order to highlight some basic formal properties of the filmic image, that, while they might be ever present within the image, are oftentimes perceptually 'drowned out' by our attention to other aspects of a film, such as its narrative. I thereby wish to foreground a fundamental distinction between the still and the moving image: by means of the continual movement by which it is produced, the film image has the capacity to oscillate between representation and abstraction.

In an attempt to investigate the relationship between synaesthetic, kinaesthetic and *kinematographic* experience, I would like to propose the following three hypotheses: first, that the astonishment, fascination, engagement, or indeed the 'illusory' qualities of the moving image are not dependent on the naturalistic representational qualities of a given image or image environment; second, that illusion and abstraction are not opposites, but each may contribute in their own fashion to a sense of spatial presence; and third, that experiences such as these are fundamentally linked to the intermodal capacities of the human perceptual apparatus. However, rather than following the line of investigation that emphasizes either the distinction between the illusory and the real, or the oscillation between awareness and abandon, which are otherwise the province of discussions of 'immersion' or 'spatial presence', I propose instead that we re-examine how such a compelling spatial involvement with the world (in both aesthetic and everyday situations) is facilitated by the manner in which perception and imagination are engaged by a particular moving image.

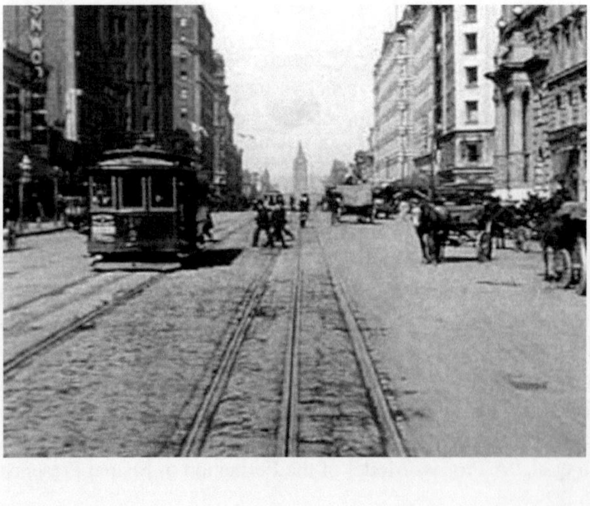

Fig. 2: *A Trip Down Market Street*, 1905.

## Apparatus-based Immersion

A short film from 1905, known as *A Trip Down Market Street,* offers a striking example of how spatial involvement may depart from realistic representation.[7] Filmed with a fixed camera from the front of a cable car, it travels through space towards the vanishing point, which eventually can be seen to be located approximately where the Ferry Building stands in San Francisco. During the (roughly) real-time travels of the camera through this space, humans, animals and vehicles cross the path of the cable-car at random, often seeming to misjudge the speed of that cable-car and just barely move out of its path in time, creating a surprising amount of suspense in a short film that would seem to depict nothing more than an everyday street scene. Such so-called 'phantom rides' as this, shot by a camera positioned in a moving vehicle, whether a car, subway or passenger train, have enjoyed a revival within film and media scholarship in recent years and have been called upon in a wide variety of texts, to act as the precursor to virtual reality, and as the paradigmatic example of the kind of spatial immersion available to viewers of film.

In film historian Raymond Fielding's 1970 account of motion picture realism, for instance, spatial immersion is achieved in an additive fashion, with various apparatuses speaking to each of the senses individually. In fact, for him, the *Trip to the Moon* ride that was introduced at Disneyland in the 1950s was the pinnacle of motion picture realism. Although it did nothing more than offer a phantom ride film depicting fictitious space travel, it did so in a room decorated in the fashion of a 1950s spaceship with everything from gauges, knobs, flashing lights and even intergalactic stewardesses that moved and shook in a manner appropriate to the image on the screen.

In a similar fashion, contemporary notions of immersion have been largely contingent on the attempt to recreate the elements of the external world as completely as possible in order to allow the viewer to be inserted in some fashion into that ever more holistic spatial construct. Formulations such as those by Oliver Grau or Allison Griffith define immersive media and account for their affective power by means of their ability to suggest an all-encompassing, overwhelming space that envelops the viewer or user.[8] However, emphasis within books such as

7 The film is in the public domain. A copy is held by the Prelinger archives and is available at http://www.archive.org/details/TripDownMarketStreetrBeforeTheFire (16.4.2011).

8 In his study, Grau seeks a common, trans-historical impetus behind a variety of significant works within the discipline of art history, such as the frescoes in the Villa dei Misteri in Pompeii, the anamorphic ceiling paintings in the Church of St. Ignatius of Loyola in Rome, in the diorama-like scenes in the chapels at the Sacro Monte of Varallo, or in a variety of Panoramas; he then asserts these works are all *avant-la-lettre* members of the same immersive tradition to which 20th and 21st century analog and digital media aspire. The common immersive impulse is, according to Grau, located in the attempt to envelop for, "these images integrate the observer in a 360° space of illusion, or immersion, with unity of time and place.

these on this particular aspect of immersive experience has been a hindrance to a better understanding not only of the immersion's basis not in an apparatus or indeed even in a particular illusory mode of representation, but rather in perceptual capacities that are quite independent of the audio-visual technology employed. Indeed the spectacular effects evoked by immersive environments may tell us more about the spectacular capacities of spatial perception in general and the human being's complex relationship to movement in space. Nonetheless the notion of realism that is at the heart of the majority of treatments of immersion, whether it be filmic or based upon a more interactive setting such as computer games or virtual reality apparatuses, tends to be based on the additive replication of three dimensional space, or in other words, the claim, that the more spatially detailed a work is, the more immersive it will be.

I would like to question this assumption that involvement and immersion is dependent on the apparative qualities of a given medium by offering some alternative examples of moving images; additionally, the part played by abstraction in spatial involvement deserves a closer examination. Two things are important to note here: one is that the trappings of 'genuine' travel (such as "real" kinaesthetic stimuli) would seem to be unnecessary to produce for the viewer a sense of sharing in the velocity of the moving image. The Austrian Psychologist Ivo Kohler already noted in 1965 that,

> Perception allows itself to be quite easily deluded [...] when stimuli are simulated (as is the case for instance [...] in scenes which have been filmed with a moving camera or a zoom lens, or else when there are pans or tilts in which the background is undifferentiated and so on). [...] That kinaesthetic information regarding the movement of one's own body was utterly lacking in such cases as these was amazingly quite insignificant.[9]

As image media can be described in terms of their intervention in perception, in terms of how they organize and structure perception and cognition, virtual immersive spaces must be classed as extreme variants of image media that, on account of their totality, offer a completely alternative reality." *Virtual Art,* p. 13. In a rather less categorical fashion, Griffiths considers in her book the ways in which media and/or institutions such as IMAX film, museums, and planetariums produce a particular mode of embodied spectatorship, defined by "the complex spatial relations and embodied modes *of* encountering visual spectacle that accompany immersive and interactive spectating." *Shivers Down Your Spine*, p 1. For Griffiths the sensation of immersion is identified by "the sensation of entering a space that immediately identifies itself as somehow separate from the world and that eschews conventional modes of spectatorship in favor of a more bodily participation in the experience, including allowing the spectator to move freely around the viewing space (although this is not a requirement)" p. 2. Despite the difference in the material they examine, each of these authors define immersion as a transhistorical phenomenon that is dependent on the illusory power of large-scale presentations that seek to envelop the viewer by surrounding or spatially overwhelming him or her.

9 Kohler: *Handbuch der Psychologie*, p. 630. Kohler writes, "Die Wahrnehmung [lässt sich] in der Tat leicht täuschen […], wenn Reizänderungen der oben besprochenen universellen Art künstlich geboten werden (z. B. bei Verwendung der Maschen Trommel oder in Filmszenen, die mit fahrender Kamera oder mit Gummilinse aufgenommen wurden, bei Drehungen oder

Furthermore, in Kohler's brief examination of the manner in which the senses somehow cooperate within consciousness to provide information about one's surroundings, he emphasizes that,

> [...] even when the stimuli would seem to be visual, it is difficult to distinguish between the information provided by vision and that which is contributed by the other senses and integrated into a vivid whole.[10]

Kohler emphasizes the extent to which consciousness effects a blending of the senses. The impact of this everyday sensory amodality deserves closer attention as well. This leads me to my next example.

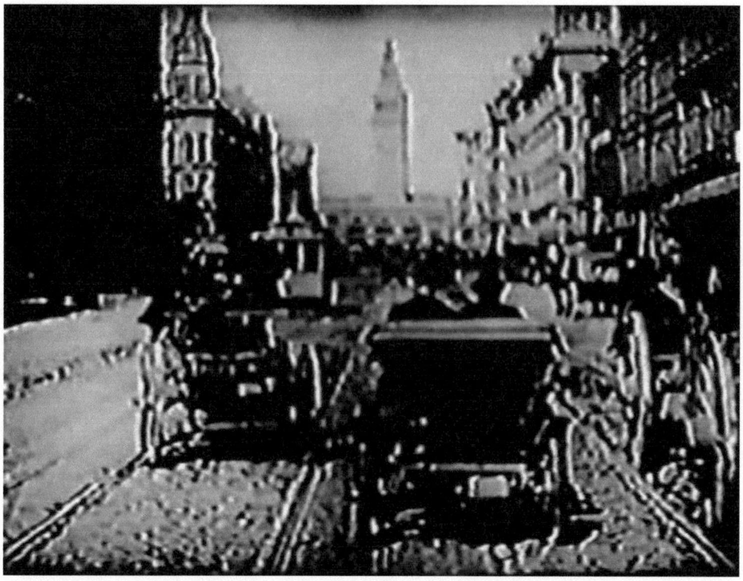

Fig. 3: *Eureka*, Ernie Gehr, 1974.

Schwankungen von vorgezeigten Objekten ohne differenzierten Hintergrund u. dgl. Mehr). Es hängt in solchen Fällen von der Größe des Gesichtswinkels ab, unter dem man diese Dinge sieht, bzw. von der Abwesenheit sonst noch sichtbarerer – und nicht mitveränderter – anderer Objekte, wie lange es dauert, bis man der Täuschung verfällt, dass nicht das Gesehene, sondern man selbst sich bewegt. Das Fehlen kinästhetischer Nachrichten über die eigene Bewegung, macht in solchen Fällen erstaunlich wenig aus." Ivo Kohler, "die Zusammenarbeit der Sinne und das allgemeine Adaptionsproblem." [rc: my translation in body of text].

10 Kohler: *Handbuch der Psychologie*, p. 619.

## The Avant-garde and Immersive Experience

A reworking of my first example, *A Trip Down Market Street,* was provided by Ernie Gehr's *Eureka* from 1974, which slows the original material by half and reprints it. While the chaotic street scene from the original film is no less suspenseful, the wear and tear on the film material itself becomes all the more perceptible to the viewer. Thus despite the fact that the viewer here may be oscillating between surface and depth perception – an oscillation which is usually viewed as the on-off switch of immersive experience – the movement towards the vanishing point is still inevitable, and may not even be key to the spatial experience offered by this film. While the image is ostensibly *less realistic* because it is slowed, it is nonetheless equally spatially engrossing.

On this basis, and this is the second point that I would like to emphasize, I would like to introduce some doubt into the assumption that it is the illusory depiction of three-dimensional space, which creates immersion, or moreover, that the ever greater 'perfection' of that representation, will lead to ever more spatial engagement and immersion. Instead the extent to which our experience of moving images takes on a degree of plasticity would seem to be equally a product of our own perceptual apparatus independent of this particular illusory 'quality'. Indeed an intense spatial involvement can come about independent of three-dimensional 'realism' or indeed, in a strict sense, of representation, and is likely, in general, a product of intermodal perception or amodal representation, and is, more specifically, related to such compound effects as intensity, vitality and rhythm.

## Einfühlung

An intense engagement not only with other humans but with space, form and colours was key to the notion of *Einfühlung,* which circulated with a particular intensity around the turn of the last century. *Einfühlung*, which is usually translated as empathy, was introduced (at least by name) by the Art Historian Robert Vischer, was popularized by Psychologist Theodor Lipps, and found its most detailed application to spatial experience in the writings of the Art Historian, August Schmarsow. *Einfühlung* was described in essence, however, some time before that in 1858 by the philosopher and physician Rudolf Hermann Lotze, who termed it a "Theory of Internal Co-experience." It was in the second of his three-volume work *Microcosm* that he wrote,

> The world becomes alive to us through this power to see in forms the joy and sorrow of the existence that they hide. [...] No form is so unyielding that our imagination cannot project its

> life into it. We do not only partake of the particular senses of being alive which are closest to our own, the joyous flight of the singing bird or the graceful fleetness of the gazelle; we do not pull on the heartstrings of our own spirits in order only to dream of the compact existence of a clam or the pleasurable monotony of its opening and closing, we do not only feel ourselves expand into the tall slim form of a tree, whose finest twigs suggest and animate the pleasurable sensation of sinking and swaying; indeed even the inanimate is the receptacle for these interpretive sensations thus transforming the dead substance and supports of a building into as many limbs of an animate body, as may be transferred to us in the form of internal tension.[11]

Lotze emphasized the significance of the experience of gravity upon our own bodies for our perception of other phenomena, indeed the significance that our recollection of the sensations of embodied experience have always and everywhere. The act of projection implied here had broad implications for aesthetic experience in general, and, in particular, for the discussion of the manner in which we perceive the formal qualities of our surroundings.

While *Einfühlung* has often carried mystical connotations (particularly in its earliest mention – as a verb in the writings of Herder and Novalis), I wish to emphasize the widespread interest that a broad variety of practitioners showed in the term, many of whom were particularly keen to debunk these mystical connotations and to investigate instead a possible psychological basis for such experience. Moreover these historical debates are useful in that they describe little discussed forms of engagement with aesthetic objects that have many similarities with the notions of immersion and presence current today. Indeed, the search for an adequate form to describe the aesthetic experience of space implied by architecture was of special interest in discussions of *Einfühlung*. Art Historian Harry Mallgrave describes Lotze's treatment of this phenomenon as follows:

> The pleasure of symmetry is due not so much to the regularity or proportion of members as to the pleasure we take in emulating this movement. This "remembrance" of the concrete world, the self-experience of our own physical condition, altogether pervades our spatial viewing. [And, continuing, he quotes Lotze] 'For all spatial forms affect us aesthetically only insofar as they are symbols of a weal or woe personally experienced by us.'[12]

11 Rudolf Lotze: *Mikrokosmos*, p. 201–202: "Kein Gestalt ist so spröde, in welche hinein nicht unsere Phantasie sich mitlebend zu versetzen wüsste .... Nicht allein in die eigentümlichen Lebensgefühle dessen dringen wir ein, was an Art und Wesen uns nahe steht, in den fröhlichen Flug des singenden Vogels oder die zierliche Beweglichkeit der Gaselle; wir ziehen nicht nur die Fühlfäden unseres Geistes auf das Kleinste zusammen, um das engbegrenzte Dasein eines Muscheltieres mit zu träumen und den einförmigen Genuss seiner Öffnungen und Schliessungen, wir dehnen uns nicht nur mitschwellend in die schlanken Formen des Baumes aus, dessen feine Zweige die Lust anmutigen Beugens und Schwebens beseelt; vielmehr selbst auf das Unbelebte tragen wir diese andeutenden Gefühle über und verwandeln durch sie die toten Lasten uns Stützen der Gebäude zu ebenso vielen gliedern eines lebendigen Leibes, dessen innere Spannungen in uns übergeben." The English translation here is drawn from a quotation in Mallgrave/Ikonomou: *Empathy, Form and Space*.

12 Mallgrave/Ikonomou: *Empathy, Form, and Space,* p. 20 f. Quoted from Hermann Lotze, *Geschichte der Ästhetik in Deutschland*, p. 80. "Und so wirken denn alle räumlichen Gebilde

One aspect of the kind of holistic engagement with objects and environments external to oneself at the heart of empathetic response deserves to be emphasized in particular. The role played by a kind of spatial memory that appears explicitly in Malgrave's account of Lotze's position is key to spatial engagement with audio-visual media.

## Vitality Affects

Contemporary perspectives on synaesthesia as a form of intermodal perception that is present to some degree in all humans have an important precursor. In order to better elucidate the implications of the 'rhythm' of the filmic image (as it was brought to bear by van Campen) I would like to draw on the work of the psychologist Daniel Stern's notion of 'vitality affects'. In his studies of pre-verbal infants, published in 1985 under the title, *The Interpersonal World of the Infant,* Stern established that babies are capable of transposing information that is perceived in one particular sensory mode into another. This doesn't mean that they translate, for instance 'hearing' into 'seeing', but rather that, percepts are encoded into what Stern calls "amodal representations," which may be recognized in any sensory modality. He writes: "These abstract representations that the infant experiences are not sights and sounds and touches and nameable objects, but rather shapes, intensities, and temporal patterns – the more 'global' qualities of experience."[13]

Such "amodal representations" as these, are given the name 'vitality affects'. These are affects, which are both experienced in one's own body, as well as being recognized in the bodies of others. These elusive qualities are better captured by dynamic, kinetic terms, such as (to quote Stern) "surging," "fading away," "fleeting," "explosive," "crescendo," "decrescendo," "bursting," "drawn out," and so on, than by the more familiar categorical affects that were already set out by Charles Darwin (angry, sad, happy and so on). Moreover they are well suited to describing the states of other human beings. Stern writes,

> Like dance for the adult, the social world experienced by the infant is primarily one of vitality affects before it is a world of formal acts. It is also analogous to the physical world of amodal perception, which is primarily one of abstract qualities of shape, number, intensity level, and so on, not a world of things seen, heard, or touched.[14]

ästhetisch auf uns, sofern sie Symbole eines von uns erlebbaren eigenthümlichen Wohls oder Wehes sind."

13 Stern: *The Interpersonal World of the Infant: A View from Psychoanalysis and Developmental Psychology*, p. 51.

14 Ibid., p. 57.

Thus Stern describes a perceptual capacity that has much more to do with qualitative, nearly atmospheric aspects of perception, than with concrete actions and events in a narrative sense. These are capacities, which we have all experienced in the earliest phases of our development, but are no longer generally a part of the linguistic repertoire that we employ when we attempt to describe things that leave an impression upon us.

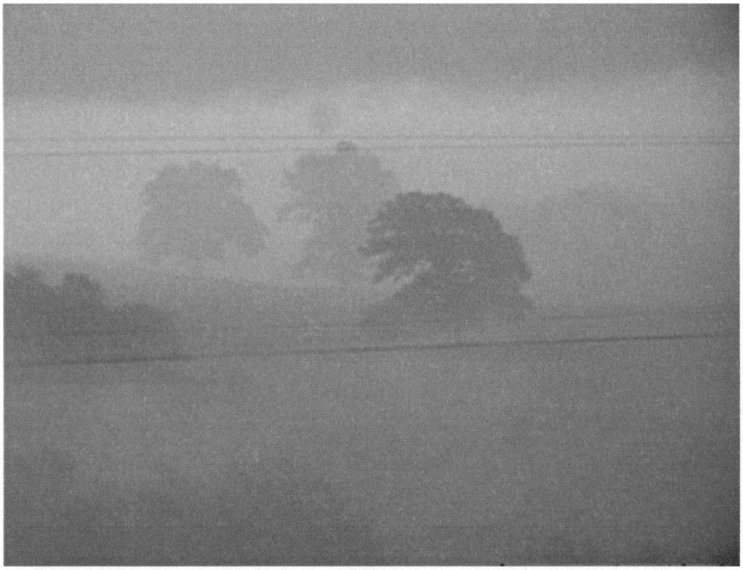

Fig. 4: *Fog Line*, Larry Gottheim, 1970.

Finally, and to close, I would like to consider one last example, Larry Gottheim's film *Fog Line* from 1970. Precisely the kind of perception that is generally neglected in our attempt to account for affect, was investigated by the filmic avant-garde, particularly in the category of film designated 'the structural film' (a category to which Ernie Gehr's *Eureka* also belongs). As it documents the uncovering of a landscape that is initially wholly obscured by fog it hovers between representation and abstraction. Gottheim's film, like several others of its time, seek to emphasize the interstitial realms of perception, where objects dissolve and reform, oscillating between representation and rhythm, formal organization and pure intensity.

If we take seriously Cretien van Campen's call to both re-tune our senses and re-consider what we say about what we experience, such films as these call an uncomplicated description of the manner in which spatial perception is processed, into question. They should encourage us to look farther than the most obvious explanation for our own fascination with the moving image, and reconfigure research into the manner in which representation and abstraction interact in our experience of space. Even the blockbusters of the last ten years are generally dealt with as a form of aesthetic experience through which the viewer is catapulted, where visceral reaction is paramount and self-determination under-examined. But the forms of involvement available to us as viewers (and users of audio visual media) point to the fact that there are a variety of ways that we can engage with moving images spatially, in a far more self-determined fashion.

## References

Cytowic, Richard E. / David M. Eagleman: *Wednesday is Indigo Blue: Discovering the Brain of Synesthesia,* Cambridge/London (MIT Press) 2009.

Fielding Raymond: "Hale's Tours: Ultrarealism in the Pre-1910 Motion Picture", in: *Cinema Journal*, Vol. 10 (1970) 1, pp. 34–47.

Gunning, Tom: "The Cinema of Attractions: Early Film, Its Spectator and the Avant-Garde", in: *Wide Angle*, 8 (1986) 3/4, p. 63–70.

Griffith, Allison: *Shivers Down Your Spine: Cinemas, Museums, and the Immersive View.* New York (Columbia University Press), 2008.

Grau, Oliver: *Virtual Art: From Illusion to Immersion.* Cambridge (MIT Press), 2003.

Joseph, Branden: "'My Mind Split Open': Andy Warhol's Exploding Plastic Inevitable", in: *Grey Room*, 8 (2002), pp. 80–107.

Kohler, Ivo: *Handbuch der Psychologie in 12 Bänden, vol. 1. Allgemeine Psychologie. Der Aufbau des Erkennens, Wahrnehmung und Bewusstsein*, ed. by W. Metzger, Göttingen (Verlag für Psychologie) 1965.

Kracauer, Siegfried: *From Caligari to Hitler* (1947), Princeton (Princeton University Press) 1974.

Kracauer, Siegfried: *Theory of Film: The Redemption of Physical Reality* (1960), Princeton (Princeton University Press) 1997.

Lombard, Matthew / Theresa Ditton: "At the Heart of It All: The Concept of Presence", in: *Journal of Computer-Mediated Communication,* 3 (1997) 2.

Lotze, Rudolf Hermann: *Mikrokosmus. Ideen zur Naturgeschichte und Geschichte der Menschheit* (1858) Vol. 2, Leipzig (S. Hirzel Verlag) 1885.

Manovich, Lev: *The Language of New Media*, Cambridge (MIT Press) 2001.

Mallgrave, Harry Francis / Eleftherios Ikonomou: "Introduction", in: *Empathy, Form, and Space: Problems in German Aesthetics, 1873–1893,* ed. Harry F. Mallgrave, translated by Harry Mallgrave / Eleftherios Ikonomou, Santa Monica (Getty Center Publication) 1994.

Panofsky, Erwin: "Style and Medium in the Moving Pictures", *transition,* 26 (1937), pp. 124–125.

Giuseppe Riva / Fabrizio Davide / Wijnand A. IJsselsteijn (eds.): *Being There: Concepts, effects and measurement of user presence in synthetic environments,* Amsterdam (Ios Press) 2003.

Simner, Julia / Catherine Mulvenna / Noam Sagiv / Elias Tsakanikos / Sarah A. Witherby / Christine Fraser / Kirsten Scott / Jamie Ward: "Synaesthesia: The prevalence of atypical cross-modal experiences", in: *Perception,* 35 (2006) 8, pp. 1024–1033.

Stern, Daniel N.: *The Interpersonal World of the Infant: A View from Psychoanalysis and Developmental Psychology,* New York (Basic Books) 1985.

van Campen, Cretien: *The Hidden Sense: Synesthesia in Art and Science*, Cambridge and London (MIT Press) 2008.

Wirth, Werner et al.: "A Process Model of the Formation of Spatial Presence Experiences", in: *Media Psychology,* 9 (2007), pp. 493–525.

## List of Illustrations

Fig. 1: *Rough Sea at Dover*, directed by Birt Acres and Robert W. Paul, 39", Great Britain, 1895.

Fig. 2 *A Trip Down Market Street*, produced by Miles Brothers, 13'52" USA, 1905; Prelinger archives collection.

Fig. 3: *Eureka*, directed by Ernie Gehr 30', USA, 1974.

Fig. 4: *Fog Line*, directed by Larry Gottheim, 11', Canada, 1970.

# Experiencing the Urban Environment in its Atmospheric Characters

HEINZ PAETZOLD

This paper engages in developing a theoretical frame to analyze the experience of urban sites in their atmospheric characters. My thesis is that only through a specific kinesthetic bodily locomotion we are enabled to fully experience urban atmospheres. Introducing the concept of atmosphere seems to be necessary once we want to reach beyond Le Corbusier's *functionalism*. This kind of urbanism favored the visual over the smell, the hearing, and the touch. There are some points of similarity between the phenomenon of atmospheric awareness and synaesthesia. Launching these concepts into the contemporary urbanism implies to renew the humanistic ideals of authors like Lewis Mumford who described the walk through the medieval city in terms of a "dilation of the senses."[1] Henri Lefebvre on his part was calling for an *urban revolution* in order to overcome consumerism and exclusionism.

## I

In recent discussions about architecture the notion of *atmosphere* has played an increasingly important role. Theoreticians like Gernot Böhme use this term in order to cope with the features of contemporary architecture.[2] Another author, Jürgen Hasse, explicitly applies this notion in order to theorize the urban environment from the viewpoint of the social geographer. In the center is the aspect of living in the city and using the urban habitat.[3] In both these strands of theory the notion of atmosphere is developed to refer to the New Phenomenology of Hermann Schmitz. His *phenomenology of felt corporality* ('Leibphänomenologie'), which is close to the philosophy of Merleau-Ponty, is centered on the bodily awarenesses. Schmitz' suggestions, which however, are to be worked through and refined for them to fit into a contemporary theory.

1 Mumford: *The City in History*, p. 343.
2 Böhme: *Atmosphäre. Essays zur neuen Ästhetik.*
3 Hasse (ed.): "Stadt und Atmosphäre".

In the following part of my paper I would like to look at the outcomes of these theories. Atmosphere is defined as something *"indeterminately outpoured into the extensiveness"* ('unbestimmt in die Weite ergossen').[4] The atmosphere has the quality of a *feeling* (Gefühl) but feeling is not localized in the inward world. *"Feelings are not private states of psychic inner worlds but spatially extensive atmospheres"* ("Gefühle" sind "nicht private Zustände seelischer Innenwelten, sondern räumlich ausgedehnte Atmosphären").[5] As an entity, atmosphere, ontologically, is beyond (and before) the split of 'ego' and 'world', subject and object. According to Schmitz, feeling covers both the awareness of a feeling in the sense of atmosphere as well as the affectively being struck by the atmosphere.[6]

Further specifics are relevant in this context. According to Hasse we have to distinguish *atmosphere* as a spatial entity from the *tuned space*. Where is the difference? The German phenomenologist Elisabeth Ströker has introduced the latter notion. She differentiated the *tuned space* ('gestimmter Raum') from the *space of the everyday*, which she labeled *space of acting* ('Aktionsraum') and against the *geometrical space* derived from the *space of intuition* ('Anschauungsraum').[7] The tuned space is without address, orientation, and theme. The tuned space has no clear *aboutness* to refer to Arthur C. Danto. Atmosphere, on the contrary, is oriented towards a specific person, a specific object, a specific event or a number of them. The tuning comes to the fore in the case in which the atmospheric feeling has become embodied in the individual consciousness. Then, in Heidegger's sense, it undercoats the whole of my being-in-the-world.[8]

Atmospheres cannot be divided. They remain persistently present, as Hubertus Tellenbach already noticed in his *Geschmack und Atmosphäre* (1968). Atmospheres are not localizable in the way things are. They occupy no secluded spot within the expanded wide spread space. According to Böhme, the atmosphere is ontologically positioned in the gap or the interstice between subject and object.[9] This means that atmospheres come into existence only by being noticed or realized by a perceiving subjectivity. In a way, the subjectivity constitutes them. But in reality, they are initiated by something beyond the reach of a subject. Something objective – medium, impulsion ('Anregungszustand') – must be there, which is stimulating the specific character of the atmosphere.

4 Böhme: *Architektur*, p. 128 and with reference to Schmitz: *Der Gefühlsraum*, §149.

5 Hasse: *Die Stadt als Raum der Atmosphären,* p. 106 with reference to Schmitz: *Gefühle als Atmosphären und das affektive Betroffensein*, pp. 33–56.

6 Hasse: *Die Stadt als Raum der Atmosphären,* p. 106. With reference to Schmitz: *Gefühle als Atmosphären und das affektive Betroffensein*, p. 48.

7 Compare Ströker: *Philosophische Untersuchungen zum Raum* and my analysis in: *Ästhetik der neueren Moderne*, pp. 29–35.

8 Hasse: *Die Stadt als Raum der Atmosphären*, pp. 107–108.

9 Böhme: *Aisthetik*, pp. 54–55. Hasse, "Stadt als Raum der Atmosphären", p. 109.

In theories mentioned so far, there are no reflections on the mental attitude and the bodily posture, which is supportive for experiencing the atmosphere of urban spots. My thesis is that the kinaesthetic activity of *strolling* is the condition of the possibility of experiencing the urban sites in their peculiar atmospheric character. In the next paragraph of my paper I shall concentrate for a moment on city strolling or more precisely on *flânerie*.

## II

Undoubtedly flânerie belongs to the very characteristics of modern urban culture. Originated in $19^{th}$ century Paris, the culture of flânerie had its early heyday in the span first between the Revolution of 1830 and the rise of department stores, and then during the construction of Haussmann's grand boulevards in the 1850's and 1860's. This first glory of flânerie was closely related to the erection of arcades.

Flânerie and the subjectivity performing it, the flâneur or the flâneuse, are translatable into foreign languages only with some difficulties. The English *strolling* and *stroller* match probably at best the semantics of the French original. Anyway, the German word *Stadtspaziergang* ('city walk') is an insipid reverberation. The same goes for *Stadtbummel* ('window-shopping') as translation of flânerie. Nevertheless, the phenomenon of flânerie can be detached from its Parisian origin.

Which kind of locomotion, then, is flânerie? Basically, it is an aimless roaming in the labyrinth of the big city. Usually flânerie begins as a simple loitering or sauntering in the city. The steady rhythm of our feet provides the necessary confidence to our forward bodily movement. One does not stroll, though, if one is in a hurry in order to get the train, the bus or the tram. Instead of walking in an upright position of the body, one's head and shoulders are bent forward and the arms are going up and down.

Paradoxically, strolling is highly intentional and at the same time inscribed into a wider structure of non-intentionality. In a specific way strolling is aimless. To give oneself over in order to be propelled by the urban crowds belongs to the very delightful experiences during strolling. The swinging steps create a rhythm of steadiness. Once this basically non-intentional state is reached, the intentionality, the attentive observation of the scene, can do its work. Steep stairs and heavily ascending streets are obstacles to flânerie. They are, as it were, brakes since one has to concentrate on the traits of the area.

Strolling is, however, no Zen of walking. Strolling lacks strong inwardness. The Buddhist teacher Thich Nhat Hanh argues that to become calm while walking is reached through attentive breathing in and breathing out.[10] The accent here is on the subjectively lived experience of breathing. Flânerie, on the contrary, is always turned towards the social world and towards the architectonic scene. Flânerie, therefore, can take the form of a bath in the crowd as Franz Hessel has described it. Looking at the others as well as been looked at by them borders on delight, but probably only on the border. Since the momentum of walking demands a continual movement further. Contrary to Hessel, Benjamin has described his own strolling as being compelled, and even as being driven. Virginia Woolf has attributed to flânerie the capacity to leave behind one's established identity and submerge into the democratic anonymity of city ramblers. Being bathed in the crowd, being driven and undergoing a metamorphosis of one's own identity are the outstanding characteristics of flânerie in the big city of modernity. It is important to keep all aspects in mind, although they might contradict each other.

Benjamin, Hessel and Virginia Woolf have rightly emphasized that flânerie is performed by isolated individuals. "Flânerie," writes a sociologist of our time, "is the sociability of 'Ones' which emphasizes and preserves the separateness of the individual." And he continues by pointing to the social and cultural context of 19th century flânerie:

> [...] it is a social practice of a generalized democratic individualism which was new to nineteenth-century Europeans. It represents the fascination with anonymity and guardedness which also manifests itself in the middle-class emphasis placed on public modesty.[11]

In contrast to the Sunday afternoon dietetic stroll, which is by twos and in contrast to the city stroll in the evening or the Italian corso, which are group events, flânerie is still today the activity of solitary individuals. The flânerie by twos succeeds most easily in foreign cities, the reason being that the two are completely devoted to viewing, hearing and smelling in order to grasp the atmosphere of the place, the architectonic scene and the doings of the crowds on the streets and on the squares.

There is no doubt that each bigger city has an atmosphere of its own, which is caused by the enactment of the everyday. The rhythm is one indicator of the atmosphere. The rhythm in New York is different than in Paris, Singapore, Tokyo or Rome. Rome is hectic whereas the crowds in New York are moving forward like a torrent of lava. In Singapore, one strolls in an unburdened leisurely slowness. In Tokyo, flânerie has something of the smooth crowding of New York, however more specified through the peculiarities of the urban areas, for example Ginza in contrast to Ueno. Generally speaking, it remains true that the rhythm of cities is modified from quarter to quarter without losing, as it were, the thorough bass of the city in question.

10 Thich: *Het is een wonder op aarde te lopen*, pp. 23–35.

11 Shields: *Fancy footwork*, pp. 63–64.

The rhythm of movement has an impact upon the experience of the atmosphere. It is difficult to determine the atmosphere of a whole city. For that reason I prefer to relate the atmospheric to specific spots and places of a city: square, street, railway-station, underground-station, market place, mall, riverside, lakeside or canal side.

## III

In order to come closer to my theme of atmospheres in the city, I need to introduce a distinction which is not recognized enough in most of other theories. We have to distinguish between the atmosphere experienced by meeting with a group or in a small number of people and the atmosphere experienced while strolling the city. In the first case I experience the atmosphere, which is produced by the specific gathering of people in a room. I read, in the way people are looking around and looking at me, whether there is a relaxed, stressed and depressed or a cheerful and cozy atmosphere. Here the mode of interactivity between people has some spatial vibrancy. Primarily the people in the room color the atmosphere, which is, of course, also tinged by the dyes at the walls, the furniture, the size of the room and the acoustics.

The second case is concerning the urban environment. Here the architecture of the houses, the design of the street furniture, the design of the square, the pavement of the ground, the acoustics, the light (night, morning dawn, bright noon), and the activities performed by the people, all these elements are main factors for creating the atmosphere of a city spot. My loneliness or being surrounded by a crowd are secondary features.

Gernot Böhme's distinction between *ingression* and *discrepancy* is on a different level. This distinction deals with how I experience an atmosphere. If I am won over and swept away through the atmosphere, say, by the cheerful atmosphere of a gathering group, Böhme labels it ingression. If my temper is in sharp contrast to the atmosphere around me, if I am mourning on a lovely summer day, Böhme calls it discrepancy.[12]

The experience of the atmospheric characters of urban spots has some similarities with the experience of a stage. I can be deeply moved by what is going on before my eyes. I can keep a distance to it. The atmosphere of a square might be experienced as frightening, as wideness, as passageway, as locality of common activities or as an aesthetically inspiring area.[13] Geographers have shown that such a typology of atmospheric characters can be used as a base for empirical research.

12 Böhme: *Aisthetik*, pp. 46–50.
13 Kazig: *Typische Atmosphären städtischer Plätze*, pp. 153–159.

## IV

What I would like to stress is the fact that the experience of the atmosphere at urban spots is made immediately. It happens before any dissecting analysis. Atmospheres take possession of us without reasoning. We experience the atmosphere first and then concentrate on the details of the scene. Atmospheres are experienced as single whole entities. Flânerie is the condition of the possibility of becoming aware of the atmosphere of an urban square, an urban riverside or a train-station. It is not true that I first have amorphous sensations and that they are synthesized through the activity of my intellect. On the contrary, first comes the bodily awareness of the whole atmosphere, and only then follows the analysis of the details.

Atmospheres of cities are not disclosed by one sense only. They are all involved. It may be better to say that the senses are fusing. Sometimes the smell is deeply impressed in memory, as is the case with railway stations and buildings in cities of the former DDR. For that reason, one might say, that atmospheres are close to synesthesia.

## V

Now comes the last step of my analysis. Any phenomenology of culture, today, has to apply the *linguistic turn* or the *symbolic turn* to philosophy. Michel de Certeau has worked through Roland Barthes' intuition of a *semiology of the city* at an important section, which is relevant to the context of my paper. De Certeau's essay *The Walking in the City*[14] is of methodological interest to the phenomenology of the culture of flânerie for two reasons:

First. Many things de Certeau has to say about the urbanism of architects and city planners do not give evidence of a good expert knowledge. He simply overlooks the fact that we find already fruitful approaches to a semiology of the city with Ildefonso Cerdà, the founder of modern urbanism. Cerdà scrutinizes the magic-poetic power of street names and the poetics of urban regions, in order to better understand the growth process of cities. De Certeau tends to identify urbanism simply with *functionalism*. However, it also covers a fruitful idea. De Certeau understands his "rhetoric of walking" as the "consequence" or the "reciprocal" of Michel Foucault's analysis of "the structures of power." The functionalist city, then, provides that frame of power, within which the "rhetoric of

14 De Certeau: *The Practice of Everyday Life*, pp. 91–110.

walking" operates and which is critically challenged, contested and thwarted.[15] Seen from a methodological point of view, de Certeau mediates the urbanistic and architectonic discourse with the urban sociologist and the cultural studies discourses.

Second – and it is as important as the first reason – de Certeau's approach sheds a new light on the phenomenology of strolling. The walking in the city space, and nota bene in the literal sense of the bodily *style* of stepping with a specific kinaesthetics of a concrete individual,[16] is theorized analytically with the conceptual equipment of post-structuralist theory. Strolling is approached from the perspective of a theory of symbols. Any philosophy of culture, today, must bring together both these poles, the phenomenological and the semiological.

Let us look a bit closer at de Certeau's approach. For de Certeau the acts and ways of *walking* in the city have their equivalent in the *utterance of statements*. Each linguistic utterance implies the acceptance and the appropriation of language as a system, that is language in the sense of *langue* (de Saussure). Correspondingly, each act of walking presupposes the appropriation of the topographical system of the given city. Furthermore, each pedestrian realizes a locus, a place, just as each *speech act* (Searle) implies the transformation of *langue* into *parole* (de Saussure). Eventually, the illocutionary aspect of the speech act, that is the socially binding force of speech acts, has its equivalent in the pragmatic constitution of relationships between topographic positions. Therefore, walking is the "space of enunciation."[17] The stress here is on the notion of space.

In the act of walking the individual realizes specific possibilities of the urban topography – for example the crossing of a square, the using of back roads instead of main streets – and gives them an *appearance*. While strolling, one can also invent, as it were, new possibilities of the urban space. This occurs if one takes a roundabout way or if one improvises new routes. In these cases one has to say that the *spatial signifier* is transformed into something other than its literal meaning.[18]

De Certeau's productive idea is that one can understand the functionalist concept of the city as a norm, which has a fixed and definitive *signified*. The factual "walking of passers-by" can be read as a "stylistic figure" which is opposed to the functionalist norm. Due to their metaphoricity "stylistic figures" transcend the norm that is embodied in the signified. In other words, the factual walking of people plays with the rules of signification prefigured by the urbanistic system. It produces within them "shadows" and "ambiguities."[19]

This can be explained by an example. The *synecdoche* is the rhetoric figure by which the part represents the whole, for example *head* instead of *man*. We

15 Ibid., pp. 99, 100; p. 96.
16 Ibid., p. 97.
17 Ibid., pp. 91–98.
18 Ibid., p. 98.
19 Ibid., p. 101.

say: "There is a 'bright head' behind," if we literally mean to say: "There is a 'bright man' behind." Following these thoughts I suggest to interpret the style of walking of the classic flâneur in the Parisian arcade insofar, in conformity with the synecdoche as he takes the realm of the arcade, which is a section of the city, for the whole of the city. The ostentatious slowing down of the speed of walking, which characterized the flâneur, as well as the joy of watching, are just some of the constitutive elements of the rhetorical synecdoche of the flâneur.

For de Certeau *synecdoche* and *asyndeton* constitute a pair. The asyndeton omits adverbs, conjunctions and copula (On your mark, get set, go!). The asyndeton spares only relicts of the spatial continuum. De Certeau attributes the mythical to the asyndeton, since both know of eminent places, for instance the holy in contrast to the profane.[20]

The rhetoric of walking, says de Certeau, articulates on top of the "forbidden" or "permitted" "literal meaning" of urban spaces a "second, poetic geography."[21] Impressively, some reflections of Walter Benjamin become analytically precise and sharp if we take the remodeling of de Certeau as a stimulating translation. Benjamin's ideas are brought to the point. Benjamin was already dealing with the magic of street names. Living for more than 20 years in the Netherlands, for me the Dutch way, in order to classify city areas in which statesmen or naval heroes are used as list of names for streets, still bears an aura of magic. The area of the city where I used to live in Amsterdam was named *Staatsliedenbuurt*, which means area of statesmen. I dwelled in the *Van der Hoopstraat*, not meaning: The Street of Hope, but alluding to the statesman Van der Hoop. The Dutch lawyer, public prosecutor and minister Joan Cornelis van der Hoop (1742–1825) who served his country under different political regimes is the point of reference. The anarchistic party settled in the Staatsliedenbuurt called itself ironically *Staatsverlangen*, which means: *desire for state*.

According to de Certeau, in such "symbolizing kernels" "three distinct (but connected) functions of relations between spatial and signifying practices" are included: "the believable," "the memorable" and the "primitive." The conclusion is: "these three symbolic mechanisms organize the topoi of a discourse on/of the city (legend, memory, and dream) in a way that [...] eludes urbanistic systematicity."[22] In other words, the symbolic of street names and names of areas make the places of a city inhabitable. They 'recall' or 'suggest' 'phantoms' concealed in the 'gestures' and in the style of walking of the people. They denominate a history. It is unnecessary to underscore that a division of city regions according to numbers would destroy all the poetics of the urban spaces even if such division would advance the urban administration.

De Certeau's rhetoric of walking, of which I presented a few aspects, derives from the presupposition that *discourse* – in accordance with Benveniste

20 Ibid., p. 101–102.
21 Ibid., p. 105.
22 Ibid., p. 105.

"the language," in which language is "as it is assumed by the person speaking and in the condition of intersubjectivity" – and *dream* resemble each other. Language and dream are based on the same convention of "stylistic procedures," respectively the same modes of symbolization. The most important ones are "displacement" and "condensation." Since language and walking correspond to each other, the extension of language through dream applies as well. Discourse, dream and walking share a comparable "register of expression." To summarize, I would say that the *rhetoric of walking* by de Certeau has a bearing for urban theory because is gives evidence of the anarchistic drift behind strolling. Furthermore, a *rhetoric* or a *poetics of walking* is relevant because it testifies that each cultural activity, among them walking is coded and recoded. This is, of course, a Foucaultian idea. The consequence of what I said is that atmospheres are symbolically coded. But how does this happen?

## VI

I had to stay a little longer with de Certeau's theorizing because from this discourse, a line from the more classical theory of symbols of Ernst Cassirer to our own times can be drawn. I would suggest relating Cassirer's concept of symbolic pregnance to the atmospheric and to synaesthesia. Symbolic pregnance and atmosphere are, as it were, at the same epistemic level. Cassirer thought that symbolic pregnance is the first grasp of a phenomenon in its complexity, which asks for further clarification and refinement by working through the various symbolic forms. Symbolic pregnance has a paradoxical structure. Logic and reason, which usually give a stable structure to our experiences, do not play the main role. Nevertheless, if a phenomenon is identified as symbolically pregnant then it has some form of perceptive identification. It can be refined in ongoing processes of symbolic activities. "The now is filled and saturated with the future: *praegnans futuri*, as Leibniz called it." I remind the reader of the definition that Cassirer gave to the concept of symbolic pregnance: "By symbolic pregnance we mean the way by which a perception as a sensory experience contains at the same time a certain non-intuitive meaning which it immediately and concretely represents."[24] This background allows us to continue. The reference to Heinz Werner phenomena of synaesthesia "reveals," as Cassirer literally says, "a fundamental behavior and character of the perceptive consciousness."[25] One does not go too far if one argues that for Cassirer the basic symbolic synthesis is not coming into existence through logical reasoning. Rather the bodily senses, which are in interaction with

24 Cassirer: *The Philosophy of Symbolic Forms. Volume 3,* p. 202.
25 Ibid., p. 34.

the environment, are the starting point of all finer cultural activities. Mumford on his part argues that only the lived putting in action of all senses in the urban realm gives some guarantee for all cultural refinements.

If we follow the theory of Richard E. Cytowic, therefore we can interpret the phenomenon of synaesthesia as "a result of a fundamentally mammalian process in which the cortex briefly ceases to function in the modern manner, permitting the senses to fuse, or, rather, we should say, perceive fusion that may be there all along but that never arises to consciousness."[26] If we concede that synaesthesia and atmosphere are parallel phenomena, we are probably able to understand some aspects of atmospheric perception. With regards to synaesthesia, I mention the aspects of being involuntary but elicited (1), their being projected outside of the mind (2), their being durable, discrete, and generic (3), their being memorable (4) and their being emotional and noëtic (5).[27] My hypothesis, is that the criteria that apply to synaesthesia are also valid for the atmospheric. There seems to be only one difference. Few and far between persons are synaesthetes in a strict sense, either one person per 300,000 (Cytowic) or one person per 100.000 people (Gage).[28] Contrary to that restriction in number with regards to synaesthesia, most people can experience urban sites in their atmospheric character.

To conclude I would like to argue that taking strolling and the atmospheres seriously would amount to demand an urbanism of possibly great variety of urban scenes. Uniformity maims and kills.

In the second paragraph of this text I used material, which had earlier been published in the essay: *Rethinking Key-words of Modern Urban Culture: Flânerie and the City as Theater*, in: Madalina Diaconu Eva Heuberger Ruth Mateus-Berr Lukas Marcel Vosicki (eds.): *Senses and the City. An interdisciplinary approach to urban sensescapes*. Wien Berlin (LIT) 2011, pp. 33–46.

## References

Böhme, Gernot: *Atmosphäre. Essays zur neuen Ästhetik*, Frankfurt am Main (Suhrkamp) 1995.

Böhme, Gernot: *Aisthetik. Vorlesungen über Ästhetik als allgemeine Wahrnehmungslehre*, München (Wilhelm Fink) 2001.

Böhme, Gernot: *Architektur und Atmosphäre,* München (Wilhelm Fink) 2006.

26 Cytowic: *Synesthesia,* p. 176.

27 Cytowic: *The Man Who Tasted Shapes,* pp. 73–79.

28 Cytowic: *Synesthesia,* p. 64. Gage: *Synesthesia,* pp. 350–351.

Cassirer, Ernst: *The Philosophy of Symbolic Forms. Volume 3: The Phenomenology of Knowledge,* translated by Ralph Manheim, New Haven / London (Yale University Press) 1985.

De Certeau, Michel: *The Practice of Everyday Life,* Berkeley, Los Angeles, London (University of California Press) 1984.

Cytowic, Richard E.: *Synesthesia. A Union of the Senses,* New York (Springer) 1989.

Cytowic, Richard E.: *The Man Who Tasted Shapes. A Bizarre Medical Mystery Offers Revolutionary Insights into Emotions, Reasoning, and Consciousness,* London (Abacus) 1997.

Gage, John: "Synesthesia", in: Michael Kelly (ed.): *Encyclopedia of Aesthetics,* Vol. 4, New York Oxford (Oxford University Press) 1998, pp. 348–351.

Hasse, Jürgen: "Die Stadt als Raum der Atmosphären. Zur Differenzierung von Atmosphären und Stimmungen", in: Jürgen Hasse (ed.): *Die alte Stadt,* 35 (2008) 2, pp. 103–116.

Kazig, Rainer: "Typische Atmosphären städtischer Plätze", in: Jürgen Hasse (ed.): *Stadt und Atmosmphäre*, pp. 147–160.

Lewis Mumford: *The City in History. Its Origins, its Transformations and its Prospects,* London/New York/Victoria/Markham/Auckland (Penguin) 1991.

Heinz Paetzold: *Ästhetik der neueren Moderne. Sinnlichkeit und Reflexion in der konzeptionellen Kunst der Gegenwart,* Stuttgart (Steiner) 1990.

Shields, Rob: "Fancy footwork: Walter Benjamin's notes on *flânerie*", in: Keith Tester (ed.): *The Flâneur*, London / New York (Routledge) 1994, pp. 61–80.

Schmitz, Hermann: "Der Gefühlsraum", in: *System der Philosophie, Vol. III: Der Raum, Second Part*, Bonn (Bouvier) 1969.

Schmitz, Hermann: "Gefühle als Atmosphären und das affektive Betroffensein von ihnen", in: Hinrich Fink-Eitel / Georg Lohmann (eds.): *Zur Philosophie der Gefühle*. Frankfurt am Main (Suhrkamp) 1993, pp. 33–56.

Ströker, Elisabeth: *Philosophische Untersuchungen zum Raum,* Frankfurt am Main (Klostermann) 1965.

Thich, Nhat Hanh: "Het is een wonder op aarde te lopen", in: Paulo Coelho et alii: *Walking*. Amsterdam: Byblos 2001, pp. 23–35.

# The Hermeneutics of Painting: Jackson Pollock and Cy Twombly

ISABELLE MOFFAT

Each time I look at a painting I am a different person. Like an utterance, the painting addresses the spectator, constituting her in the process. The way in which the specific cognitive effort of viewing shapes the subject is comparable to the effect of an act of hailing or interpellation – a mechanism theorized in Louis Althusser's theory of ideology as an introduction into a system of ideological recognition. The mechanisms of this encounter are the subject of this paper.

My discussion of this encounter as a cognitive experience draws in part on Norman Bryson's notion of a "hermeneutic effort." In *Vision and Painting* (1983) Bryson uses the term to explain what he calls painting's "specialized relationship between denotation and connotation, where connotation so confirms and substantiates denotation that the latter appears to a level of truth."[1] His reading of Giotto's *Betrayal* analyzes the information conveyed in this highly interpretative representation of Christ and Judas and concludes:

> [...] the point is not that such interpretation makes any authoritative claim to accuracy, but on the contrary that because it requires a certain amount of hermeneutic effort, because it must extract meaning from the image under conditions of difficulty and uncertainty, the connotations are experiences as *found*, not made.[2]

In the context of Bryson's argument, this notion of the found information guarantees its claim on the effect of the real; it will appear *natural* because the spectator feels it is her effort that has discovered this knowledge. Here I am not so much concerned with the iconographic "reading" of an image, involved in the analysis of narrative or of connotative elements. Rather I am curious about the extra-perceptual experience of space, inferred by the spectator in a process of cognitive reconstruction of spatial relations in the works of two abstract painters, Jackson Pollock and Cy Twombly.

To begin with, I am interested in the metaphoric associations of the way in which space is conceived. It is not merely the ubiquity of spatial expressions, such as 'seeing behind something' or 'looking forward to something', doing right and acting gauche, that have left traces of spatial reasoning and its connotations in language that is relevant here, but more specifically I want to consider the

1 Bryson: *Vision and Painting,* p. 62.
2 Ibid., p. 64.

implications on a spectator of a 'hermeneutic effort' that entails both the visual perception and its interpretation. Namely, the spectator's work of discovery, finding a figure in the dark, re-cognizing a correspondence of color or tone, of following a line from beginning to end, of analyzing a composition – of getting it, whatever 'it' may be. This process is intimately related to a cognitive pleasure principle – a system that acknowledges and rewards this discovery.

Artists, I argue, create according to deeply ingrained assumptions of knowledge production and traces of these epistemological models find their way into the works they produce. The manner in which this information is formulated and perhaps communicated is neither straightforward nor predictable – nor does it necessarily manifest itself formally, but it contributes to the complex set of relationships that constitute the encountering subject. The manner in which the spectator may infer information about form and space from the handling of paint in the works of the two artists discussed here is quite distinct: whereas Pollock's work holds out for the promise of unraveling knowledge, full discovery is never an option in Twombly's renderings. These epistemological positions are not "represented" but inferred in a process of cognitive operations that present this non-perceptual knowledge as real and begins to intertwine perception and cognition.

## Pollock

The dialogue with Pollock's work shaped Clement Greenberg's theory of modernism and his model of painting's role within it. In Pollock's drip paintings from 1947–50, the critic saw the fulfillment of his theory of modern art and consequently the replacement of traditional hierarchical composition by an all-over treatment of the painting's surface. His frequently harsh comments on Pollock's work after 1951 are indicative of incongruities with a model that could not accommodate the strictures of his own theory with the practice he encountered.

Within Greenberg's model there was no conceptual space to allow for what I take to be the diachronic nature of Pollock's drip paintings. Not surprisingly, in light of the strict modernist prescriptions, I wonder if this view of Pollock's work may disqualify me, in Greenberg's eyes. If I were to take him literally, my inability to take in these works "at-once" stems from my lack of training and expertise.

Unlike the correctly formalist viewing experience, prescribed by Greenberg, and on occasion with similar authoritarianism by Michael Fried, even viewing Pollock's drip paintings, I cannot shut off my diachronic sense of exploration. I follow the drips around and across the canvas, mentally noting where they cross over or under one another. For me the layers of web-like pourings invoke an inferred sense of space related to their temporal execution. I am not referring to the actual time it may have taken the artist to execute the work, the duration of the paint drip that hit the surface first till the last of that drip was applied or to a notion of process. Mine is a knowledge gained by inference: the web exists in narrative time because I attempt to unravel it; the story of its execution is recorded within the successive layers of paint. At the same time, these layers create an optical space contained between the first and the last layers, and this internal space gives a horizontal, three-dimensional structure to the web, causing it to project out from the flatness of the canvas, to hover between picture plane and viewer almost like a holographic image or a 3D computer animation.

The space is neither stable nor constant. Pockets develop here and there and the sequential logic I can infer is continuously destabilized by the optical play in which the colors are engaged. The space 'within the web' then is not strictly speaking illusionistic. It is not the window or fictitious space of illusionistic painting nor is it the effect of a contour line suggesting inside/outside that Michael Fried described as typical of naïve illusionistic abstraction.

Perhaps I don't actually see space between the layers of paint but infer it from the sequential, temporal distance I assume. At the same time, I don't seem to be able to stop wondering about the architecture of this structure. Perhaps then the space, within the layering, could be described as deictic – it is based on my viewing experience that uses contextual clues.[3] It is an inference I cannot keep myself from making.

## Greenberg's Pollock

In his review of Pollock's 1947 show, Greenberg wrote that the artist "points a way beyond the easel, beyond the mobile, framed picture, to the mural, perhaps – or perhaps not. I cannot tell."[4] One year later Greenberg reiterated his praise, again trying to theorize where exactly it was Pollock was going. "Since Mondrian," Greenberg wrote, "no one has driven the easel picture quite so far away from itself; but this is not altogether Pollock's own doing. In this day and age the art of painting increasingly rejects the easel and yearns for the wall."[5] Greenberg emphasized that Pollock was caught up in the progress of painting, driven by the force of the medium's development.

After 1951 Greenberg claimed that it was Pollock's reluctant and troubled withdrawal from this newfound space that had caused the artist insurmountable

3 I will discuss the notion of deixis further when I develop the way in which the subject is constituted before a painting. I am referring to the deictic aspect of shifters as Emile Benveniste has articulated it in his 1956 essay *The Nature of Pronouns*.

4 Greenberg: *Collected Essays and Criticism Volume 2,* p. 125. Incidentally Pollock, in his 1947 application for a Guggenheim fellowship, wrote almost the same words.

5 Ibid., pp. 201 f.

difficulties. The drip paintings, Greenberg asserted, had led to a place from which Pollock could not move forward:

> One of the unconscious motives for Pollock's 'all-over' departure was the desire to achieve immediate, denser, and more decorative impact than his late Cubist manner had permitted. At the same time, however, he wanted to control the oscillation between an emphatic physical surface and the suggestion of depth beneath it as lucidly and tensely and evenly as Picasso and Braque had controlled a somewhat similar movement with the open facets and pointillist flecks of color of their 1903–1913 Cubist pictures [...]. Having achieved this kind of control, he found himself straddled between the easel picture and something else hard to define, and in the last two or three years he has pulled back.[6]

In the critic's teleological model this possibly was the very end: one hundred years of modernism, of the medium explicating itself as it expressed its intrinsic flatness, had run its course. In his failure and retreat, Pollock had proven Greenberg's theory by default.

And this default Greenberg argued with great determination, motivated perhaps by his historical self-interest. As Robert Storr has pointed out, the waning of Greenberg's critical approval for Pollock in 1952, after the reintroduction of figurative elements, showed traces of a personal investment:

> Thus, at the very moment when Greenberg codified his ideas about the new art (in the 1955 "'American-Type' Painting"), he both granted Pollock credit for past achievement and foreclosed his future [...]. The capriciousness of his remark ['Jackson, well, he had his ten-year run'] resonates with brutality if not outright vindictiveness toward an artist who did not heed his counsel.[7]

If Greenberg wanted to salvage his historical determinism, if the progressive crisis of easel painting had come to a resolution in Pollock's drip paintings and the easel painting as such was supposed to have died of natural causes, Pollock and the other Abstract Expressionists could certainly not have re-introduced figurative elements, or employ what Greenberg derisively called 'good' painting. The most threatening aspect, however, of accepting Pollock's post-1951 work was that it retrospectively showed not only the arbitrariness of Greenberg's artistic prophesies, but, more damagingly, might force a retrospective recognition of 'skill' and 'good' painting in the supposedly 'pure' drip paintings. These 1951 paintings demonstrated that Pollock had abandoned neither composition, or invention, nor all reference.

The effects of Greenberg's refusal to come to terms with these complexities and ambiguities of artistic practice, his insistence on simply shutting them out by dismissing Pollock's later painting are evident throughout his discussion of the relationship between spontaneous or automatic inspiration and controlled composition in the artist's work; there, a conflict is generated by his insistence on the importance of so-called "deskilling" and of inspiration, as the critic defines the terms.

6 Ibid., pp. 225 f.

7 Storr: "No Joy in Mudville", p. 189 (note 62).

The two terms are linked by Greenberg's theory of immediacy: the picture had to look spontaneous and effortless while at the same time retaining a sense of strict compositional control. Much of this, according to Greenberg, was achieved by Pollock's move away from a gesture based on the "habits or mannerisms of fingers, wrist, elbow, and even shoulder that are brought into play by the use of a brush, knife, or any other implement that touches the picture surface,"[8] in favor of the use if sticks, basting syringes and the like to drip the paint onto the canvas. This deskilling practice supposedly freed Pollock from any virtuosity or 'handwriting'; without his 'touch', Greenberg's argument implied, there remained only the underlying conceptual structure to identify the Pollockness of his paintings.

> Like Mondrian, Pollock demonstrates that something related to skill is likewise unessential to the creation of aesthetic quality; namely, personal touch, individuality of execution, handwriting, 'signature'. In principle, any artist's touch can be imitated, but it takes hard work and great skill to imitate Hsia Kuei's, Leonardo's, Rembrandt's, or Ingres's. Mondrian's touch can be imitated, or rather duplicated, with no effort at all, by anybody. So, almost, can Pollock's touch in his 'drip' period. With a little practice anybody can make dribbles, spatters and skeins of liquid paint that are indistinguishable from Pollock's in point purely of handwriting. But Mondrian's and Pollock's quality can no more be duplicated that Leonardo's or Rembrandt's. Again, it is driven home that, in the last analysis, conception, or inspiration, alone decides aesthetic quality.[9]

There are two problems raised here, the first created by Greenberg's radical separation of conception from execution, and his privileging of the former over the latter. Given the complex build-up of layers in Mondrian's paintings, it is far from certain that 'anybody' would be capable of copying them, even with considerable practice. Neither is it clear that Mondrian's work is lacking 'individuality of execution' – in fact, a case could be made that what is surprising about his paintings, as is also true in the case of Robert Ryman's, is how much 'individuality of expression' there is in such a strict or highly simplified format. What is true of Mondrian is perhaps even clearer in the case of Pollock, as Greenberg himself seems to imply ("so, almost..."). If anyone's hand can be duplicated and inspiration alone differentiates art from decoration, then how explain the particularities of the hand that are themselves an inherent part of an artistic vision?

The second problem is that, as an exclusive strategy, deskilling also narrows the range of technical options available to the artist. This limitation made it more difficult for Pollock to find a way to develop an art based on this notion, a difficulty identified by Greenberg and perhaps somewhat intensified by his writing. Greenberg caught Pollock in a ferocious double-bind: having declared the artist entirely dependent on inspiration rather than talent, he then concludes that the artist must have been paralyzed by fear of losing this ephemeral advantage – after all, he was forbidden to fall back on experience, skill, or his 'touch' – if he

8 Greenberg: *Collected Essays and Criticism Volume 4*, p. 248.
9 Ibid., pp. 247 f.

wanted to do his best work. For, not accidentally, it is just this charge, of recourse to proficiency and 'good' painting that Greenberg leveled against Pollock's post-drip paintings. Since proficiency, painting skill, and intentionality were definitely things of the past, it was with disdain that Greenberg declared:

> In the decrepitude of his art, from 1952 to his death in 1956, during which time he displayed proficiency in an obvious enough way to win admission to any guild of 'good' painters, that past did more than cling; it closed in. Pollock himself was among the first to register this. His vision exhausted itself, at least for the time being; he was filling in with 'good' painting, and it was not enough.[10]

But if the past had "closed in" on Pollock, it had done so with no less vengeance than Greenberg himself in his drive to allow Pollock's work to develop or be interpreted in only one direction and that defined by him. Greenberg further complicated the problem of understanding the relationship between concept and execution in Pollock's work by conflating the artist's dislike of "madeness," with an aversion to the intentionality of the stroke per se, an interpretation that suited Greenberg's thinking more, but that unilaterally redefined the artist's search for expression:

> Last but not least came Pollock's revulsion from 'madeness' from the look of the intended and arranged and contrived and trimmed and 'tickled.' To him, almost all drawing with a brush or pencil began to look too deliberate. That in escaping 'madeness' he went over into something like anonymity or impersonality of execution did not particularly strike Pollock – or any one else – at the time.[11]

Greenberg was propping up history here. What he referred to as anonymity relates Pollock to the Color-Field painters that Greenberg saw as the heirs of his theory of painting development. Pollock did not go into "anonymity of impersonality of execution." His dislike of "madeness" had to do with his often stated wish to express his feelings, not illustrate them, connoting to him a sense of authenticity, searching for a technique to control what he took for self-expression. Whereas "madeness" connoted contrivance and inauthenticity, the duplication of feeling, not its articulation, it was not touch, or the stroke as such that Pollock abhorred.

The evolution of the gestural into a ready-made, its reification into the "Tenth Street Touch," in Greenberg's phrase, is a better explanation of Pollock's supposed "revulsion from 'madeness.'" What had seemed to him personal and authentic in the expressive gesture – notwithstanding our perspective on such an assumption – and in controlled arbitrariness, turned out to be just another language of painting. The abundance of 'spontaneous' art drew attention to the fact that even gestural painting was not immediate and direct, and that such an extremely personal idiom could be coopted too.

To that extent, Greenberg was right to note that

10 Ibid., p. 250.
11 Ibid., p. 248.

> By 1955 at the latest the expressive possibilities of abstract painterly appearance – of pure painterly, pure *malerisch* appearance – had been exhausted for the time being. Painterly Abstraction had turned by and large into an assortment of ready-made effects. The smears, swipes and lumps of paint left by brush or spatula, and the shapes in which liquid paint disposed itself when it spilled on a flat surface, had begun to connote the mannered and stereotyped far more than the spontaneous or fresh. The look of the accidental had become an academic, conventional look.[12]

But the challenge posed by Pollock's work was not how to survive the death of easel painting but how to continue as an artist after painterly gesture had become a sign, a trope in the Abstract Expressionist vocabulary. Not only has the overlay of Greenberg's interpretation of Pollock's situation distorted the reading of the work of this period, it has also made illegible aspects of work, such as Twombly's, that is engaged in a dialogue with Pollock's paintings from a perspective different from the critic's. Twombly sought alternative routes to address and respond to the swift exhaustion of Abstract Expressionism.

## Twombly

By the early 1950s the gestural had fallen into disrepute, so much so, that the younger generation of artists, such as Twombly, Robert Rauschenberg, and Jasper Johns began a dissection of the stroke as such. From the art of the Abstract Expressionists, some of whom were seen as admired idols, others as mediocre epigones, the younger artists sought to distill something new. But their investigation was not necessarily fired by a sense – propagated by Greenberg at the time and promulgated by successive critics – that painting had run its course. Even if the look of the gestural had become a mannerism and without denying the break that did occur in the mid-1950s when the stroke was de-naturalized and subjected to rigorous analysis, the reaction of artists such as Twombly, Rauschenberg, and Johns makes clear that there were valid and lively alternatives to packing up canvas and easel, brush and paints. While the "demise" of modernist painting in general, and as we saw of Pollock's work in particular is dated to his 1951 Betty Parsons Gallery show, the transformation into the mannerism of the Tenth Street stroke took place in the first half of the 1950s. It was in this period that all three artists produced their early mature work, more or less initiating the projects with which they have remained occupied. Twombly in particular took lessons from Pollock and the fate of Abstract Expressionism in order to develop a practice of painting that was self-aware and that did not assume unmediated access to expression.

Like Pollock, Twombly exploits the spaces created between wall, support, and spectator, but he takes further Pollock's move towards the spectator by re-

12 Ibid., p. 180.

versing the process, by moving out from under Pollock's web, unearthing the layers in reverse order, scratching into the paint as if offering the negative of Pollock's drips and making the stroke (or sometimes scratch) itself, both literally and conceptually, his subject matter.

This process began in the early 1950s when Twombly went from painting turbulent, brusque non-recognizable imagery, taken, for example, from Luristan bronzes and from African fetish works,[13] to focusing on the stroke itself. The grey, black, and off-white 1951 *Min-Oe* is an example of this very early work that shows the influence of Kline, de Kooning, Motherwell and Tworkov, but also already has the surface ambiguity characteristic of Twombly's later work. The densely layered surface offers no clues as to the exact temporal progression of the process. Hence, in some areas, the black "background" seems to have been roughly painted in last, whereas, in other places, it is submerged under layers of white and gray. As in Pollock's paintings, such temporal ambiguity also creates a sense of multiple inferred internal spaces.

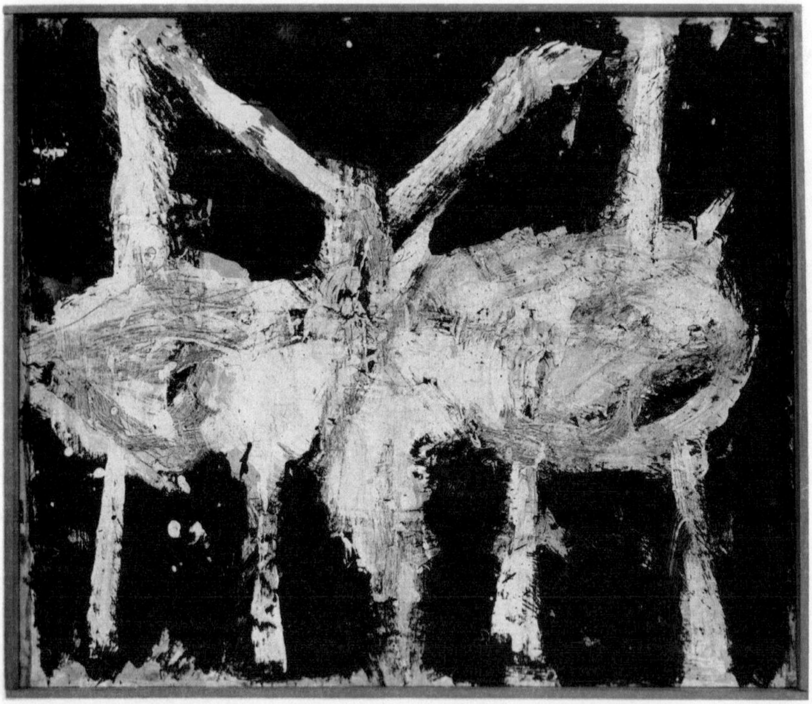

Fig. 1. Cy Twombly: *Min-Oe*, 1951.

This effect is particularly clear in *Didim*, also from 1951, which is at first strangely reminiscent of Kline's calligraphic paintings. But here as well, the apparently simple black grid turns out to be both painted over the beige background

13 See Varnedoe: "Inscriptions in Arcadia", p. 55, note 36 and p. 15.

as well as painted into with this same beige color, a device that brings the spatial relationship of colors into play as the dirty white recedes and advances continuously, oscillating without being fixed. These rough 1951 paintings with their large obstructing objects and ambiguous figure/ground – if these terms can apply to this complex process of signification at all – relationships, show Twombly steadily working his way through Abstract Expressionism and Art Brut, particularly the work of Dubuffet.

The same kind of spatial ambiguity created by the multilayered and disorienting paint application is found in many of Twombly's later works. He has continued to induce an unexpected sense of pictorial space by constructing intricate backgrounds that in their roughness of application and dirty yellow-white coloring give the appearance of carelessness and connote spontaneity. This is not to imply that these qualities betray a disingenuous mannerism but simply to note Twombly's subtle insistence, within his own informal approach, on classical painting with its rules of composition and balance.

His trip to Italy and Northern Africa with Rauschenberg had a great impact on Twombly's imagery. *Tiznit* (1953), for example, brings together drawings of various objects from his North African Sketchbook, apparently "tribal items" displayed in the Pigorini ethnographic museum in Rome.[14] Twombly's use of these loose drawings of various objects and surfaces in 1953 is similar to Johns' use of his own very different found two-dimensional imagery. Both appear to be searching for a language without content, utterances without meaning, in order to explore painting's possibilities 'after abstraction'; but while Johns, with *Flag*, *Target* and *Map*, chose an iconography literally flattened (images that only exist in two-dimensional state, even if they represent three-dimensional terrain as is the case with maps), and conceptually impoverished from overuse, Twombly chose highly charged, ritualistic objects. Instead of using them as *objet trouvé*, however, he enlarged and distorted them to non-recognizability. *Tiznit*, to illustrate, combines three 'objects' from different parts of Twombly's sketchbook, enlarging them, so that they take up the entire page, dividing it vertically. But the painting, unlike the sketches or the drawn study, relates the separate images, intertwining them with each other and with the background, finally transforming the various objects into a strange new language. Or, so it appears: the all-over quality of the drawings is obfuscated by the thickness and texture of the paint. As if unwittingly, a sense of modeling and depth works itself through the image, giving it a landscape-like feel, a quality Twombly had scrupulously avoided before by exclusively dividing the picture plane vertically.

Another important early work anticipating Twombly's paintings of the mid-1950s is *La La* (1953), in which the artist once more plays with the assumptions of over and under painting. Scratched into a light blue surface, the strokes seem to emerge from underneath the paint, as much as they are inscribed into it, divid-

14 Ibid., p. 17.

ing the still-wet paint. Both this process of drawing *into* paint and the spatial paradox are characteristic of Twombly's later work. This two-fold paradox entails a conundrum for the viewer as the deduction of a temporal sequence of paint application or over/under relationship is obscured and therefore the latent spatial inference is undermined.

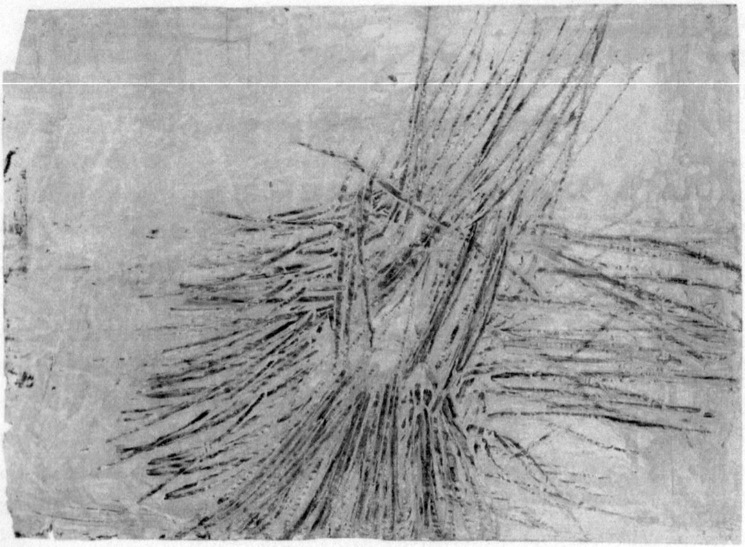

Fig. 2. Cy Twombly: *LA LA*, 1953.

Much has been made of Twombly's story about drawing in the dark while in the Army in 1953–54: according to Kirk Varnedoe, "Twombly has since affirmed that the drawings he did in Augusta, in a hotel room rented on weekend leaves, established 'the direction everything would take from then on.'"[15] To Varnedoe (and Pincus-Witten), drawing in the dark was part of an attempt at "deskilling":

> Unlike the 'automatic drawing' of the Surrealist," Varnedoe writes, "which aimed to elicit a smooth, uninterrupted flow of unconsciously motivated line, this exercise in reduced control seems to have been intended to impede and slow down the artist's graphic skill, and force into it some of the distortions of children's drawings. The 'blind' practice contributed to the scrawling cursiveness and the looping, elongated proportions that are the hallmark of the Augusta drawings, and the nocturnal, uncensored manner of rendering may also account for the more candid opening of the imagery onto a psychosexual subconscious.[16]

Varnedoe is here employing partially modernist terms; when Pollock used sticks to drip paint, Greenberg made the same argument and thereby placed him in

15 Ibid., p. 19.
16 Ibid., p. 20.

company with Picasso and Duchamp. But it is misleading to describe Twombly's activity in such terms, since, in his case, it is not a formal tool, a pictorial element – the deskilled stroke versus the virtuoso – but rather a more fundamental decision to investigate the stroke (and its history, according to the often quoted dictum from the artist's 1957 text) and to divest it of 'direct' and 'unmediated' expressiveness. That is why Varnedoe's second point, that the nocturnal setting facilitated more explicit imagery, is naïve too. It contradicts his preceding argument of non-automatic, intentional 'deskilling'. Varnedoe's writing here is reminiscent of Greenberg's paradoxical assessment of Pollock as working automatically, not from skill and talent – while at the same time being in tight control of paint and composition.

The notion of a camouflaged virtuosity and the intentional masking of his proficient hand has become a trope in the writing on Twombly.[17] Though it was used by early champions to convince detractors of the value and beauty of Twombly's work by implying that it was intentional deskilling, not an inherent lack of skill, that motivated the artist's aesthetic, it constitutes an extension of modernist criticism, implying a logical continuation, though a drastic one, from Pollock's use of a basting syringe to 'remove' his virtuosity from the picture, to Twombly's 'fake' clumsiness. But this analysis overlooks that Twombly's hand is not erased, not masked, it is rather very distinct. Instead what is masked is a certain contrivedness of his line. The unease and 'clumsiness' so often described by critics then translates not into aesthetic terms but into an idea of time: it accentuates the effort, the successive states of hesitation, execution and regret.

Another recurring theme in the reception of Twombly's work are accusations of aggression, originating perhaps in a vague association of the 'clumsy' with the aggressive, sometimes taking the form of a sense of frustration projected onto the works. The inability to decipher what superficially looks like language, to unravel the secrets supposedly locked up in Twombly's work appears to have infuriated many spectators. Some have approached it with more sophistication than others, but the underlying frustration is often conspicuous; typical is, for instance, Linda Norden's reaction when she speaks of the "maddening approximation to writing. Maddening because we want to read these images and can't."[18] Certainly there is no code, no translation that offers a glimmer of future understanding in Twombly's work. The anger this frustrated search has sometimes entailed however is interesting.

What Twombly's sojourn in the Army might probably have provoked is a return to the alphabet and to simple signs and logograms; instead of inventing a formal language based on his drawings of fetish objects and ritualistic pieces,

17 See, for example, Robert Pincus-Witten *Learning to Write* where he writes "Fearing slickness, [Twombly] drew as if with his left hand." Quoted in Varnedoe: "Inscription in Arcadia", p. 59, note 75.

18 Norden: "Not Necessarily Pop", p. 151 f.

Twombly's variations of his slashes, scribbles, doodles, and triangular shaped marks become a shorthand for the *illegibility* of such language. The series that begins with a suite of paintings of white chalk and crayon on gray/grey background, of which only the monumental *Panorama* still exists, anticipates Twombly's striking blackboard paintings of the 1960s.[19] *Panorama*'s white chalk marks, unlike those in much of the later work, are applied in an all-over manner; obviously related to Abstract Expressionism's compositional dicta and most specifically to Pollock's all-over drip paintings, *Panorama* is at once whimsical and devastating. Its strokes already have the paradoxical quality that is Twombly's trademark beginning in the mid-1950s: their accidental look and deceptively simple background momentarily obscure the delicate but precise composition. But as the sense of artistic control gradually manifests itself and eventually becomes ubiquitous and unavoidable, expression is thrown into question – by a balanced and precise blow at the dead center of the myth of the expressive stroke.

Twombly's work between 1955 and 1957 (the year of his move to Rome) continues to investigate the possibilities of the stroke, and to examine the process of producing meaning. Indeed, the stroke and its entangled relationship with the ground is the predominant subject of these paintings from mid-decade. The figure/ground relationship is consistently questioned by the scratchings into the surface, bringing into play, as in earlier work, any clear sense of over- and underlayers. As in *La La*, in *Free Wheeler* (1955) Twombly has painted his housepaint ground over crayon and pencil marks, and then scratched into the wet paint, inscribing and exposing at the same time. In *Free Wheeler*, however, many more kinds of marks, some in red, gray or black, succeed each other through many more layers of paint, giving a greater variation in the intensity of the line.

Twombly's project here is very similar to Rauschenberg's in that they both create an illusion of haphazard composition and erratic, hurried creative process, when in fact they carefully construct this very impression. Robert Rosenblum wrote in 1956 that on encountering *Factum I* and *Factum II* together "one is forced to admit that the same combination of impulse and discipline that produces more conventional pictures is also operating here," and called this admission "a premise of unreasonable reason."[20]

Twombly, too, suggests such rapid and unpremeditated acts of creation while, at the same time, drawing attention to the deliberateness of the composition and of the quality of line. While the clusters of doodles and swirling marks may at first give an impression of unrehearsed and illicit scribbling, Twombly's often quoted comment – "Each line now is the actual experience with its own innate history"[21] – literally describes the trace of the physical execution as the

19 The painting measures 8'4'' x 11'2'' feet. Varnedoe dates Panorama to 1954 whereas it is usually dated 1955; his explanation is found on p. 60, footnote 88.

20 Quoted in Ferguson: *Hand-Painted Pop*, pp. 29 f.

21 Cy Twombly L'Esperienza moderna No.2 (August–September 1957), p. 32. Quoted in Varnedoe: "Inscription in Arcadia", p. 27.

line displays the weight and labor of its making. It refers to its own production and the effort it took to scratch and scrawl into the thick mush of paint.

This notion of physical effort emphasizes the slowness and temporal suspension of the stroke and its execution. The marks in *Free Wheeler* and *Untitled* (1956),[22] for example, are not light strokes sweeping easily across the surface of the work; labored and repeatedly redrawn, covered up and multilayered, Twombly's web of strokes gives a sense of both time and depth as each stroke carries with it the expanded time it took to produce.

The gravity (or gravitas, one is tempted to say) in Twombly's line implies an analysis and deconstruction of spontaneity and of the expressive possibilities of the gestural, thus exposing the aspirations to unmediated and direct expression ascribed to the Abstract Expressionist painters as flawed. The rapidity and looseness implied by the 'gestural' in Abstract Expressionist painting of the early decade is subverted in Twombly's work of the mid-1950s, in which it is demonstrated that no stroke can comply with such claim of self-referentiality. Rather Twombly draws attention to the difficulty of self-expression; if it is possible to trace one's self, his work seems to suggest, it is through a labored and painfully uncertain route, since whatever one produces is always mediated by hand, medium and consciousness. It is as if Twombly makes visible the time it takes to translate the utterance from head to hand and depict the delay in thought. At issue, then, is the illegibility of essence, the impossibility of ever fully understanding a subjective utterance, even for the enunciating subject itself.

Twombly's blind drawings from 1953 only underline this point by showing that abandon is impossible, and automatism equally controlled by inclination and intention. It is the illusion of pure self-expression, one to which Pollock repeatedly confessed, that Twombly unravels and destroys.

The work of Pollock and Twombly maintain variant epistemological positions, suggesting models of the way in which knowledge about the world and the self can be obtained. The distinct viewing experiences, the 'hermeneutic effort' in which the spectator engages the work, find an equivalent in the way the work addresses the subject. One might say, that some of Pollock's work presents a "temporalized web"[23] that holds the promise of unraveling the successive marks back to an originary gesture, to the first mark. Even as unlikely (literally and conceptually) as this is, the spectator's response is also contingent on the cognitive pleasure in which this notion may result. The inability to 'decipher' Twombly's marks, on the other hand entails a productive ambiguity that precludes such an assumption. The palpable aggression towards Twombly's early work encountered in so much of the initial reception then may not stem from an outraged propriety concerning graffiti and

22 "Untitled, Plate 7" in *Cy Twombly*, Houston.

23 A term I borrow from Georges Didi-Huberman.

clumsiness but rather from the work's insistent refusal to be understood in a conventional way, of not being legible within an uncomplicated model of signification.

## References

Althusser, Louis: *Lenin and Philosophy and Other Essays*, New York (Monthly Review Press) 2001.

Bryson, Norman: *Vision and Painting – The Logic of the Gaze*, New Haven / London (Yale University Press) 1983.

Fergurson, Russell (ed.): *Hand-Painted Pop: American Art in Transition, 1955–62*, Los Angeles (The Museum of Contemporary Art) 1992.

Greenberg, Clement: *Collected Essays and Criticism Volumes 2: Arrogant Purpose 1945–1949*, ed. by John O'Brian, Chicago/London (The Chicago University Press) 1986.

Greenberg, Clement: *Collected Essays and Criticism Volumes 3: Affirmation and Refusals 1950–1956*, ed. by John O'Brian, Chicago/London (The Chicago University Press) 1986.

Greenberg, Clement: *Collected Essays and Criticism Volumes 4: Modernism with a Vengeance 1957–1969*, ed. by John O'Brian, Chicago/London (The Chicago University Press) 1993.

Norden, Linda: "Not Necessarily Pop. Cy Twombly and America", in Russel Ferguson (ed.): *Hand-Painted Pop: American Art in Transition, 1955–62*, Los Angeles (The Museum of Contemporary Art) 1992.

Storr, Robert: "No Joy in Mudville: Greenberg's Modernism Then and Now", in Kirk Varnedoe / Adam Gopnick (eds.): *Modern Art and Popular Culture: Readings in High and Low*, New York (The Museum of Modern Art, Abrams) 1990, pp. 160–191.

Varnedoe, Kirk: "Inscriptions in Arcadia", in: *Cy Twombly: A Retrospective*, New York (Museum of Modern Art) 1994.

## List of Illustrations

Fig 1. Cy Twombly: Min-Oe, 1951, bitumen and house paint on canvas, 34 x 40 inches (86.4 x 101.6 cm), Collection Robert Rauschenberg. © Cy Twombly.

Fig. 2 Cy Twombly: LA LA, 1953, house paint and wax/oil crayon on paper, 19 3/8 x 27 ¼ inches (50 x 69 cm), Collection Robert Rauschenberg. © Cy Twombly.

# *Modernities*

# *Correspondances* – Synaesthesia, Senses, and Modernity

GERHARD SCHARBERT

*Je finis par trouver sacré le désordre de mon esprit.*

Arthur Rimbaud

On the 10th of October 1863, the English poet Algernon Charles Swinburne received a letter from his Parisian colleague Charles Baudelaire to recommend his old friend Nadar. Baudelaire took this opportunity to thank Swinburne for his exuberant review of the *Fleurs du Mal* he published in the journal *The Spectator*, and mentioned a strange experience that happened to him in a similar situation when he met a German composer: "One day, Mr R. Wagner jumped on me to thank me for a text I wrote on *Tannhäuser*, and told me: 'I never thought that a French writer could understand so easily, so many things.' As I am not particularly a patriot, I took for me all the grace of his compliment."[1] Richard Wagner had good reasons to be happy and delighted, as he met an understanding man, a man of taste, who was able to put aside the prejudices of his nation and time, virtues the composer regrettably lacked at times. It must also be mentioned that Paris, the capital of the arts, did not treat Wagner well. The so-called high society, reacting in a philistine and nationalistic way, pretended that the noble image of Civilisation Française has been severely damaged by these circumstances. Baudelaire was entirely devoid of the kind of nationalism represented by the outcry against. Baudelaire immediately and clearly recognized the modernity of Wagner's music, in spite of the ignorance and the stifling nationalism of the majority of his contemporaries. This musical event had nothing to do with such ideological swamps. In a letter to the creator of these sounds, dated 17th February 1860, Baudelaire described his listening experience in the finest French prose:

> […] j'ai éprouvé souvent un sentiment d'une nature assez bizarre, c'est l'orgueil et la jouissance de comprendre, de me laisser pénétrer, envahir, volupté vraiment sensuelle, et qui ressemble à celle de monter dans l'air ou de rouler sur la mer. Et la musique en même temps respirait quelquefois l'orgueil de la vie. Généralement ces profondes harmonies me paraissaient ressembler à ces excitants qui accélèrent le pouls de l'imagination. […] Il y a partout quelque chose d'enlevé et d'enlevant, quelque chose aspirant à monter plus haut, quelque chose d'excessif et de superlatif. Par exemple, pour me servir de comparaisons empruntées à la peinture, je suppose devant mes yeux une vaste étendue d'un rouge sombre. Si ce rouge re-

1 Baudelaire: *Correspondance*, vol. II, p. 325. (All translations by Franck Loric).

> présente la passion, je le vois arriver graduellement, par toutes les transitions de rouge et de rose, à l'incandescence de la fournaise. Il semblerait difficile, impossible même d'arriver à quelque chose de plus ardent; et cependant une dernière fusée vient tracer un sillon plus blanc sur le blanc qui lui sert de fond.[2]

The world would have to wait for almost half a generation before other artists would represent such visions on a canvas, and a few more years before films would adopt such visions.[3] Baudelaire, in his essay "Richard Wagner et *Tannhäuser* à Paris", which he wrote shortly after his enthusiastic letter, added verses from his own poem *Correspondances*, showing that he took good note of Wagner's ideas about the *Gesamtkunstwerk*. But the thoughts of the Frenchman seemed to reach far beyond the field of contemporary music theatre, to a cosmos in the brain that would obey the same laws as cosmic bodies:

> Nature is a temple where living pillars
> Let escape sometimes confused words;
> Man traverses it through forests of symbols
> That observe him with familiar glances.
>
> Like long echoes that intermingle from afar
> In a dark and profound unity,
> Vast like the night and like the light,
> The perfumes, the colors and the sounds respond.[4]

A tiny detail makes this self-quote remarkable: in the version included in *Fleurs du Mal*,[5] the word 'Nature' is written with an initial capital letter. Why Baudelaire, in his letter to Wagner, abstained from writing it the same way? How clear was it for him that the physics of vibrations and nerves, which lied underneath 'Nature', would also undermine 'the man'? As Baudelaire made absolutely no reference to his experiences with drugs, which acoustic and physiological aspects one could have read about in a publication of the French psychiatrist Jacques-Joseph Moreau de Tours dated 1845. It seemed that such flooding of the audible in the visual world, which Baudelaire so vividly described in his poetic self-

2 Baudelaire: *Correspondance*, vol. I, p. 673: "I often felt a strange feeling, it was the pride and pleasure to understand, to let myself being penetrated, invaded, a really sensual voluptuousness that felt like rising in the air or rolling on the sea. And music, at the same time was inspired by the pride of life. Eventually, these deep harmonies seemed to me like these stimulants that hasten the pulse of imagination. [...] There is everywhere something joyful and exciting, something that rises higher, something excessive and superlative. For example, to use a comparison taken from painting, I figure before my eyes a vast field of dark red. If this red stands for passion, I see it going through all nuances of red and pink, to reach the incandescence of a blaze. It would be difficult, even impossible to reach something fieriest; however, a last rocket traces a whiter furrow on the white background."

3 Thanks to Wolfgang Hagen for his anti-deconstructivist and media history analysis of such *Gedankenformen* [forms of ideas].

4 Baudelaire: *Œuvres*, vol. II, p. 784.

5 Id.: *Œuvres* I, p. 11.

quote, was an effect of the direct influence on the brain and the nervous system. "The sense of hearing […] is made extremely sensitive by the action of hashish",[6] declared Moreau in a comment about Théophile Gautier whom he quoted later in the same book:[7]

> One should, at least partly, attribute the extreme development of the sensitivity of hearing to the powerful influence of music on the persons intoxicated by hashish. One can test the limits of words to picture all the kinds of emotions that harmony can inspire. The coarsest music, the simple vibration of the string of a harp or a guitar brings you to a delirious state or plunges you into a sweet melancholia. Depending on your state of mind, the moral shattering can be transmitted to the body, fibres of muscles and soul vibrate in unison and choreic or hysteriform movements happen.[8]

One can almost hear in Moreau de Tours a pre-nietzschean critic of Wagner as he describes the direct vibration of muscle and nerve fibres as an effect of music, which can be compared to Saint Vitus dancers and hysterics. But this discussion is not about a *Zukunftmusik.* Moreau simply described the effect of a psychotropic substance on the physiology of hearing. Effects which, in spite of our drug-saturated everyday life, remain striking and shocking for the persons who are not familiar with the effect of hemp. That such effect arguably belongs to the field of pathology is a matter for medical doctors rather than for Wagner's admirer. Baudelaire only *compared* the opening of physical and psychological space through music with the effects of drug.[9] But Moreau clearly assigned these phenomena to the field of hallucinations and consequently to pathology:

> From the over-excitation of memory and imagination, an excitation strong enough to leave only a very small space for outer perceptions, associated to the overall excitation of the thought and the confusion of ideas, arises a specific mental state on which I already attracted the attention, and which the state of dreaming. This state modifies the sensations caused by harmony in such a way that, although coming from outside and originating, starting from the real world, they look like these imaginary creations the state of dreaming produces. In short, they bear all the characteristics of the psychological facts one calls hallucination.[10]

Moreau de Tours represents a strong and unique connection, an identification between the vibration – one could almost say a resonance – of physiology and psychology, the condition of dreaming, and the obvious psychopathology of the

6 Moreau de Tours: *Du hachisch,* p. 71: "Le sens de l'ouïe […] est rendu extraordinairement impressionnable par l'action du hachisch."

7 Gautier: *Le club des hachischins,* quoted after: Moreau de Tours: *Du hachisch*, pp. 21–25. Moreau de Tours also published this article in two other notable medical and psychiatric publications: *Annales médico-psychologiques* (*Description des effets du hachich, par un feuilletoniste de* la Presse, pp. 490–493) and in the then famous book by Brierre de Boismont *Des hallucinations* (pp. 378–383), published the same year as *Du hachisch*.

8 Moreau de Tours: *Du hachisch*, p. 72.

9 Baudelaire: *Œuvres* II, p. 785.

10 Moreau de Tours: *Du hachisch*, p. 82f.

physical media of what has been called the psyche. Although one cannot compare the intensity of these phenomena with everyday life,[11] for Moreau de Tours, their nature is organic because they act directly and concentrate their effects on organs.[12] In 1845, maybe he was not able to imagine that such effects could be the same in the media and aesthetic strategies, which lifted the traditional boundary between the common experience of hearing and an ecstatic and increased listening experience. The affect and the physical were concerned because they were the targets of an acoustical event, which *was* the affect itself. This is exactly what Baudelaire heard in Wagner's music, and somehow already knew through his experience with hashish and opium. Perhaps, as a man of letters was he better prepared for this experience than most his contemporary music professionals. It suggests the importance of the form of words as well as the voice as an acoustical event in his work.[13] He was also very well versed in the theories of Denis Diderot and Etienne Bonnot de Condillac on aesthetics and the origins of language. They drew far-reaching conclusions from the affective and vocalic roots of language. Baudelaire quoted Diderot in his text on Wagner: "the music was *the noted and rhythmic cry or sigh of passion.*"[14]

Condillac expressed the idea in his *Essai sur l´origine des connaissances* of 1746 that thought was preceding language, since people had "the custom to link any idea to arbitrary signs."[15] The faculties of the soul were based on what physical senses absorbed, and on what the person imagined of external impressions, which were "[...] the germ of language and of all the arts that help us to express our thoughts."[16] The necessity to develop a system for language arouse from the natural cries,[17] which were the first thoughts. Therefore, linguistic expression and all kinds of imagination were given a system, and poetry was measured. Such thought deeply influenced French physiology – let me mention Jean Georges Cabanis and Xavier Bichat – it should not come as a surprise that a poet, who had to measure the advancement of poetry to the meter of physiology, chose to illustrate the physical experience of listening to music. In France, at that time, German romantics and their successors were described by categories of pathology,[18]

11 Ibid., p. 83.

12 Ibid., p. 79.

13 One could think of remarkable poems in the *Fleurs du Mal* such as *Le Crépuscule du Soir* or *Le crépuscule du Matin,* and in the *Petits Poèmes en Prose* such as *Le Mauvais Vitrier*, *Le Crépuscule du Soir* and *Une Mort héroïque*.

14 Baudelaire: *Œuvres* II, p. 788.

15 Condillac: *Essai sur l'origine des connaissances humaines*, p. 114.

16 Ibid., p. 149.

17 Ibid., p. 114.

18 On this matter, see: Béguin, Albert: *Traumwelt und Romantik*, on illness as a metaphor ibid. p. 393. Baudelaire notes that Wagner's works, despite the "sincerity of their taste" and a "perfect understanding of classical beauty", through Romanticism, they remain linked to the Christian Middle-Age: "S'ils font rêver à la majesté de Sophocle et d'Eschyle, ils contraignent en même temps l'esprit à se souvenir des Mystères de l'époque la plus plastiquement ca-

and Wagner was considered one of them when his music was first heard in Paris. The early modernity inherited this judgment as a stigma and Baudelaire commented on it in a famous review of the Salon de 1859: "Romanticism is either a heavenly or hellish blessing, which got us eternal stigmata."[19]

But the *feelings* to which Wagner's music is addressed are reasonably definite, according to their *nervous intensity.*[20] "[...] (Dramatic) music (should) [...] adapt to the feeling with the same accuracy as language, but obviously by other means [...]."[21] This nervous intensity reaches the nervous system and the brain and has a number of effects:

> Nerves start to vibrate with the melody since the very first measures; all the flesh that can remember shakes. Every well formed brain has two infinities, heaven and hell, and in every image of one of these infinities, the brain recognize a half of itself.[22]

Music moves the nervous system like a drug, it makes it vibrate and brings it to the threshold of two physiological infinities, the joy of the 'good trip' and the hell of the 'bad trip', which Baudelaire knew too well. This split in two infinities revealed by drugs – in reality, they represent two vectors included in a continuum – illustrate the artistic ideal Baudelaire could only insinuate in the *Paradis Artificiels*, in which he described an *Ideal Artificiel.*[23] In his text about Wagner in Paris, he used music as another example of his views. In it are linked together – *concaténées*[24] – all the elements, as in a well made poem, by Baudelaire's own standards, which is surprisingly consistent with the poetic postulates of Novalis.[25] One can recognize, in the poem *Correspondances* and its references to German romanticism, many elements of synaesthesia, a condition that contemporary medical research from both countries, especially in the field of the physiology of senses, already had discovered. The questions of what is communicated by the senses and what the consequences are for the intellect, could be answered by the emerging physiology of senses in the first half of the 19th century, not only by philosophy. Johannes Müller, in his treatise *Über die phantastischen Gesichtserscheinungen* published in 1826, was confronted to the medical and psychological evaluation of such phenomena, which could not be easily classified as either

tholique." (original quote in Baudelaire: *Œuvres* II, p. 791). So much or so little for (or against) the later Nietzsche.

19 Baudelaire: *Œuvres* II, p. 645: "Le romantisme est une grâce, céleste ou infernale, à qui nous devons des stigmates éternels."

20 Ibid., p. 806.

21 Ibid., p. 787.

22 Ibid., p. 795. My preference goes to the editor of the Pléiade (*Cette leçon est certainement preferable*) who favoured to read *vibrent à l'unisson* (p. 1465) in the manuscript rather than *vivent à l'unisson* (p. 795), which appears in the later editions. It seems that the insightful Claude Pichois rejected the direct biblical reference of the expression, which prevailed before.

23 Baudelaire: *Œuvres* I, p. 403, in *Le poème du Hachisch.*

24 Baudelaire: *Œuvres* II, p. 803.

25 See Friedrich: op.cit., p. 21.

spiritual or material.[26] The boundary between these fields was becoming less and less clear, if one considers the experimental medical science and biology of the time. For Johannes Müller, such phenomena belonged to the field of the physiology of senses, even though they were traditionally assigned to psychology or early psychiatry, which tagged them as 'errors', 'illusions' or 'fantasies'. Thenceforth, began the exploration of the proximity between internal impressions, memories, and perception of senses, synaesthesia and bodily sensations.

In France, around the middle of the 19th century, this approach lead to the transfer of experimental research on the psyche to the expending fields of neurophysiology and pharmacology. The psychiatrist Jacques-Joseph Moreau de Tours – which I already mentioned – a student of Jean Dominique Esquirol, introduced a hallucinogenic drug in this research and as a result founded psychopharmacology. In the context of a more general classification, he systematically made accessible an interpretation of delusional and extraordinary perceptions and sensations by conducting his experiments on himself. Moreau's key concept was the *sens intime* (intimate knowledge) which, as a perception or consciousness of the body, can give information about the status of the individual, independently from the faculty of judgment and intellectual introspection. Perceptions, feelings and *sens intime* form a continuum, which appears more clearly in intoxication and madness because cognitive functions are disrupted. The great influence of the experiments was the result of the participation of the French artistic and literary elite, and because they refuted the theories which considered modernity as the history of the dissociation of the sensory experience from embodiment. Including synaesthesia in this process of transformation of the theoretical concepts of senses, in the context of the complexity of sensory experiences, forces to reevaluate the aesthetic consequences of modernity from an epistemological perspective. As Baudelaire precisely wrote, because of the *intensité nerveuse* energized by the "accumulation de force vitale […] réservoir d'électricité humaine"[27], maybe Wagner was the *truest representative of modernity,* in spite (or because) of approximated knowledge of antiquity.[28] On this matter, Baudelaire's keywords are *will power, desire, concentration, nervous intensity, explosion.*[29] We will encounter Rimbaud in the same context, but it is Baudelaire who saw the implications of his intoxicating experience with music for the poetic form in general, which immemorial and long forgotten connection with the spheres of intoxication, madness and sound would reach a whole new level in the heart of modernity.

26 Müller: *Über die phantastischen Gesichtserscheinungen.*
27 Ibid., p. 800.
28 Ibid., p. 806.
29 Ibid., p. 807 (Emphasized in the original).

In the large study on the effect of hashish of 1860, which quite unusually included the word *Poème* in the title,[30] music gives the rhythm to important parts. It shows that Baudelaire was looking for a medium in which language could express modernity.

> Musical notes become numbers, and if your mind as the gift of mathematics, the melody, the harmony you listen, while keeping its voluptuous and sensual nature, is changing to a vast arithmetical operation in which numbers generate numbers, and which phases and creation you can follow with an unexplainable ease and an agility equal to the one of the performer.[31]

A little later, Arthur Rimbaud consciously appropriated these ideas. It is not without reason that he wrote about Baudelaire: "Baudelaire is the first foreseer, the king of poets, a real god."[32] The young rebel was the one who would express the synaesthetic relationships of the senses, which his elder hid in his poetics of modernity, for example in the *Fleurs du Mal* – or, to be more direct – he gave it an almost kinaesthetic expression. In his famous and much quoted poem *Voyelles*, the subject seems to be straightforwardly cognitive synaesthesia:

> A black, E white, I red, U green, O blue: vowels,
> I shall tell, one day, of your mysterious origins:
> A, black velvety jacket of brilliant flies
> which buzz around cruel smells,
>
> Gulfs of shadow; E, whiteness of vapours and of tents,
> lances of proud glaciers, white kings, shivers of cow-parsley;
> I, purples, spat blood, smile of beautiful lips
> in anger or in the raptures of penitence;
>
> U, waves, divine shuddering of viridian seas,
> the peace of pastures dotted with animals, the peace of the furrows
> which alchemy prints on broad studious foreheads;
>
> O, sublime Trumpet full of strange piercing sounds,
> silences crossed by Worlds and by Angels:
> –O the Omega! the violet ray of Her Eyes![33]

A section of the chapter "Délires II" of his text *Une saison en enfer* is titled "Alchimie du verbe":

> I invented colors for the vowels! [...] I made rules for the form and movement of every consonant, [...] It was first a study. I wrote silences, nights, I wrote down the unutterable. I made the whirling world stand still.[...] I got used to elementary hallucination: I could really very

30 Hans Georg Coenen vigorously defends the very Romanesque separation between 'poème' and 'prose' in his *Französische Verslehre*. (Id.: *Französische Verslehre*, p. 1).
31 Baudelaire: *Œuvres* I, p. 419.
32 Rimbaud: *Œuvres complètes*, p. 253.
33 Ibid., p. 53.

> see a mosque instead of a factory, a drum corps of angels, horse carts on the highways of the sky, a living room at the bottom of a lake; monsters and mysteries; a vaudeville's title filled me with awe.[…] At last, I began to consider my mind's disorder a sacred thing.[34]

Colors of vowels is an old romantic theme which already appears in A.W. Schlegel[35] and drew the attention of Ferdinand de Saussure,[36] while numerous drug eaters reported similar synaesthetic perceptions. Here, Rimbaud referred to his own sonnet *Voyelles*, one of the most commented poems of literature.[37] This short piece of the young Rimbaud – in which he implemented his theoretical ideas on poetic *writing* – is a key work which shows that the literary self-reference, at this important point of the *Saison*, is absolutely programmatic. Rimbaud invoked the memory of his own experiment to combine a drug-based filtering of senses and a writing practice – meaning that their irreconcilable temporal and physiological distance lifted itself. Contrarily to the reading of most interpreters, the enormous importance of a written possibility to unify acoustic and physiological vibrations and the visual perception of a text is addressed in *Voyelles*, not primarily by the sound of vowels but by their typeface (graphic appearance on the page) – *la forme et le mouvement* – to describe this double nature, Rimbaud formed out of the word *vibrer (to vibrate)*, the neologism *vibrements (vibring)*.[38] Here, one could say that learning to write is synaesthetic. The contemporary critics intuitively recognized it.

He illuminates every letter with obscure associations, the fly which shape can recall the A,[39] refers to one of the strangest and most terrifying poems of the *Fleurs du Mal*, *Une Charogne*, in which waves of flies are buzzing around a piece of carrion to picture the strangeness of organic processes:

> All that was going up and down like a wave,
> Or rushed crackling;
> It seemed that the body, swollen with a vague breath,
> Lived by multiplying.[40]

34 Rimbaud: *Œuvres*, pp. 106; 108.

35 In his *Betrachtungen über Metrik*. The extract is quoted in: Lange, Wolf-Dieter (Ed.): op. cit., Bd. II, p. 17.

36 de Saussure: *Linguistik und Semiologie*, pp. 478–480.

37 Rimbaud: *Œuvres*, p. 53.

38 Following Antoine Adam in his reading of *Voyelles* (Rimbaud: *Œuvres* BdP, p. 900).

39 Rimbaud: *Œuvres*, p. 53: "A, noir corset velu des mouches éclatantes / Qui bombinent autour des puanteurs cruelles".

40 Baudelaire: *Œuvres* I, p. 31.

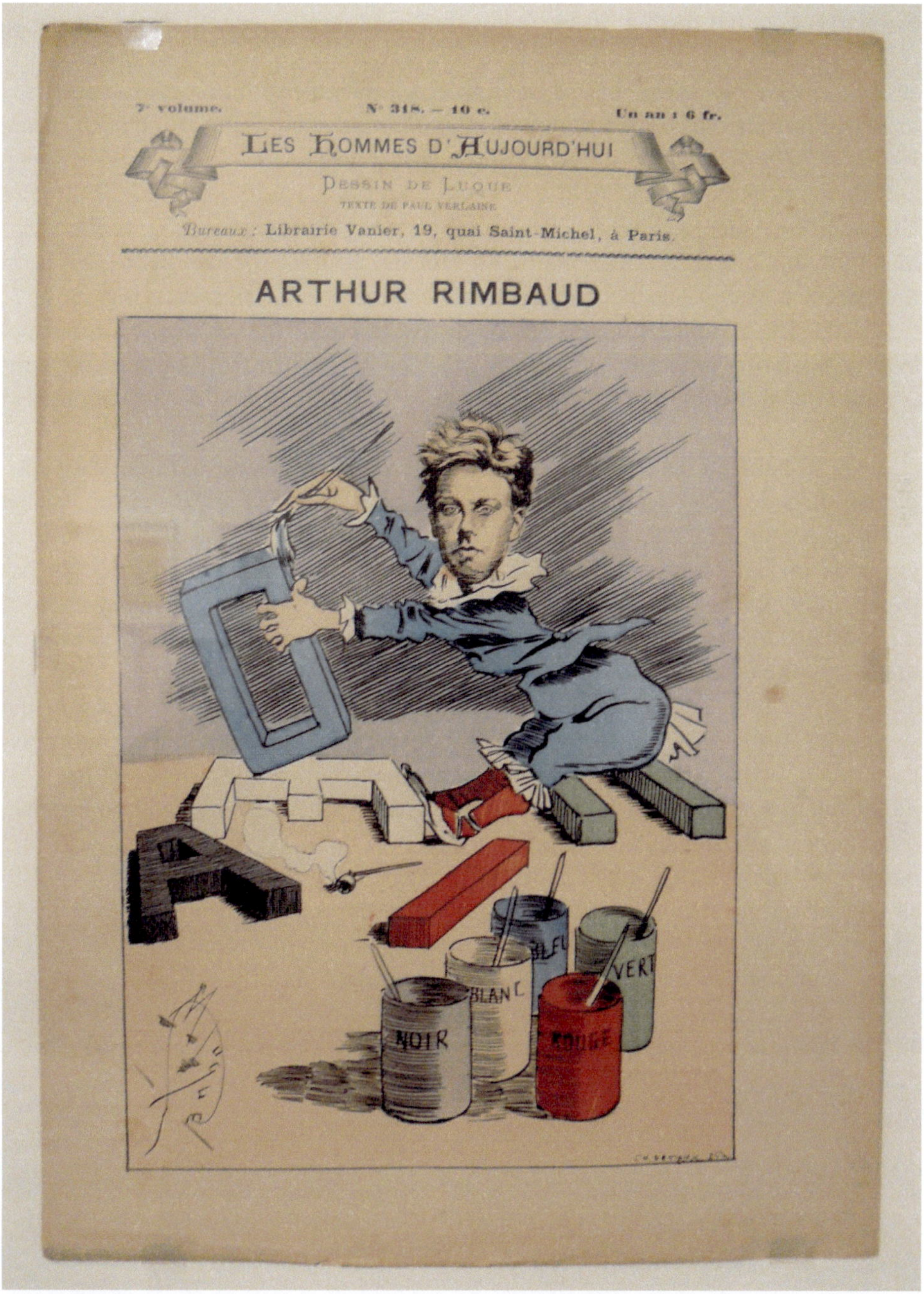


Fig. 1: Caricature of Rimbaud by Luque, 1888.

Similarly, E in the form ε, in the Latin font used until a recent past in European schools and also in France,[41] smokes over water, icicles, *frisson d'ombelles* (shivers of umbels),[42] a 'white' spiral movement comparable to intoxicating vapours. I as a haemorrhage, (red) pen stroke of an ignorant teacher,[43] the laughter distorted by anger or excitement of beautiful lips. U as a sequence of two successive up and down strokes, which enclose a wide depression in the middle and furrows and ripples on the swell of the sea which evoke the swaying grass and the wrinkles of a studious forehead. Finally, O, Omega, a violet silence, the lightning in the eyes of a beauty one can only call with capital letters. *Aphrodite, stay close.*[44]

This was an experiment, literally to *write* under the influence of a drug. Walter Benjamin noted the curious aberrations of the handwriting after the consumption of mescaline.[45] "Ce fut d'abord une étude"[46] means 'writing exercises' literally.

"Je m'habituai à l'hallucination simple"[47] (I made myself familiar with simple hallucination) is an ironic reference to a psycho-pathological concept of the medical doctor Alexandre-Jacques-François Brierre de Boismont developed in his book on hallucinations in 1862, in which he was making a distinction between *hallucinations simples* and *hallucinations composées.*[48] Rimbaud chose this concept to show his dissatisfaction regarding the dissociation of perception in modern lifestyles.

The poems of Rimbaud and the late texts of Baudelaire responded in the same way to the direct interconnections between relationships, nerve and transportation networks, as if a major city of the nineteenth century imposed itself on its inhabitants. 1845 – the year Moreau de Tours defined[49] in his book on hashish, *aliénation mentale* (mental illness) as a mental state in which the 'irreconcilable' outer and inner worlds of perception interpenetrated, and which he previously simulated by the use of drugs – was the year the well-known psychiatrist and chief editor of the *Annales médico-psychologiques* Jules Baillarger identified many 'automatisms' in the physiology of spiritual life, which could eventually

41 In the case of Rimbaud, the handwriting of the letters is self explanatory. See Rimbaud: *Œuvres*, p. 900.

42 Ibid., p. 53.

43 One can think about the *crayon* (de sanguine) with which Georges Izambard scribbled over *Le cœur du pitre*.

44 Kittler: *Musik und Mathematik Band I*, p. 337. This interpretation can be suggested by a very sensitive translation of a prayer to this goddess by Lucretius and a hymn like *Soleil et chair/Credo in unam*. This last verse can also be understood as an answer to the religious and Christian idea concluding Baudelaire's *Une charogne*.

45 Benjamin: *Über Haschisch*, pp. 129ff.

46 Rimbaud: *Œuvres*, p. 106.

47 Rimbaud: *Œuvres*, p. 108.

48 Brierre de Boismont: *Des hallucinations* [...], p. 19. Baudelaire already referred to this author (in the *fusées*. *Œuvres* I, p. 656). The first edition of 1845 was published the same year as *Du hachisch*.

49 Moreau de Tours: *Du Hachisch*, p. 172f.

confirm such interconnections.[50] The diagnosis made in the 19th century, stating that the *moi* was dissociated, was experimentally proved by Moreau de Tours and was not only a threat in the enclosed spaces of hospitals and asylums. The shock and trauma of a monstrous urban modernity, which transportation systems, residential developments and working methods scattered the conventional ego. This modernity began to condense into an aesthetics which fate it was, ironically, to be later identified with this threat.

## References

Baillarger, Jules: "Théorie de l'Automatisme (1845)", in: *Recherches sur les maladies mentales I,* Paris (Masson) 1890, p. 494.

Baudelaire, Charles: *Correspondance en deux volumes. Texte établi, présenté et annoté par Cl. Pichois avec la collaboration de J. Ziegler* (Bibliothèque de la Pléiade), Paris (Gallimard) 1973.

Baudelaire, Charles: *Œuvres Complètes en deux volumes. Texte établi, présenté et annoté par Claude Pichoi* (Bibliothèque de la Pléiade), Paris (Gallimard) 2004.

Béguin, Albert: *L'âme romantique et le rêve. Essai sur le romantisme allemand et la poésie française*, Paris (J. Corti) 1979.

Béguin, Albert: *Traumwelt und Romantik. Versuch über die romantische Seele in Deutschland und in der Dichtung Frankreichs*, ed. by Peter Grotzer, Bern/ München (Francke) 1972.

Benjamin, Walter: *Über Haschisch. Novellistisches. Berichte. Materialien*, Frankfurt am Main (Suhrkamp) 1972.

Brierre de Boismont, Alexandre-Jacques-François: *Des hallucinations ou histoire raisonée des apparitions, des visions, des songes, de l'extase, des rêves, du magnétisme et du somnambulisme*, Paris (Germer-Baillère) 1845.

Brierre de Boismont, Alexandre-Jacques-François: *Des hallucinations ou histoire raisonée des apparitions, des visions, des songes, de l'extase, des rêves, du magnétisme et du somnambulisme*, Paris (Germer-Baillère) 1862.

Coenen, Hans Georg: *Französische Verslehre*, Darmstadt (Wissenschaftliche Buchgesellschaft) 1998.

Condillac, Étienne Bonnot de: *Essai sur l'origine des connaissances humaines. Ouvrage où l'on réduit à un seul principe tout ce qui concerne l'entendement humain*, Paris (Libraires Associés) 1787.

50 Baillarger: "Théorie de l'Automatisme (1845)", in: *Recherches sur les maladies mentales I*, p. 494. Rimbaud would return later to such ideas. The concept of "automatisme" was very important for French psychiatry, see for instance Despine, Janet and de Clérambaud.

Condillac, Étienne Bonnot de: *Essai sur l'origine des connaissances humaines* [...], *éd. établie par R. Lenoir*, (Les Classiques de la Philosophie VI) Paris (Colin) 1924.

Friedrich, Hugo: *Die Struktur der modernen Lyrik. Von der Mitte des neunzehnten bis zur Mitte des zwanzigsten Jahrhunderts. Erweiterte Neuausgabe*, Reinbek bei Hamburg (Rowohlt) 1979.

Gautier, Théophile: "Description des effets du hachich, par un feuilletoniste de la Presse", in: *Annales médico-psychologiques* (1843) t. II, pp. 490–493, and in: Brierre de Boismont, Alexandre: *Des hallucinations* [...], Paris (Germer-Baillère) 1845, pp. 378–383.

Hagen, Wolfgang: "Walter Ruttmanns Großstadt-WEEKEND. Zur Herkunft der Hörcollage aus der ungegenständlichen Malerei", in: Nicola Gess / Florian Schreiner / Manuela, K. Schulz (ed.): *Hörstürze. Akustik und Gewalt im 20. Jahrhundert*, Würzburg (Königshausen & Neumann) 2005, pp. 183–200.

Kittler, Friedrich: *Musik und Mathematik Band I: Hellas, Teil 1: Aphrodite*, München (Wilhelm Fink) 2006.

Lange, Wolf-Dieter (ed.): *Französische Literatur des 19. Jahrhunderts* 3 vols., Heidelberg (Quelle & Meyer) 1980.

Moreau de Tours, Jacques-Joseph: *Du hachisch et de l'aliénation mentale. Études psychologiques*, Paris (Fortin, Masson et Cie.) 1845.

Müller, Johannes: *Über die phantastischen Gesichtserscheinungen. Eine physiologische Untersuchung mit einer physiologischen Urkunde des Aristoteles ueber den Traum, den Philosophen und Aerzten gewidmet*, Koblenz (Jacob Hölscher) 1826.

Rimbaud, Arthur: *Œuvres Complètes. Édition établie, présentée et annotée par Antoine Adam* (Bibliothèque de la Pléiade), Paris (Gallimard) 2005 [1972].

Rimbaud, Arthur: *Œuvres Complètes. Édition établie par André Guyaux. Avec la collaboration d'Aurélia Cervoni* (Bibliothèque de la Pléiade), Paris (Gallimard) 2009.

Scharbert, Gerhard: *Dichterwahn. Über die Pathologisierung von Modernität*, München (Wilhelm Fink) 2010.

de Saussure, Ferdinand: *Linguistik und Semiologie*, Frankfurt am Main (Suhrkamp) 1997.

## List of Illustrations

Fig. 1: Caricature of Arthur Rimbaud by Luque. Published in: Les Hommes d'aujourd'hui 7e vol. No 318, 1888.

# Synaesthesias of Reading. Rilke's Cross-Modalities

JAN SÖFFNER

Malte Laurids Brigge, the narrator of Rilke's famous novel, describes the readers in the Bibliothèque Nationale in Paris as nearly anaesthetized. You can bump into them and they won't even notice. However, if you "excuse yourself, [the reader] nods toward the side on which he hears your voice, his face turns to you and does not see you, and his hair is like the hair of a person asleep"[1]: The reader's sensitivity receives voices. All the other senses seem packed into this auditory. Evidently, for Rilke, reading – even silent, private reading – entails vocalism.

At another point, Malte states, "I am sitting and having a poet" – "Ich sitze und habe einen Dichter" – which is an unusual phrase even in German.[2] This poet's voice "sounds like a bell in pure air"[3] – and that means: Malte does not just read to decipher meanings; reading, for him, is a synaesthetic experience, conjuring up the environment of clear air wherein the bell-like voice sounds.

Such vocal synaesthesias are the topic of my chapter, largely in reference to Rilke's *Sonnets to Orpheus*. My main argument is twofold: First, that the implied synaesthesia is not just sensual, but also emotional; second, that voice (Stimme) and existential mood (Stimmung) are closely related in Rilke's notion of the reading experience.

## 1.

Before I turn to Rilke's poetry, let me elaborate a bit on the relation of existential mood and voice. The emotive attunement of the voice is a major issue in and mystery of emotional communication. First of all, the emotional timbre of the voice is an embodied enaction, related to certain tensions and relaxations of the body. A warm and gentle sound is created through a relaxing of posture, soften-

1 Rilke: *Notebooks*, p. 27: "[…] entschuldigst [du] dich, so nickt (der Leser) nach der Seite, auf der er deine Stimme hört, sein Gesicht wendet sich dir zu und sieht dich nicht, und sein Haar ist wie das Haar eines Schlafenden" (Rilke: *Sämtliche Werke*, Vol. 6, p. 741).

2 The translation by Burton Pike, "I am sitting and reading a poet" (Rilke: Notebooks, p. 27) does not render this phrase very well.

3 Ibid., p. 29: "[…] klingt wie eine Glocke in klarer Luft." (Rilke: *Sämtliche Werke*, Vol. 6, p. 745).

ing of the palate, and loosening of muscles. Vocalizing a 'growl' timbre, on the other hand, requires tensing the abdominal muscles, diaphragm, and larynx. In the line with a Darwinian approach to emotions, one could argue that such a posture can be understood as physical preparation for a fight, preparing the body to absorb blows and emit loud sounds to scare the opponent. Therefore, it should not be a surprise that a growl timbre is often perceived as aggressive. Aggressiveness and growling can be heard coming from aggressive characters in the Chinese Jinghu opera, Japanese Noh theatre, and Death Metal.[4]

Moreover an emotional state like this implies an interaction. It is not just personal. Hearing a growl reveals the aggressive mood of a *shared* situation, while a warm voice discloses *shared* feelings of kindness. Furthermore, this frequently occurs subliminally. We participate in situations through vocal clues. The nuanced tone of our own voice and the voices we hear allow people to share what Matthew Ratcliffe calls "existential feelings"[5] – feelings considering the world we find ourselves in.

I chose the term 'existential moods' to 'existential feelings' for this chapter, because I wish to refer to what in German would be called 'Stimmungen' – moods that are not merely personal, but can be part of a shared atmosphere.[6] In English you could say that a landscape has a certain *atmosphere*, or that it *creates* a particular mood; in German, the landscape itself would have a mood, as would a voice and its timbre.

Rilke works with a similar concept of the timbre of the voice and shared moods.[7] The first stanza of the 26th poem of the second part of the 'Sonnets to Orpheus' begins:

> Wie ergreift uns der Vogelschrei…
> Irgendein einmal erschaffenes Schreien

4 Cf. Tsai, Wang; Wang, Shau, Hsiao and Auhagen: "Aggressiveness of the Growl-Like Timbre."

5 Ratcliffe: *Feelings of Being*.

6 The freshest and most inspiring approach to Stimmungen in literature can be found in Gumbrecht: *Stimmungen Lesen*. I am widely following his approach.

7 Rilke, who used the term "Stimmungsbild" (pictured 'Stimmung') for a particular way of poetic descriptions, had a strong notion of 'Stimmung' as an embodied but nevertheless subliminal, participatory ways of sensed reality – as can be seen from the following quotation: "Wer nur über die Brücke der Stimmung mit dem Dichter gehen will, der ist gebannt durch die körperhafte Wirklichkeit der Alpenlandschaften, über der doch so ein unbeschreiblich feiner Zauber liegt. Der fühlt heimlichen Schauer einer ungebannten Macht mit, der diese Menschen von Fleisch und Blut doch so unvermerkt überkommt" (Rilke: *Sämtliche Werke*, Vol. 5, p. 314–315; "Who is ready to walk with the poet over the bridge of Stimmung, will be caught by the bodily reality of the landscape of the Alps, upon which such an indescribably subtle enchantment is laid. He will sense [in synchrony] with [the poet and the landscape] the secret shiver of an untamed force, overcoming these people of flesh and blood without them noticing"; my translation).

> Aber die Kinder schon, spielend im Freien
> schreien an wirklichen Schreien vorbei.[8]

Voice and vocalism, are as inseparable from moods as they are from musicality. Accordingly, the etymological root of Stimmung also refers to the tuning of instruments, hence to overtones. When Paul Hindemith set Rilke's *Life of Mary* to music, he accordingly counted on the opposition of harmonic and dissonant overtones to trace the redemption and condemnation exposed in the poetry. Crucially, musicality embraces *both* the concordant and the discordant. And so it does in Rilke. He does not condemn the strident bird cries. Phylogenetically or by the work of God, bird cries have been once created (they are "einmal erschaffen"), and thus they participate in the natural order – even if they are discordant. Children's cries are different, though. The dissonance at play here is linked to their free will – it takes place "im Freien" and in the context of playing, not only as a consequence of sharing the natural order. Rilke continues (the Children):

> Schreien den Zufall. In Zwischenräume
> dieses, des Weltraums (in welchen der heile
> Vogelschrei eingeht, wie Menschen in Träume –)
> treiben sie ihre, des Kreischens, Keile.[9]

Rilke owes these 'gaps' of the cosmos or world-space (Weltraum) to the Greek etymology of the word 'harmony': (the carpenter's) 'joints', or the work of 'fitting flushes'. Moreover, this metaphor does not just refer to harmony in the physically musical sense, but also to the antique, medieval and renaissance concept of World Harmony, in which a cosmic symphony was produced by the order of planets in movement, subliminally sounding through the world. The concept was profoundly astrological. Just as believers in astrology conceive of constellations as taking their real and readable shape in the firmament, their influence is understood to be subliminally present in the messy, unreadable immanent world. World Harmony was also thought to be inaudible to the material ears, but could still affect matter, particularly the order of the human organism as a microcosm. As Leo Spitzer[10] has convincingly argued, the German term Stimmung as a shared, existential mood, is in the tradition of this World Harmony. Stimmung is a kind of afterlife of this concept. It, indeed, still holds the latency and sharedness of an order that can only be subliminally felt, one that remains a background feeling, even when separated from the sound of the rotating planets.

8 "How bird-cries strike us.../ or any other outcry [once created]./ But the children, at play outside ["im Freien", which also means in liberty]/ – they already cry past real cries." (Translation by Graham Good, my annotations).

9 "Cry Fate [rather 'chance']. Into the gaps/ Of world-space (in which the intact/ bird-cry enters like dreams engulfing dreamers [literally: like people enter dreams])/ they force/ their wedges of screams." (Translation by Graham Good, my annotations).

10 Spitzer: *Classical and Christian Ideas of World Harmony*.

Rilke picks up this tradition and relates the existential moods back to music, albeit without reference to the transcendental order. Rather, he focuses on the overtones that echo the Stimmung of the cosmos in a completely immanent manner. His point is about how emotional mood and acoustic timbre can become one – as in the case of the captivating bird cries. And how they can fall apart: if children force the wedges of their cries into the interstices of the cosmos, it is the individual, the subjective cry, which puts the atmospheric order out of joint. The cry does not share the world anymore, but has become a personal expression.[11]

Traditionally, World Harmony was often linked to the sublime substance of gas- and fire-like ether – which, according to antique, medieval and early modern natural philosophy, was the substance filling the space of the heavens. In the late 19th century, though, the word 'ether' was reintroduced for something equally subliminal, something of an equally non-material materiality: radio transmissions. Rilke uses both these technological and cosmological backgrounds of ether in a prominent metaphor for shared emotionality in another poem to Orpheus, when he writes:

> Die Antennen fühlen die Antennen,
> und die leere Ferne trug...
>
> Reine Spannung. O Musik der Kräfte! (I, 12)[12]

The relation of the subliminal radio-waves and of electrical and musical tension present in the ether and waiting to be re-embodied, the already sensual acoustic waves in the air and the bodies, the attunement of overtones and of moods are brought together on the base of Stimmung.

## 2.

The extent to which Rilke cared about the sharedness and atmospheric character of existential moods, as embodied in vocalism, is set out in the first Sonnet to Orpheus in the second part of this collection:

11 Thus Rilke, at the end of the poem, calls for the god of song (presumably Apollo, who oversaw World Harmony in the neo-Platonic tradition) to make a chorus out of these children, "tragend als Strömung das Haupt und die Leier", carrying the head and the lyre as a flow.

12 Graham Good translates: "Antennae answering antennae,/ and out of empty space… // Pure tension! Music of the powers!"; but literally the lines read: "The antennas feel the antennas,/And the empty distance carried// Pure tension. Oh music of the forces."

Atmen, du unsichtbares Gedicht!
Immerfort um das eigne
Sein rein eingetauschter Weltraum, Gegengewicht,
in dem ich mich rhythmisch ereigne.

Einzige Welle, deren
Allmähliches Meer ich bin;
Sparsamstes du von allen möglichen Meeren, –
Raumgewinn.

Wie viele von diesen Stellen der Räume waren schon
Innen in mir. Manche Winde
Sind wie mein Sohn.

Erkennst du mich, Luft, du, voll noch einst meiniger Orte?
Du, einmal glatte Rinde,
Rundung und Blatt meiner Worte.[13]

If this poem is spoken naturally, the many enjambments and tremendous diversity of verse length obfuscates the rhymes. Thus, the poetic scheme is heard only subliminally. It is as latent in speaking as breath itself.

Another striking point is the use of the first person. As Paul de Man and others have noticed, Rilke's use of the first person does not necessarily refer to the speaker. Instead, it often refers to relations. In this poem, the first person seems to partially lie in vocalism. If "I occur rhythmically in the air" the reference must be to the voice. On the other hand, in the second-to-last stanza, the exhaled breath makes the atmosphere something that was "in me". Here, the first person refers to a breathing *body* instead of the voice this body produces. The question becomes even more difficult to answer in reference to the second stanza. Here, Rilke mingles wave concepts: those of the sea, and those of sound, which are their own time-space: a space without inside and outside and without surface.[14] For this time-space – an acoustically shared phenomenon taking on and dynamically bringing forth space – once again he uses the first and the second person. Both refer to the shared environmental enaction of breathing as a relation that physically inhabits the material world. There is no chiasm between the subject of the poem and the world surrounding this subject in Rilke's poetry, when the first person is used for the phenomena of the world (as Paul de Man has ar-

13 "Breathing, you invisible poem!/ World-Space in constant interchange/ with itself [literally: cosmos constantly exchanged purely around its own being]. Counterweight/ in which I rhythmically become [literally: occur].// Single wave,/ I am your gradual/ sea [literally: of which I am a gradual sea], the thriftiest [of all seas] possible:/ Saving [literally: gaining] of space.// How many of these places in space were once/ inside me. Many a wind/ is like a son [to me].// Do you know [recognize] me, air, full of places that were/ once mine?/ You, once smooth rind,/ rounding and leaf [or sheet] of my words. (Translation by Graham Good, my annotations).

14 For this notion, cf. Hermann Schmitz: *Der Leib, der Raum und die Gefühle*.

gued).[15] The subjective focus is not interchanged with a focus departing from the objects. Rather the focus is already shared with the world.

To turn to the last verses: here too, the relation between the first and the second person does not seem to be a relation of exchanging messages or addressing an Other as Other. It is rather, what Rilke himself refers to when he conceives of intransitive love, i.e. love that, unlike transitive love, does not have any object it is *about*.[16] Again, the material *relation* is crucial to understanding this concept – intransitive love is relational and enactive. The breathing atmosphere, in this tercet, is not only constituted of what is exhaled from a corporal body, but also of the trees which, in becoming trees, have produced oxygen and absorbed carbon. The trees and corporal body coexist in the metaphor of the wind instrument and paper (both made of trees), to which Rilke evidently refers, as prostheses of the voice; by physically sharing a world, words and world thereby become one. Everything is linked in a chain of transformations of matter occurring in the world.

But *how* then, as the first verse of the stanza states it, is the air supposed to "*recognize*" the persona? The only answer is: by *participating* in the waves, the sounds, the breathing activity; by materially sharing the form of and taking part in the phenomenon. Here, understanding is an atmospheric way of participatory sense-making.[17] The air neither recognizes *as* a persona, nor has it any recognition *about* a persona. There is no hermeneutic recognition at stake here, but rather what Shaun Gallagher and Dan Zahavi would call "Second Person Interaction."[18] Recognition is not about referential meaning (in the forth sonnet of the first part, Rilke accordingly writes: "Tender ones: enter now and then/ this *breath* that does not *mean* you.")[19] Recognizing occurs without reference, but within the context of sharing and participating; it indicates at the same time inhabiting an environmental and embodied relation, and sharing a phenomenon, not communicating issues or referring to them. The air's recognition is not *about* anything, but rather consists in becoming part of. Consequently, 'I' and 'Thou' are not used to demarcate a dialogue between two discrete entities.[20] Rilke rather dislocates the speaker and the reader and makes of both a *participatory relation occurring in the world* instead of persons or entities. Using the pronoun "ich" ('I') in this way, does not necessarily denote personification. An unexamined use of 'I' merely gives a face to a phenomenon and makes it addressable (as the rhetorical terms personification or prosopopoeia would imply). If Rilke's use of personal pronouns refers instead to shared phenomena provided with their own experiential *gestalt*. Personal pronouns in his poetry are much more about inspiration and

15 Cf. *Allegories of Reading*.
16 Cf. Schiwy: *Rilke und die Religion*, p. 101.
17 Cf. Di Paolo and De Jaegher: "Participatory Sense-Making".
18 Cf. Gallagher and Zahavi: *The Phenomenological Mind*.
19 "Oh ihr Zärtlichen, tretet zuweilen / in den Atem, der euch nicht meint" – here Good's translation "[…] not really meant for you", as smooth as it might read, is profoundly misleading.
20 Cf. Schiwy: *Rilke und die Religion*; Magnússon: *Dichtung als Erfahrungsmetaphysik*.

giving a soul to the things in the world than giving an addressable face or a mask – as the terms prosopopoia or personification would imply. It speaks more to what the poem shares by virtue of vocal inhabitation, than to the fact of dialogically addressing persons.

As stated above, something similar holds for Stimmungen.[21] If, as Matthew Ratcliffe would argue, existential feelings latently orient our actions in the world; if, as Martin Heidegger would have it, Stimmungen disclose the world; if existential moods, by inhabiting the world, give it its emotional form and enacted intrinsic judgment, then recognition, here too, is not *about* anything. This fact is made prominent in Rilke's poetry as well: when the existential mood vocally shares a body, it shares the action of breathing and the acoustics of sound waves. "Gesang ist Dasein" – singing is existence or being there (I,2) writes Rilke to define what orphic poetry is. It is intransitive, i.e. participatory. Stimmung and Stimme recognize by resonance i.e. by participating in one another – not by referring to one another. Recognition is something shared, something emerging *inter*corporally by inhabiting a shared space. There is no persona expressing herself or himself, speaking about his or her world, evoking or constituting a reality by speaking or writing. Rather, there is an enactive relation, from which sense emerges in its particular, individual, but nevertheless shared *gestalt*.[22]

When one turns this particular way of making sense not by referring, but by sharing, it becomes clear, at what kind of sense-making Rilke's poetry was aiming. His point was neither to make the poem aesthetically refer to itself, nor to make it refer to the world. It was to make the poem part of the world, let the world speak as the poem, and to make a poem speak by sharing the world. And it becomes easy to see, that this is also what happens to the readers in the Bibliothèque Nationale: the text becomes a synaesthetical (instead of referential) habitat of their bodies, just like the surrounding world is a habitat. Only that the textual habitat is stronger.

Another conclusion can be drawn from both the 'breathing' of poetry and the bell-like voice of Malte's poet. The crucial issue in this is shared vocalism. Reading, in Rilke, implies at least a subliminal kind of factual synaesthetic vocalisation and embodiment that makes 'voice' more than just a metaphor for the index of subjectivity (e.g. for the 'author' as a subject). Vocalism, here, is understood as corporally *sharing* rather than deciphering the subject 'behind' the text.

21 Cf. Angelika Jacobs: "Vom Symbolismus zur 'Stimmung'", pp. 112–116.

22 Rilke also theoretically conceived of this fact. In a letter (7.3. 1896 to Bodo Wildberg) he wrote (quoting "Dr. Klaar", who is Alfred Klaar, president of the association "Concordia" in Prague): "'Stimmung' is in a situation what individuality is in a character. 'Stimmung' makes a particular, specific, individual situation out of a general one; just like individuality coins a character into being the 'One' that is like no other" ("Stimmung verhält sich zur Situation wie Individualität zum Charakter, die Stimmung macht die allgemeine Situation zu einer besonderen, spezifischen, individuellen, wie die Individualität den Charakter mehr oder weniger zum 'Einen' stempelt, dem kein zweiter gleichkommt." Rilke: *Gesammelte Briefe*, p. 18, my translation).

The embedded situatedness of poetry shows that Rilke's poetry is less about signification than it is about *synaesthesia*.

## 3.

As early as 1904, Rilke wrote the poem *Orpheus, Eurydice, Hermes*; this work offers more insight into his poetics of *sharing* and inhabiting – and into its relation to its opposite, which would be both addressing persons and saying things *about* the world or referring to it. Here Eurydice appears as:

> Die So-Geliebte, daß aus einer Leier
> mehr Klage kam als je aus Klagefrauen;
> daß eine Welt aus Klage ward, in der
> alles noch einmal war.[23]

By the force of poetry, a lost world is brought back into being – even though it is brought back *as lost*. The world of poetry, the world where everything is there for a second time, is a world one *inhabits*. The second world emerges synaesthetically *within* the world, as the senses are compressed into sharing the song of a poet. And as Gabriele Brandstetter has convincingly argued: it is a kinaesthetic world, a world where turning back is a danced movement, which instead will be lost as a dance, as soon as it is 'only' poetry,[24] i.e. part of the world of Hermes, who instead is the "Gott der Botschaft" ('God of the message'), the god of talking *about* the world.

According to this double nature of finding oneself in the world (i.e. by poetry and by observation), the senses of Orpheus are "entzweit" ('split in two'). While his gaze focuses at the objects in front of him, "His hearing stayed behind like a scent" ("blieb sein Gehör wie ein Geruch zurück"): the gaze alone is addressing. The synaesthetic comparison of senses of smelling and listening instead focus on a way of sensing which avoids addressing. These senses are the place where the intransitive lovers walk. The gaze, on the other hand, is the object producing action. Making a world accessible to observation makes objects arise as objects, subjects as persons. Gaining addressable entities goes hand in hand with creating a subject-object dichotomy and thereby with *transitive* love. The gaze means losing acoustic spatio-temporality as a shared space. The world with addressable agents, though, is Hermes' world; and this is the world wherein which

23 "The so-beloved, that out of one lyre / more grief came than from all grieving women: / so that a world of grief arose, in which / all things were there once more." (Translated by A.S. Kline).

24 Brandstetter: "Poetik der Ent-Wendung".

Orpheus' power is insufficient to keep him from losing his love. Hermes, sending Eurydice back to the underworld, states that "He" has turned around – Eurydice replies, "Who?" For her, there was no addressable Other present, no gaze felt, because all that was *shared* was intransitive action. Euridice's walk followed the steps, not the person.

The threshold between the states of sharing and addressing sheds some light on the concept of 'orphic metamorphosis' ("Orphische Verwandlung") and orphic poetry in Rilke's later works. When Rilke states: "Once and for all times it is Orpheus, if it sings" ("Ein für alle Male/ Ist's Orpheus, wenn es singt" I,5), he is creating the very same paradox of addressing and sharing. On the one hand, song, here, is depersonalized: 'it' sings just like 'it' rains, and this *impersonality* is orphic agency. This is analogous to Malte, who 'has' a poet by sharing his voice and by inhabiting the synaesthesias of reading. On the other hand, the phrase is within a volume of *Sonette an Orpheus* – poems addressed to Orpheus, not sharing his agency, but written for him. The sonnets thereby have two sides; they are sound-poems, etymologically speaking (because this is the meaning of 'sonetto'), *and* thought-poems in the literary tradition of the sonnet. The poems can be shared as a latently felt voice in reading, but they also say something *about* poetry. Orphic metamorphosis mediates between these incompatible realms – just as Orpheus does when he tries to restore a face to Eurydice, when his gaze tries to make her a personification of herself instead of sharing the path with her in walking. They take place in the space between the two phenomenological modes of discerning discrete persons and objects bearing qualities on the one hand – and shared interactions and existential moods on the other hand. Orphic metamorphosis mediates between a world to talk about or gaze upon, and a world inhabited and musically shared, between reading poetry as deciphering texts and developing concepts, and reading poetry as a synaesthetically and kinaesthetically shared enaction. Between words referring to meanings and words whose meanings consist in a felt sensuality.

Seen from this point of view, of course the act of *describing* or referring, the fact of being thought-poems, contradicts sharedness. If the poems talk about all this sharedness, therefore they produce this very contradiction: they are – in their being about something – transitive and stand on the side of Hermes. But discerning this contradiction is not the only, and perhaps not even the important point, since making this point is itself profoundly hermeneutic. Consequently, one could also make the opposite point by stating that the essential issue is orphic metamorphosis, not Herme-neutics, sharing a corporal transformation, not building mental models of transformation: understanding must be like the air understanding sounds – not like a hermeneutic mind understanding allegories. Rilke's poetry is not as much about the allegories of reading, as it is about the synaesthesias of reading.

## 4.

The last sonnet to Orpheus begins with the stanza:

> Stiller Freund der vielen Fernen, fühle,
> wie dein Atem noch den Raum vermehrt.
> Im Gebälk der finstern Glockenstühle
> Lass dich läuten. […][25]

Here the 'I' and the 'thou' seem to have at least something to do with poet and reader. And as in the reading hall of the Bibliothèque Nationale, *silent* reading is addressed. The friend is a silent one, and one of the many distances lying between him and the poet he has. Nevertheless, synaesthetic and emotional sharedness still play a crucial role – becoming one with the phenomena remains the major issue. Again through breath, the friend shares the enlarged space and is embedded in that world. Both Malte's poet and this friend resound like bells, in a shared Stimmung and with a shared Stimme, they both resonate. The poem thereby describes the subliminal embodiment of a voice in silent reading; the "Glocke in klarer Luft" is a tone of voice generated by a subliminal intonation sharing a mood.

Ultimately, this is the point about inhabiting a poem. And the first tercet is about this very meaning or sense (Sinn) of poetic synaesthesia:

> Sei in dieser Nacht aus Übermaß
> Zauberkraft am Kreuzweg deiner Sinne,
> ihrer seltsamen Begegnung Sinn.[26]

Rilke here uses both the *via crucis* and the crossroads as a metaphor for poetic cross-modality. The strange and unforeseen encounter of the senses and the meaning in reading is the orphic metamorphosis. The particular sense emerging from this encounter, the semanto-sensual existential mood intrinsic in this poetry, is the crux of the synaesthesias of reading.

The last verse of the cycle then turns to *kin*aesthetics as a means of reading *in* the world:

> Und wenn dich das Irdische vergaß,
> zu der stillen Erde sag: Ich rinne.
> Zu dem raschen Wasser sprich: Ich bin.[27]

25 "Silent friend of many distances, feel/ how space is still increasing through your/ breath. Among the dark belfries' beams/ let yourself ring out [literally: Among the dark belfries/ let yourself be chimed]." (Translation by Graham Good, my annotations).

26 "Be in this night's immensity [literally: this night consisting of immensity]/ magic at the crossroads [or *via crucis*] of your senses – be/ their strange encounter's meaning."

The Sonnets to Orpheus end by bringing a new twist to Heraclite's paradox that we can *and* cannot step twice into the same river. In the second poem I quoted, the air recognized the sound by sharing its waves; likewise, here the earth understands the flow of those moving upon it by being their firm ground, and the flowing water understands the 'being' of those that step into it by flowing around them. Rilke, again, develops a sensual form of participation in which poetry itself can be embodied, and understood *by* that embodiment. Reading a poem has to become part of the reader's embodied habitat, and the reader's embodied habitat has to become one with reading a poem. Therefore, poetry neither refers to the world nor to itself. It shares and inhabits the world.

But to return to the earthly that forgot the 'thou'. The *Seinsvergessenheit* Heidegger mentions when he talks about philosophy, appears in Rilke as a forgetfulness of this very need of poetry to share the world, to be embedded in it. Moreover, this lack of participation is rather a fact of *being forgotten* by the earthly than for the earthly to *forget* itself. When – as he often does – Rilke attacks concepts of *poiesis* and poetic creation and instead points on participation,[28] this necessity of inhabiting is the point he is trying to make. Without subliminally sharing, without being embodied and embedded *in the* world, poetry can neither refer to it nor bring forth a world of its own.

## Conclusion

All this may seem fairly metaphysical, but I think it is not. In reading them loudly at least, poems indeed *do* change one's embodied tone of voice; the implicit mood of a poem comes through the partially unintended timbre the voice assumes. And understanding a poem does not only consist in acquiring the knowledge to describe it. It also consists in acquiring the knowledge to (at least subliminally) enact it. The Stimmung of reading, thus embodied, considers reading as an action embedded in the world. And this embodied embeddedness gives

27 "[And] if the earthly has forgotten you/ say to the still Earth: I flow./ And tell the flowing stream: I am." (Translation by Graham Good).

28 This is an often overlooked but nevertheless explicit, important and repeated claim of Rilke. A poet can, yes, 'make sense' i.e. create a self-referential meaning or a meaning referring to the world. But a meaning 'in the world' cannot be produced by poetry, since the world itself cannot be produced either. In the 12th Sonnet of the first part of the Sonnets to Orpheus, one can accordingly read: "Even if the peasant cares and acts/ there where the seed in the summer is transformed/ he himself is never enough [for this transformation]/ The earth donates." ("Selbst wenn sich der Bauer sorgt und handelt, / wo die Saat im Sommer sich verwandet, / Reicht er niemals hin. Die Erde schenkt", my tranlstion). Something similar holds for poetry whose meaning lies in the sensual transformation of actual bodies instead of the 'production' of meaning.

one's reading of a poem its subliminal orientation. And this is what I mean by stating that Rilke's poems are about inhabiting a poem and letting a poem inhabit one's own embodied existence.

It is difficult to determine *how* poetic meanings become embodied as a timbre, though. There is a huge explanatory gap between the meaning of a poem and its embodiment. Thinking about it in terms of synaesthesia might help with this; indeed, silent reading makes the embodied relation with the text even more synaesthetic than the attuned voice does. Instead of being a manifest embodied action, the intrinsic Stimmung is now something subliminally sensed and enacted. Like Rilke describes it for the readers of Bibliothèque Nationale, the text itself becomes the immersive environment of the body.

In this sense, it is correct to say that one can *have* a poet like one *has* furniture at home; indeed, Rilke discusses that in the same passage, and at this point in the novel we should consider Malte as having lost his own furniture. He has exchanged his home, the place where his habitus and habitat met, with the reading room. Losing the place one inhabits equals losing a form of existence – and, in a similar way, having a poet equals having him *as* a form of existence.

Reading, therefore, is the act of sensually embodying a text and making it so much a part of one's sensual habitat that it becomes more important than the actual environment. The absorption of the reader in the Stimmung, is thus the opposite of disembodiment or decontextualization. When the readers turn to who has spoken to them without seeing the person, they behave like Eurydice in the poem. They remain unaware of the "who." And in *this* scene there *is* no Hermes, no God of Hermeneutics.

## References

Brandstetter, Gabriele: "Poetik der (Ent-)Wendung. 'Orpheus und Eurydike' als Choreographie, in: Armen Avanessian / Gabriele Brandstetter / Franck Hofmann (eds.): *Die Erfahrung des Orpheus*, Munich (Fink) 2010, pp. 187–197.

Chen-Gia Tsai / Li-Ching Wang / Shwu-Fen Wang / Yio-Wha Shau / Tzu-Yu Hsiao / Wolfgang Auhagen: "Aggressiveness of the Growl-Like Timbre – Acoustic Characteristics, Musical Implications and Biomechanical Mechanisms," in: *Music Perception* 27 (2010), pp. 209–221.

De Man, Paul: *Allegories of Reading*, New Haven (Yale University Press) 1982.

Di Paolo, Ezequiel / Hanneke De Jaegher: "Participatory Sense-Making. An Enactive Approach to Social Cognition", in: *Phenomenology and the Cognitive Sciences* 6 (2007) 4, pp. 485–507.

Gallagher, Shaun / Dan Zahavi: *The Phenomenological Mind*, London (Routledge) 2008.

Gumbrecht, Hans Ulrich: *Stimmungen Lesen*, Frankfurt am Main (Suhrkamp) 2010.

Magnússon, Gislí: *Dichtung als Erfahrungsmetaphysik. Esoterische und okkultistische Modernität bei R. M. Rilke*, Würzburg (Königshausen & Neumann) 2009.

Jacobs, Angelika: "Vom Symbolismus zur 'Stimmung'. Zur Poetik des Gefühls beim frühen Rilke", in: *Blätter der Rilke-Gesellschaft* 25 (2004), pp. 99–127.

Rilke, Rainer Maria: *Briefe aus den Jahren 1892–1904*, Leipzig (Insel) 1939.

Rilke, Rainer Maria: *Sämtliche Werke*, ed. by Ernst Zinn, 7 Vols., Frankfurt am Main (Insel) 1955–1998.

Rilke, Rainer Maria: *The Notebooks of Malte Laurids Brigge*, transl. by Burton Pike, Champaign, London/Dublin (Dalkey Archive Press) 2008.

Ratcliffe, Mattew: *Feelings of Being. Phenomenology, Psychiatry and the Sense of Reality*, London (Oxford University Press) 2008.

Schiwy, Günter: *Rilke und die Religion*, Frankfurt am Main (Insel) 2006.

Schmitz, Hermann: *Der Leib, der Raum und die Gefühle* (1998), Bielefeld/Locarno (Sirius) 2007.

Spitzer, Leo: *Classical and Christian Ideas of World Harmony. Prolegomena to an Interpretation of the Word 'Stimmung'*, ed. by Anna Granville Hatcher, Baltimore (Johns Hopkins University Press) 2008.

# The Temporal Gap
# On Asymmetries within the So-Called "Audiovisual" Regime (in Sensory Perception and in Technical Media)

WOLFGANG ERNST

## Introductory remarks

Terms like *audiovisual media* (condensed to *AV Media*) and *audiovisual perception* are so commonly used that the link between both components, the auditory and the visual, seems almost self-evident. Media-archaeological analysis though (in accordance with the cybernetic approach encompassing signal transfer both in humans and in machines) sharpens attention for asymmetries, discontinuities and asynchronicities within this apparently complementary complex. With synaesthesia being defined as phenomenon of multisensory cross-integration and cross-sensory mapping, the question arises to what degree the signal processing involved needs to be differentiated according to its channels of transmission – an approach which is familiar to communication engineers. Among neurobiological theories of synaesthetic effects there is the explanation of aberrant wiring in the cerebral cortex, thus once more reactivating the once famous electronic model of brain functions. Based on the theorems of information theory, such processes within human cognition and within technological systems can be compared and correlated (with human-machine interfaces increasingly coupling both). This media-communicative perspective provides a link between the sensory and the cultural analysis of synaesthetic and kinaesthetic effects.

The bias of this approach is a critique of the totalizing notion of the *audio-visual* as such. More specifically, there seems to be a privileged affinity – or even resonance – of the auditory (or sonic) sensual channel to the temporal frequencies of nerve cell signalling on the one side and a privileging of spatial schemes by visual signal input on the other side. The asymmetries between the auditory and the visual in signal processing (in sensory perception which means aisthesis – and in technical media which means electronic operations) can be specifically addressed under the aspect of its different temporal configurations (the temporal gap, both in its techno- and neurodynamical significance). This involves the question if there is a human or technical sense of time at all. Research into synaesthetic mixing of the senses inevitably leads to questions of synchronization of sensory signal transmission by the rhythms of pulse trains. Digital signal processing (starting with telegraphy and the Morse code) is close to the signal transmission within human nerves where optical and acoustic perception is translated into impulses which are communicated to the brain in form of pulse trains. To an astonishing degree, the neuroscientific vocabulary to describe the cognitive ti-ming processes within the human brain, resemble the description of technological tempor(e)alities.

## The visual alphabet, clocks and numbers versus electro-acoustic space (McLuhan)

Auditory information is radically time-based and thus requires short-time pre-semantic memory buffers in the human brain. The privileged relation between the frequencies of oscillations within the human brain and auditory sound wave perception[1] might be related to one of the wonders of cultural engineering: phonetic speech and more specifically its visual expression, the vocal alphabet. "Although periodic sound stimuli are relatively rare in nature (and sinusoids virtually absent), such stimuli are especially important for humans because of their role in vocal communication."[2] The musicality of speech is in its vocal sound, most expressively in oral poetry which led early Greece to the specific modification of writing towards the phonetic alphabet, that is: adding explicit symbols for vowels.[3] But visual spatiality took revenge when writing and reading became the dominant practice of acquiring knowledge. The neuronal ratio of sound-sight mapping is indeed coupled to external symbolic operations: "As an intensification and extension of the visual function, the phonetic alphabet diminishes the role of the other senses of sound and touch and taste in any literate culture," Marshall McLuhan wrote in 1964 in his classic Understanding Media.[4] By phonetic writing, sound became spatialized, privileging and separating optical reading over the other senses.[5] This heating up of one sense for symbolic information processing was enhanced by the printing press and culminates in the communication theory from the engineering point of view with its linear, sequential and logic diagram of sender – channel – receiver, and the separation of *figure* and *ground,*[6] *thing* and *medium.*[7]

1 Kaernbach: *Echogedächtnis*, p. 132 f, referring to Cowan: *On short and long auditory stores*, p. 341–370.
2 Purves et al. (ed.): *Principles of Cognitive Neuroscience*, p. 153.
3 Ernst/Kittler (ed.): *Die Geburt des Vokalalphabets aus dem Geist der Poesie.*
4 McLuhan: *Understanding Media*, pp. 81–88 (84).
5 McLuhan/Powers: *The Global Village*, p. 74.
6 Ibid., pp. 25–36 (25).
7 On this distinction, see Heider: *Ding und Medium*, pp. 109–157.

The phonetic alphabet, written in distinctive symbols, and its kinaesthetic decoding by reading corresponds with mechanical cinematics in its technical meaning, like the clock-work of timing relates to the mathematical position system of numbers: "Great cultural changes occurred in the West when it was found possible to fix time as something that happens between two points."[8] The phonetic alphabet has been the technology that preconditioned "the visual and uniform fragmentation of time."[9] But with the 19th century emergence of the electromagnetic field, a discontinuity in this hierarchy took place: "In the space-time world of electric technology, the older mechanical time begins to feel unacceptable."[10] Linear perception has been replaced by synchronisation – which is a sort of synaesthetic effect within the temporal regime of perception itself. Thus another dimension of synaesthesia takes shape, which takes place in the human senses when being coupled to technological agencies such as electronic sound or video recording. Electricity as such is principally of the same nature like the acoustic world by being potentially everywhere simultaneously; electronic recording media carry this further into the manipulation of time: "By electric tapes, synchronization of any number of different acts can be simultaneous."[11] The mechanical principle of serial analysis and synthesis as known from the printing press and from cinema has been superseded by electronic immediacy.

> Today in the electric age we feel as free to invent nonlinear logics as we do to make non-Euclidian geometries. Even the assembly line, as the method of analytic sequence for mechanizing every kind of making and production, is nowadays yielding to new forms.[12]

A principle which is (algorithmically expressed) recursive function in computing. Only with the electric image the ground returned – a stochastic ground, though, as expressed in Bill Viola's videotape Information (USA 1973).[13] The information of an electronic image can actually be measured in terms of digital communication engineering.[14]

8 McLuhan: *Understanding Media*, pp. 145–146 (145).
9 Ibid., p. 147.
10 Ibid., p. 147.
11 Ibid., p. 152.
12 Ibid., p. 85.
13 See the (in fact impossible) 'video still' reproduction in: Herzogenrath: *TV-Kultur*, p. 293.
14 See Shannon: *A Mathematical Theory of Communication*, pp. 379–423 and 623–656.

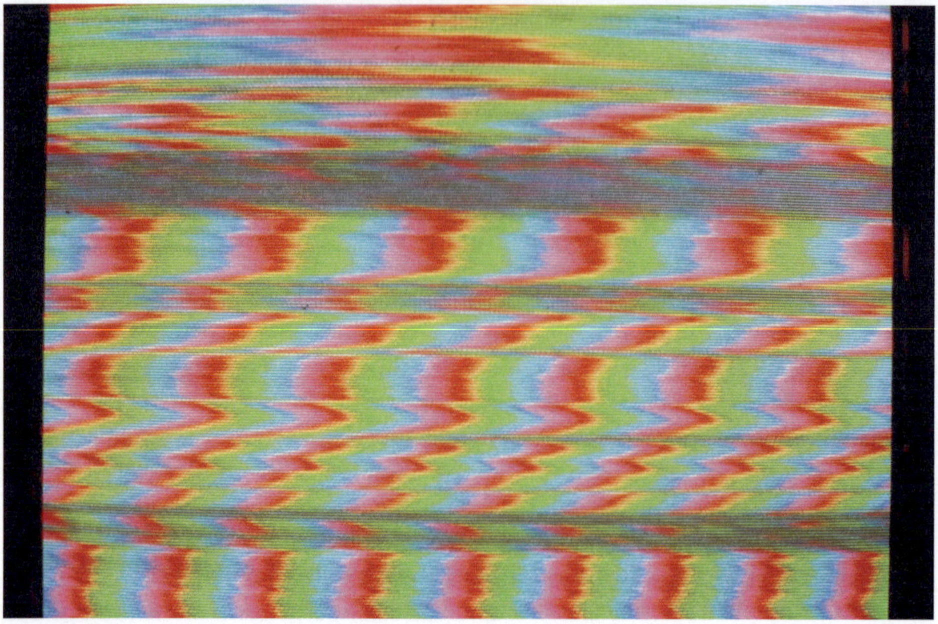

Fig. 1: Bill Viola, *Information*, USA 1973. Colour video, sound, 30 min.

McLuhan argues for a non-linear, right-hemispheric brain mode of communication[15] rather than *euklidic*, left-hemispheric space of analytic geometry.[16] Today, this categorization is not as obsolete as it appears in McLuhan's historicized media theory. In the neurosciences of the 1980s it has been proposed that time and number are represented by the same representational currency. Both perceptions are almost synaesthetically linked within the human brain. "Time and number are fundamental non-verbal aspects of cognition,"[17] being located in the brain area which is in charge of sequential ordering (the number form).

## Articulation in "sonic" time: resonances

In its ancient Greek sense syn-aisthésis means sympathetic sensation. This reminds not only of cross-modal metonymies but as well of sympathy within the temporal field, which is familiar from the phenomenon of resonance as a special form of energy transfer. Acoustic space is without centre; it rather consists of

15 McLuhan: *Understanding Media*, p. 30.

16 Ibid., p. 89.

17 Purves (ed.): *Principles of Cognitive Neuroscience*, p. 51 (referring to the interpretation of Meck and Church).

infinite resonances.[18] It is this dynamic state to which the human brain responds in a privileged way since its own internal timing processes are oscillatory to a high degree.

> Resonance refers to the tendency of [...] numerous [...] objects to vibrate in an ongoing manner determined by the details of their physical structure. Depending on the frequency components of these ongoing vibrations, longer-lasting stimuli can generate the perception of a tone if the vibrations are relatively coherent, but are perceived as noise if they are incoherent.[19]

This is mirrored in the mechanism of vocal-consonant speech, between pure tone and noise.

It is not an oxymoron but by reference to both cultural and neurological studies into the stimulation of brain hemispheres that McLuhan could claim when humans watch TV, their eyes function like ears.[20] Research into synaesthetic cross mapping of auditory and visual senses inevitably lead to questions of synchronization between sensory and signalling pulse trains. Loosely in accordance with Gotthold Ephraim Lessing's *Laocoon* theorem from 1766, there is a privileged affinity of the auditory (or sonic) sense resp. channel to the frequencies of nerve cell signalling, as opposed to visual signal processing:

> Like other wave phenomena, sound waves can be described in terms of four characteristics: waveform [...], frequency [...], amplitude [...] and phase. Because the frequency of sound waves is within the range of nerve cell signalling (at least of low frequencies), the auditory system can use this information directly in responding to sound stimuli; in vision, the frequencies of light waves are many orders of magnitude greater, and the response to frequency is only indirect via the energy content of different frequencies.[21]

By nature (physis), sound waves belong to the mechanical world, while light is within the range of the electro-magnetic spectrum, thus being of completely different media qualities. In a certain sense, visual perception is the only *radio* organ humans are provided with, while ears cannot listen to radio (in its technical, Hertzean sense) at all, just in translation by loudspeakers as interface. In the world of so-called audio-visual media, we are confronted with media-induced temporal affects of epistemologically different kinds. Where sound waves and light though converge is in their common analysis as periodic events, counted in frequencies. In media-archaeological perspective, the earliest devices to create optical illusions of movement like William George Horner's Zoetrope have their predecessors in the study of acoustic oscillations, like Ernst Florens Chladni's famous visualizations of such sound figures in 1787.[22]

18 See Cramer: *Symphonie des Lebendigen.*

19 Purves, p. 152.

20 McLuhan/Powers: *The Global Village*, p. 84.

21 Purves: *Principles of Cognitive Neuroscience*, p. 153.

22 See Gethmann: *Zauberscheiben und Schwingungsverhältnisse*, pp. 51–79 (60 f).

## Asymmetries: rhythms for example

The science of Education differentiates between three types of learning: auditory, visual and synaesthetic. This asymmetry differentially unfolds in time. But let us be cautious with the use of the term: 'symmetry' is a geometrical concept itself; it is deprived of the temporal axis. Here the appropriate equivalent is rather synchronicity.

The ear is privileged as a substitute for the missing *sixth sense* (the temporal sense), whereas the eye is concentrated on synchronous distribution of objects in space. In between happens kinetics (movement as temporal integration of successive spaces), which leads us to rhythm. Let us remember ancient Greek theories of music, such as Aristoxenos' notion of elementary tempora units of expression (chrónoi) and deviations (arrhythmia) in prosody and dance, which anticipated on the field of time-critical articulation which later has been detected as (a-) synchronous oscillations of neurons in the human brain.[23] Michel Chion discusses the neurodynamic element within the context of cinema:

> Rhythm […] is an element of film vocabulary that is […] neither specifically auditory nor visual. […] when a rhythmic phenomenon reaches us via a given sensory path, this path, eye or ear, is perhaps nothing more than the channel through which rhythm reaches us. Once it has entered the ear or eye, the phenomenon strikes us in some region of the brain connected to the motor functions, and it is solely at this level that it is decoded as rhythm.[24]

Is the audio-visual divide thus suspended in the temporal dimension? On the more structural level of perceptual distinction it opens again: "For the sense of sight those distinctions (except for color) are spatial ones; but for the sense of hearing they are mainly temporal. To put it directly: what the sense of hearing hears is essentially time."[25] But what characterizes hearing is not that it senses mechanical waves as such but their distinctions; just as "sight does not perceive electromagnetic dynamics but the minute distinctions between electromagnetic waves."[26] This brings audio-visual perception close to the Aristotelian definition of time as measurement of movement by numbers, which here is: frequencies.

23 Aristoxenus: *Elementa Rhythmica*. See also Emmanuel: *La Danse Grecque antique d'après les monuments figurés*.
24 Chion: *Audio-Vision*, p. 136.
25 Ibid., p. 136.
26 Turner/Pöppel: *The neural lyre*, pp. 277–309.

## Asymmetries between the auditory and the visual

The asymmetry within the so-called audio-visual media is disclosed in the filmic subgenres of *photo film* and *still movies*: long shots with quasi-photographic endurance.[27] One can cut out a single frame in a film, copy it and produce a long (seemingly) immobile sequence (in fact, the medium – whether mechanically the cinematograph or electronically the video monitor – moves constantly), but the accompanying audio track, cut out of one frame, in fact is a sample in its technical sense which – being reproduced, would rather result in a single signal. An image (i.e. a portrait) can be visually frozen in the *photo film*, but not a spoken word.

Neurobiologically the model of multimodal integration and intermodal analogies has replaced the notion of distinctly separate senses.[28] This replacement is itself a product of the epistemology of system theory (objectified in network-based communication media). The limbic system within the human brain represents the quasi-medium to translate between the separate senses by hyper-binding and hyper-connectivity, reminding of *wiring* in electronic engineering.[29] But nota bene: what today, in multi-media technologies, looks like an analogy to this brain intermodality (the indifference of signal processing regarding the phenomenological senses), is in fact based on a strict techno mathematical uniformity: the alphanumeric binary data processing, indifferent to analog components which play a decisive role (chemical transmitters) within the brain. Here, the different sensual regimes appear only on the interface level as formats.

The media-archaeological perspective accentuates the electronic differences in what appears like an audio-visual integration. When, for use in sound film, the photocell is used for reading visual information into sound again, it is the cold electronic *eye* itself, which transforms this without reference to any auditory or visual meaning, just operating on the principles of photonic effects and electromagnetic induction. The filmmaker Oskar Fischinger in the early 1930s inscribed geometric patterns on the sound track of the cinematic celluloid, which is a media-archaeological approach to sound. Artists in the 1920s (notably Raoul Hausmann's Optofonetika) and 1930s used the photo cell device for artistic sound synthesis; Lászlo Moholy-Nagy declared media art being of both the optical-kinetical and the acoustic-musical regime.[30] Vice versa the cathode ray tube has been used for visualizing sound. But these media components themselves remain indifferent to aesthetic or simply functional practice in media culture.[31] Different

27 See Hámos/Pratschke/Tode (eds.): *Viva Fotofilm.*

28 See Daurer: *Audiovisuelle Wahrnehmung.*

29 See Marks: *On colored-hearing synesthesia*, and Cytowic: *Synesthesia.*

30 See Thoben: *Technical Sound-Image Transformations.*

31 Ibid.

from art films which try to evoke sonic impressions by using graphics and colour (which is a kind of synaesthetic rhetoric), the photo cell allows for actual transformation of image into sound: no synaesthesia, but signal transformation, not sensual, but electro physical transducing.

The basic asymmetry between the auditory and the visual is in its different tempor(e)alities.

> According to Helmholtz' experiments with human nervous reactions a tenth of a second signifies [...] the threshold separating [...] experience from measurement. [...] But since operating below the differential thresholds of sensual physiology counts to the possibility conditions of technical media – of film i.e. – the historical apriori of the Humanities is at the same time the physiological apriori or technical media. [...] Unaccessible to experience and thereby to understanding in history is, [...] the real or what only media can register.[32]

Hermann von Helmholtz detected that the run-time (speed of propagation) of signals in the motoric nerves of a frog counts around 24 meter/sec. This speed recalls a synchronization problem within humans, when technical audio-visual synchronicity might lead to irritation when compared to physical signal run-times in real nature;[33] a lightning stroke is seen more immediately than the accompanying thunder is heard. The media psychologist Hertha Sturm once experimentally explored the temporal domain of human perception and noted that while every day perception always includes a slight temporal delay of reaction involving a kind of inner speech ("subvokales Ansprechen"[34]), electronic media force their audience into immediate affection. Immediate media interfaces deprive humans of their natural chance of delayed perception.[35] Does nothing or everything happen within this half-second? Electronic immediacy, the almost missing microtemporal gap, is comparable to the essential "time of non-reality" (Norbert Wiener) in digital switching between zero and one.[36] There is asynchronicity in signal processing time regarding humans on the one hand and electronic machines on the other, a difference in phase delay of signal transfer between technology and human physiology. But quasi-technological timing can be detected within human neuroprocessing itself, a kind of chrono-engineering. Pre-emptive activity is what apparently is stimulated in the pre-frontal cortex of the brain, which does not simply react to incoming sensations, but time critically tends to anticipation (familiar from the difference between *live* and *real-time* signal transmission in communication media).

32 Siegert: *Life does not count.*
33 See Sander: *Die fehlende Halbsekunde,* pp. 290–293 (292).
34 Sturm: *Wahrnehmung und Fernsehen: Die fehlende Halbsekunde*, pp. 58–65 (61).
35 Sturm: *Fernsehdiktate*, p. 55.
36 See Pias: *Time of Non-Reality*, pp. 267–282.

In order to undo the run-time difference between auditory and visual signals, in sound film, the audio track has to be "protentional" (to use Edmund Husserl's term)[37] in comparison to the image frame it is meant to accompany in human perception. Affect, in this context, is a temporal interval: "in-between time after before but before after."[38] Just because the nerve lines are so short, humans mostly do not remark the signal transfer delay and thus avoid the experience of being always one step behind presence.[39] Although, to human senses (the binaural system) the auditory signal delay is noticeable as temporal gap (the echo effect), the optical information is perceived as immediate (the literal speed of light, even though light itself is a frequency event out of the electro-magnetic spectrum, thus a wave form just like sound). In terms of communication theory, when applied to the macro-temporal channel called *tradition* or *transmission* as well, the auditory and the visual are being transmitted in two different channels. What Warburg declared as the somewhat subconscious visual memory in cultural history (pathetic formulae such as gestures since antiquity), and what Walter Benjamin identified as the optical unconscious ("Optisches Unbewußtes"), goes different ways when compared to the auditory.

The Platonic cave metaphor is mostly remembered for its apparent pre-cinematic setting (dispositive).[40] Most readers overlook Plato's remark on the audio event: While the inhabitants of the cave can be betrayed by shadows, which they take for the movements of real beings, the sound which enters the cave from outside is reflected at the inner wall with echo delay. The slow speed of sound (as compared to the proverbial speed of light) irritates the visually orientated perception; the auditory perception connects to the real, the visual to the imaginary, with the human ears being the substitute for the missing time organ, being much more sensitive to subtle changes in frequency than the eyes are to changes in movement.

The auditory and the visual channel are incommensurable; it was by means of the signal delay manifested in the echo effect that Aristotle (in Peri Psyches) identified the existence of an *in-between* (to metaxy), a substantiated *in-between*[41] which is avant la lettre a term for *media* as channel (thus defined by Claude Shannons "Mathematical Theory of Communication").

37 Husserl: *Vorlesungen zur Phänomenologie des inneren Zeitbewusstseins.*

38 Angerer in her review of *Brian Massumi: Ontomacht*, referring here to: Massumi: *The Bleed*, p. 29.

39 von Helmholtz: *Ueber die Methoden, kleinste Zeittheile zu messen, und ihre Anwendung für physiologische Zwecke*, pp. 169–189 (189).

40 See Baudry: *Cinéma*, pp. 1–8.

41 See Alloa: *Metaxu*, pp. 247–262.

## The audio-visual interrelation in human perception and in technical systems

The term *AV Media* presupposes complementarity but breaks apart in respect to temporal signal processing. An originary media-archaeological gap opens between the audio regime and the visual regime and is embodied in the phonograph and the cinematograph (esp. silent film). The first one is based on physical pressure (physical media), the latter on the photochemical impression of light (like photography before). Later, the mechanical audio recording technologies was extended by electronic media like radio, which is a direct transmission of electronically amplified sound waves and television, and is a direct transmission of light (embodied in electromagnetic signals).

There is a friction between the *real* and the *imaginary*: audio signals pervade the human auditory system in other ways than the visual, which touches the imaginary. But let us be aware that signal processing in the human brain, first of all does not originally differentiate between auditory or visual or other sensual qualities; what is being communicated to the brain by the different receptors (eyes, ears) is first of all pulse trains. It is only in the temporal integration that the modality of the senses is generated. Audio perception within humans is a mechanical vibration of signal trains translated into neuro-electric impulses, which are synthesized in the brain; visual perception is a parallel processing of light waves translated in electro-chemical transmitters.

Sound happens in time but involves space as well.[42] The physical propagation of acoustic waves requires a runtime, which can be noticed by the human binaural perception. The run time of acoustic signals can be measured by autocorrelation: folding a delayed signal onto its original. Within architectural space, the various space lengths traversed by the sound waves can be measured and thus unfolded.[43] All of a sudden, space itself becomes a function of sonic time. While one-dimensional sound recording can be realized in linear *writing* like the mechanical phonograph, image recording (video) required a decisive modification of the medium, the rotating magnetic tape writing *head* in oblique, counter-directive way to cheat the temporal axis.[44]

42 Introduction to the chapter "Ton versus Bild", in: Doelker: *Kulturtechnik Fernsehen*, p. 185.
43 Ehrenstrasser: *Stochastische Signale und ihre Anwendung*, pp. 90 f.
44 See Zielinski: *Zur Geschichte des Videorekorders*.

## Media-synaesthetics: audiovision with Bill Viola

The video artist Bill Viola, referring to Julian Jaynes' cultural archaeology of shifting brain functions,[45] concentrates on the acoustic properties of space in a somewhat synaesthetic argument: "If there is a space of thinking, either real or virtual, then within it there must also be sound, for all sound seeks its expression as vibration in the medium of space."[46] The message of sound within the spatial medium is temporality. Once the impression of space is being identified as a function of vibrations (which modern techniques of architectural acoustics pioneered by Wallace Sabine around 1900 perform by impulse-response-measuring), its conception becomes dynamic. Jean-Baptiste Joseph Fourier analyzed this in his 1822 *Théorie analytique de la chaleur*. Temporal reverberations (Fourier uses, in his introduction, a term well acquainted from musicology: "resonance") replace rigid geometrical proportions; such vibrations themselves can be translated into a 'geometrical' order of a second degree: frequencies, that is: mathematizable quantities (spectra). All of a sudden, space itself becomes temporalized, phenomenologically noticeable by the physical nature of refraction ("the bending of sound waves due to a change in speed as they pass through different media"),[47] of diffraction ("sound turning a corner, when the edge of a barrier generates a new series of waves"),[48] and by reflection (the rebounding of sound waves off a surface). Furthermore, such sonic phenomena are interference and resonance (sound waves reinforcing themselves). "With multiple surfaces this becomes an echo, and it is then possible to hear one's own voice, possibly multiple in times, as it existed at a previous point in time. One can sing with one's self."[49] This effect was actually matched by a technology, which was to affect the human temporal sense fundamentally: sound recording, starting with the Edison phonograph. It is by no means accidental that Viola chose as a title for his reflections on the electronic video image, what looks at first glance like an oxymoron: "The Sound of One Line Scanning." Different from the cinematographic image, the electronic image is close to sound by its essentially temporal and time-critical nature; the auditory is immanent to the electronic image. It is a media-inherent logic, which in the late 1920s led John Logie Baird to record electromechanical television lines on gramophone, discs, his Phonovision storage system – from television to sound.[50] Media-archaeological remembrance tells us that video image recording was born out of sound recording (with the notable

45 Jaynes: *The Origin of Consciousness in the Breakdown of the Bicameral Mind.*

46 Viola: *The Sound of One Line Scanning*, pp. 39–54 (40).

47 Ibid., p. 41.

48 Ibid., p. 42.

49 Ibid., p. 42.

50 See McLean: *Restoring Baird's Image.*

time-critical feature that the interrupted line jump differentiates the gramophonic recording of the television signal from uninterrupted sound recording).

Human perception confronted with electronic images is affected on the level of its internal *sense* of being-in-time, which is otherwise rather located within the auditory channel of perception, as distinct from the durability, which is the message of visual configurations, which is the co-existence of bodies in space. Lessing's differentiation,[51] re-actualized for the *new medium* of sound film by Rudolf Arnheim ("Towards a New Laocoon")[52] and by Clement Greenberg for modernist painting[53] remains neuro-scientifically intact: under what semiotic or media-technological condition differ the auditory and the visual aesthetics? There seem to be space-based and time-based forms of such modalities, but practically they intermingle in a rather fuzzy way, as evident in the effect of failing lip synchronization in films. A special application of spatio-temporal video warping is applied when dubbing a video with another soundtrack. Once more, time counts and here closes the differential audio-visual gap:

> The new soundtrack rarely matches the lip motion of the original video, and particularly disturbing are cases when the mouth moves but no sound is heard [...]. The mouth motion can be accelerated or slowed down using an appropriate time flow [...].[54]

Around 1900, as expressed in Henri Bergson's *Matière et Mémoire*, solid matter began to be perceived as an image-like vibrating element. What used to be an image as a stable configuration of bodies in space dissolved into time in the electronic image. Here the temporal gap between technological and human perception opens. The video image, with its divisions into lines and frames, "is a living dynamic energy field, a vibration appearing solid only because it exceeds our ability to discern such fine slices of time."[55] A synaesthetic transfer (audio-visual metonymy) took place in time, when the vibrational acoustic character of the cathode ray-based image was discovered. This is not a media-theoretical, epistemological or philosophical fancy but technologically positive. The videotape has evolved out of electromagnetic sound recording and its association with cinema is misleading since film and its grandparent, the photographic process, are members of a completely different branch of the media-genealogical tree (the mechanical/chemical). Actually the video camera as an electronic transducer of light into electrical impulses bears a closer relation to the microphone than to the mechanical film camera.

51 See Lessing: *Laocoön*.
52 Arnheim: *Neuer Laokoon*, pp. 81–112.
53 See Hoesterey: *Der Laokoon-Faktor in der Moderne*, pp. 169–181.
54 Rav-Acha et al.: *Evolving Time Fronts: Spatio-Temporal Video Warping*.
55 Viola: *The Sound of One Line Scanning*, p. 44; See also Lazzarato: *Video Philosophie*.

"Evidence of synaesthesia, the crossover between and interchangeability of the senses, has been reported in individuals since the earliest civilizations,"[56] but with electronic communication technologies, the focus sharpens: "Synaesthesia is the natural inclination of the structure of contemporary media."[57] "The material that produces music from a stereo sound system, transmits the voice over the telephone and materializes the image on a television set is, at the base level, the same."[58]

With the shift from analogue waves to digitally coded signals a further epistemological shift takes place, when all kinds of functions are being integrated by the one and only binary code – completely decoupled from any sensual analogy on its basic level and ironically therefore mightier than any other medium before to produce hallucinatory multi-media effects. Digital data processing certainly provides "even more potent translation possibilities beyond basic sensory inputs."[59] It is this beyond which is the techno mathematical challenge to human synaesthesia. Discussing synaesthesia we are stuck with the phenomenological level, but – in accordance with the discourse analysis stimulated by Michel Foucault's *Archaeology of Knowledge* – we are led to inquire what are the formative principles, the temporal drives, the generative codes.

## References

Alloa, Emmanuel: "Metaxu. Figures de la médialité chez Aristote", in*: Revue de Métaphysique et de Morale*, 106 (2009) 2, pp. 247–262.

Angerer, Marie-Luise: "Review of: Brian Massumi, Ontomacht. Kunst, Affekt und das Ereignis des Politischen, Berlin (Merve) 2010", in: *Zeitschrift für Medienwissenschaft*, online http://www.zfmedienwissenschaft.de, September 2010.

Aristoxenus: *Elementa Rhythmica. The Fragment of Book II and the Additional Evidence for Aristoxenean Rhythmic Theory*, edited, translated and introduced by Lionel Pearson, Oxford (Clarendon Press) 1990.

Arnheim, Rudolf: "Neuer Laokoon. Die Verkoppelung der künstlerischen Mittel, untersucht anläßlich des Sprechfilms" (1938), in: Arnheim, Rudolf: *Kritiken und Aufsätze zum Film*, ed. by Helmut Diederichs, Munich/Vienna (Hanser) 1977, pp. 81–112.

Baudry, Jean-Louis: "Cinéma. Effets idéologiques produits par l'appareil de base", in: *Cinéthique*, 7/8 (1970), pp. 1–8.

56 Viola: *The Sound of One Line Scanning*, p. 49.
57 Ibid., p. 49.
58 Ibid., p. 49.
59 Ibid., p. 50 f.

Chion, Michel: *Audio-Vision: Sound on Screen*, New York, NY (Columbia Univ. Press) 1994.

Cowan, Nelson: "On Short and Long Auditory Stores", in: *Psychological Bulletin*, 96 (1984), pp. 341–370.

Cramer, Friedrich: *Symphonie des Lebendigen. Versuch einer allgemeinen Resonanztheorie*, Frankfurt am Main / Leipzig (Insel) 1996.

Cytowic, Richard E.: *Synesthesia. A Union of the Senses*, New York, Berlin (Springer) 1989.

Daurer, Gerhard: "Audiovisuelle Wahrnehmung", entry to the Website of the *exhibition See this Sound* (Linz, Austria, 2009), http://beta.see-this-sound.at/kompendium/text/33 (accessed November 2010).

Doelker, Christian: *Kulturtechnik Fernsehen. Analyse eines Mediums*, Stuttgart (Klett-Cotta) 1991.

Ehrenstrasser, Gottfried: *Stochastische Signale und ihre Anwendung*, Heidelberg (Hüthig) 1974.

Emmanuel, Maurice: *La Danse Grecque antique d'après les monuments figurés* [1896], Reprint Genève, Paris (Slatkine) 1984.

Ernst, Wolfgang / Kittler, Friedrich (eds.): *Die Geburt des Vokalalphabets aus dem Geist der Poesie*, Munich (Fink) 2005.

Gethmann, Daniel: "Zauberscheiben und Schwingungsverhältnisse. Simon Stampfer, Félix Savart und die Erfindung der stroboskopischen Methode", in: Daniel Gethmann / Christoph B. Schulz (ed.): *Apparaturen bewegter Bilder*, Münster (LIT Verlag) 2006, pp. 51–80.

Hámos, Gusztáv / Pratschke, Katja / Tode, Thomas (eds.): *Viva Fotofilm. bewegt/unbewegt*, Marburg (Schüren) 2010.

Heider, Fritz: "Ding und Medium", in: *Symposion*, 1 (1927) 2, pp. 109–157.

von Helmholtz, Hermann: "Ueber die Methoden, kleinste Zeittheile zu messen, und ihre Anwendung für physiologische Zwecke", in: *Königsberger Naturwissenschaftliche Unterhaltungen*, 2 (1851) 2, pp. 169–189.

Hoesterey, Ingeborg: "Der Laokoon-Faktor in der Moderne. Zum Problem der Mediendifferenzierung in den Künsten", in: *Komparatistische Heft*, 5/6 (1982), pp. 169–181.

Husserl, Edmund: *Vorlesungen zur Phänomenologie des inneren Zeitbewußtseins*, ed. by Martin Heidegger (*1928), 2. ed. Tübingen (Niemeyer) 1980.

Jaynes, Julian: *The Origin of Consciousness in the Breakdown of the Bicameral Mind*, Boston (Houghton Mifflin) / London (Allen Lane) 1976.

Kaernbach, Christian: "Echogedächtnis", in: Nicolas Pethse and Jens Ruchatz (ed.): *Gedächtnis und Erinnerung. Ein interdisziplinäres Lexikon*, Reinbek (rowohlts enzyklopädie) 2001, pp. 132–133.

Lazzarato, Maurizio: *Video Philosophie*, Berlin (b_books) 2002.

Lessing, Gotthold Ephraim: *Laocoön. An Essay on the Limits of Painting and Poetry* [orig. 1766], trans. E. A. McCormick, Baltimore/London 1984.

Marks, Lawrence E.: "On Colored-Hearing Synesthesia: Cross-Modal Translations of Sensory Dimensions", in: *Psychological Bulletin,* 82 (1975), pp. 303–331.

Massumi, Brian: "The Bleed. Where the Body meets Image", in Welchman, John C. (ed.): *Rethinking Borders*, Minneapolis/London (University of Minnesota Press) 1996, pp. 18–40.

McLean, Donald F.: *Restoring Bai's Image*, London (The Institution of Electrical Engineers) 2000.

McLuhan, Marshall: *Understanding Media. The Extensions of Man*, New York, Toronto, London (McGraw-Hill) 1964.

McLuhan, Marshall / Powers, Bruce R.: *The Global Village. Der Weg der Mediengesellschaft in das 21. Jahrhundert*, Paderborn (Junfermann) 1995.

Pias, Claus: "Time of Non-Reality. Miszellen zum Thema Zeit und Auflösung", in: Volmar, Axel (ed.): *Zeitkritische Medien*, Berlin (Kulturverlag Kadmos) 2009, pp. 267–279.

Purves, Dale (ed.): *Principles of Cognitive Neuroscience*, Sunderland, MA (Sinauer) 4th ed. 2008.

Rav-Acha, Alex, et al.: "Evolving Time Fronts: Spatio-Temporal Video Warping", chap. 4 "Spatially Varying Time Flow", http://www.vision.huji.ac.il/videowarping (accessed November 2010).

Sander, Uwe: *Handbuch Medienpädagogik*, Berlin/Heidelberg/New York (Springer) 2008.

Shannon, Claude E.: "A Mathematical Theory of Communication", in: *Bell System Technical Journal*, 27 (1948), pp. 379–423 and 623–656.

Siegert, Bernhard: "Life Does Not Ccount. Technological Conditions of the Bifurcation between Sciences and Humanities around 1900 (especially Dilthey)", lecture (typescript) at the summer academy of the Rathenau Stiftung für Wissenschaftsgeschichte, Berlin (July 1994); printed German version: "Das Leben zählt nicht. Natur- und Geisteswissenschaften bei Dilthey aus mediengeschichtlicher Sicht", in: Pias, Claus (ed.): *Medien. Dreizehn Vorträge zur Medienkultur*, Weimar (VDG) 1999, pp. 161–182.

Sturm, Hertha: *Fernsehdiktate. Die Veränderung von Gedanken und Gefühlen. Ergebnisse und Folgerungen für eine rezipientenorientierte Mediendramaturgie*, Gütersloh (Verl. Bertelsmann-Stiftung) 1991.

Sturm, Herta: "Wahrnehmung und Fernsehen: Die fehlende Halbsekunde. Plädoyer für eine zuschauerfreundliche Mediendramaturgie", in: *Media Perspektiven*, 1/84 (1984), pp. 58–65.

Thoben, Jan: "Technical Sound-Image Transformations", in: Dieter Daniels / Sandra Naumann with Jan Thoben (ed.): *See This Sound. Audiovisuology. Compendium. An Interdisciplinary Survey of Audiovisual Culture*, Cologne (Walther König) 2010, pp. 425–431.

Turner, Fred / Ernst Pöppel: "The Neural Lyre. Poetic Meter, the Brain, and Time", in: *Poetry*, August (1983), pp. 277–309.

Viola, Bill: "The Sound of One Line Scanning", in: Dan Lander, Micah Lexier (ed.): *Sound By Artists*, Canada (Art Metropole & Walter Phillips Gallery) 1990, pp. 39–54.

Zielinski, Siegfried: *Zur Geschichte des Videorekorders*, Berlin (Wissenschaftsverlag Spiess) 1986.

## List of Illustrations:

Fig. 1: Bill Viola, Information, USA 1973. Videotape, colour, sound, 30 min., in: Wulf Herzogenrath et al. (eds.), TV-Kultur. Das Fernsehen in der Kunst seit 1879, Amsterdam and Dresden (Verl. d. Kunst) 1997, 293.

*Arts of Synaesthesia*

# Why Is Green a Red Word?

DITTE LYNGKÆR PEDERSEN

Green is red because the two vowels 'e' are red and they are dominating my perception of the word green. I have used this question as a working title for a long-term project on synaesthesia. It reminds me of the big spectrum of colors and the complementary issues this phenomenon brings up. Under the umbrella of Why is Green a Red Word? I have made a series of conceptual and documentary video works, exhibitions, talks and a book.

Between 2003 and 2010 I searched for synaesthetes and researchers around the world that would share their views on multi sensory perceptions. With an autobiographic approach I used the video camera as an instrument to collect, remember and discuss what I learned. I also used the camera to experiment on how to translate and imitate the synesthetic experience. In this process I found myself being fascinated by how language is an inadequate medium in describing the sensations, and at the same time how problematic a materialization is, because the synaesthetic experience often happens in the minds eye.

How does interpretation overlap, replace and become truths? How do we translate sensory experiences? How does one reduce such a phenomenon down to something one can identify with? These are some of the questions that guided the years of research.

My main interest has been to discuss the subjective versus the objective reality and provoke imagination, rather than visualizing and materializing synesthetic sensations. I have not found any correct materialization of synesthetic attributes. I believe I have found a few ways of illustrating the phenomenon and how it feels or how it is experienced. I have done this by focusing on the discourse around the phenomenon, power of imagination and by avoiding colors. Illustration is not a correct rendering, because it is something in itself, something totally new. With respect to understanding synesthetic experiences, the translation takes place in the absence of an original, because each type of synesthesia has its own original, known to only one person. Art is considered a descriptive language, and I think it creates a space between the familiar and the unknown. I believe aesthetics strikes and seduces the eye, so how the eye weaves these impressions into a context is a chance procedure to begin with. How far can descriptive languages lead us, and to where? Art is considered a communicating language, and the prerequisites for communication are agreements/accords. What agreements do we have in art? Is it our ability to imagine which makes art a communicating and mediating language?

Using synaesthesia as a starting point for a discussion can perhaps tell us more about ordinary perceptual experiences and its relationship to thinking, memory and language. I like to get lost in first-person reports and the absurdity it poetically conveys including the dynamics between synaesthetes and researchers. With this process, I intend to create some kind of confusion and a social space for imagination, and emphasize a better understanding of each other.

My main challenge has been how to create a collective imaginative space in order to relate to people's stories. But as every synaesthete I met came up with new spectrums of aesthetic sensations I realized there were probably no collective imaginative space to be found, but only solitary ones.

Imagination and concentration is essential in understanding effects of synaesthesia. These effects are reported so vividly and with such detail that an illustration – for example a drawing – would always seem incomplete. But I believe that the will to describe and the will to understand go hand in hand. In order to see or feel the reality of another person, you need to come close to his or her actual experience. By provoking translating processes, there is a chance to get a glimpse of it. I have done a few translation experiments, both with the purpose of fulfilling my own desire to experience another type of synaesthesia, but also to provoke a translation process in the viewer of the video.

One experiment is a video featuring a young synaesthete Gregory Sean Kielian. He takes us on an aesthetic journey through the lines and shapes of the buildings and sculptures in the landscape around Berkeley University. The image appears in black and white, while he speaks about his colors, then it slowly fades into regular colors. He also makes a color analysis of the lines appearing on his personal identity card. During the interview, Kielian and I play a game where we look for colors in the immediate surroundings that could match any of colors we assigne to letters of the alphabet. We find a few – in the sky, the rooftop of a building, the trees, the swimming pool etc., but they are only similar to our synaesthetic colors, and we do not have the same colors for any letter. The camera follows our search.

Another example is a video based on an experiment, which finds its origin in my desire to imagine and understand (by illustrating it) what another person perceives. Lisa Nyberg experiences Spatial Number Forms Synaesthesia. I gave Nyberg a very long questionnaire, with questions like: how many centimeters from your arm is January? How tall are the days of the week? Based on her written answers I made drawings of her time related answers. In the video Nyberg comments and corrects my attempts to translate her three dimensional perception of time into a two dimensional illustration.

In this text, I will share with you some personal notes and how I have worked with synaesthesia in my art practice.

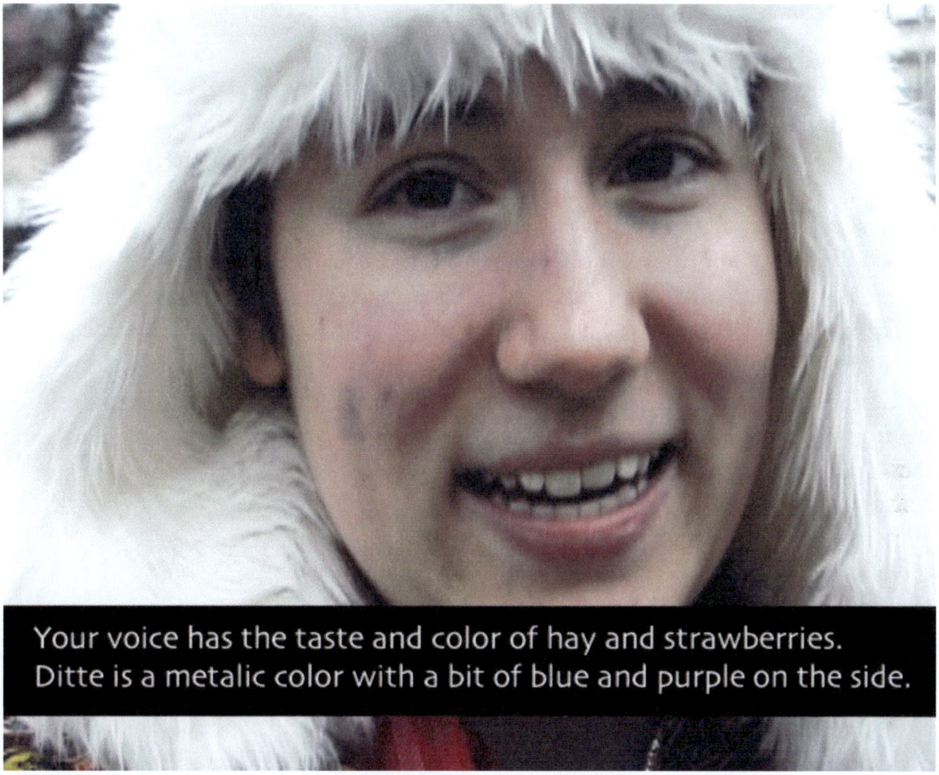


Fig. 1: Video still from the video *A Study Of A Name – Ditte*, 2006.

I will introduce myself and some of the people who kindly took part in my projects by describing a short video *A study of a name – Ditte* about my voice and the synaesthetic connotations to my name.

In casual situations, when people ask me what my art is about, I try not to mention synesthesia, especially in those situations where I don't know how much time people have to listen to my answer. However, sometimes I slip and it is guaranteed that they will ask "What color is my name?"

It almost appears as a test of what I am saying is true. Thankfully it is also the easiest way to demonstrate how the colors work. It can be exhausting, in a sporty way, to be at a party and describe 10 names one after the other.

For me, it is funny, how these types of conversations or Q and A sessions almost remind me of the premises of the synaesthetic nature itself. Simply because the structure of the conversation repeats itself in a completely automatic way and is always the same.

I also experience that the question "What color is my name?" comes up at a time in the conversation when people need a time-out from all the complex issues related to the topic. At one point in my own project, when I interviewed synaesthetes, I would get carried away in theories and sensory descriptions That was before I decided to use this question as a break. Later I compiled it into a video as a portrait of my voice and my name.

In the video *A Study Of A Name – Ditte* I ask different types of synaesthetes, who I have met around the world, to describe their synaesthetic reaction(s) to my name or my voice. In one scene two persons are discussing the colors of my name and are trying to find an agreement on how it looks. To me this could be a sign of the way we are taught to think. We live in a time where we have to make a lot of choices and defend our opinions constantly. The way they do it in the video is a bit unusual for a synaesthete. If you have synaesthesia, there is nothing to choose from. It is just what it is. But of course I do not want take away their joy of sharing an experience.

In another scene the synaesthete suggests that I should get a nickname if we were going to become good friends, because my name tastes like garden soil and harsh plastic to him.

## I am not Kandinsky

In 1998, I experienced synaesthesia during a lecture on Vassily Kandinsky. It was an informative moment. I was the only one in the classroom who noticed colored letters and numbers and a spatial perception of time around my waist. For me every single graphic letter has its own color. When someone talks to me in a foreign language, colors appear when I can picture how the meaningless sound could be spelled. *Kjileos* is not a word but a chance assemblage of colored letters.[1]

I did not know what to do with this realization of suddenly being a synaesthete and I felt a bit alienated. It reminded me of the fact that we experience the world very subjectively. I somehow wanted instinctively to believe that we experience the world objectively.

1 Kjileos: Oddly enough, this "word" has a balanced color composition. J, L and O light white shades (not the same nuances). K and S are strong colors – turd-brown/charcoal grey and glistening burgundy, respectively – that look good with the other letters. E is a warm pink-red (a bit reminiscent of the label on a coke bottle). I will conclude by confessing that I just now had a surprising personal insight: I had previously assigned an obviously wrong color to the letter "I". Hoping to find logical rules or patterns in my color system, I discovered when a researcher tested me that capital "I" is always white, but small "i" is yellow when it's not next to another white letter. In Kjileos, "i" is beside "j", one of the white letters, but it still appears to be yellow so I can toss that theory. In any case, small "i" is white when it stands alone, but when next to other colors, the dot begins to shine yellow. If there is a pattern, I have not yet figured it out.

I was struck with the fundamental 'angst' of not having the same frame of reference as others – of standing alone without a language. So I left it there and did not do anything about it.

But it became an obsession during my final year (2003) in university, when I decided to talk about it and turn it into a research project and include this aspect as a fundamental inspiration in my art practice. I was attracted to how reality can be experienced as being stranger than fiction. This phenomenon takes place more in our brains than we ourselves can ever understand. As we know we experience the world subjectively, we can't help to have the intuitive desire to believe we experience it objectively.

There is always a level of personal surprise and involuntarily realizations coming along with my research and interviews. Sometimes, I am not ready to discover more details in my own synaesthetic reality. One question would lead to the next and never be answered, to such an extend that it would no longer be productive and I would have to leave the project and rest my ideas and desires for a while. It could last months or even years. Therefore my synaesthesia project is what you would call an ongoing and never ending research-based art project and I do other art works as well.

My approach was driven by curiosity with an intention to collect material and represent a group of people before an audience who probably never heard of this phenomenon. I had no scientific, academic, journalistic or artistic ambitions at hand. I was very curious and I used the camera as an instrument to document in order to contribute to the oral history of synaesthesia. I realized that the synaesthesia research community is rather small and international.

I travelled to find people who share my interest. After I had visited the annual conferences of the American and UK synesthesia associations, I ended up being kind of lost in translations. I focused on first person reports and anecdotes. My experiments and interviews became very technical in terms of specific details of synesthetic patterns of each individual. Very often the subject would be carried away and discover new aspects of their perceptions during the interview.

## Exhibition

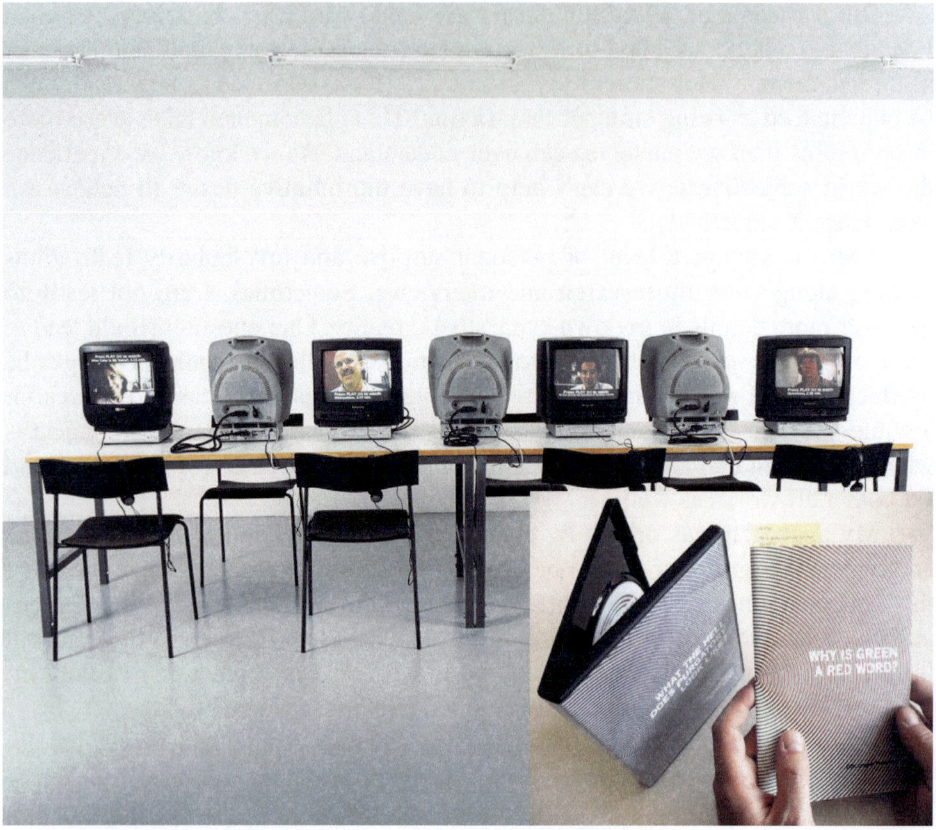


Fig. 2: Installation shot of video archive, gallery Peep, Malmö 2004.

In 2004 I created an exhibition of the material using the aesthetics of a conference setting or a laboratory. I presented synaesthetes and scientists on two different monitors. At the bottom floor of the gallery I installed videos, which were driven by intuitive studies and experiments. This way the top floor represented the consciousness and the basement the unconscious method of research. I chose not to illustrate any of the synaesthetic imagery and used very little color. In the entrance I projected questions, which could lead to a synaesthetic, diagnose. The walls were covered with descriptions of synaesthetic sensations that I edited from email correspondence with Swedish synaesthetes. Something I would call Found Poetry. I was invited to design one page in a national newspaper in Sweden, and I decided to use this opportunity to make a personal add where I searched for people who experience synaesthesia. I opened an email account and started a forum. I received many letters from people who saw the ad. The archive of sensory descriptions in the exhibition was also inviting the audience to contribute with their own descriptions by adding them on the walls.

After this exhibition I was so lost in details and science that I was no longer able to make art out of it after all. Again, I found myself being mostly attracted to how language failed in describing the sensations, and the big challenge of how to create an imaginary space in order to relate to people's stories. It is a common human predicament that language falls short, all the more so for synaesthetes, who are never satisfied with the words and means with which they choose to describe their experiences. What can translate the sensory codes and expand the framework of comprehension to encompass abstract sensory descriptions? I realized I was dealing with questions of intersubjectivity, the limits within language and the power of imagination and fantasy. I was somehow still convinced there was no collective imaginative space to be found, but only solitary ones.

I felt a resistance to start making illustrations, because an illustration could end up being just a bad copy of the sensation, a reduction, which does not serve as an evidence to the science and at the same time not even be art. I put the material to rest.

In 2010 I decided to revisit the material and give the public the opportunity to meet some of the people I have met. One of the amazing things that an exhibition on synesthesia can trigger very easily is that people get the chance to find out for the first time ever that they have synesthesia and are part of our club. Hopefully they want to be found. I wish that sometime in the future, the public will have adapted to all your brilliant academic and scientific research to the extend where a show on synesthesia will not have the affect of a spectacle. Yes, maybe it will become a natural thing we all experience according to levels of awareness.

## Speaking up about synaesthesia and impossible or non-existent questions

This summer, I found out that my partner does not hear certain frequencies. We were sitting in the garden enjoying the sounds of the insects – at least that is what I thought we were doing – until I found out these sounds were not a part of his reality.

If we wish to resolve the mystery of synaesthesia, a great exercise is to share details in what seems obvious about the way we sense the world. To get into the details of the synaesthetic sensation one needs to ask impossible questions or non-existent questions. Impossible questions are those that do not exist in general usage; they can be asked, but they cannot be answered by anyone. The questions appear to be illogical, the words twisted and turned around as in poetry. Impossible questions can sound naive or idiotic, but they are effective as warm-up, or instructive for a person in the process of discovery. Do you see the year? How big is your year? etc.

By speaking about our sensory inputs, we can slide together into the deeper reality that exists in everyone, but so seldom surface up to our consciousness. Surprising details in these individual experiences could play a role in learning processes for a student as well as for a teacher. Synaesthesia being a seemingly unresolved phenomenon, it reproduces itself in the media. Every month, I feel I come across an article that says the same as 20 years ago. "Look what we found – it is so amazing and crazy," instead of saying "look what we found and this is what we did with it!"

I made a DVD-BOX, which consists of a video compilation and a booklet. It presents *What the Hell Does Purgatory Look Like?* (video, 8 min. 2005) and additional 29 bonus tracks, featuring conversations with researchers, people who experience different types of synaesthesia and artistic experiments from 2003–2010. The booklet presents sketches, images and texts including "I spy something" – Ditte Lyngkær Pedersen's works on synaesthesia by Dr. Sabine Flach & Dr. Gerhard Scharbert 2010.

Fig. 3: Bonus track: *Code Breaking – A Study Of The Film Close Encounter Of The Third Kind.* Video stills, 2004.

Steven Spielberg's film *Close Encounter Of A Third Kind* from 1977 is a brilliant sci-fi movie where aliens communicate with UFO researchers in tones accompanied by colors. It reminds me of synaesthesia. I feel that each synaesthete I meet is like an alien trying to convey his or her reality of perception to me. Being a synaesthete and meeting many others, naturally leads to a desire to convey the experience and at the same time understand the mind of others. Either by materializing the experience or somehow finding out how it could be useful.

The video is an experiment where I translated the colors in the Spielberg's film according to my synaesthetic chromatic response to specific letters in the alphabet, in order to break their code of communication. My decoding of the colors in the film creates a combination of letters, which could spell the word *Obey*.

## From the video compilation

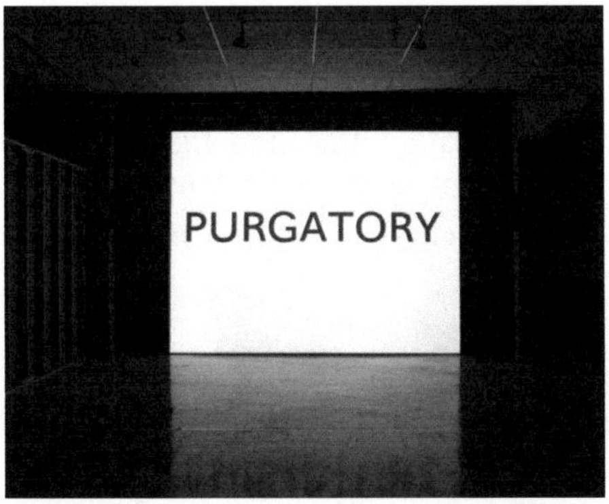


Fig. 4: *What The Hell Does Purgatory Look Like?* Video installation view, 2005.

The concept is to provoke an alternative way of editing moving images. It is the result of my desire not to use colors in my project, but instead to stress imagination and create an imaginative space that allows art and synaesthesia to be an inner experience of images, to touch the sphere of perception.

• The video *What The Hell Does Purgatory Look Like?* is composed of a constant frame that shows the word PURGATORY on a white background with voice-overs consisting of nine synaesthetes' descriptions of each letter that spells purgatory. "Colors of a day, old bruise" or "it tastes like a sweet cheese on bitter greens wrapped in an apple with lemon squeezed on" are some of the responses by various types of synaesthetes.

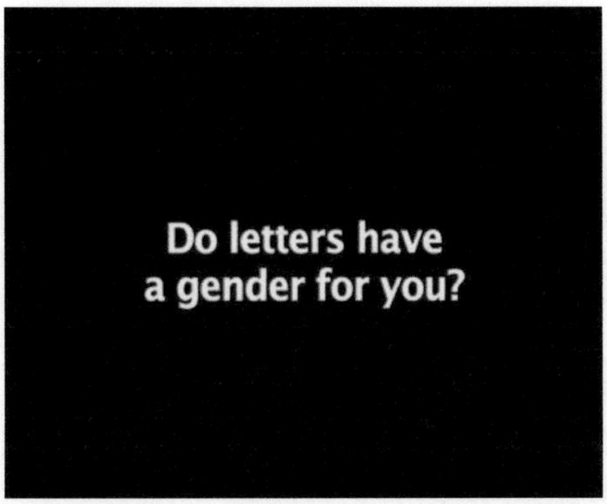


Fig. 5: Bonus track: *A Study Of Questions*. Video still, 2004.

*A Study Of Questions* is a video loop presenting a series of questions that point out and defines the different types of mixed sensations and concepts leading to synesthesia. The questions appear on a black background to the sound of heartbeats and atmospheric sounds.

## What is true is what we understand; what we understand is what we can imagine

I am actually not convinced there is a direct link between synaesthesia and art. A person who experiences gustatory lexical synesthesia – the kind that produces taste – is not necessarily a good cook. However, I am open to a link to creativity, and I do believe as Dr. Sabine Flach and Gerhard Scharbert suggest in their text: "that synaesthesia can help us develop a sense of abstraction, which is also a component in the experience of art and a talent in the human being?"

I see rich opportunities in using the art space to confront and inform an audience with synaesthesia. Due to the belief that the art space is an autonomous place, which can provoke a conversation about the hidden and less obvious reality of mankind and the way we organize ourselves in societies. I also think it is important to be a bit careful or even strategic with how we talk about synaesthesia and how we share our knowledge about it so we do not create a distance to non-synaesthetes. When we focus on synaesthesia, we sometimes forget to hear how non-synaesthetes sense, associate and remember things.

## The visible invisible art

I have searched for the possibilities of translating these immaterial concepts. Both for the individual synaesthete and for those who do not recognize what is being described and want more insights. What does this procedure imply, and is it even possible?

First and foremost I can observe that it is apparently not possible, but that the possibilities are found in the will of the one who wants to translate, and who is not satisfied with interpretation. The procedure demands a definite presentation ability, detailed source information and descriptions. I will admit that since this project began, I have difficulty ignoring people's extra senses. When I know about someone's synaesthetic system, it becomes a part of my image of them. For example, I know someone who has Spatial Number Forms Synaesthesia – which is a spatial and visual perception of time. I listen to how she has a kind of time archive on top of her head where she systematically puts everything having to do with time. When she enters a room, I imagine an invisible hat on her head.

Within my artistic practice I create spaces for free speech, secrets and collective or personal statements of unspoken or oppressed realities. I am driven by the idea that art is a space for imagination – which can serve as a collection of experiences and visions the public could relate to. Through fiction and visual representation, feelings are provoked and we create a relationship to the imagined, which could sooner or later become reality.

As an artist I can recognize the necessary effort to overcome, or come to terms with, the non-translatable. The familiarizing and translating process synaesthesia provokes can be a metaphor for artistic production and reflection. Through a critical process, where ideas must materialize into an indefinable language, the translation replaces that which it tries to translate.

## List of Illustrations

Fig. 1: From the video *A Study Of A Name – Ditte*, Video still (interview with Emily Brown, NYC 2005), (6:30 min. 2006).
Fig. 2: Installation shot of video archive, gallery Peep, Malmö 2004. / Detail of the archive as DVD-BOX.
Fig. 3: Code breaking – *A Study Of The Film Close Encounter Of The Third Kind.* Video stills. (2 min. 2004).
Fig. 4: *What The Hell Does Purgatory Look Like?* (video 2005, 8 min.) Installation shot, video program Movies Without Pictures, the Swiss Institute, New York 2007.
Fig. 5: *A Study Of Questions*. Video still. (5 min. 2004).

# Interview with Kate Hollett

SABINE FLACH & JAN SÖFFNER

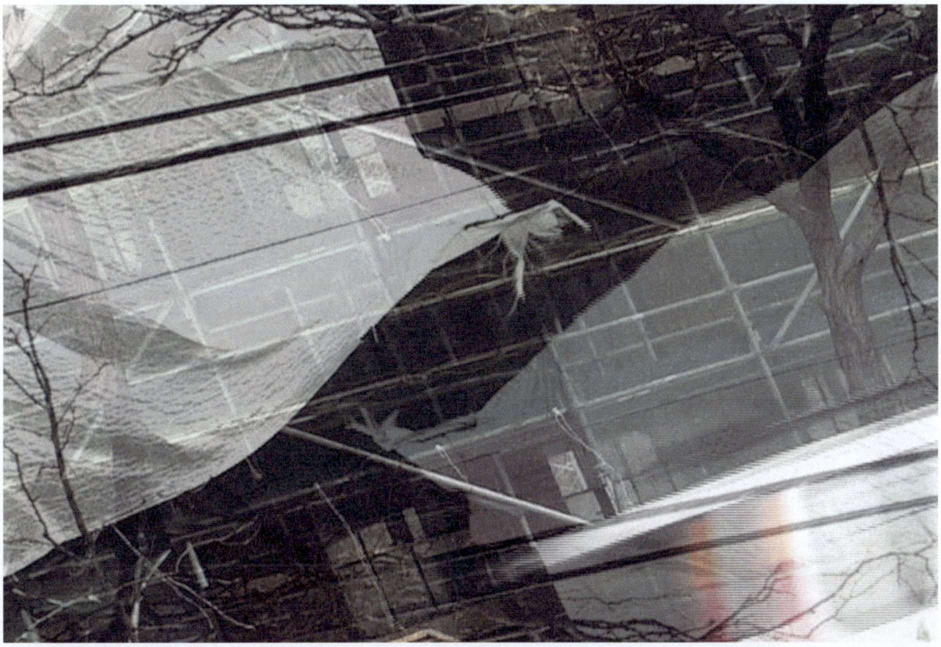

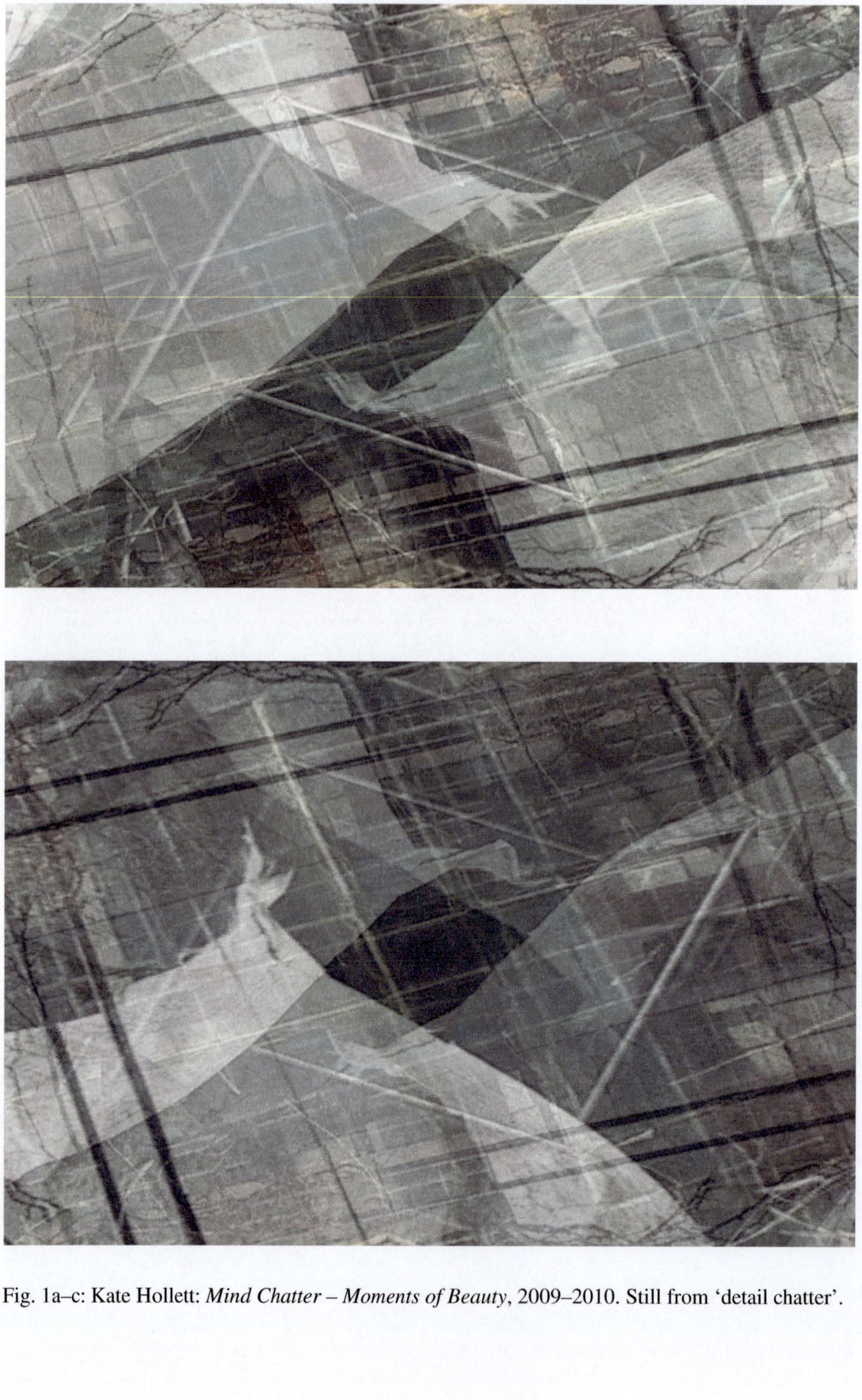

Fig. 1a–c: Kate Hollett: *Mind Chatter – Moments of Beauty*, 2009–2010. Still from 'detail chatter'.

*SF&JS: Would you please describe the idea for Mind Chatter?*
KH: The idea for Mind Chatter emerged out of past work dealing with issues of emotional connection and communication. Mind Chatter was a complete 180 degrees turn from the work I had been doing for the past 12 years. I had been working with the concept of love – emotions and communication – connection, working with love as a visual language, specifically by working with the words "I Love You."

I initially started the work on love to try to find the meaning of love when my mother became terminally ill and eventually died from cancer. I deconstructed love by using the different meanings of what "I love you" can mean by using various forms of media. First in paint, then video and video installation to multi-media, each media form lead into the other as the search continued. The "I Love You" project expanded to include videos filmed all over the world, with over 2,000 people simply saying the words "I Love You," to an interactive video installation, website and a multi media event including art, dance, music, poetry and interactive video art.

What initially was a search for meaning after my mother's death became a universal search for ways to connect using media. With more and more of our time spent in front of a computer void of sensory communication, how do we emotionally connect to one another?

The project morphed and grew to take on a shape of it's own created out of the individual expressions of love. With each expression of love, the definition of love expanded, yet it ultimately revealed a disconnection. There were moments of love, yet the media reflected a separation, not just in a technical aspect as individual clips but also as emotional separation. The participants all had very individually felt meanings of love. It revealed the isolation that exists within time and space. Our memories shape our definitions, and with each person having unique experiences of love, connecting in a shared meaning of love seems less likely. How do we connect in love with so many ways to feel it? It was frustrating. What started out of a search for meaning lead me to see the separation; a disconnection.

With Mind Chatter, I tried to realise the disconnection by expanding it, examining it closely and taking it apart. Similarly to the "I Love You" project, I started with myself. It is from here that I can get a clear view of my subjective perspective when approaching a subject. What did I bring into the equation when I examined disconnection of emotions and communication?

If I wanted to look at the disconnection I had to reverse the process of the "I Love You" project. Rather than work with what one might call issues of the heart, I looked at issues of the mind. The idea for Mind Chatter began as a collection of thoughts using a digital recorder. If love was an emotion, what was in my thinking?

In the process of gathering as many of my thoughts as I could, I realised different kinds of dialogue or 'chatter' – that perpetual voice talking as we travel through life. There was chatter that consisted of details – grocery lists, appointments; emotional thoughts; media triggered thoughts like an internal TV channel connecting to advertising or image, and chatter that came from relationship issues to name a few.

What I found was that there were very few moments when the chatter really related to the world around me. Thoughts of the past, thoughts of future events; living is very much an auto piloted endeavour lead by timelines.

It was from the experiences shooting that I found the connection and fully realised the concept for Mind Chatter. Ideas of connection and disconnection are on my mind all the time. It is in everything I do, whether it is a dinner party, relating to the neighbours, interactions with strangers, connection to beauty, media, language, communication, love. As a result, I have come to trust that when I want to shoot something even if I have no idea why I want to, I shoot anyway.

It was the moments in time, those raw and rare moments where something in life grabs hold of you and stops the thoughts, that I realised the connection of emotions and thoughts. The only thought that can be heard is the connecting thought and emotion. For example, when we see something beautiful, like a rose or the sun glittering in a droplet of dew even if for a nanosecond, the chatter stops; I call these 'moments of beauty'.

It became clear that separation existed between the internal dialogue and the external world. This formed the basis for the piece.

I deconstructed connection based on types of mind chatter and coupled the audio with video of random street scenes. The work attempted at creating disconnection by separating the two experiences of visual experience and mind, or inner dialogue of time. It attempts at breaking away from any from of narrative.

In more esoteric terms I would say the concept of the work is to challenge ideas of identity as predetermined as it interrogates the layers of subjective and objective experience that presume a whole self travelling coherently through space and time. It attempts to expose the interactions between consciousness and the world, and the mediating role played by memory and emotion.

Layers of thought, words and emotion disconnected from the present, the "real" world we exist in. We live a virtual existence of the past, repeating and reflecting images and experiences that play out our individual stories with the hope of finding connection. We are disconnected from each other by forms of media yet connected in a virtual world outside of concrete realities. The more we have feelings of disconnection, the more we work at rationalizing our fears.

*SF&JS: Is Mind Chatter for you a film or rather an installation? Could you please describe the way, the artwork should be presented to the audience?*
KH: Mind Chatter – Moments of Beauty is an installation although it can be viewed as a film. The installation is intended to represent the world through my eyes, the connections and disconnections as revealed by travelling in my world, so the audience is taken inside my head.

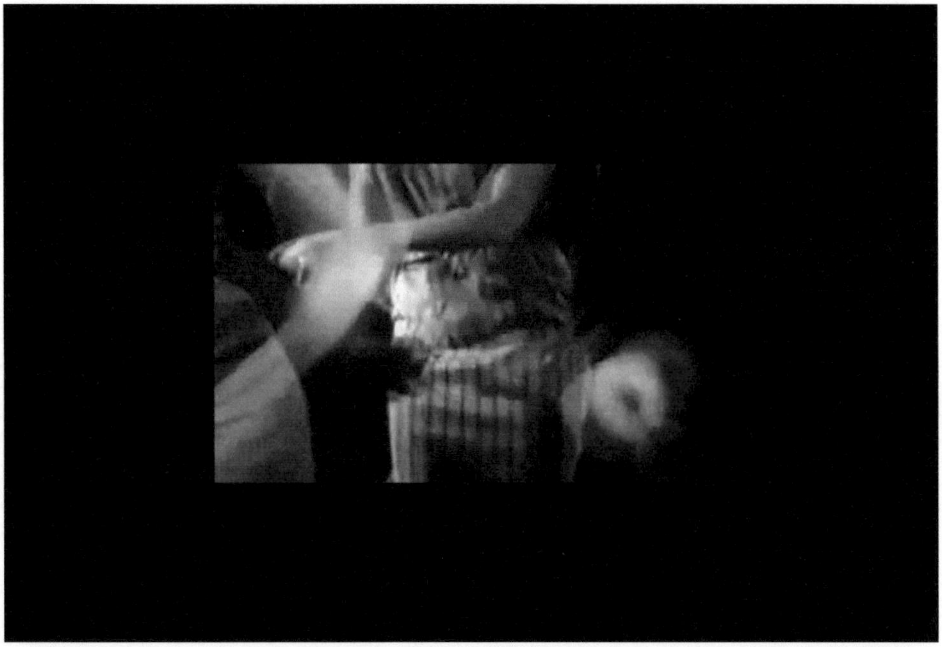

Fig. 2: Kate Hollett: *Mind Chatter – Moments of Beauty*, 2009–2010. Still from 'media chatter'.

Imagine, a giant head, large enough to walk into and stand. Inside there are three screens each mounted on one side of the head. The entrance to the head is on the fourth side and at the back of the head. The inside is padded. The film plays on different screens, sometimes together, sometimes one scene on one screen, one scene on another playing in around, with volume levels see-sawed. At times one scene, in particular, like the scene with three chairs in the sun, is played on all three screens. The viewer is bounced around experiencing mind chatter as if inside my head, reflections that radiate and rebound.

The first section portrays layers of mind chatter created when memory and reflection absorb and process the experience of people and common objects. As this chatter becomes more and more intense an effort is made to break it down as the mind seeks out underlying pain and emotion as in the second section. The moment becomes a mirror into the past.

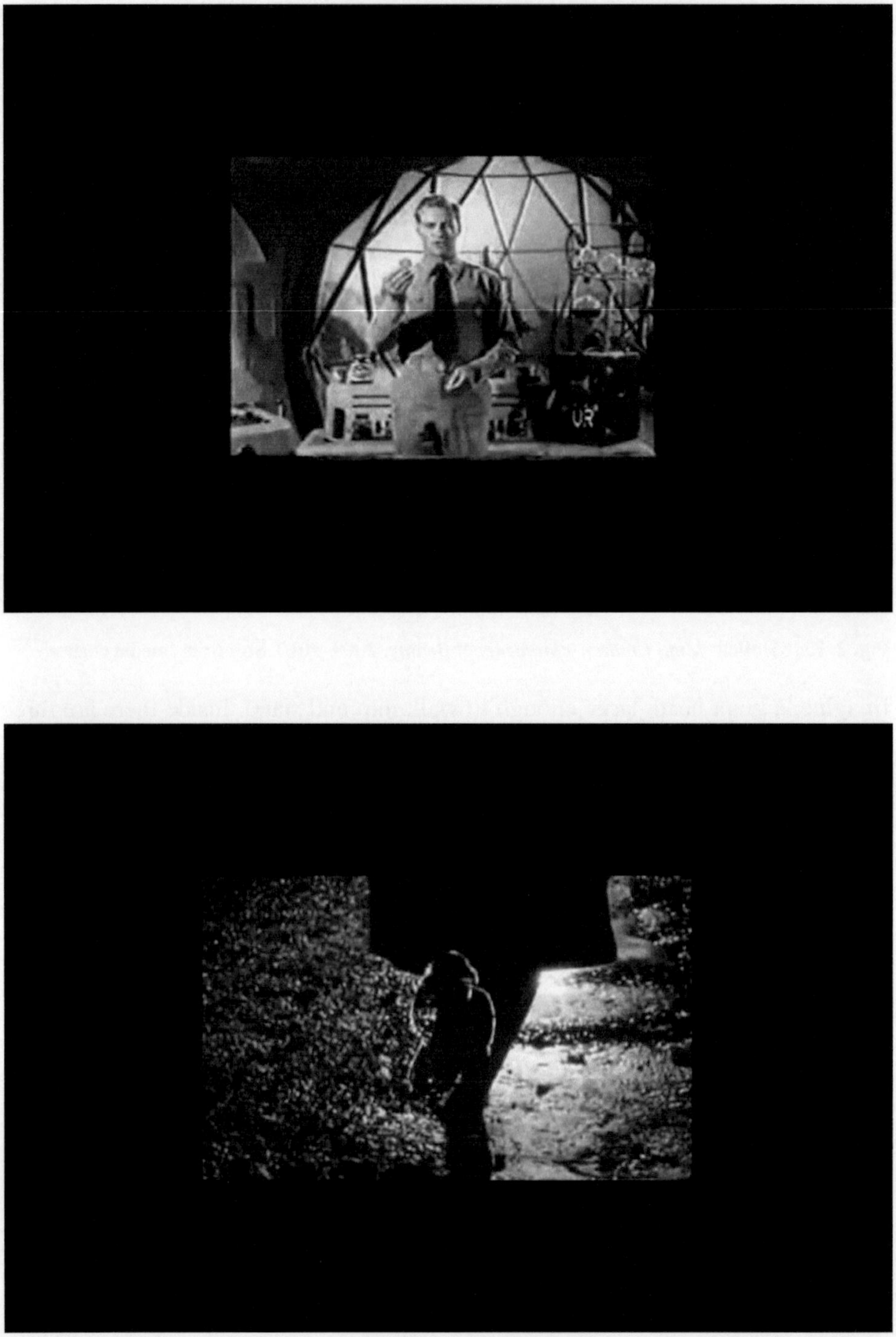

Fig. 3a–b: Kate Hollett: *Mind Chatter – Moments of Beauty*, 2009–2010. Still from 'media chatter'.

In the third section, pain and emotion culminate in stark imagery that bring the chatter to a halt; leaving a sense of calm and a recognition of the beauty that lies beyond the constant conscious striving to hold onto identity. In the media chatter section, a remembrance of simpler moments is portrayed in media representations from the past. These also signify another form of experience that brings constancy to identity, but they are laden with comparisons to an unattainable world of ideals, and therefore, bring feelings and thoughts of insecurity and inadequacy. Feelings of trauma hidden under layers of experience become penetrate the meditation and calm. Memories are triggered and a struggle between image and memory ensues.

Then there are moments, words that repeat the same discussion, repeating, repeating rationalization for unrealised emotions, fear, and insecurity. We use words to calm the fear, trying desperately to solve the problem, somehow knowing that this is out of our control and it is this lack of control that ensures repetition. Everyday life is happening all around us, people living, walking, chatting, and passing through our lives as we repeat messages of fear. We are not connected, walking past moments of simplicity, connection, banal moments in life that remind us that we are not alone. Time holds everything, what we choose to see is what it represents. When these moments, these visual moments of acceptance are ignored, they will expand, forcing us to get out of ourselves. When life is spent in the mind, time and space play tricks on us, building moments of drama until the mind is forced to let go.

Finally in the last section we see and hear a moment that is connected. The connection both giving and taking feelings of joy, peace and sorrow. The connection to what is now opens us up. This in turn is reflective of lost connections, the feeling that this connection is rare. Yet as it is no longer part of a visual scripted expression, it reminds of the hope that exists in the future.

*SF&JS: If Mind Chatter is an installation could you please describe the interaction of the piece with the environment? This means: what role does the question of place and space play? Are there necessary conditions for you to choose a location?*

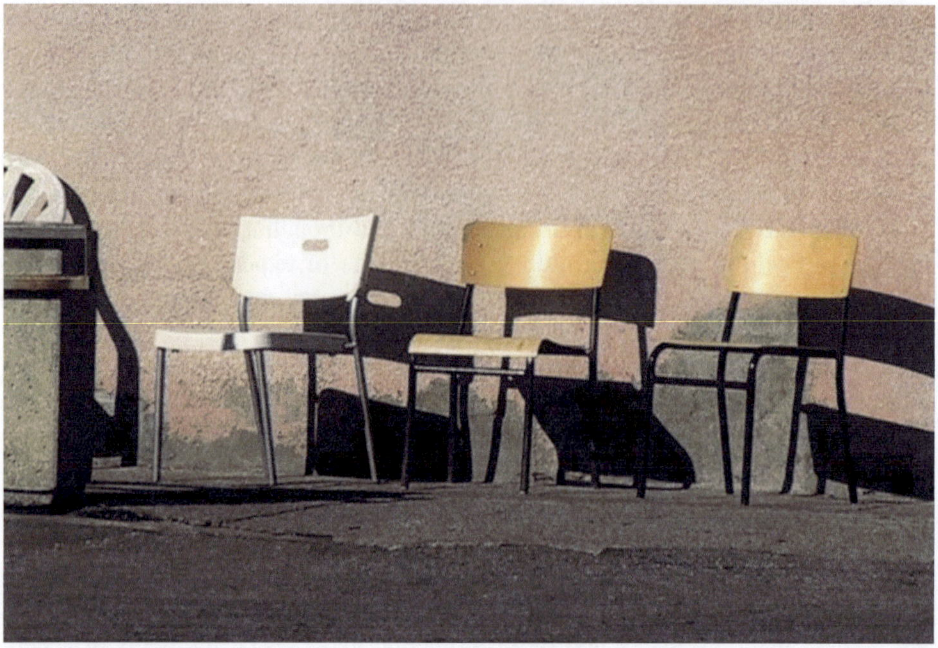

Fig. 4: Kate Hollett: *Mind Chatter – Moments of Beauty*, 2009–2010. Still from 'moment of beauty #1'.

KH: The very notion of mind chatter is about dis"place"ment, the installation is an important factor in presenting the disconnection of space and time by attempting at realizing the experience of being in one's head. The location of the giant head can be anywhere as it is not interactive with the visual surroundings, we are 'seeing' the outside world as if through my mind.

*SF&JS: Would you please describe the way you choose the filmic scenes? How did you choose the scenes and develop the storyline?*
KH: The video is taken during a walk that I did as a ritual, a 20 minutes walk from home to the grocery store. I have walked that way many times. Walking is part of my process. I film random events and images that caught my attention without thinking about why and with no intent. In a way, they are connecting moments for me artistically.

The media chatter was chosen based on personal memory of pop culture and advertising that triggered memories. Coffee Crisp, Kentucky Fried Chicken, McDonald's, scenes from Barbarella that gave me nightmares, all of these were reflective of emotional connections.

The scenes represented a timeline based on real time. The creative manipulation of the video was emotionally driven by the visuals and the chatter layered to reflect the same emotion even though it was clear that the two were not related, they were connected for me through emotional expression.

*SF&JS: Does it play a role if the audiences know where the film was shot?*

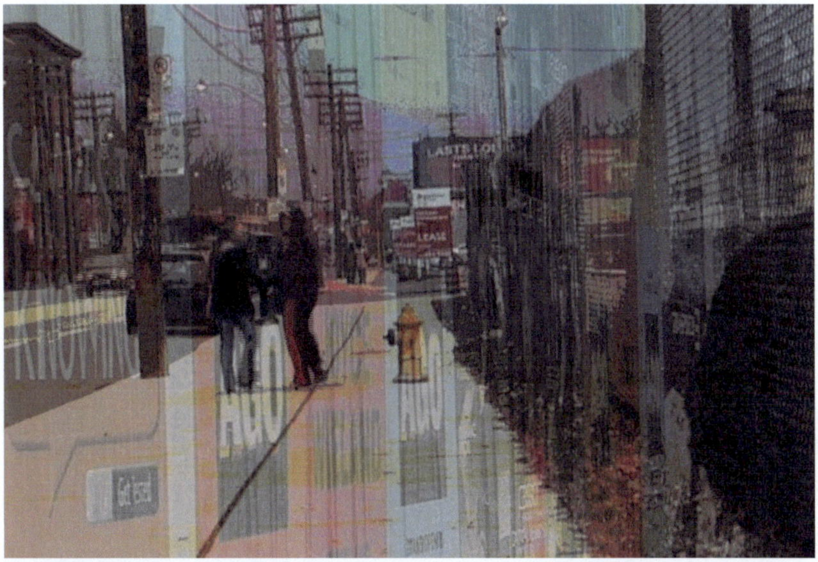

Fig. 5: Kate Hollett: *Mind Chatter – Moments of Beauty*, 2009–2010. Still from 'relationship chatter'.

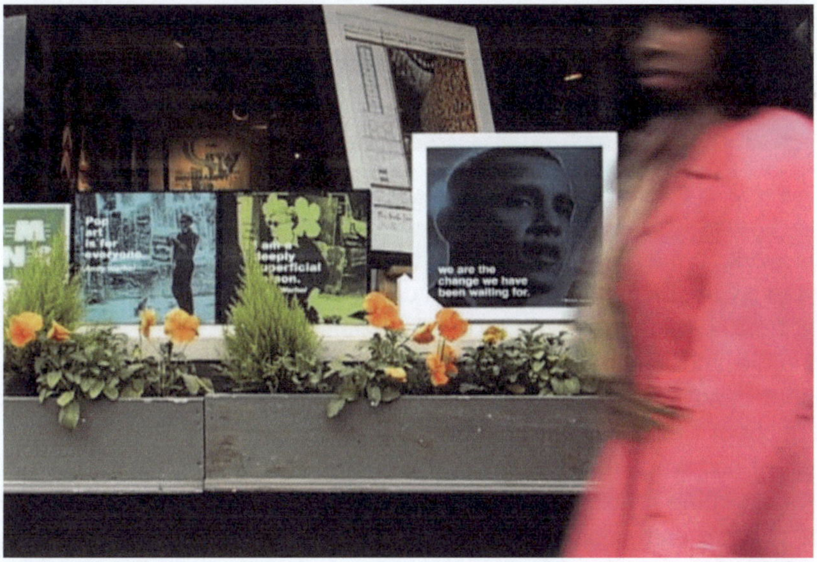


Fig. 6: Kate Hollett: *Mind Chatter – Moments of Beauty*, 2009–2010. Still from 'chattering chatter'.

KH: It was intended to reflect everyday life, everyday captured moments so in a way yes, however, it does not have to be specific to a town or street address.

*SF&JS: Mind Chatter works with cross dissolves – so the spectator often seems to see with doubled senses: Whatever is represented – events, spaces, places, objects, persons, acts and emotions – is on the verge of disintegrating. Often it seems to re-integrate in abstract forms – often, the abstract forms themselves disintegrate and re-integrate in what is presented. All this makes me think of synaesthetic phenomena. Is synaesthesia, in this work, just an issue, or also a guideline and a structural principle?*

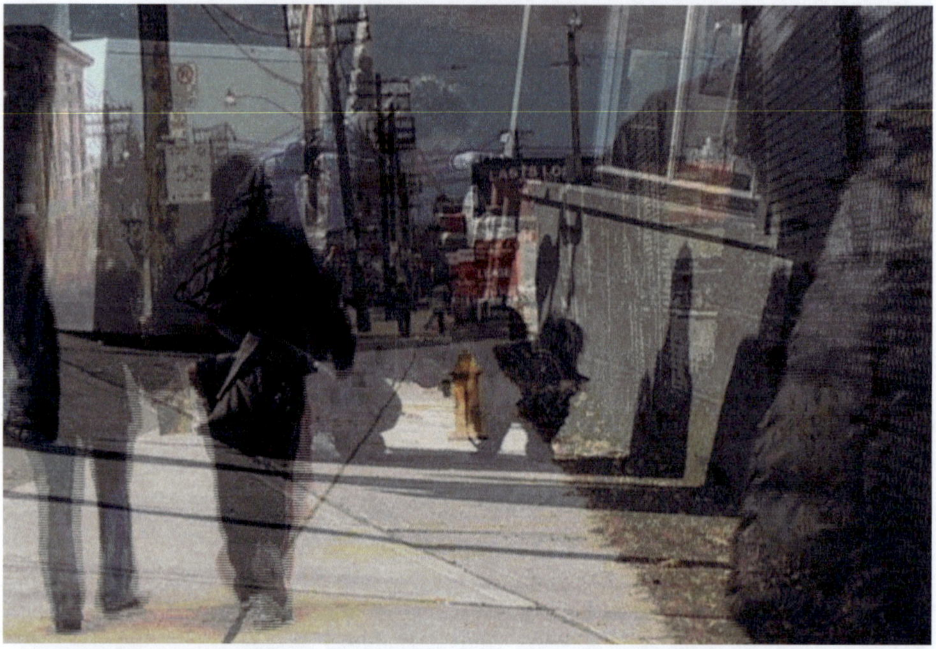

Fig. 7: Kate Hollett: *Mind Chatter – Moments of Beauty*, 2009–2010. Still from 'chattering chatter'.

KH: In this work, synaesthesia is an issue not a structural principle. The work was created to try to come to terms with the conflicts of inner and outer realities, at the same time, I wanted to deconstruct the connections we make on a daily basis. The audio and visual were created at different times then put together. Nothing about it was structured on any principle or school of thought, it was created more out of a desire to understand how connection works.

For years I had worked at trying to form connections in my work, yet it always lead to revealing a disconnection. So after fighting with myself about the meaning of positive and negative ways to manifest connection, I gave into the dark side. I flipped it around and I tried to deconstruct it and create disconnection both working with both content and various media i.e. audio and visual as separate forms.

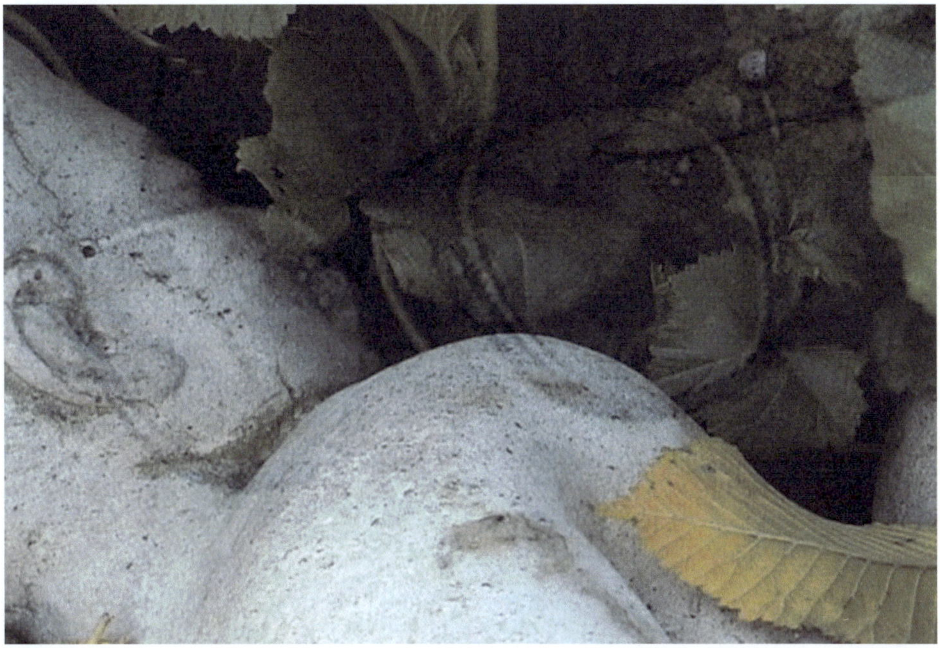

Fig. 8: Kate Hollett: *Mind Chatter – Moments of Beauty*, 2009–2010. Still from 'chatter that you can't hear'.

*SF&JS: Another question coming to mind when being exposed to this work is the question about the background and the foreground, of what becomes an issue of conscious cognition and what remains unseen, unheard, unthought. The spectator feels to be put on the verge of latency and manifestation, of conscious and subconscious experiencing. What role does the subliminal play in Mind Chatter?*
KH: The sound files were randomly made at all times of the day and night. It was an attempt at trying to capture, as they happen, the thoughts that play out or 'talk' in the background of our mind while other things in life are happening. Of course, it is impossible to actually record all of one's thoughts as they happen, we think far too quickly.

In a way, the audio is an attempt at revealing subconscious and conscious thought. And as one can hear, there are thoughts about many things, emotional thoughts, relationship thoughts, thoughts that others may have, and thoughts about "what's for dinner" which is not what one would consider a subconscious thought. The sections in the film where there is no 'thought' is a thought of not thinking. It also works at revealing differences between chatter and non-chatter or moments of beauty.

The visuals were shot during a daily walk, a regular event. I filmed whatever caught my eye, trusted that is was relevant to my process. Intuitively working with both visual and audio is important, it is in this way one can 'see' without knowing, the mind is pulled into subconscious connections, ways that help us navigate our way in the world. The visuals related to the audio only through subconscious connection and this is only realised once the two media were reviewed and merged into one work.

*SF&JS: Do you have any specific interest in cognitive and neurosciences and if yes, which one? Do these works then play a role for your art? Assuming yes, which one?*
KH: In the search for connection, my work has travelled down many forms of inquiry; this involves emotional research in the sciences, including cognitive and neuroscience, and social sciences, to issues of time and communication. This includes but not limited to the work done by neuroscientists – Dr. Uri Hassen, Dr. Vittorio Galese, and Dr. S. Masters, anthropologist – Dr. Helen Fisher, Dr. Eric Fromm, philosophers like Slavoj Zizek and Michel Foucault, media specialists like Marshall McLuhan and Clay Shirky, to organizations like The School of Mind and Brain, the ZFL Institute, The Wellness Trust and The Association of Neuroesthetics.

In a very purist form, my work is interdisciplinary as it crosses art with other forms of study outside of art. In artistic terms, the work is Interdisciplinary using many forms of media to explore meaning. The various areas of research and media used are integral to the exploration, representing the study of communication as part of the purpose for understanding connection and disconnection.

The research I do does play a big role in my work and it's development, however, it is creatively driven. That is to say I am driven by my desire to understand emotional connection, individually and collectively; that includes and starts with understanding my emotional connections and the environment I find myself in. I often find that my work falls into empirical knowledge after the fact; this then perpetuates a direction for further research. I know I am on the right track when this happens.

*SF&JS: How should Mind Chatter address the senses? And in which way? Is it relevant for you to show the emotional state the actors of the film are in or should the art-piece address the emotions of the audience? Or both?*
KH: I am not sure I would call any participant in the piece an actor. It is documentary in the way I express my emotions and mind chatter, and the people in the film are real people. In a way, this does address the senses as it shows conflicting sensory experiences between what is seen and what is heard. It is intended to address the disconnection we all experience in a sensory way. Our feelings navigate our vision of the world and how we interact with it. The piece was intended to address the emotional states of the audience by revealing the emotional disconnection.

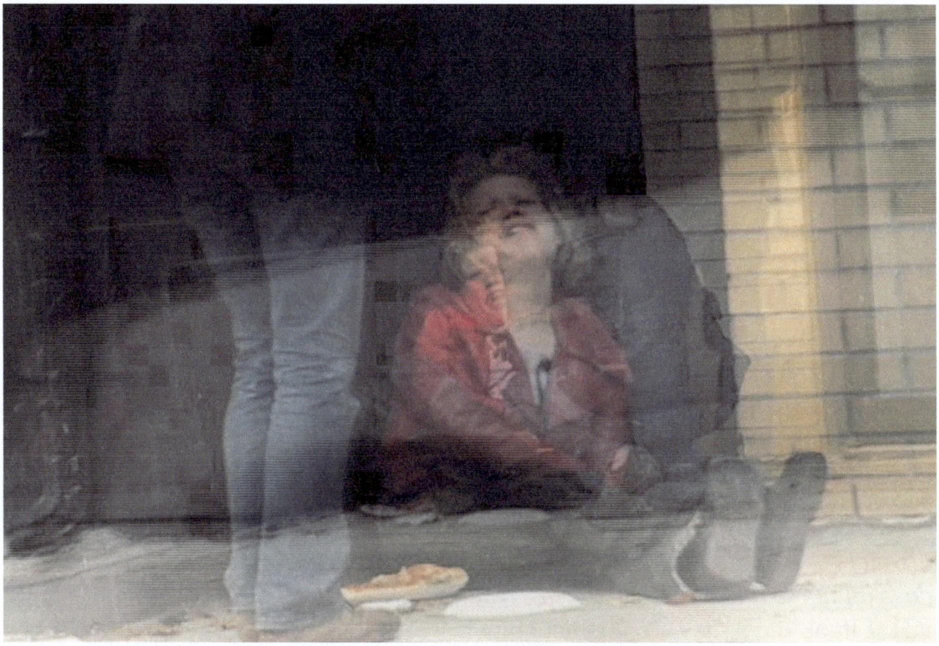

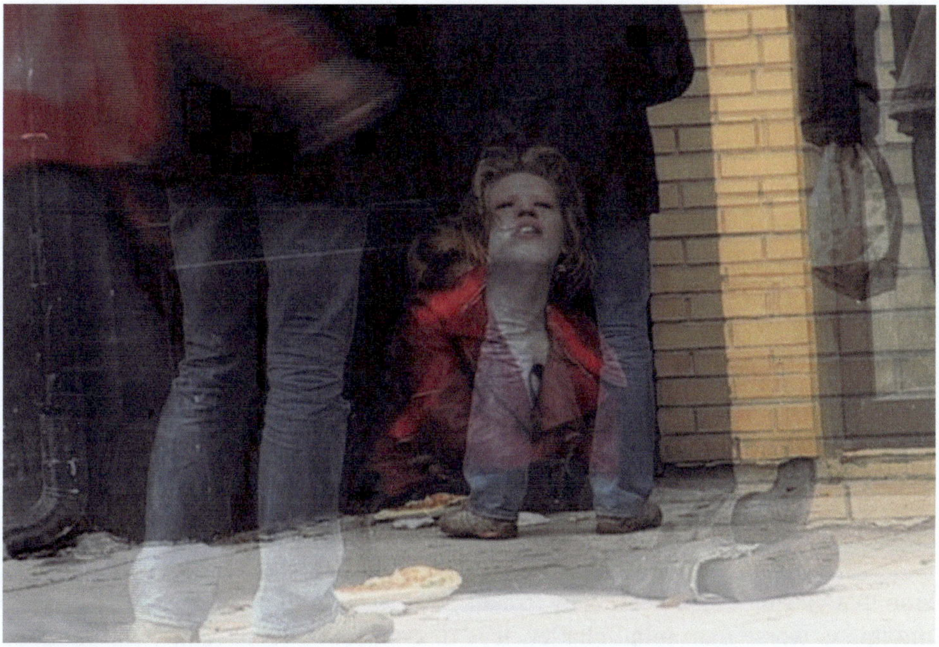

Fig. 9 and 10: Kate Hollett: *Mind Chatter – Moments of Beauty*, 2009–2010. Still from 'emotional chatter'.

The tension between the pubic construction and maintenance of a complete persona is explored in terms of the intensely private negotiations that feed the outward expression of who we are in the eyes of others and how we are to ourselves. The camera plays a dual role that reflects physical engagement with the world and as it prompts various thoughts and feelings that chatter away in the mind. Common images are presented as a collage as sound is used to express the layers of reflection that accompany each physical encounter. Together sound and image try to express the distance between what we experience and how it reflects back on how we are in each moment.

With more and more of us connected through digital media, our sensory experiences are felt through reflection not real tangible experiences. We are becoming more and more separated in a real sense yet connected like never before, the dichotomy is reflected in the work.

*SF&JS: The mentioned features of this work raise the question, if the mind of this chatter can be 'cartesian', if it can be a self-present mind, one with clear and distinct issues present. What kind of psychology did you have in mind – and how does all his relate to the 'chattering' voices present in your work?*

KH: I think the issues are distinct and clear. Although this is my mind chatter, it can be reflective of the fact that we, as a society, are inundated with information overload and sensory stimulation, albeit mostly audio & visual senses, we are often disconnected from our reality in the present. And even then, reality is always individual; we see what we can connect with using memory. Memories are of the past; time, in a linear sense, is in the future, so finding a clear connection to the present is never clear.

If I had to label it with any psychological term, the work is based on one of post-traumatic stress disorder. We live in a world where we are exposed to all kinds of stressful issues, images that show us horrors like 9–11, terrorists beheadings, tsunami, wars – violent, sad, hard and painful issues so difficult to comprehend. It is hard to understand unless we can connect. If we can, then one would wonder why the world is not suffering from post-traumatic stress disorder on an on-going basis. I mean, it makes sense that if we have much going on inside and outside of ourselves all the time, we would experience disconnection. In a way, we have to. If I were walking and not filming, would I connect to the woman crying on the street? If I was late for a meeting, probably not, but if I was paying attention, it would bother me to see her in pain. I might even go up and ask if I could help, but this is only based on my reality of her pain.

On the other side of it, there are "images" that are based on creating an illusion that consumerism is the way to feel good, belong to a social way of life. To me this is worse than mind chatter, it is disconnection from reality of emotions one may not know how to deal with, like the feeling of helplessness or alienation. In Mind Chatter, it is the emotions that feed the mind chatter.

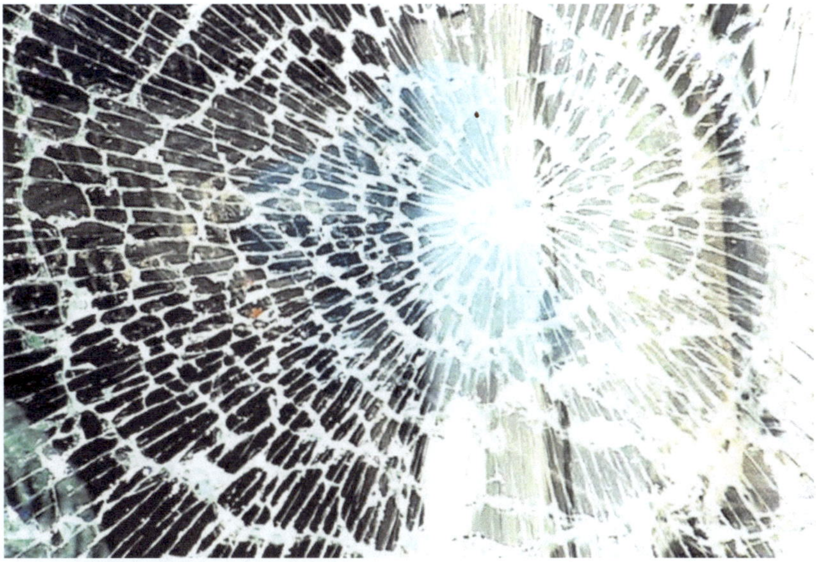

Fig. 11: Kate Hollett: *Mind Chatter – Moments of Beauty*, 2009–2010. Still from 'chattering chatter'.

*SF&JS: Could you describe the process of encoding and decoding as being part of the emotional process in your artwork? Or are questions about codification misleading for considering your artwork?*

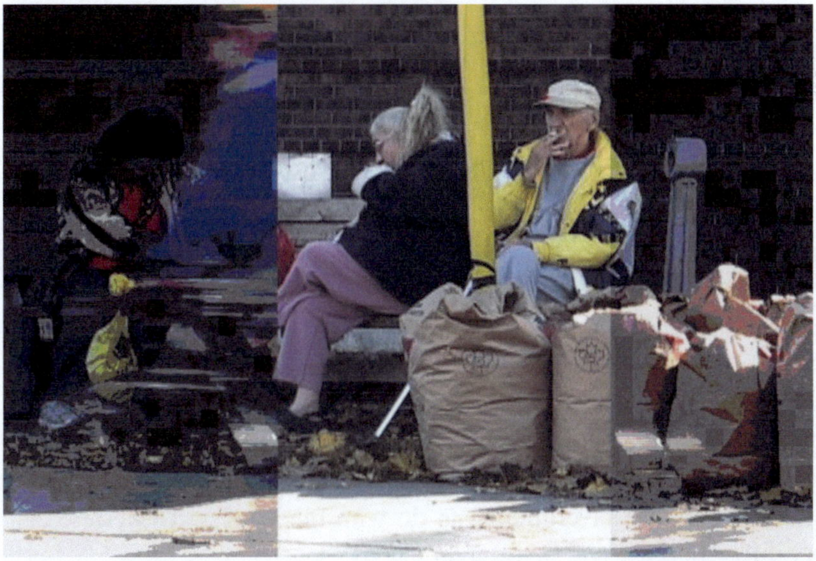

Fig. 12: Kate Hollett: *Mind Chatter – Moments of Beauty*, 2009–2010. Still from 'relationship chatter'.

KH: It is interesting that you used the word 'encoding'. Encoding is more about digital technology to me. And in a digital sense, the media is encoded, so yes the piece is encoded, however in an esoteric sense it does not really play into its development and creation.

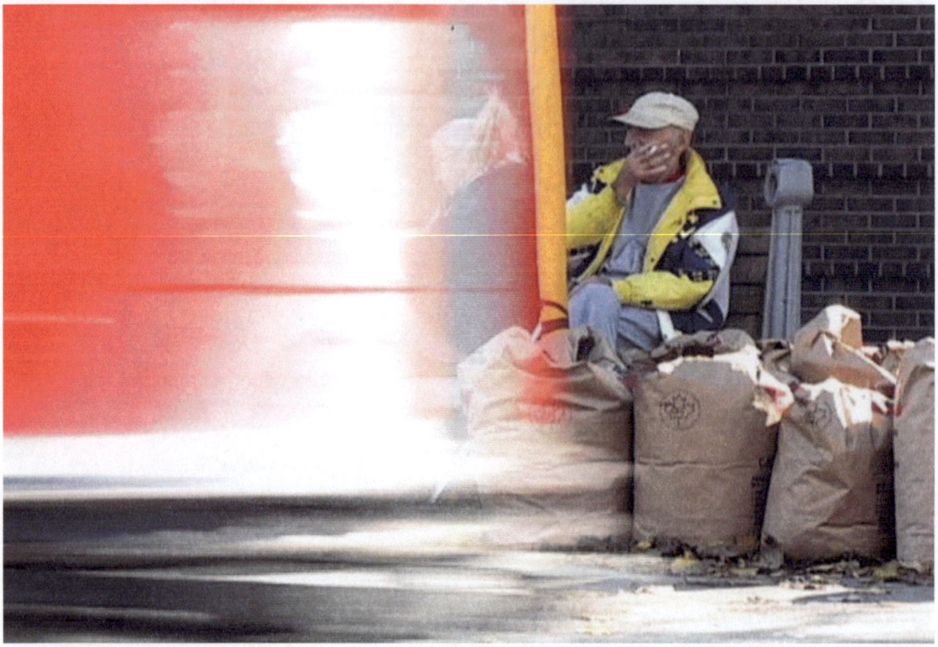

Fig. 13: Kate Hollett: *Mind Chatter – Moments of Beauty*, 2009–2010. Still from 'relationship chatter'.

The challenge was to really capture the full extent of what I felt, connected with in terms of memory, and what I saw, this process does not involve any conscious form of codification. I believe in this work, any codification that is done by the audience takes the form of subjective experiences felt with the work. There are symbols and images, like the advertising in the media chatter section, that have codified meaning for me personally, however, it is intended to be reflective of subjective meaning and experiences that can be understood on a larger scale. So yes, I would say that and questions of codification are misleading when considering my work.

*SF&JS: Do you consider the chatter of the voices as referring to what we see or rather an inner monologue? And can you please explain, who is talking?*
KH: The chatter, the person talking is my voice, I am talking. They are my thoughts and the thoughts have nothing to do with the visuals. They were captured at very different times and in different places.

The thoughts are meant to be reflective of my inner dialogue and at the same time represent in an empathetic way, the inner dialogue we all have. Although to be fair, it is impossible to capture the thoughts in one's brain as they happen, the brain is far too fast, so what you hear is an attempt at retrieving the process by layering and connecting fragments of this inner dialogue.

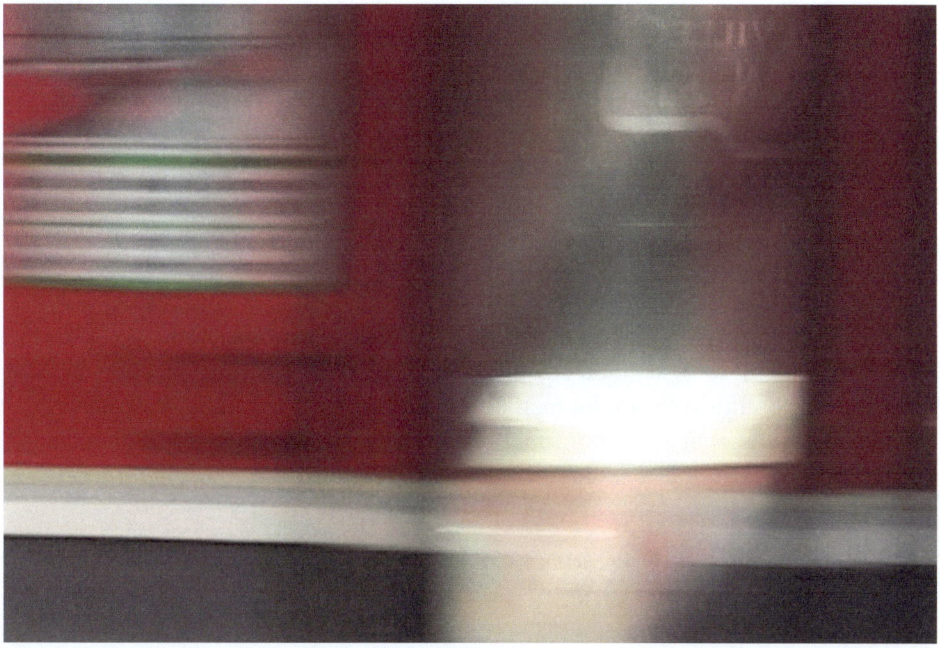

Fig. 14: Kate Hollett: *Mind Chatter – Moments of Beauty*, 2009–2010. Still from 'relationship chatter'.

*SF&JS: Chattering is a verbal activity. Many things are spoken, but many things also seem to be made unspoken by uttering them. By overlapping, the words thereby erase each other. What words and phrases mean seems to be involved in the same process of disintegration and re-integration like the sensual aspects of your work: They too become manifest and fade away into latency. How do sensual and semantic meaning interact in your work?*

KH: Well put. I think that the words and visuals were both used to reflect the way I felt in mind and body, thinking and feeling. You know the feeling of being lost in thought, for example, you are going to the office or riding the subway, you'll start to realise that you've started drifting into your thoughts. The thoughts, often motivated by emotions, can take over, often to the point of forgetting to get off at the right floor or subway stop until something brings you back, often it is jarring and sometimes it has the effect of moving images that finally penetrate the thoughts.

In the visuals, the same phenomenon can happen: there can be an aspect of something that happens that pulls us in and out of our worlds. The visuals represent this type of flow.

*SF&JS: Verbal messages, in your work, sometimes seem to become a polyphone background, in which the subjective experience starts to dissolve. Inner and outer voice, thinking and perceiving intermingle in an all-embracing chatter.*

*Would you agree to state that this is about a collective chatter that speaks through the person?*

KH: The many layers are representational of the innumerable thoughts of our thinking. As well, the layering is used to replicate the repetition of our thoughts, especially when it comes to the relationship thoughts… They repeat over and over, rationalising fears. Shere Hite reported in "Women and Love, A Cultural Revolution in Progress" (1987, Knopf), that 92% of women in relationships say they spend a large amount of time trying to figure out the relationship they are in – Mind Chatter…

The chatter is also, as mentioned, 'inner and outer voice' thinking so in this way, they are still disconnected, and disconnected from the visuals, random sound bites coming from many memories and forms of thinking. Yes, it is about collective chatter that speaks through the person. The chatter is the person, the chatter is you, it is me it is anyone who can relate to this inner and outer dialogue.

*SF&JS: Do you see a difference in experiencing your art-pieces alone or being surrounded by others and assumed, that would agree that there is a difference – which one?*

*Would you say that there is an ongoing exchange between inner and outer forms of representation in your work that 'creates' the feelings?*

*Could you describe the role, the spectator plays for you in your artworks? Would you say that she has a constitutive part already in your planning? Assuming yes, what kind of part?*

KH: The last three questions seem to come to the same place for me, to talk about the intended effects…. versus experiential results of the piece.

As described, the intent is to reveal the disconnection of one's mind and emotions and how this translates in our relationship with the world.

Certainly as the person who is expressing the mind chatter it has a personal connection, and as a personal connection, the viewer is taken into my world with the intent of connecting to the feelings. Knowing that the mind chatter and visuals were not connected in an experiential way, that is, separate recorded times and irrespective of each other, it was my intent to reveal the disconnection. However, what I found was that the audience tended to try to connect the two by trying to form a narrative. Many people asked me about the woman crying, if is represented me, if I knew her or they commented on aspects they could relate to, there was a general heaviness and uneasiness in the emotional reactions. We want to put the images and feelings together, to make 'sense' of what we 'see', when there is a separation, this creates longing and quite often, a connection to loss, so the response was to try to find the connections.

What was surprising for me was that the "I Love You" project is all about trying to see emotional connection, yet it revealed a disconnection; and with the Mind Chatter piece, it was about trying to create disconnection yet the work revealed a connection. The viewer tried to form connection.

The spectator is heavily involved in the work I do by helping to shape the definition of love. As all of my work examines emotional connection and disconnection, each aspect is a creative experiment and research project attempting to form a collective shape from meaning and communication.

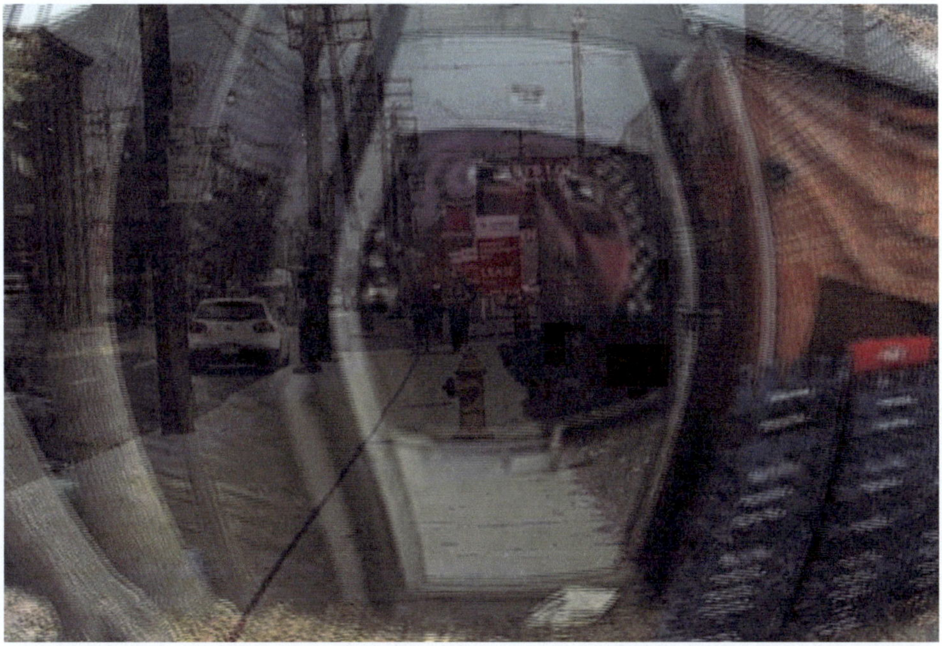

Fig 15: Kate Hollett: *Mind Chatter – Moments of Beauty*, 2009–2010. Still from 'chattering chatter'.

*SF&JS: Time, in your work seems to be in a constant process of disintegration and re-integration. The visual experience of this work entails flashing impressions that interrupt the flow of images, repetitions that interrupt the ongoing evolvement of what could be thought of as narrated, time lapses that speed up the course of time, images of static objects that seem to freeze it. How does the 'Chatter' relate to these temporal structures?*

KH: Time is very relevant. Memories are not real-time based. Emotions can be felt in an instant and seem timeless, and at times, emotions can cause pain that seems to last forever. We are constantly shifting timelines in our mind. We may count time but it is not how we experience it. Yes, we are young and grow old and there is much that can be drawn onto the straight line of time, but even in that process of aging, we feel time pass at different speeds. Like when we are young, time seems to pass so slowly, and as we age, time travels faster.

Time is also extremely interesting in an age when everything is speeding up. Information, experiences, relationships… I think it is important to understand how time affects us, so the film tries to reveal quite manifestations of this lateral connection by layering visual time variances, like we might experience emotionally everyday.

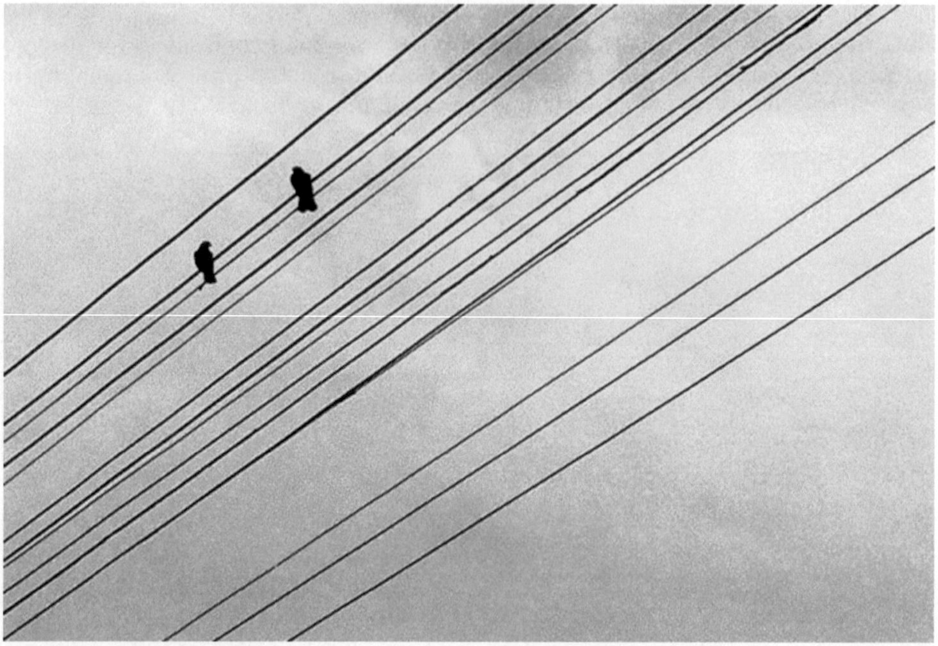

Fig. 16: Kate Hollett: *Mind Chatter – Moments of Beauty*, 2009–2010. Still from 'moment of beauty #1'.

*SF&JS: In Synaesthesia the question about representation (our an outer world) and (self-sufficient) presentation is very prominent. Synaesthetic experiencing is beyond the very question of what is 'really' out there and what is not. Do you think, something similar also applies for Mind Chatter?*
KH: Yes, I think the film presents the same characteristics of synaesthesia. The film works directly with the ideas of an inner and outer world. It attempts at revealing this by separating the two and by showing the outer world as only reflective of an inner world. As mentioned above, I would be surprised if it wasn't more common in varying degrees in many people.

You could you say the process of creating Mind Chatter was an act of synaesthesia… In a way, it was a subconscious creation of 'disconnection' which in of itself is synaesthesic.

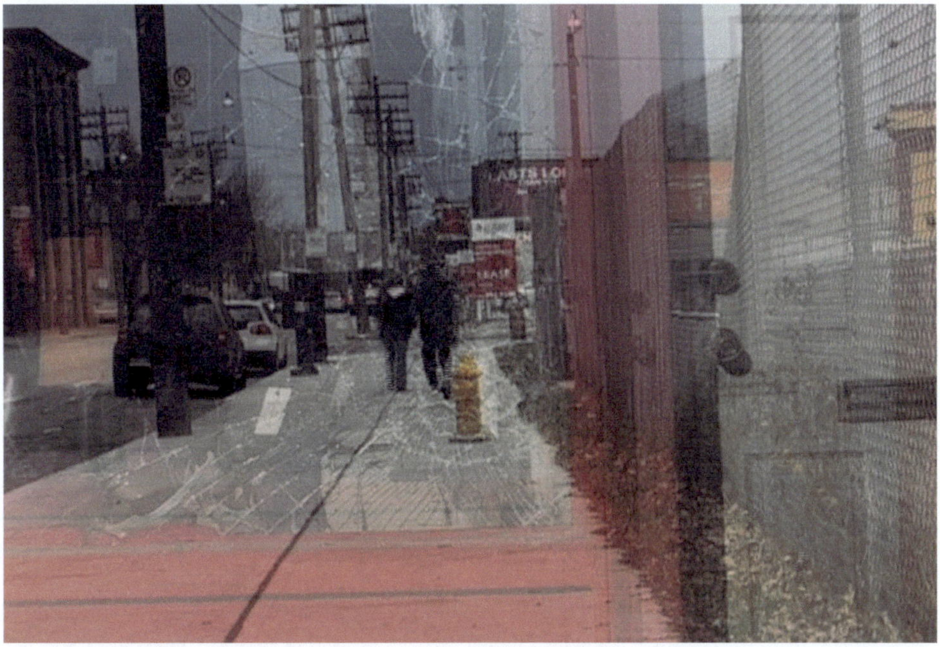

Fig. 17: Kate Hollett: *Mind Chatter – Moments of Beauty*, 2009–2010. Still from 'relationship chatter'.

# List of Illustrations

All images: Kate Hollett: *Mind Chatter – Moments of Beauty*, 2009–2010.

# natur, wissenschaft und die künste
# nature, science et les arts
# nature, science and the arts

Edited by

Julia Burbulla, Bernd Nicolai, Ana-Stanca Tabarasi-Hoffmann, Philip Ursprung & Wolf Wucherpfennig

Nature, Science and the Arts is an international scholarly series dealing with the history of cultural interplay between arts, humanities, natural sciences and technology, both on the level of theoretical reflection and in artistic enunciations. It is not restricted to any particular epoch, society, medium or region. By publishing contributions to this new interdisciplinary research area, the series illuminates the traditional connection between two ways of interpreting the world, a connection that has been largely marginalized since Wilhelm Dilthey's strict dissociation between humanities and natural sciences.

Vol. 1 Julia Burbulla
Allumfassende Ordnung. Gartenkunst und Wissenschaft in Gotha unter Ernst II. von Sachsen-Gotha-Altenburg (1772–1804).
ISBN 978-3-0343-0038-4. 2010.

Vol. 2 James King
Beyond *The Great Wave*. The Japanese Landscape Print, 1727–1960.
ISBN 978-3-0343-0317-0. 2010.

Vol. 3 Sabine Flach, Daniel Margulies & Jan Söffner (eds)
Habitus in Habitat I. Emotion and Motion.
ISBN 978-3-0343-0530-3. 2010.

Vol. 4 Sabine Flach & Jan Söffner (eds)
Habitus in Habitat II. Other Sides of Cognition.
ISBN 978-3-0343-0531-0. 2010.

Vol. 5 Glon Emmanuelle
Cinéma dans la Tête. L'esthétique du film à la lumière des neurosciences.
ISBN 978-3-0343-0603-4. 2011.

Vol. 6 Julia Burbulla & Ana-Stanca Tabarasi-Hoffmann (Hg.)
Gartenkunst und Wissenschaft. Diskurs, Repräsentation, Transformation seit dem Beginn der Frühmoderne.
ISBN 978-3-0343-0547-1. 2011.

Vol. 7 Dorothea Baumann
Music and Space. A systematic and historical investigation into the impact of architectural acoustics on performance practice, followed by a study of Handel's Messiah.
ISBN 978-3-0343-0615-7. 2011.

Vol. 8 Joerg Fingerhut, Sabine Flach & Jan Söffner (eds)
Habitus in Habitat III. Synaesthesia and Kinaesthetics.
ISBN 978-3-0343-0532-7. 2011.

Vol. 9 Sixto Castro & Alfredo Marcos (eds)
The Paths of Creation. Creativity in Science and Art.
ISBN 978-3-0343-0511-2. 2011.